Pattern Making

Published in 2019 by Laurence King Publishing Ltd.
361–373 City Road
London EC1V 1LR
United Kingdom
Tel: +44 20 7841 6900
Fax: +44 20 7841 6910
e-mail: enquiries@laurenceking.com
www.laurenceking.com

ISBN: 978-1-78627-196-9

Front cover photograph: Sebastian Reuter/Getty Images for IMG

Book design by The Urban Ant
Screengrab editors: Chen Chen, Brad Dary

Printed in China

Pattern Making

Techniques for Beginners

Francesca Sterlacci

Editors: Barbara Arata-Gavere and Barbara Seggio

Instructors: Francesca Sterlacci, Barbara Arata-Gavere, and Barbara Seggio

LAURENCE KING PUBLISHING

Contents

Brief Contents

Chapter 3 Bodices page 132

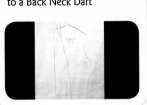

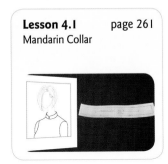
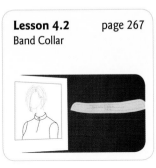

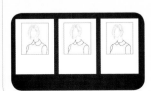

How this Book Works

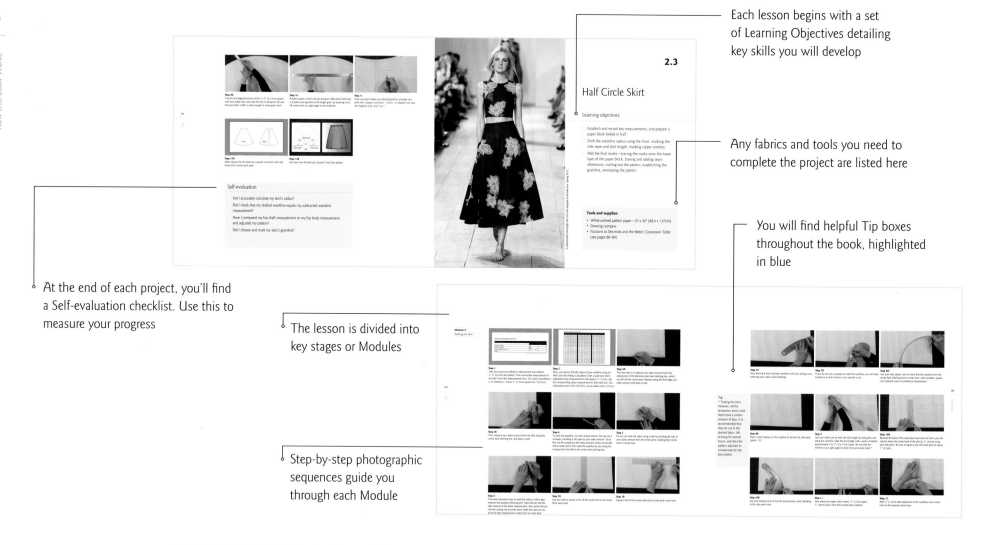

Each lesson begins with a set of Learning Objectives detailing key skills you will develop

Any fabrics and tools you need to complete the project are listed here

You will find helpful Tip boxes throughout the book, highlighted in blue

At the end of each project, you'll find a Self-evaluation checklist. Use this to measure your progress

The lesson is divided into key stages or Modules

Step-by-step photographic sequences guide you through each Module

You can also view the video lessons from the University of Fashion—see **www.universityoffashion**

Preface

In between the design "concept to creation" process lies the process of pattern making. Whether a design is created via draping (3D) or through the flat pattern (2D) method, the result is a pattern, which is later cut, fit, and sewn in fabric. Critical to the pattern making process is learning how to draft a set of blocks or slopers, which serve as the foundation for creating numerous design variations. A complete library of blocks consists of a basic sleeve, skirt, torso, pants, and jacket. These blocks save fashion industry brands time and money when creating hundreds of new styles each year.

By learning pattern making terminology, the function of various pattern making tools, along with basic drafting techniques, not only provides a designer with a solid foundation for executing more complex designs, but also for understanding computerized software programs.

Considered the "architects" of fashion design, pattern makers have the ability to draft a pattern using a two-dimensional method while thinking of the design in a three-dimensional way. With a solid foundation in pattern making, designers can play a more meaningful role in the industry by utilizing zero-waste techniques and other sustainable methods such as recycling and upcycling existing garments.

As technology continues to impact the fashion industry, new paradigms and strategies have emerged in the field of fashion education. In 2008, the University of Fashion (UoF) identified a solution in addressing student learning needs in an Internet dominated world. By creating an online video library with hundreds of lessons in key design disciplines, the UoF provides the perfect teaching tools to teach fashion design to aspiring designers, fashion college students, home sewers, industry professionals looking to upgrade their skills, and the fashion-curious. To reinforce that learning further, the UoF has partnered with Laurence King Publishing. The books work on their own, with step-by-step sequences based on the videos. But they can be used in conjunction with the videos on UoF's website to create the ultimate learning experience. We wish you every success with your projects.

Francesca Sterlacci

Introduction to Pattern Making

PATTERN MAKING, pattern cutting, or flat patterning is the process of creating a two-dimensional diagram or template of a garment, drafted on a flat surface. This can be constructed using a series of body measurements, or it can be transferred from a previously made fabric version of the garment—a draped muslin (toile). Slopers (or blocks) are basic patterns that are drafted containing a certain amount of ease for the wearer's comfort, and these are created without seam allowances. Slopers are used as the foundation or template for creating design variations that are subsequently cut and sewn in fabric. A sloper that is draped without wearing ease is known as a "moulage."

In the fashion industry, patterns are drafted on white unlined pattern paper, or sometimes on dotted white pattern paper. In the home-sewing industry, patterns are printed and sold on tissue paper (although when drafting your own patterns it is not advisable to use tissue paper, as it is easily torn while working). Slopers are drafted on white pattern paper and then copied onto a hard paper, or card, called "oaktag." They can then withstand repeated use when creating design variations. The process of changing a finished pattern from one size to another is called "grading."

Ancient Pattern-making Techniques

To understand the evolution of pattern making, we must look right back to early man, who fashioned protective clothing out of animal skins, furs, and foliage to keep warm. While these early humans were not concerned about fashion, but rather with protecting themselves from the elements—snow, rain, wind, and sun—there would still have been a degree of pattern-making skill involved in these ancient garments. Each covering was tailor-made to fit the individual wearer, and pre-planned so that it could wrap around the figure, protect strategic sections of the body, and be fastened with a primitive string or bone closure.

The process of weaving fibers to produce textiles emerged during the Neolithic era, and in prehistoric Egypt—around 5500 BCE—linen made from flax was being produced in sufficient quantities that garment styles began to emerge. By the eighth century, in ancient Greece, clothing took the form of three main garments: the peplos, chiton, and himation. A peplos was a large, rectangular piece of cloth, formed into a cylinder that measured the length of the wearer from shoulder to ankle, plus approximately an extra 25" (64cm).

Left. White unlined pattern paper
Center. White dotted/numbered pattern paper
Right. Oaktag bodice sloper

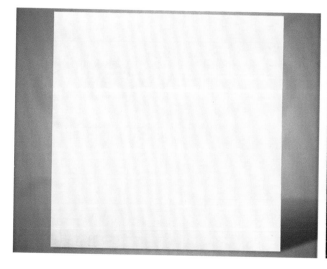
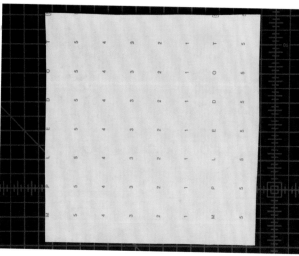
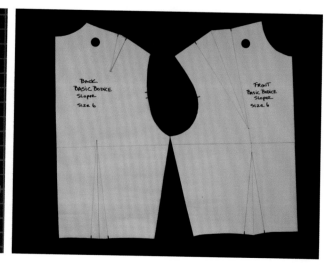

This extra allowance enabled the fabric to be folded along the topline to create a cuff, called an *apoptygma*, which ended below the waist and was then belted with a *kolpos*. Today we refer to this effect as a "peplum." A peplos was fastened at the shoulders with a pin or brooch (known as a fibula), and the armholes were allowed to drape and form a cowl. The chiton was also constructed from a body-length cylinder of fabric, and it became popular in two styles: the Ionic and the Doric. Unlike the peplos, the Ionic chiton did not fold over to create an over-blouse, but instead, the fabric was wrapped around the body and pinned along the shoulder to create a sleeveless garment. For an elbow-length version of the same garment, a wider piece of fabric was pinned with fibulae in as many as eight places along the arm. The Doric chiton was a combination of a sleeveless chiton and a peplos, but the *apoptygma* ended above the waist, approximately 18" (46 cm) from the shoulder, so that when the garment was belted at the waist it created a caplike effect rather than a peplum. The himation was made from a large, rectangular piece of fabric about 4 to 6 feet (1.2–1.8 meters) wide and 6 to 8 feet (1.8–2.4 meters) long, worn draped under the left arm and over the right shoulder. It was worn as a wrap or shawl that covered a chiton and peplos.

Pattern Making & Form-fitting Clothing

Pattern making as we know it today evolved from the introduction of more form-fitting clothing in the Middle Ages. Prior to this, garments had largely consisted of loose-fitting shifts that were draped and belted, so did not require much planning for bust fullness, fit around the shoulders and arms, or waist shaping. But clothes that conformed to the shape of the body required a more architectural approach. Tailors and dressmakers began to author guides on how to cut and sew clothing for men, women, and children, and guilds were also formed that offered apprentices the opportunity to learn the techniques of the trade.

Clockwise from left. Peplos; Ionic chiton (elbow-length); Doric chiton; Himation

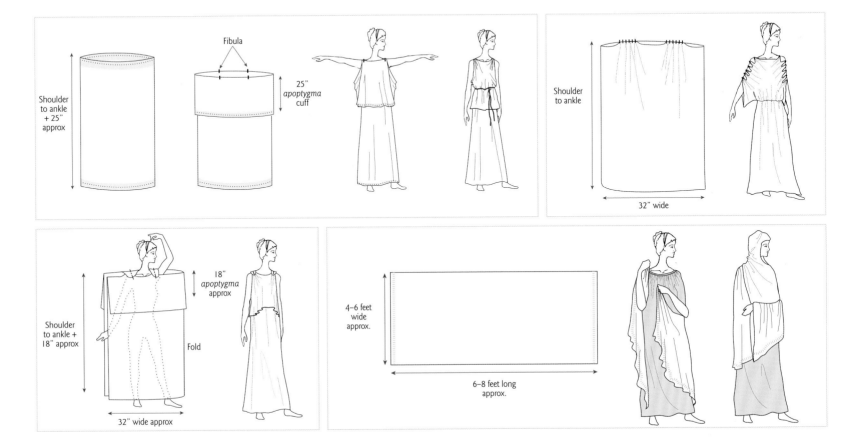

Pattern-making Publications & Guides

The earliest surviving tailors' patterns appeared in Juan de Alcega's *Libro de geometria pratica y trac a para* in 1580, and by the late 1700s, pattern drafts for professional tailors had also appeared in publications such as Garsault's *Descriptions des arts et métiers* and the *Encyclopédie Diderot et D'Alembert: Arts de l'habillement*. In 1809, the American publication *The Taylor's Instructor*, by Queen and Lapsley, appeared, and numerous other journals specific to the professional tailor followed throughout the nineteenth century. Soon the home dressmaker was able to access full-size patterns, too, although these were primarily aimed at women whose time was spent on charitable work, sewing for the poor.

During the early 1850s, magazines such as *Godey's Lady's Book*, *The World of Fashions*, and *Petersen's Magazine* began presenting small pattern diagrams of new clothing styles. Later, *Mme. Demorest's* offered full-scale patterns through mail order. Butterick first introduced patterns in graded sizes in 1863, and this company was eventually joined by three more—McCall's, Vogue, and Simplicity. Patents were also issued that included solutions for properly identifying pattern pieces (by Robert S. O'Laughlin in 1899, and George M. Laub in 1907), and for conveying the order of garment assembly with numerical symbols (William P. Ahnelt in 1907, and Alice Audrey Maxwell in 1908). Hannah G. Millard's "Dressmaker's Pattern Outfit," a comprehensive solution for reading patterns, was patented in 1920. This explained garment cutting and construction procedures for pattern makers, and came with a step-by-step instruction sheet

and diagram. Millard's patent was then secured by Butterick and named the "Deltor," after Butterick's magazine *The Delineator*. In 1925, Max Herzberg of the Excella Pattern Company patented the "Pictograph," which printed all of the instructions on the pattern pieces themselves, eliminating the need for a separate reference sheet altogether.

Pattern Making & the Industrial Revolution

The Industrial Revolution was a time of significant technological change in fashion. The introduction of steam power and the power loom were just two of many innovations that made the mass production of textiles possible, and this development went hand in hand with the rise of garment factories, thus changing the industry forever. Since garment factories were now producing ready-to-wear clothing for a growing market, systems of standardized sizing evolved to facilitate this. For example, in the U.S., measurements in inches were obtained from Civil War soldiers and used to help standardize clothes for the male population, while in 1863, Butterick patented size specifications for women for the patterns they produced. Beginning in the 1940s, the American Society of Testing and Materials (ASTM) began issuing standards that would apply to sewing machine technology and sizing standards.

Below, left to right;
Godey's Lady's Book;
A McCall's pattern envelope; Garsault's
Descriptions des arts et métiers;
*L'Encyclopédie Diderot et D'Alembert:
Arts de l'habillement*

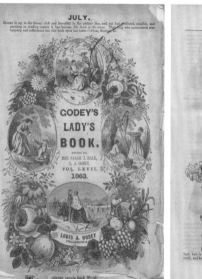

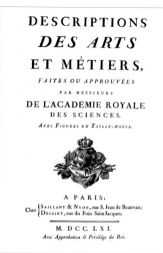

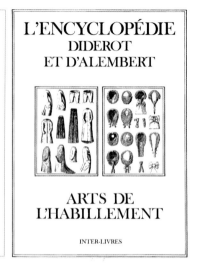

Pattern Making & the Fashion Industry Today

Technological advances are once again having a significant impact on the fashion industry—especially in the areas of pattern making and grading, where a variety of computer programs are available that streamline these processes. However, many small companies that cannot afford a computerized pattern system still rely on the drafting and fitting of a complete set of slopers based on the body measurements of their "average size" customer. Slopers are custom-fitted, basic patterns from which patterns for many different styles can be developed. A sloper "library" consists of a whole set of basic slopers: a bodice, straight sleeve, fitted torso, straight skirt, pant (trousers), and jacket. Some companies create their slopers by using standardized body measurements, such as those provided by the ASTM; others use sizing data collected by companies that produce dress forms (tailor's dummies) specific to particular countries or regions. The Alvanon dress-form company, for example, scans thousands of men, women, and children in one country, then uses that data to create dress forms based on the average person in that country. Another source of sizing data is [TC]^2, who in the early years of the twenty-first century, body-scanned over 10,000 subjects through their SizeUSA and SizeUK apparel-focused survey. The data, consisting of demographic information for each subject and over 200 standard measurements, is available for purchase.

Bespoke & Couture Pattern Making

For commercial production, patterns are made to fit several standard body sizes. In bespoke clothing, however, custom-made, couture slopers must be developed for each client, created from a personal set of measurements. Tailors use this technique almost exclusively when creating suits and coats. Alternatively, the process can begin with draping muslin (calico) on a dress form to produce a three-dimensional fabric template (muslin/toile) that can then be converted into a two-dimensional sloper. A client can opt for a made-to-measure dress form that is an exact replica of their body, created using body-scanning technology or based on a series of measurements. However, this can be very expensive and uneconomical, especially if their weight tends to fluctuate. A less expensive solution is to use cotton batting (wadding) or strips of muslin to pad out specific areas of a standard-size dress form so that it mimics the client's own body. A further option that some find helpful is the use of a commercial padding system that utilizes pre-formed foam shapes and a body covering to achieve a close match.

Left. An Alvanon dress form, representing a client body type
Right. A dress form padded to represent a client's body measurements

Right. Fabulous Fit patented dress form padding system

Architects of Design

Pattern makers are the architects of fashion design, and drafting a set of foundation slopers that fit the body accurately is the first challenge they face. Once those basic slopers are created, a pattern maker must then be able to interpret a design sketch in order to adapt or alter the slopers in terms of proportion and style lines to create a garment that fits well. In contrast to a draper, who has the advantage of seeing a design take shape in three dimensions, the pattern maker must combine the sensibility of an artist with the eye of an architect to envisage how a two-dimensional draft will transform into a three-dimensional garment. They must then be able to fit the sample prototype and correct the pattern. While there are standard pattern-making techniques used in the industry, many pattern makers develop their own approach over the years, and it can be fascinating to watch a pattern maker at work, as they will often have unique ways of solving fit issues. The relationship between a fit model (one whose body measurements match a company's mid-size range) and a pattern maker is key, since the fit model will provide valuable feedback as to how a design fits, and whether or not the pattern or design needs to be adjusted and cut for a second or third fit, prior to releasing the pattern for production.

The mind of a pattern maker is analytical. Pattern drafting deals in fractions of inches and centimeters, and patterns must be drafted so that they are cut on grain and can be assembled accurately, meaning seams must match and notches must be added in key spots to act as the road map for the garment's construction. Trueing—that is, making sure that seam allowances are at the appropriate angles and that seam lines align with each other—is just one of the analytics that the pattern maker is responsible for. Some patterns, especially those for outerwear garments, can consist of more than 100 individual pieces, and each of those pieces must be annotated and properly trued. Pattern makers have the ability to construct and dissect a pattern just like an engineer, architect, or surgeon, which is why some designers who started out with a career in architecture or medicine are able to design with the mind of a pattern maker.

Left. Charles Frederick Worth:
"The Father of Couture." (mid-1800s)
Right. Paul Paul Poiret popularized the
"column silhouette." (early 1900s)

The Father of Couture

By the time the English designer Charles Frederick Worth arrived on the Paris
fashion scene in the mid-1800s, with his wife as muse, the world was ready for
its first fashion house. The "Father of Couture" soon attracted the attention of
the French aristocracy, becoming official court couturier to Empress Eugénie of
France. Over the years his client list grew to include other nobles, too, such as
Queen Victoria and members of the royal families of Spain, Russia, Italy, and
Germany. Women also came from as far as the United States to be fitted for
dresses at the House of Worth. Worth did not let his customers dictate design,
which had been the practice up until that time, but rather designed clothes
that he felt suited their body type. His clothes utilized precision pattern-making
techniques to achieve their highly tailored design and construction.

Paul Poiret

Although Paul Poiret was known as the first designer to use draping techniques
instead of pattern making, his actual patterns were based on the concept of
straight lines and constructed rectangles. As an advocate of modern fashion in
the early years of the twentieth century, Poiret was one of the designers who
freed women from the corset and created the concept of a column silhouette,
a meaningful departure from the restrictive and fussy style employed by Worth
50 years earlier. Poiret's emphasis on Far Eastern culture and kimono-like
shapes resulted in patterns with flatness and planarity. His work would inspire
generations of designers, including those who, today, continue to explore the
possibilities of taking two-dimensional forms and placing them on a three-
dimensional body.

Gilbert Adrian

Legendary American film and fashion designer Adrian created signature styles for
Hollywood movie stars throughout the 1930s and '40s, designing for the likes
of Joan Crawford, Greta Garbo, Marlene Dietrich, and Carole Lombard. Adrian's
power suits for women were pattern-making marvels; they were drafted with
insets and seaming details that absorbed the fullness of the bust, thus creating
a unique dartless clothing concept. The organza dress he designed for Joan
Crawford for the movie *Letty Lynton* was a pattern-making masterpiece, notable
especially for its extravagant sleeves, which inspired a spate of imitations and
became the springboard for the use of shoulder pads in women's clothing.

Halston

Like Poiret and Madeleine Vionnet before him, Halston's design philosophy in the
1960s and '70s was all about easy, wearable clothes. His understanding that clothes
should be as effortless as possible was reflected in the patterns he created for his
collections. Whether he was reinventing the shirtdress in Ultrasuede® or creating
space age, architectural, made-to-measure pieces, the simplicity of his patterns
demonstrated a keen design sensibility.

Left. Geoffrey Beene was the master of using the female body to dictate the direction of his style lines (Fall/Winter 1995)
Right. Thierry Mugler—broad-shouldered suits and "Glamazon" silhouettes are his legacy. (Fall/Winter 1989–1990)

Geoffrey Beene

One of several top fashion designers who started out with a career in medicine, Geoffrey Beene brought a love of the female form and an appreciation for detail and fit to his designs. In the early 1990s, Beene produced some of the most minimal and yet complex clothing patterns in the industry. He used the curves of the female body to dictate the direction of his style lines, and the results were masterpieces of fit and form.

Thierry Mugler

Mugler took power-dressing to new heights during the late 1970s and 1980s. Expert pattern making and tailoring techniques, as well as his use of shoulder pads, were significant design elements throughout his collections. A combination of catwomen, dominatrix, and his "Glamazon" silhouette, inspired by 1930s' costumers Adrian and Edith Head, are his legacy. These power-suits played a key role in fashion, as women took on the issue of equality in a male-dominated corporate world.

Left. Gianfranco Ferré—the "architect of fashion," known for designs incorporating geometric planes. (Fall/Winter 2013)
Right. Azzedine Alaïa—known for his curvaceous cut, earned him the nickname the "King of Cling." (Fall 1991)

Gianfranco Ferré

Ferré began his career as an architect before finding his path in the world of fashion in the late 1970s. It was, therefore, no surprise that his designs and patterns would look like architectural blueprints. Best known for his magnificently designed blouses, Ferré's patterns were made up of planes and architectural shapes that framed the face and flattered the wearer.

Azzedine Alaïa

Alaïa began his career as a tailor at Christian Dior and then as a freelance designer at Guy Laroche and Thierry Mugler, before opening his own atelier in the late 1970s. He turned his knowledge of pattern making and tailoring into an art form by designing some of the most form-fitting, curvy, and sexy clothes on the market, earning him the name the "King of Cling."

Left. Alexander McQueen's "bumster" pants and sharp-edged tailoring were his trademarks. (Spring 1999)
Right. Yohji Yamamoto—known for marrying de-constructivism with exemplary pattern-cutting skills. (Spring/Summer 2017)

Alexander McQueen

McQueen entered the fashion industry at age 16, as an apprentice on Savile Row to tailors Anderson & Sheppard and Gieves & Hawkes, where he acquired his knowledge of bespoke menswear. He later made these sharp-edged tailoring and pattern-making skills his trademark, whether producing exceptional suits for women or displaying his genius for drop-dead-gorgeous eveningwear.

Yohji Yamamoto

Yamamoto's anti-fashion statements marked a whole new era in the fashion world in the late 1980s, and his deconstructivist philosophy was the antithesis of the form-fitting, highly tailored pattern-making techniques of Alaïa and McQueen. However, a sense of form and pattern cutting was still evident in many of his designs.

J. W. Anderson

J. W. Anderson studied menswear at the London College of Fashion, while
working as a window dresser at Prada, and launched his eponymous menswear
label and his capsule collection for women in 2010. Known for his androgynous
aesthetic, Anderson combines dressmaker pattern techniques with precision
tailoring methods to express his concept of "the homogenous wardrobe."

Zero Waste & Subtractive Pattern Cutting

The philosophy of designing clothes
with patterns that limit the amount
of waste and toxicity in the process,
and that promote a sustainable natural
life cycle of products, is part of the
ongoing "slow fashion" movement.
Designers and manufacturers are
making strides and are focusing on
the three "Rs": Reduce, Reuse, and
Recycle. It is estimated that 15 to 20
percent of the fabric used to produce
clothing winds up in U.S. landfills
because it is cheaper to dump the
scraps than to recycle them. Designer Madeleine Vionnet, creator of the bias
cut, was the first to utilize this zero-waste pattern-cutting philosophy. American
designer Yeohlee has been part of the zero-waste fashion movement since the
1980s, designing clothes at the pattern-making stage with little to no waste in
the process. Other zero-waste designers include the English designer Zandra
Rhodes; the Australians Mark Liu, Susan Dimasi, and Chantal Kirby; and Holly
McQuillan from New Zealand.

Another method for saving fabric is simply not to cut the fabric at all,
but drape it directly onto a dress form then tuck, layer, and sew the garment
together—a technique that falls somewhere between traditional pattern
making and draping. These experimental garments break the boundaries of
typical garment shapes and belong to the genre of work made famous by the
Japanese designers Issey Miyake and Rei Kawakubo. Today, British designer
Julian Roberts calls this technique "subtraction cutting"—designing with
patterns, rather than creating patterns for designs. Its basic premise is that the
patterns do not represent the garments' outward shape, but rather the negative
spaces within the garment.

Learning Pattern Making

Pattern making begins with learning how to make a set of basic patterns known as slopers. Unlike the three-dimensional draping method, the entire garment pattern is drafted on a flat surface, most often from measurements, using pattern paper, rulers, and curve rulers, as well as specialized tools specific to pattern making. Slopers are drafted without seam allowances.

To create a perfect sloper, whether it is a sleeve, bodice, skirt, or pant, you should first cut your drafted pattern (with seam allowances added) out of muslin, and then test it for fit. This is an inexpensive way to test your patterns, and muslin is an easy fabric to work with when it comes to making quick adjustments. Each of your muslin pattern pieces must be cut following the same grainlines that you would use for cutting your actual garment. Once you have transferred any necessary corrections back to the pattern, you can then transfer this revised pattern to durable oaktag (without seam allowances) to become part of your sloper library.

The lessons that follow in this book will provide you with a solid grounding in the concepts and techniques of pattern making. In the process, you will produce a complete set of slopers, which you will be able to use as the basis for your own designs in the future. You will begin by drafting a basic straight sleeve, using a set of measurements and the appropriate specialist tools to produce a pattern complete with grainlines and notches. The resulting sleeve sloper will then act as a foundation for producing a series of sleeve variations—a format that is repeated in subsequent chapters, covering skirts, bodices, collars, and pants in turn.

As you complete the lessons you will also become acquainted with pattern-making terminology, relating both to parts of the body (apex, crotch depth, inseam, outseam, and so on) as well as to the patterns themselves (grainline, notches, trueing, etc.). Once you have mastered the contents of this book, you will be ready to create just about anything your creative mind can dream up!

Below. Julian Roberts—pioneer of "subtraction cutting", designing with patterns instead of making patterns for designs.

Getting Started

Sleeves

The best way to begin learning how to make patterns is by drafting a basic straight sleeve sloper, which is why a lesson for this appears first in the book. This lesson provides you with an easy-to-read chart that lists all of the necessary measurements that you will need to draft your women's sleeve for U.S. sizes 4 to 16 (equivalent to British sizes 8 to 20, European sizes 36 to 48, and Asian sizes 7 to 17). You will learn the intricacies of establishing the correct cap (or sleeve head) height, and of how to shape the cap so that your sleeve will fit into an armhole with ease.

Once you have perfected a straight sleeve sloper—the foundation for just about all your future sleeve patterns—you will learn how to convert it into a fitted sleeve sloper with a dart at the elbow. This fitted variant is another item that you will need in your sloper library, since it is the foundation for variations such as a two-piece suit sleeve. The lesson on transferring your fitted sleeve to oaktag will then introduce you to the key process of converting paper drafts into oaktag slopers.

When your sleeve slopers have been drafted you will be ready to learn how to design a number of sleeves, beginning with a bishop sleeve. Here you will encounter the concept of "slash and spread," a technique for creating fullness—in this case, at the sleeve wrist—that you will be able to apply to many areas of other garments, such as flared skirts, dresses, coats, and pants. A short puff sleeve follows the same "slash and spread" principles, but this sleeve is gathered, at the bottom of the sleeve as well as at the sleeve cap. The next lesson then shows you how to a create petal sleeve—a novelty sleeve that is used in childrenswear as well as in eveningwear. This design replaces the sleeve inseam with a unique overlay along the center of the sleeve.

Skirts

The skirts chapter begins with drafting the basic straight skirt from measurements. We make this easy by providing you with a measurements form, on which you can record all of the measurements that you will extract from either your dress form or from a live figure. You will learn about creating wearing ease and about darts—how to space the darts along the waistline, and how long to make each dart. You will finish with a muslin version that you can test for fit, before converting your final draft into an oaktag sloper.

Another popular skirt style is the circle skirt. Circle skirts can be constructed with four different levels of fullness: a quarter circle, half circle, three-quarter circle, and full circle. To make drafting each of these skirts easier, we provide a series of forms and charts for you to use, so that you can record your measurements easily, and make any necessary calculations.

Bodices

A tight-fitting bodice, known as a 'moulage' or mold, will become the foundation for many of your future dress, blouse, and jacket designs. We will teach you how to draft this bodice, either from body measurements, or from measurements provided on our women's global size chart. We have provided several charts and diagrams to assist you in the measuring and drafting process, beginning with a color-coded diagram illustrating each of the measuring points. This diagram works in tandem with a measuring points chart, whereby you will be able to record each of your measurements. Also included is a worksheet to assist with key calculations as you draft. Once you have extracted the necessary measurements, you are ready to begin drafting.

You will be guided through the process, using our easy-to-follow, alpha-numeric system for mapping, marking, and connecting key points, such as the darts, armholes, necklines, and side seams. You will also learn where to position the darts, as well as intake amounts for each of the darts. By learning how to true the front and back darts, the waistline, and the side seams, you are ready for the next step, transferring the Moulage Bodice Sloper to oaktag and then how to add ease to create a sleeveless bodice and a bodice sloper with sleeve ease.

Once you have transferred your Front & Back Shoulder Dart Bodice Sloper to oaktag you will be ready to learn how to pivot and manipulate darts. You will start by learning how to pivot the front shoulder dart to the side seam to produce a bust dart, before referring to the initial lesson in this chapter to recap how to transfer a sloper to oaktag and add another sloper to your bodice sloper library. Next, you will learn how to produce a front sloper with a single waist dart by pivoting the same shoulder dart, but this time to the waist. Another location for this dart is the armhole. Again, we demonstrate how to do this by pivoting the shoulder dart on your Front Shoulder Dart Bodice Sloper.

Once you have learned how to move a single dart, you will be ready for a two-dart bodice variation, following our easy method for transferring a shoulder and a waist dart to a neck and a French dart. Once you have mastered, you will have lots of fun exploring other dart combinations. You will also learn how to pivot a dart on the back bodice, transferring a shoulder dart to a neck dart.

A fitted torso sloper is probably one of the most important slopers in the fashion industry, providing the foundation for blouses, dresses, and jackets. Again using your Front & Back Shoulder Dart Bodice Sloper, you will learn how to draft a fitted torso sloper, transfer it to muslin, test it for fit and make any necessary corrections, and then transfer it to oaktag.

This chapter concludes with instructions for drafting two types of sleeve—a raglan sleeve (with one- and two-piece variations) and a kimono sleeve. These lessons employ slopers drafted previously in this chapter, as well as the straight sleeve sloper that you will have drafted at the very start of the book. The skills that you acquire here will then provide you with a jumping-off point for all sorts of future sleeve variations.

Collars

You will begin this chapter with learning how to draft a mandarin collar and a band collar. The mandarin collar is designed to meet at center front, while the band collar has a slightly rounded top edge and is drafted so that you will learn how to plan for a button and buttonhole at the neck. This knowledge can then be applied to other areas of a garment, such as waistbands and sleeve cuffs.

Once you have mastered the band-style collar you will learn how to draft a convertible collar. Convertible collars build on the method used for mandarin and band collars, except here you will plan for a wider collar that sits higher on the back of the neck and has a slight roll and stand. A convertible collar, as the name suggests, can be worn open or closed at the front neck, and is perfect for blouses or shirtwaist dresses.

The next type of collar you will learn how to draft is a roll collar, of which three variations are included in the Peter Pan series. A roll collar differs from a convertible collar in that it cannot be worn open at the neck because the shape of the collar's neckline will more closely follow the shape of the garment's neckline. We will draft one that sits flat on the body's neckline, one that has a slight stand, and a third one with a higher stand. Each of these lessons can be stylized to produce a rounded edge at center front, a pointed collar tip, or any shape that you can imagine.

A sailor collar lesson then builds on the methods covered in the Peter Pan lesson. However, here you will learn how to stylize a collar with a V neckline and an extended back, which has many other design possibilities as well.

Pants (or Trousers)

To draft a pant sloper you will start by using another set of our custom-made forms and charts. We will demonstrate how to measure and extract your body measurements from a pant form (or a live model) and then record those measurements on our custom-made chart. You will also be provided with an illustration of key body-measurement points, as well as various hem-width amounts for your sloper's leg sweep.

Once you have established the necessary measurements, you will be ready to start drafting your pants. You will learn how to position your darts at the waist and how long each dart should be. Depending upon the waist-to-hip differential, it may be possible to have a single dart either front or back or both, instead of the two-dart back that is drafted in this lesson. Then you will learn how to determine your front and back crotch extension and ankle circumference.

Annotating your pattern with the proper grainlines and notches forms part of this lesson, as with others. And, as elsewhere, once your drafting is complete, you will need to cut your pattern out in muslin, fit it on a body or pant form, make any corrections needed, and then transfer it to oaktag. Once the sloper is perfected it will give you the means to create all sorts of other pant styles, from straight-legged to stovepipe, flared, bellbottom, and cropped variations.

Pattern-making Tools

Pattern making always begins with **white unlined pattern paper**, and **paper scissors** or **pattern shears**. This type of paper is the best choice for beginners since it is easier to use than other papers, such as those marked with 1" (2.5cm) marks or dots. For turning your paper draft into a sloper you will need **oaktag** (a thicker paper, or card, that is manila-colored on one side and green on the other). You will need a **women's dress form** and **pant form** to extract measurements from, and to test your patterns for fit. A **cutting mat** will protect your table surface, and its self-healing qualities will enable you to sink your **pushpins (drawing pins)** into it while drafting patterns. You will also need

weights to hold your patterns in place, an **awl** to mark your dart vanishing points, and a **notcher** to create notch marks in key positions on your patterns. In addition, you will need an assortment of measuring tools to draw your pattern lines, including a **tape measure, 36" (91cm) metal ruler, yardstick, 18" (46cm) clear plastic ruler, hip curve, L square, styling curve**, and a **French curve**. To mark your patterns you will need a **pencil sharpener**, an **eraser**, a **2HB pencil** or a **mechanical pencil, a red and a blue pencil**, tracing paper, size 17 (27mm) dressmaker pins, and a **needlepoint tracing wheel**. And to close darts and hold your drafts in place you will need clear **Scotch tape** and **removable tape**.

1 Sleeves

Designing sleeves begins with drafting a straight sleeve sloper. By referencing the sleeve measurement chart supplied with this lesson, you will draft a basic straight sleeve from a series of measurements. Once you have transferred the straight sleeve to oaktag, this sloper will become the foundation for all of the sleeve variations in this chapter. Next, you will convert the straight sleeve to a fitted sleeve and then transfer that sleeve into oaktag. Fitted sleeves are used in bridal and evening wear or wherever a tight-fitting sleeve is desired.

The bishop sleeve lesson introduces you to the 'slash and spread' method to add fullness to the sleeve and teaches you how to draft a sleeve placket with a button/buttonhole cuff. The puff sleeve lesson expands on the slash and spread method, but this time you will add fullness to both the sleeve cap and hem, and then finish the hem edge with a narrow cuff band. And finally, the petal sleeve lesson introduces you to the 'one-piece sleeve' concept. The petal sleeve is popular in childrenswear, as well as eveningwear.

Straight Sleeve Sloper

Learning objectives

☐ Extract measurements from the chart, preparing and marking the essential guidelines onto paper

☐ Shape the sleeve, using a French curve to draw in the sleeve cap, transferring marks to the underside with a tracing wheel, cutting out the sleeve

☐ Add the final markings, drawing in guidelines and where to create notches

Tools and supplies:

• White unlined pattern paper—16 x 28" (41 x 71 cm)

A well-balanced straight sleeve adds the perfect touch to this classic yet elegant dress from the Brock Collection. (September 2016)

Straight Sleeve Measurement Chart

US size (UK size)	4 (8)	6 (10)	8 (12)	10 (14)	12 (16)	14 (18)	16 (20)
Sleeve cap (sleeve head)	6" (15.2cm)	6⅛" (15.6cm)	6¼" (15.9cm)	6⅜" (16cm)	6½" (16.5cm)	6⅝" (16.8cm)	6¾" (17cm)
Bicep circumference	11" (27.9cm)	11½" (29.2cm)	12" (30.5cm)	12½" (31.6cm)	13" (33cm)	13½" (34.3cm)	14" (35.6cm)
Elbow circumference	9¼" (23.5cm)	9¾" (24.8cm)	10¼" (26cm)	10¾" (27.3cm)	11¼" (28.5cm)	11" (29.9cm)	12¼" (31cm)
Inseam (underarm length)	16" (40.6cm)	16¼" (41.3cm)	16½" (41.9cm)	16¾" (42.6cm)	17" (43.2cm)	17¼" (43.8cm)	17½" (44.5cm)
Wrist	7¼" (18.4cm)	7½" (19cm)	7¾" (19.7cm)	8" (20.3cm)	8¼" (21cm)	8½" (21.6cm)	8¾" (22.2cm)

Step 1

Using the Straight Sleeve Measurement Chart, find the measurements that are specific to your particular size.

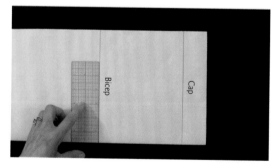

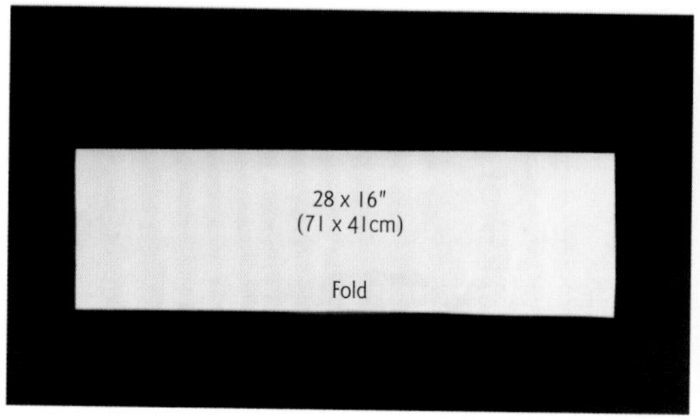

Step 2

For this lesson you will need a piece of white unlined pattern paper, 28 x 16" (71 x 41cm), folded in half lengthwise, with the fold facing you. This is the centerline of the sleeve.

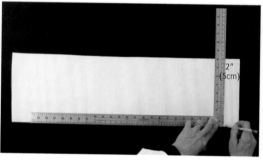

Step 3

Square a line off the fold, at 2" (5cm) down from the top. This is the capline of the sleeve.

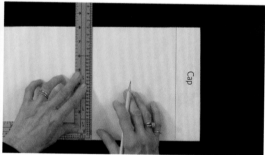

Step 4

Next, referring to the sleeve chart, come down by the measurement of your sleeve cap (head), make a dot, and square a line across. This is your bicep line.

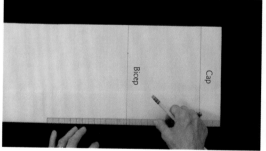

Step 5

Measuring up from the fold along the bicep line, measure half the distance of your bicep circumference and place a mark.

Step 6

To find your elbow line, divide your underarm measurement in half then subtract 1½" (3.8cm). Measure down from the bicep line by this measurement and place a mark.

Step 7

Now square a line across to form the elbow line.

Step 8
Next, measuring from the fold up the elbow line, measure half the distance of your elbow circumference and make a mark.

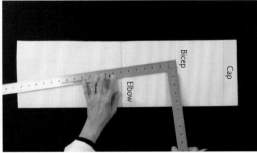

Step 9
Refer to the sleeve chart for your sleeve's inseam measurement. Now measure down from the bicep line by the length of your inseam, intersecting your elbow line. This is the inseam. Then make a mark.

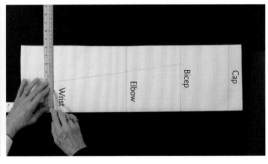

Step 10
Square a line across from the fold line to this mark to form your wrist line.

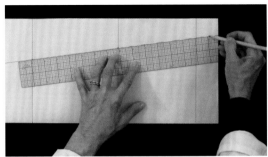

Step 11
In preparation for shaping the sleeve cap, extend your inseam with broken lines from the bicep line to the cap line.

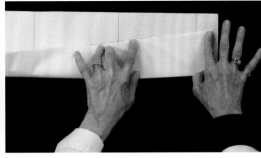

Step 12
Divide the cap in half lengthwise from above the bicep line and make a crease.

Step 13A
Fold the sleeve center over to meet the inseam line and make a crease.

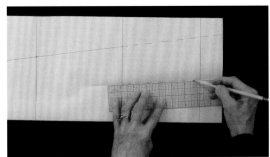

Step 13B
Mark the crease with a broken line.

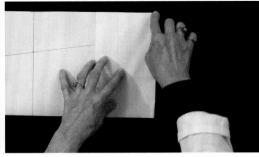

Step 14
Now fold the sleeve cap line down to meet the bicep line and form a crease.

Step 15
Measure up ¾" (2cm) from the intersection of the two crease lines toward the cap line and place a mark.

Tip
Always be sure that as you use your curve tool, your underarm seam is a right angle to the armhole.

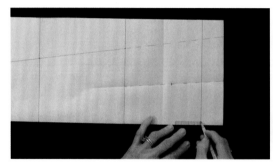

Step 16A
Place a mark ¼" (6mm) away from the fold on the capline.

Step 16B
Place two marks on the bicep line—one at ¼" (6mm) from the bicep/inseam intersection, and another at 1" (2.5cm) in.

Module 2:

Shaping the Sleeve Cap

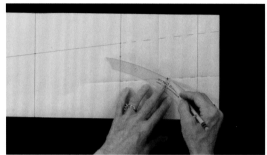

Step 1A
To form the cap, place your French curve at the ¼" (6mm) cap mark (made in 16a above), with the point in the direction of the 1" (2.5cm) mark at the underarm.

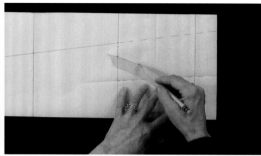

Step 1B
Intersect the ¾" (2cm) mark (made in Step 15 on p. 173) and shape the upper cap.

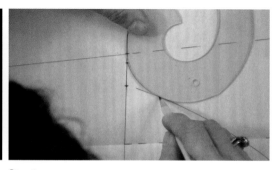

Step 2
Flip your French curve over and shape the lower underarm, intersecting the ¼" (6mm) mark at the side seam/underarm intersection, blending to create a nice smooth curve.

Step 3
The final steps begin with transferring your bicep, elbow, and wrist line onto the underside using your tracing wheel and carbon paper.

Step 4
Now cut out your folded sleeve draft.

Opposite: The Misha Collection adds lacing detail to this otherwise basic straight sleeve. (September 2016)

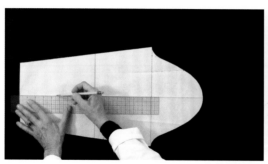

Step 1
Open the sleeve and, with your plastic ruler, draw in your bicep line, elbow line, and the centerline of your sleeve.

Step 2
To add your notches, start by placing a mark halfway between the crease line and the underarm section on the right side of the sleeve. Measure in ¼" (6mm) from this mark and, with your French curve, re-blend your front armhole.

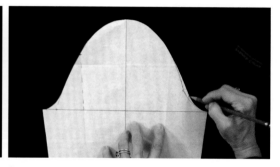

Step 3
Using your red pencil, mark the area that will be cut away later.

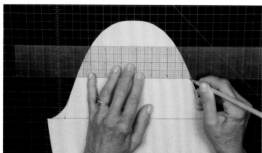

Step 4
Measure down ½" (1.3cm) from the crease line on the right side, and place a dash. That will be your front armhole notch.

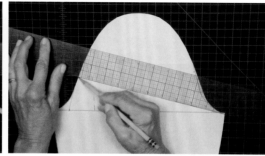

Step 5
The back sleeve will have two notches. One at the same level as the front notch, and the other ½" (1.3cm) lower.

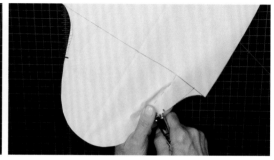

Step 6
Now you are ready to create your front and back notches.

Step 7A
The last step is to trim away the excess from the front armhole.

Step 7B
You have now finished your Straight Sleeve Sloper. To transfer your straight sleeve sloper to oaktag (card), follow the steps as outlined in Lesson 1.3, Transferring the Fitted Sleeve to Oaktag.

Self-evaluation

☐ Is the sleeve cap a smooth curve?

☐ Did I scoop out the lower portion of the front armhole?

☐ Are my front and back notches placed properly?

☐ Have I marked the sleeve centerline?

☐ Did I transfer my bicep and elbow lines onto the front sleeve?

A fitted sleeve is the perfect touch for this sexy mini dress by Oday Shakar. (September 2016)

Creating a Fitted Sleeve from the Straight Sleeve Sloper

Learning objectives

☐ Make the sleeve draft—preparing paper blocks, copying the straight sleeve sloper, adding guidelines, cutting out the sleeve draft

☐ Shape the fitted sleeve—spreading the sleeve at the elbow and creating the elbow dart

☐ Add the final markings— tracing the sleeve draft onto a new sleeve block, connecting the marks and trueing the sloper, adding notches and grainline, annotating the sloper

Tools and supplies:

- Straight Sleeve Sloper (see Lesson 1.1)
- Three blocks of white unlined pattern paper— each 16 x 28" (41 x 71cm)

Module 1:

Lesson Prep

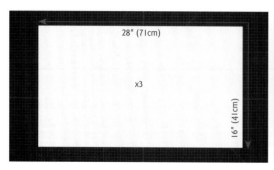

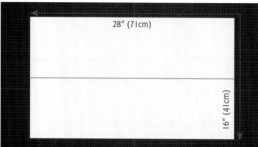

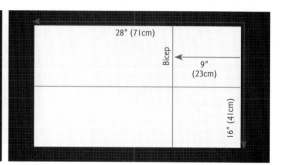

Step 1

For this lesson you will need to prepare three blocks of white unlined pattern paper, each measuring 16" (41cm) wide and 28" (71cm) long.

Step 2

The first step is to draw in your sleeve guidelines. With your yardstick or L square, draw a line along the middle of the paper in the length direction. This is the sleeve center.

Step 3

Measure down 9" (23cm) from the top of the paper and square a line across the width of the paper, perpendicular to the sleeve centerline. This is the sleeve's bicep line. Repeat these steps for the other two pattern paper blocks.

Module 2:

Copying the Straight
Sleeve Sloper

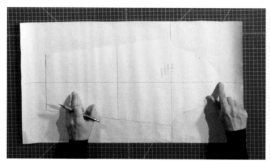

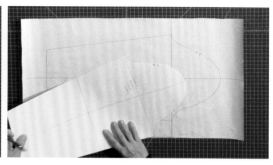

Step 1

The first step is to copy your straight sleeve sloper onto paper. Place the oaktag (card) sloper onto one of the prepared paper blocks, aligning the sleeve center and bicep of the oaktag sloper to the sleeve center and bicep of the paper block.

Step 2

Once you have matched the guidelines, begin tracing around the straight sleeve sloper. Starting at the sleeve back, trace the back cap, the notches, and underarm, then move round to the inseam, back elbow guideline, and wrist. Next, trace the front underarm, elbow guideline, armhole, notch, and front sleeve cap.

Step 3

Remove the oaktag sloper from the sleeve draft.

Step 4

With your L square, connect the elbow, making sure that your line is perpendicular to the sleeve centerline.

Step 5

Now carefully cut out the sleeve draft along the pencil lines with your paper scissors.

Tip

The Straight Sleeve and Fitted Sleeve Sloper are tight-fitting sleeves with a minimum circumference ease, used for the purpose of creating other style variations.

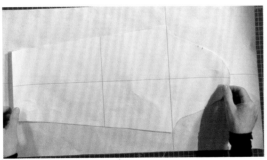

Step 1
Slip your second prepared sleeve block underneath the straight sleeve draft, lining up the center and bicep guidelines.

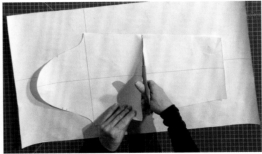

Step 2
Reposition the paper draft on the table so that the back of the straight sleeve draft is facing you. Now cut along the elbow line from the back underarm to the front underarm, but leave ¹/₁₆" (2mm) connected.

Step 3
Match up the centerline and the bicep line of the sleeve to the paper block. Use small pieces of Scotch tape to secure the sleeve to the paper at the sleeve cap center, at the front bicep line, and the back bicep line.

Step 4
You will be spreading the sleeve at the elbow line, so insert a pin in the paper block and the cutting mat at the front elbow line. Spread the elbow for a total of 1" (2.5cm). Measure this with your ruler and tape down both sides of the elbow line to the paper block below. Secure the front and back wrist with tape.

Step 5
Remove the pivot pin from the front elbow line and tape down the elbow line here.

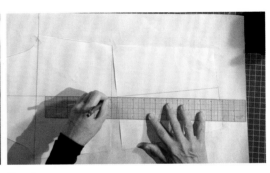

Step 6
Extend a new grainline from the elbow to wrist in line with the centerline above the elbow.

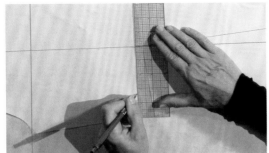

Step 7A
Now we will create the elbow dart. Measure the back elbow from underarm to centerline with your clear plastic ruler. Divide that number into thirds and place a mark at each third. In this case, each section measures approximately 1⅝" (4cm).

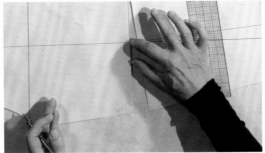

Step 7B
The second mark will be the vanishing point of the elbow dart.

Step 7C
Position your ruler at the vanishing point of the dart and draw the lower leg of the dart to the back underarm.

Step 7D
Reposition the paper draft so that you can close the dart. Finger press the lower leg of the dart and fold the bottom leg up to meet the top leg of the dart. Note how we cup the paper and reposition the sleeve to make it easier to manipulate so that we can flatten the dart.

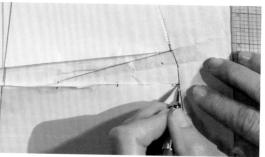

Step 7E
Once you have closed and flattened the dart, use your ruler and pencil to reconnect the back underarm. With your tracing wheel, trace the dart area, then open the dart to see the perforated lines of the dart pickup. True the new dart underarm with your pencil and ruler. Add a notch to the upper dart/underarm intersection.

Step 8
Connect a straight line from bicep to wrist. This will become your new underarm seam.

Step 1
Slip your third prepared sleeve block underneath both layers of the fitted sleeve draft. Line up the bicep and centerlines, then pin the layers together at both the top and bottom.

Step 2A
Use your tracing wheel to trace around the outside edge of the sleeve, pressing hard so that the perforations reach the bottom layer. Trace the wrist, along the front underarm and sleeve cap, then trace the back sleeve cap from the underarm to the center. Trace the back underarm and the new dart line to the wrist.

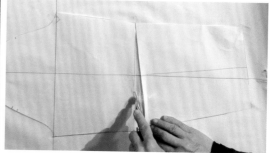

Step 2B
Trace the elbow line from the back underarm to the front underarm, and trace the lower leg of the dart and the dart's vanishing point.

Step 2C
Trace the new sleeve centerline from elbow to wrist.

Step 3
Now trace all of your notches. Begin with the front notch, then complete the center sleeve cap notch and the back cap notches.

Tip
A single elbow dart intake is between ¾" (2cm) and 1" (2.5cm).

Step 1

Remove the centerline pins and separate the two top layers from the bottom layer, in preparation for trueing the sloper.

Step 2

We will begin the trueing process by connecting all of the sleeve lines and notches, using the tracing wheel markings as our guide. Start by drawing in the elbow line of the sleeve with your clear plastic ruler, following the tracing marks. Then draw in the new centerline of the sleeve, from elbow to wrist.

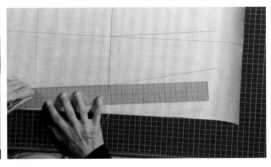

Step 3

Connect the back underarm from the wrist to the elbow dart, and then from the elbow dart to the bicep—again, using the tracing markings as your guide.

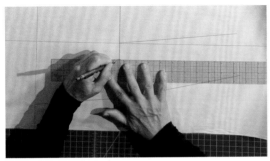

Step 4

Next, draw the lower leg of the dart to the vanishing point then mark the dart's vanishing point. Note that the elbow line forms the upper leg of the dart.

Step 5

Move to the front underarm and, following the tracing marks, draw a line connecting the front wrist to the front elbow line, and then continuing from the elbow to the bicep.

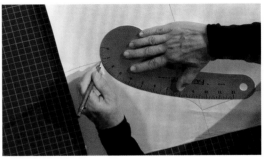

Step 6A

Now rest your styling curve on the tracing marks and true the back lower armhole. Reposition the curve and true the back sleeve cap.

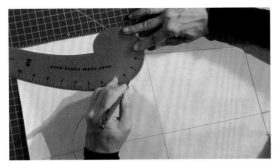

Step 6B

Flip the curve to true the front sleeve cap, following the tracing lines, then reposition the curve and true the front lower armhole.

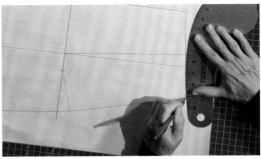

Step 7

Move to the wrist and, with the styling curve, follow the tracing lines and true the front wrist to the sleeve center. Flip the curve and true from the sleeve center to the back wrist.

Step 8

Next, mark the notches. Mark the elbow dart notches, both back sleeve cap notches, the center cap notch and the front cap notch. Notch marks should always be placed perpendicular to the seam, and no longer than $1/4$" (6mm).

Step 9
You should now annotate the sleeve sloper. In the area under the back sleeve cap, write "Fitted Sleeve Sloper," and "Size 6," or whatever your particular size is.

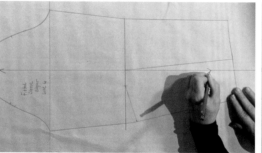

Step 10
Add grainline arrows on the centerline, the first at 2" (5cm) below the cap, and another 2" (5cm) above the wrist.

Step 11A
Note that the centerline of the sleeve will shift below the elbow once the dart is sewn. However, the sleeve must be cut on grain using the arrowed line as the guide.

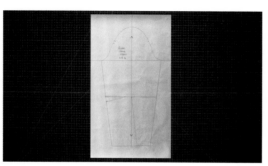

Step 11B
You have now finished drafting a Fitted Sleeve Sloper from your Straight Sleeve Sloper.

Tip
Remember that the sleeve is cut along the grainline/centerline, but once the dart is closed the actual center of the sleeve shifts.

Self-evaluation

- [ ] Have I copied my straight sleeve sloper properly?
- [ ] Did I slash into the elbow line and spread my dart no more than 1" (1.3cm)?
- [ ] Have I calculated my elbow dart length accurately?
- [ ] Did I remember to true my elbow dart at the underarm seam?

Transferring the Fitted Sleeve to Oaktag

Learning objectives

☐ Transfer the sloper—preparing the oaktag, matching the sloper to the oaktag guidelines, tracing the lines using a tracing wheel

☐ True the sloper—joining marks and smoothing curves

☐ Add the final marks—cutting out the pattern, notching lines and marks, punching a hole at key intersections and dart vanishing points

Tools and supplies:

- Fitted Sleeve Sloper (see Lesson 1.2)
- Oaktag (card)—16 x 28" (41 x 71cm)

Use your drafted fitted sleeve sloper to create a three-quarter length sleeve like this from Christian Dior. (Haute Couture, Spring/Summer 2015)

Module 1:

Lesson Prep

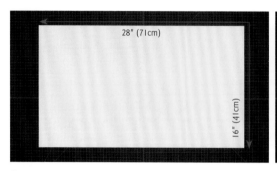

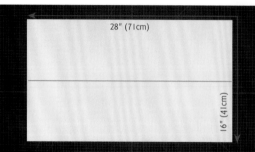

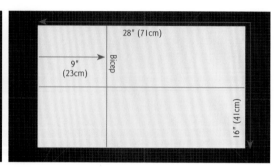

Step 1
Cut a piece of oaktag approximately 16" (41cm) wide and 28" (71cm) long.

Step 2
Draw a vertical line through the center, along the length of the oaktag. This is the sleeve center.

Step 3
Measure down 9" (23cm) from the top and square a horizontal line across the width of the oaktag. This is the sleeve bicep line.

Module 2:

Transferring the Sloper

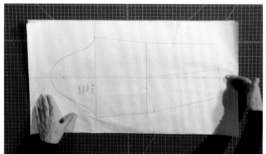

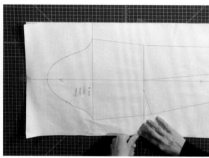

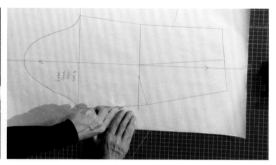

Step 1
Place your paper fitted sleeve sloper over the oaktag, matching the paper sloper's center- and bicep lines to those of the oaktag.

Step 2
Once the center- and bicep lines are aligned, use tape to secure the paper sloper to the cutting mat. Tape the cap (head), hem, and at the elbow on both sides of the sleeve.

Step 3A
Use your tracing wheel to trace the outer edge of the sleeve onto the oaktag. Begin at the wrist, pressing hard on the tracing wheel so that the marks transfer to the oaktag. Trace along the front underarm seam and along the sleeve cap, both back and front, then trace the back underarm seam.

Step 3B
Next, trace the sleeve elbow line, the lower leg of the elbow dart and dart vanishing point, and the new sleeve centerline from below the elbow to the wrist. Trace the two back sleeve cap notches, the center sleeve notch, and the front sleeve notch.

Step 4
Separate the paper sloper from the oaktag.

Tip
Trueing is an important part of the transfer process. It's the last chance you have to confirm that your underarm seams align, and your sleeve cap curves are smooth.

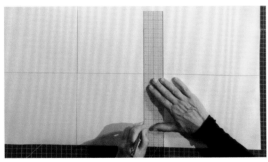

Step 1
Using the tracing perforations as your guide, begin the trueing process by drawing in your sleeve's elbow line, using your clear plastic ruler, from the front to the back underarm seam.

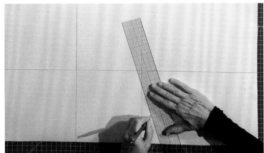

Step 2
True the lower leg of the elbow dart.

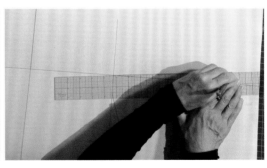

Step 3
True the new sleeve centerline from elbow to wrist, again following the tracing line.

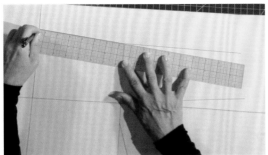

Step 4
True the front underarm seam from the wrist to the elbow, and then from the elbow to the top of the underarm/bicep.

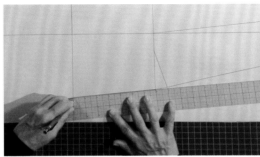

Step 5
True the back underarm seam from the wrist to the dart, then pivot at the dart intake line and finish the line at the back underarm/bicep.

Step 6
With your styling curve, true the back underarm and sleeve cap, repositioning the curve to connect the tracing marks to get the best curve. Do the same on the front sleeve cap and underarm.

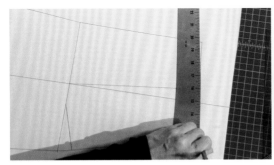

Step 7
Use your hip curve to true the wrist from the front underarm seam to the sleeve center, then flip the curve and finish trueing the wrist from the center to the back underarm seam.

Step 8
Mark the back cap notches, the center sleeve notch, and the front cap notch.

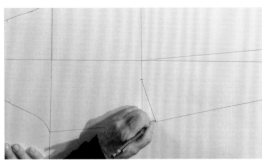

Step 9
Mark the elbow dart's vanishing point as well as both sides of the dart intake.

Step 10
Add two arrows on the center grainline, one at about 2" (5cm) from the top cap, and the other about 2" (5cm) from the wrist.

Step 11
In the top back cap area, add the annotation "Fitted Sleeve Sloper" and "Size 6," or whatever size your particular sloper happens to be.

Step 12
Use your paper scissors to cut the sleeve out carefully and precisely along the pencil lines. Always cut with the oaktag flat on the table, holding it down with your free hand. Never lift it to cut in mid-air, where you will have less control. Remove any excess as you cut, to make it easier to manipulate the oaktag.

Step 13
Now, with your notcher, notch the front cap notch, the sleeve center, and the two back cap notches. Notch both elbow notches, the wrist center grainline notch, and the new sleeve centerline notch. Then notch the elbow line on the front underarm seam.

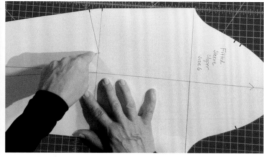

Step 14A
With your awl, create holes at the bicep/sleeve center intersection, the elbow/sleeve center intersection, and the vanishing point of the elbow dart.

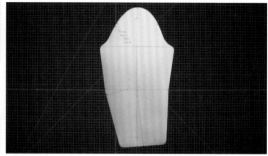

Step 14B
You have now transferred your Fitted Sleeve Sloper to oaktag.

Self-evaluation

- ☐ Did I copy all of my paper sloper's guidelines, notches and grainlines accurately?
- ☐ Have I trued my oaktag sleeve so that all of my curved lines are smooth and my straight even?
- ☐ Did I use a notcher to notch all of my sleeve notches?

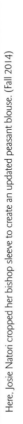

Bishop Sleeve

Learning objectives

☐ Prepare paper blocks, copy the straight sleeve sloper and draft the bishop sleeve—adding guidelines, shaping the bottom and creating fullness with the slash & spread method

☐ True the pattern—taping the drafted pattern onto a new block, using drafting tools to true the marks into smooth lines

☐ Make the final pattern—transferring the pattern to a new block, cutting, notching and annotating the pattern

☐ Make placket facing and button cuff patterns—drafting a placket facing to match the placket slit, drafting the button cuff

Tools and supplies:

- Straight Sleeve Sloper (see Lesson 1.1)
- Three blocks of white unlined pattern paper— each 20 x 28" (51 x 71cm)
- Square of white unlined pattern paper— 14 x 14"(35.5 x 35.5cm)

Here, Josie Natori cropped her bishop sleeve to create an updated peasant blouse. (Fall 2014)

Module 1:

Lesson Prep

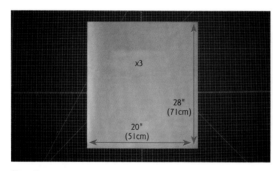

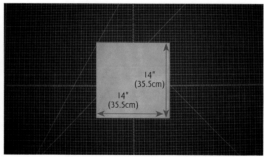

Step 1

For this lesson you will prepare three pattern paper blocks, each measuring 20" (51cm) wide by 28" (71cm) long.

Step 2

You will also need to cut a single pattern paper block that is 14" (35.5cm) square.

Module 2:

Transferring the Straight Sleeve Sloper

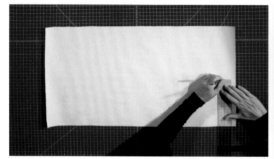

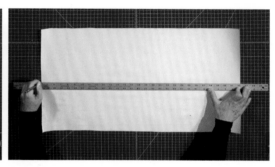

Step 1

Take one of the 20 x 28" (51 x 71cm) paper blocks and measure over 10" (25.5cm) from the length edge at the top of the block (here shown rotated to the bottom of the photograph).

Now measure over 10" (25.5cm) from the length edge at the bottom of the block.

Step 2

Draw a line connecting these points through the center of the paper. This is your sleeve center.

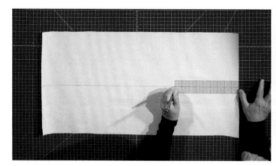

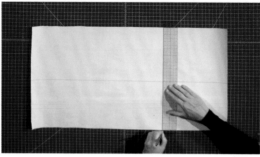

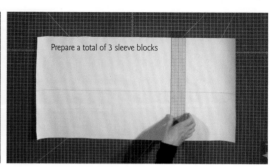

Step 3

Measure down 9" (23cm) on the centerline from the top of the block and place a mark.

Step 4

At this mark, square a line across, perpendicular to the centerline, with your clear plastic ruler. This is your bicep line.

Now repeat these steps to prepare the two remaining 20 x 28" (51 x 71cm) pattern paper blocks.

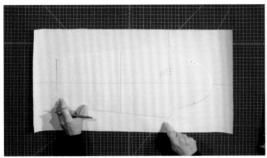

Step 5
Place your straight sleeve sloper oaktag on one of your 20 x 28"
(51 x 71cm) paper blocks, matching up the centerline and
bicep of the sloper to the center and bicep marks on the paper.

Step 6
Use weights to hold the sloper in place, then trace the sleeve
onto the paper. Remember to mark the sleeve notches at the cap.
Remove the sloper from the paper.

Module 3:

Bishop Sleeve Prep

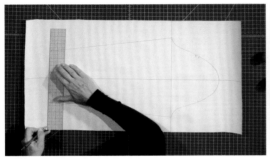

Step 1
Extend the horizontal line at the wrist for 3" (7.5cm) on each
side of the sleeve's underarm seam.

Step 2
Using your L square, square a line down from the bicep to the
3" (7.5cm) mark at the wrist. This is your new underarm seam.
Square a line down from the bicep mark on the other side.

Step 3A
On the back section of the sleeve, along the bicep line, measure
the distance between the underarm and the centerline with your
tape measure.

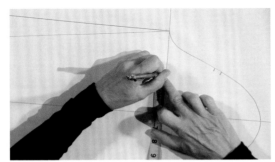

Step 3B
Divide that number in half, and place a mark on the bicep line.

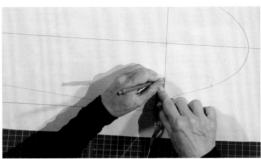

Step 3C
Do the same on the front section of the sleeve.

Step 4A
On the back section of the sleeve, rest your L square on the
bicep line at the midway point and then square a line down to
the wrist.

Step 4B
Extend that line up to the cap of the sleeve.

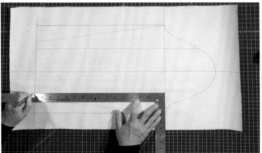

Step 4C
Square a line on the front section of the sleeve, just as you did for the back, from bicep to wrist.

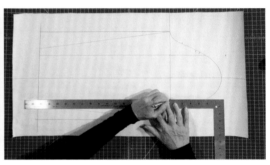

Step 4D
Extend that line to the cap, just as you did on the back.

Step 5
Cut the sleeve out, beginning at the cap, but do not cut along the length end of the sleeve at the wrist.

Tip
The amount of fullness at the bottom of the sleeve will depend upon the weight and type of fabric. The lighter the fabric, the more gathers the sleeve can support.

Module 4:
Drafting the Sleeve

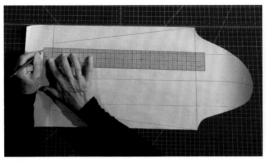

Step 1
Next, you will reshape the bottom of the sleeve to accommodate the bend of the elbow and to create a blouson effect. Extend the sleeve length at the back midway point, 1" (2.5cm) down, and place a mark.

Step 2
Use your hip curve to blend the sleeve edge from the lowered back midway point to the underarm/hem intersection on the front sleeve.

Flip the hip curve as you go, to create a nice smooth curve.

Step 3
Use your hip curve to blend a curve on the back sleeve edge, from the back underarm seam/hem intersection to the 1" (2.5cm) lowered back midway point.

Step 4A
Extend the back midway line into the lowered sleeve edge area with your ruler.

Step 4B
Cut along the new curved sleeve edge.

Step 5
Slash into the back midway line, from the sleeve bottom edge up to within 1/16" (2mm) away from the cap.

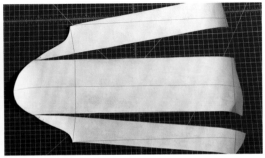

Step 6
Slash into the front midway line, from the sleeve bottom edge up to within 1/16" (2mm) away from the cap.

Module 5:

Creating the Pattern

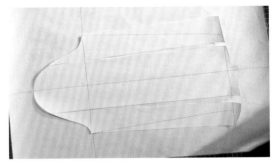

Step 1
Slip your second 20 x 28" (51 x 71cm) pattern paper block under the sleeve, matching the bicep line and the centerline on the sleeve to those on the paper block. Pin or tape the sleeve centerline at the cap and at the sleeve bottom edge.

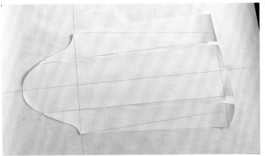

Step 2
Insert a pin through the paper and into the cutting mat at the back cap/midway pivot point.

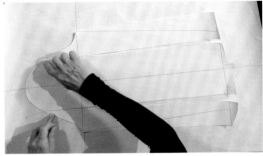

Step 3
Insert another pin at the front cap/midway pivot point.

Step 4A
Pivoting from the back cap, spread the bottom edge of the back sleeve by 2" (5cm) or more, depending on the desired fullness. Tape the sleeve edges down on both sides.

Step 4B
Pivoting from the front cap, spread the front sleeve by 2" (5cm), or by whatever amount you used on the back, then tape both sides down to the paper.

Step 5
Now remove the pins at the cap and secure the cap to the paper with tape.

Step 6
Tape down the underarms at the bicep. Note how the bicep line of the sleeve is raised as a result of the slashing and spreading.

Step 7A
At the sleeve edge, divide the distance between the back midway line and the underarm section in half, and place a mark.

Step 7B
Use your yardstick to draw a line connecting the new mark to the back cap notch.

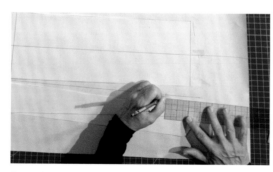

Step 7C
Measure up 3" (7.5cm) on the new line from the sleeve's bottom edge for the placket opening and make a mark.

Step 8
Blend the sleeve's bottom edge, both front and back, where the sleeve was spread, flipping your curve to get a nice smooth line.

Step 9
Use your styling curve to blend the back cap and the front cap.

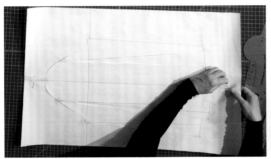

Step 1
Place the sleeve draft over the third 20 x 28" (51 x 71cm) piece of pattern paper, matching the bicep and centerlines of the sleeve to those on the paper. Pin both pieces of paper together on the centerline, both top and bottom.

Step 2A
Use your tracing wheel to trace the sleeve through to the new paper, beginning at the back underarm at the sleeve bottom edge and continuing all around the sleeve.

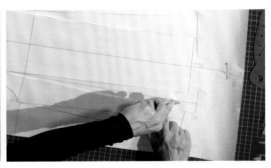

Step 2B
Trace the sleeve placket and the placket cross mark.

Step 2C
Trace the sleeve center at the bottom edge.

Step 2D
Trace the sleeve cap notches—back, center, and front.

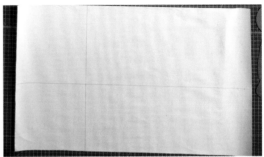

Step 2E
Then separate the draft from the paper.

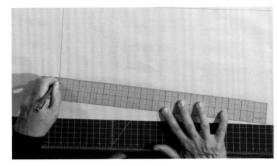

Step 3A
The next step is to pencil in all of your tracing lines, beginning at the bottom edge of the back underarm.

Step 3B
Use your styling curve to pencil in all of the cap tracing marks, flipping the curve over to form nice curved lines.

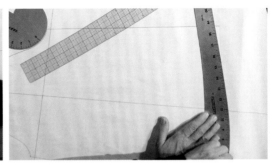

Step 3C
Use your hip curve to pencil in the bottom edge of the sleeve, flipping the curve to get a smooth line.

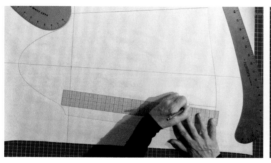

Step 3D
Draw the placket line to the cross-mark.

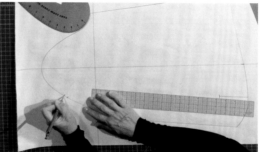

Step 4
Mark your sleeve center notch on the bottom edge. Then mark the back cap notches, and the center cap and front cap notches.

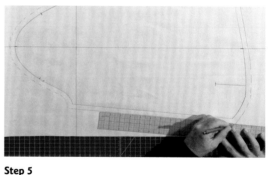

Step 5
Add ½" (1.3cm) seam allowance all around the pattern, working from the back underarm/bottom edge, then around the sleeve cap back and front, down the front underarm seam, and along the sleeve's bottom edge.

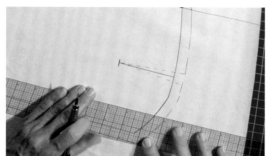

Step 6
At the placket slit opening, add ¼" (6mm) seam allowance, reducing to nothing at the point.

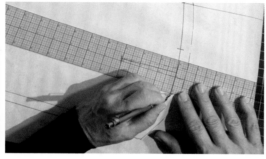

Step 7
Next, add notches 1" (2.5cm) away from the ¼" (6mm) line on both sides of the placket opening. This is where the sleeve gathers will stop.

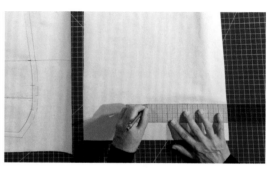

Step 8A
To draft a placket facing, start by drawing a line 6" (15cm) long, at 4" (10cm) in from the edge of your 14" (35.5cm) square pattern paper block.

Step 8B
Line up the placket line of the sleeve with the line on your pattern block.

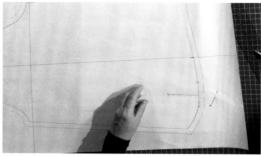

Step 8C
Pin the sleeve and the paper block together, above and below the placket slit opening.

Step 8D
With your tracing wheel, trace the stitching line from notch to notch at the bottom of the sleeve.

Step 8E
Trace the centerline of the placket slit opening and cross mark the top of the placket slit.

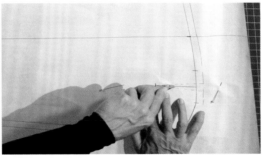

Step 8F
Trace the stitching line on both sides of the placket slit.

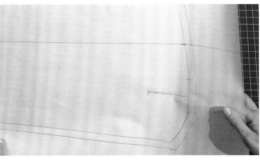

Step 8G
Remove the pins and separate the sleeve from the facing draft.

Step 8H
Pencil in the tracing marks of the sleeve stitching line at the bottom edge with the styling curve.

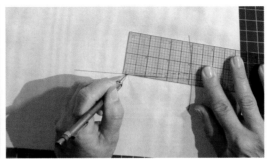

Step 8I
Pencil in the tracing marks for the slit cross-mark and the ¼" (6mm) stitching lines on both sides of the slit.

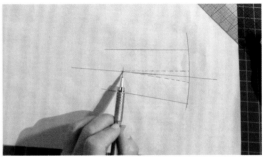

Step 8J
Add 1" (2.5cm) from the stitching line of the slit on both sides to create a facing. Now locate the top of the slit centerline.

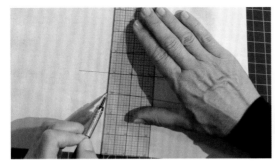

Measure up 1" (2.5cm) from the top of the slit centerline, then square off at this point. Add ½" (1.3cm) seam allowance to the bottom edge of the facing.

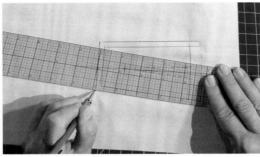

Step 8K
Erase excess pencil lines and add ¼" (6mm) seam allowance all around the placket slit facing.

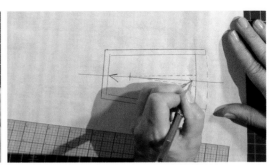

Step 8L
Add arrows on the centerline to denote the grainline.

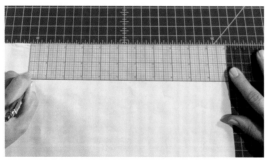

Step 1
Using your 14" (35.5cm) square pattern paper block, square off a cross grain line 2" (5cm) away from the top of the paper.

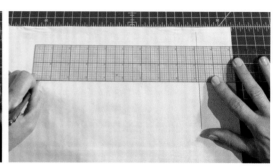

Step 2
Now draw a lengthwise grainline 2" (5cm) away from the right side edge of the paper.

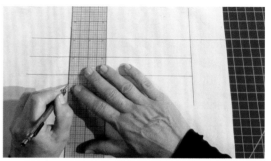

Step 3
For this lesson we will be making a 1" (2.5cm) wide cuff. Begin by measuring down 1" (2.5cm) from the cross grain line and draw a line across for 9" (23cm). This is the cuff's foldline.

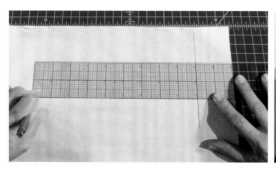

Step 4
Now measure down 1" (2.5cm) from the foldline and draw a line across.

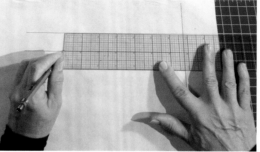

Step 5
On the foldline, measure across by your body wrist measurement, adding ½" (1.3cm) for ease, and place a mark. This represents the cuff circumference. For example, a US size 6 (UK size 10) wrist measures 6¼" (15.9cm) plus ½" (1.3cm) ease, totaling 6¾" (17.2cm).

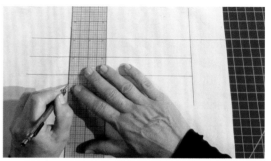

Step 6
Square a line down from the cross grain line on the cuff circumference mark.

Step 7
Now add a 1" (2.5cm) button extension from the cuff circumference line.

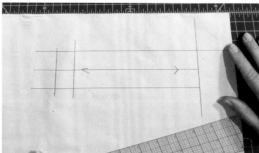

Step 8
Add grainline arrows at both ends of the foldline.

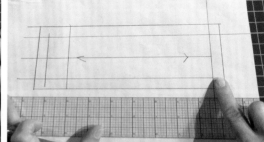

Step 9
Add ½" (1.3cm) seam allowance all around the cuff. If you have decided to make a cuff wider than 1" (2.5cm) then you will need to shorten your sleeve's length accordingly. For example, for a 2" (5cm) cuff, shorten your sleeve length by 1" (2.5cm). This leaves 1" (2.5cm) for the sleeve's blouson.

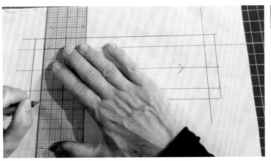

Step 10
With your plastic ruler, extend all of your seam lines into the cuff seam allowances.

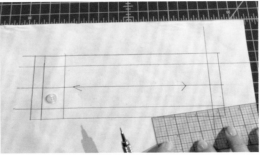

Step 11A
The size of your button extension will be double the button's width, so it depends on the button you will be using. Our button is ½" (1.3cm) so our extension is 1" (2.5cm).

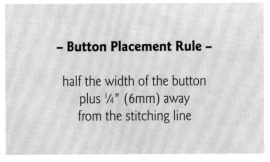

– Button Placement Rule –

half the width of the button
plus ¼" (6mm) away
from the stitching line

Step 11B
The Button Placement Rule = half the width of the button, plus ¼" (6mm) away from the stitching line.

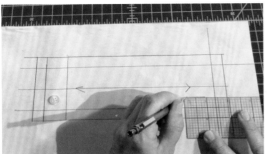

Step 12A
For this ½" (1.3cm)-wide button, place your ruler on the center of the cuff, measure over ½" (1.3cm) from the stitching line and draw a ½" (1.3cm) line for the button width plus ⅛" (3mm) ease.

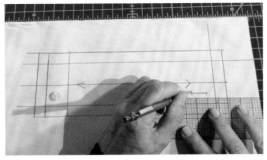

Step 12B
Cross-mark both ends of the buttonhole line. Then erase any extra lines.

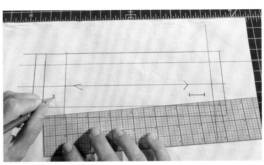

Step 13
Mark the button placement at ½" (1.3cm) away from the stitching line on the center of the cuff extension.

Module 8:

Cutting, Notching &
Annotating the Pattern

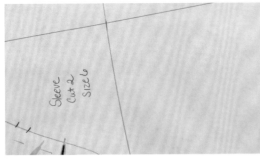

Step 1A
Annotate the sleeve pattern with "Sleeve," "Cut 2," and "Size 6," or whatever your particular size is.

Step 1B
Add arrows to the sleeve centerline to denote the grainline.

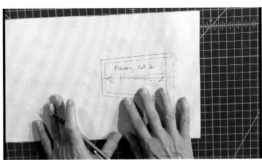

Step 2
Annotate the facing with "Facing" and "Cut 2."

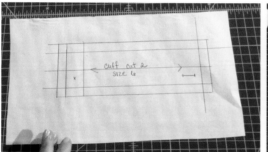

Step 3A
Annotate the cuff with "Cuff," "Cut 2," and "Size 6," or whatever your particular size is.

Step 3B
Cut out the cuff pattern.

Step 3C
Notch the cuff foldline and extension on both sides of the cuff.

Step 4A
Cut out the facing piece.

Step 4B
Notch the facing on the slit stitching lines and on the center slit line.

Step 5A
You will also need to annotate where the sleeve gathers are at the sleeve's edge. Write "Gathers" and add arrows to indicate where the gathers begin and end, on both sides of the slit.

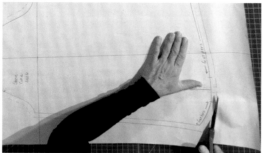

Step 5B
Cut the sleeve out and then notch all of your sleeve notches.

Step 6
You have now finished your Bishop Sleeve pattern.

Self-evaluation

☐ Have I added equal amounts to the sleeve underarm seam at the wrist?

☐ Have I divided my sleeve evenly along the bicep?

☐ Have I drafted my sleeve placket on the back sleeve?

☐ Is my button and buttonhole placed properly on my cuff?

Puff Sleeve

Learning objectives

☐ Preparing paper blocks, copying the straight sleeve sloper onto paper

☐ Draft the puff sleeve—determining the sleeve length, measuring the bicep to divide the sleeve into sections, slashing the sections to widen the sleeve, taping onto a new block, trueing the marks to create smooth lines

☐ Make the final pattern—transferring the pattern to a new block, cutting, notching and annotating the pattern

☐ Make a banded cuff pattern—drafting a cuff to match the bottom edge of the sleeve

Tools and supplies:

- Straight Sleeve Sloper (see Lesson 1.1)
- Three blocks of white unlined pattern paper— each 16 x 18" (41 x 46cm)

Module 1:

Lesson Prep

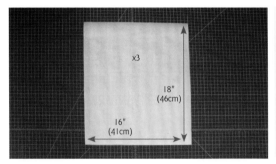

Tip
When planning and estimating the amount of gathers to add to your puff sleeve, always consider the weight of your fabric. The lighter the fabric, the more gathers you can add.

Step 1
For this lesson you will prepare three pieces of white unlined pattern paper, measuring 16" (41cm) wide by 18" (46cm) long.

54

Module 2:

Measuring & Tracing the Sleeve

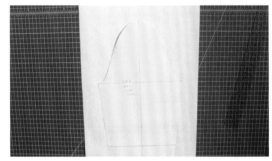

Step 1
Center your straight sleeve sloper on the 18" (46cm) length side of one of your pattern paper blocks.

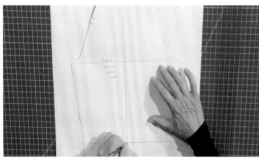

Step 2
Place center marks on the pattern paper at the bicep and elbow intersection, and at the center cap.

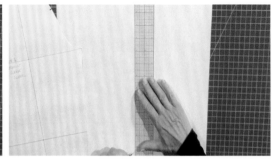

Step 3
Draw a vertical line through the center of the paper, connecting those marks.

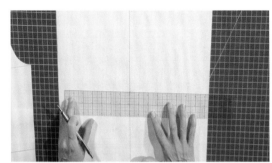

Step 4
Square off a line at the bicep and draw a horizontal line across the paper.

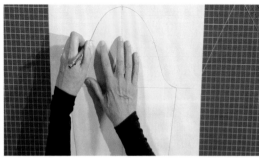

Step 5
Matching the sloper's center and bicep guidelines to the paper, trace the sloper from the elbow line and cap on one side to the other side, onto the paper, marking the cap notches as you go. Then remove the sloper.

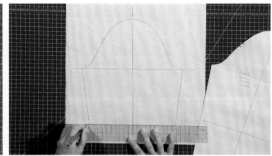

Step 6
Draw a horizontal line connecting the elbow line markings.

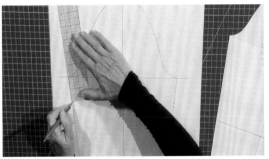
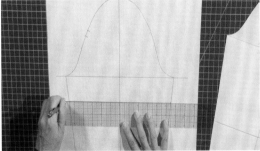

Step 7A
Determine the desired underarm length—usually 2" (5cm) to 5" (12.5cm) below the bicep line—and place a mark.

Step 7B
At the desired underarm length mark, square a line across. This is your sleeve length.

Module 3:

Puff Sleeve Prep

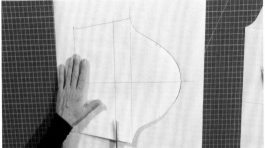
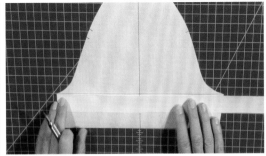
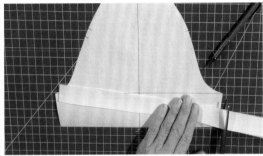

Step 1
Using your paper scissors, cut the sleeve out along your new sleeve length line.

Step 2A
Take a strip of paper 1" (2.5cm) wide and a few inches longer than your bicep measurement.

Use this paper strip to measure your bicep, then cut the paper at that measurement.

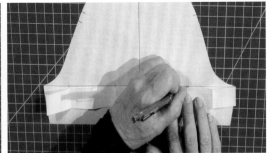

Step 2B
Divide the strip in half, in half again, and then in half one last time, until you end up with eight equal sections.

Step 2C
Unfold the strip and line it up with the bicep line of the sleeve.

Step 2D
Transfer each of the eight sections onto the sleeve's bicep line.

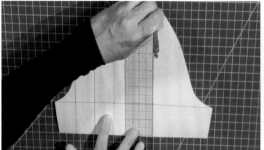

Step 2E
Draw length lines connecting each section from the cap to the sleeve's bottom edge. Make sure that your lines are perpendicular to the bicep line.

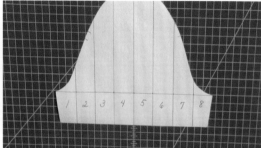

Step 3
Number each section, from 1 through to 8, beginning at the back sleeve.

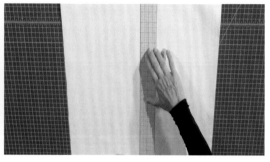

Step 4
Place your second 16 x 18" (41 x 46cm) pattern paper piece on the table, find the center of the paper, and draw a vertical line through it. This represents the center of the sleeve.

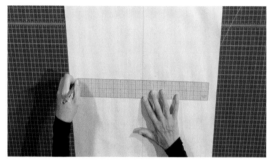
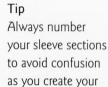

Step 5
Measure down 9" (23cm) from the top of the paper and square a line across off the centerline. This represents the bicep line. Repeat these steps to prepare the last pattern paper block.

Tip
Always number your sleeve sections to avoid confusion as you create your sleeve fullness.

Module 4:

Drafting the Sleeve

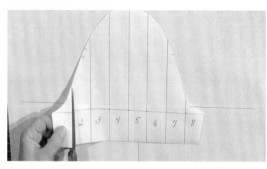

Step 1
Place your sleeve on top of your second pattern paper block. Slash along the first length line of the sleeve, from the bottom edge to within 1/16" (2mm) of the cap.

Step 2
Slash and separate along lines 2, 3, 4, 5, and 6, keeping line 7 connected to within 1/16" (2mm) of the front cap, as you did for the first section on the back cap.

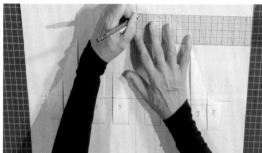

Step 3
Starting at the cap, measure over 1/2" (1.3cm) off the centerline on the new paper block and place a mark. Do the same on the bicep line.

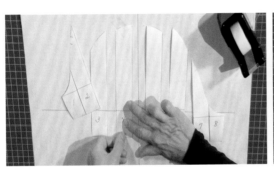

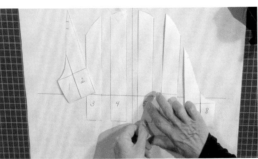

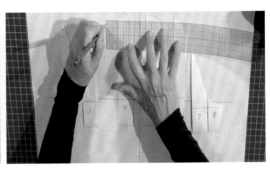

Step 4
Use tape to attach back piece #4 to the new paper, both top and bottom, matching the ½" (1.3cm) marks on the back cap and the bicep line.

Repeat this step for piece #5 on the front cap.

Step 5
Measure 1" (2.5cm) away at the cap from piece #4 and place a mark. Position piece #3 on this mark, making sure that the bicep is level.

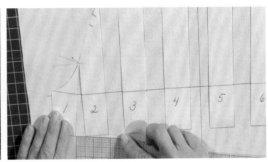

Tape piece #3 to the new paper, both top and bottom.

Step 6
Repeat this process for pieces #6, #2, and #7, remembering to always align the bicep. If you are looking for a fuller sleeve then you can separate the sections by more than 1" (2.5cm). It really depends on the desired fullness and the weight of your fabric. The thinner the fabric, the more fullness you can add.

Step 7
Insert a pin into the cap on piece #1 and pivot the piece so that it sits ½" (1.3cm) away from piece #2. The bicep line curves up as you pivot.

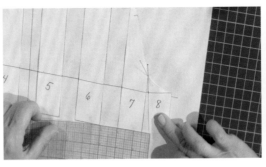

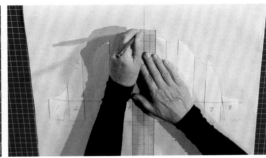

Step 8
Tape the sleeve edge of piece #1, then remove the pin and tape the cap pivot area.

Step 9
Repeat this process for piece #8, pivoting the piece to spread out by ½" (1.3cm) at the bottom.

Step 10
The next step is to blend the cap. Begin by raising the cap ½" (1.3cm) at the sleeve center.

Step 11
Blend the new cap with the styling curve, from the raised ½" (1.3cm) mark at the center, blending to nothing at the front underarm. You will notice that piece #2 is outside of the blended curve, which is fine.

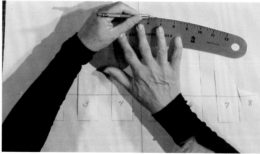

Step 12
Be sure that your cap's centerlines are at a right angle, and that you have a nice smooth line.

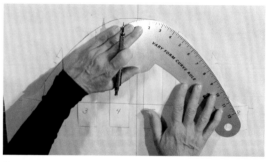

Step 13
Next, blend your back cap in the same way as you did on the front. You'll notice that your section #5 piece will extend beyond the blended line.

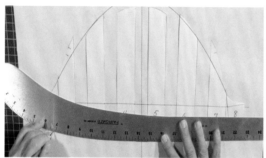

Step 14
Lower the sleeve edge ½" (1.3cm) at the center and blend the edge, using your hip curve, to the underarm. Do the same for the other side.

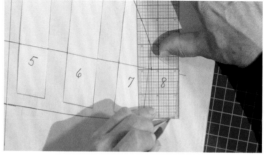

Step 15
Using a red pencil, adjust your front underarm by squaring off at the bicep/underarm intersection on the front.

Note how the sleeve extends out at the underarm once it has been squared off.

Step 16
Place a notch mark at 1" (2.5cm) away from the underarm/side seam intersection on the bottom edge of the sleeve.

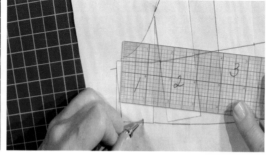

Step 17
Repeat the process of squaring off the underarm and notching the back, in the same way as for the front.

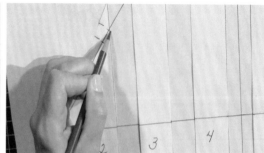

Step 18
With your red pencil, mark your back notches on the new sleeve cap, in line with the old notches.

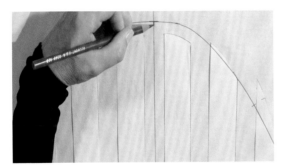

Step 19
Do the same for your front cap notch and sleeve center notch.

Module 5:

Creating the Pattern

Step 1
Place your sleeve draft over the second paper block, matching the center and bicep line of the sleeve draft to those on the paper. Then pin them together at the top and bottom.

Step 2
With your sleeve draft aligned and placed on top of the paper block, use a tracing wheel to trace the sleeve through to the new paper. Trace the underarm, the front and back cap, and the sleeve bottom edge.

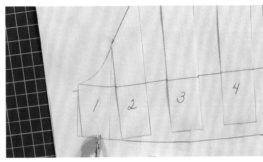

Step 3
Trace the notches on the bottom edge, the back cap, the center, and the front cap.

Step 4A
Remove the pins and separate the draft from the pattern.

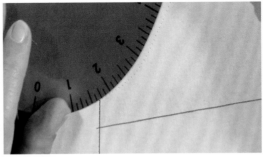

Step 4B
Use your straight ruler and styling curve to draw in all of your tracing marks.

Step 5
Be sure to square off the underarm intersections.

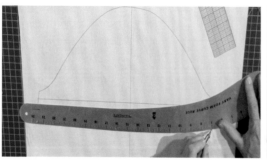

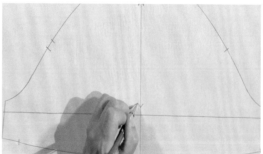

Now use your hip curve to blend the sleeve edge.

Step 6
Re-mark your notches on the sleeve edge, and the front and back cap, and add an arrow for the grainline on the centerline.

Step 7
Re-blend the cap area, as well as any other areas that need to be re-blended.

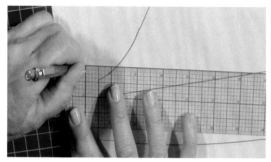

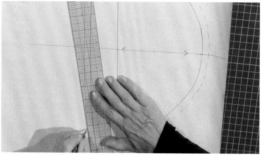

Step 8
Add ½" (1.3cm) seam allowance, beginning at the back underarm. Be sure to square your line at the back underarm.

Step 9
Proceed to add ½" (1.3cm) seam allowance all around the cap, from back to front, remembering to square the front underarm before adding seam allowance to the sleeve bottom edge.

Module 6:

Drafting the Banded Cuff

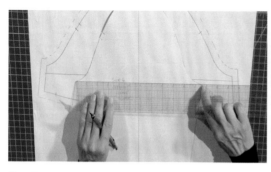

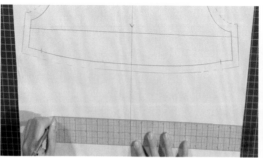

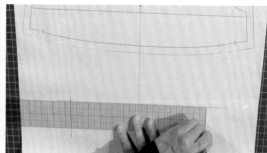

Step 1
In preparation for drafting the banded cuff, measure the bicep of your straight sleeve sloper.

Step 2
Square a line off the center of the paper, below your puff sleeve draft pattern.

Step 3
Square off one end of that line, measure over by your bicep measurement from that point, and square off another line. For a US size 6 (UK size 10) this will measure 11½" (29.2cm).

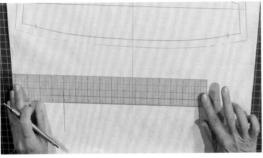
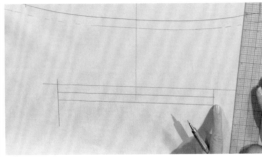
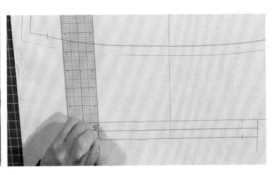

Step 4
Measure down from the horizontal edge the desired cuff width—in this case ½" (1.3cm). Then draw a line across from end to end. This represents the band's edge.

Step 5
Measuring down another ½" (1.3cm), parallel to the first line, and draw another line across. This is the band's self facing.

Step 6
Mark your notches, 1" (2.5cm) in from the outer edges on both sides, top and bottom. These will match the notches on your sleeve's bottom edge, where the shirring starts and stops.

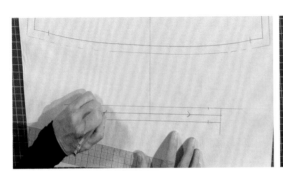
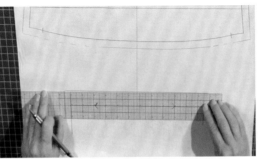
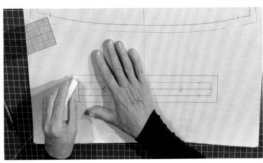

Step 7
Draw grainline arrows on the horizontal line.

Step 8
Add ½" (1.3cm) seam allowance all around the band—the top horizontal edge, the underarm, the bottom horizontal edge, and the other side of the underarm.

Step 9
Make sure all of your ends are squared off before you erase any extra lines.

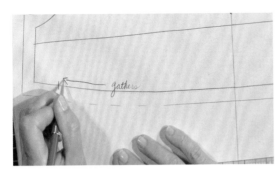
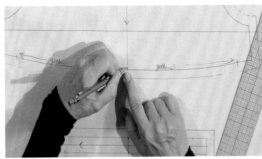
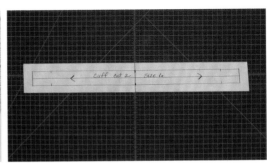

Step 10
Write "Gathers" above the stitching line of the sleeve edge, between the two notches on both sides, and add arrows to indicate the gathers.

Step 11
Add notches at the center of the cuff and the center of the sleeve's edge.

Step 12A
Annotate the sleeve cuff with "Cuff," "Cut 2," and "Size 6," or whatever your size may be.

Step 12B
Annotate the sleeve with "Sleeve," "Cut 2," and "Size 6," or whatever your size may be.

Step 13
Cut out both the cuff pattern and the sleeve pattern with your paper scissors.

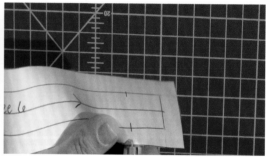

Step 14
Use your notcher to notch both ends of the shirring notches on the banded cuff.

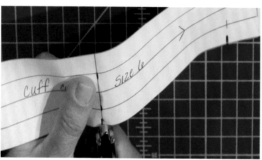

Then notch the center of the band, both top and bottom.

Step 15
Make your sleeve notches next, starting with the notch at one end of the shirring, then the sleeve center, and then the other shirring notch.

Complete the sleeve cap notches next: back, center, and front.

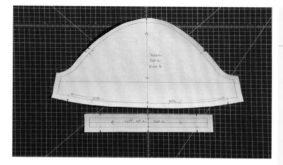

Step 16
You have now finished drafting your Puff Sleeve with Banded Cuff.

Self-evaluation

☐ Have I divided my sleeve hem into eight equal sections?

☐ Did I number each of the sleeve sections before cutting them apart?

☐ Were my sleeve sections aligned with the center and bicep line of the paper?

☐ Is the curve of my sleeve cap blended smoothly?

☐ Did I measure my sleeve bicep properly to draft my banded cuff?

While the petal sleeve is most often used in childrenswear, Alberta Ferretti adds soft gathers to her sleeve to create a demure floor-length dress. (Spring/Summer 2015)

Petal Sleeve

Learning objectives

☐ Preparing paper blocks, copying the straight sleeve sloper onto paper

☐ Draft the petal sleeve—determining the sleeve length, marking the petal style lines, annotating the draft

☐ Make the final pattern—transferring the front and back shapes to a new block, trueing, annotating, cutting and notching the pattern

Tools and supplies:

- Straight Sleeve Sloper (see Lesson 1.1)
- Two blocks of white unlined pattern paper— each 16 x 18" (41 x 46cm)

Module 1:

Lesson Prep

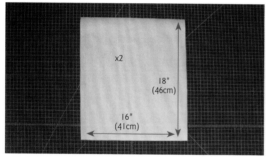

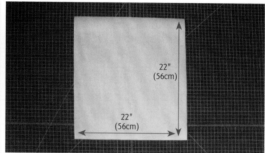

Step 1

For this lesson you will need to prepare two pieces of white unlined pattern paper. The first one should measure 16" (41cm) wide by 18" (46cm) long.

The second piece is a 22" (56cm) square.

Module 2:

Measuring & Tracing the Sleeve

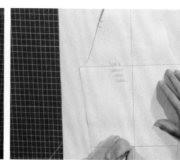

Step 1

Center your straight sleeve sloper on the 18" (46cm) length side of your pattern paper.

Step 2

Place center marks on the pattern paper at the bicep/elbow intersection and at the center cap.

Step 3

Draw a vertical line through the center of the paper, connecting those marks.

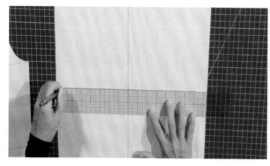

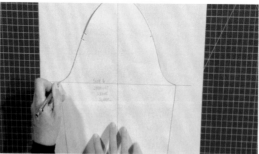

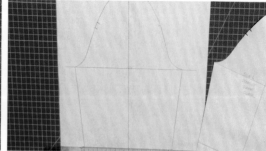

Step 4

Square off a line at the bicep and draw a horizontal line across the paper.

Step 5

Matching the sloper's center and bicep guidelines to the paper, trace the sloper onto the paper, from the elbow line and cap on one side to the other side, marking the cap notches as you go. Then remove the sloper.

Step 6

Draw a horizontal line connecting the elbow line markings.

Module 3:

Petal Sleeve Prep

Step 1
Determine the desired sleeve length. For this lesson we are measuring down 3" (7.5cm) from the sleeve underarm. Place a mark at the underarm at 3" (7.5cm) on both back and front.

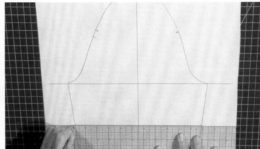

Step 2
Connect the underarm marks while keeping the line squared off at the sleeve center.

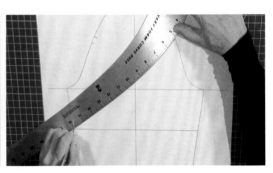

Step 3
The style line for the petal sleeve crosses at the center of the sleeve, from notch to hem. Use your hip curve to draw a curve from the front notch to the underarm/hem intersection.

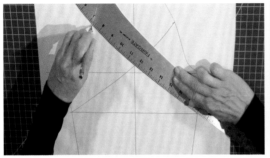

Step 4
Flip the curve over and connect a line from the middle of the back notches to the front underarm/hem intersection. The front and back cap measurements must be equal and the style lines must meet at the center of the sleeve.

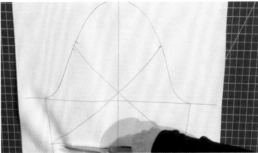

Step 5
Cut the sleeve across at the hemline, in preparation for drafting the petal sleeve.

Tip
The underarm length of a petal sleeve should never extend past the elbow.

Petal Sleeve

Module 4:

Drafting the Petal Sleeve

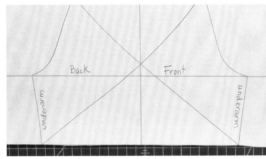

Step 1
The next step is to annotate your draft. Write "Front" and "Back" on the bicep line, and "Underarm" on both sides of the sleeve's underarm.

Step 2A
With your 22" (56cm)-square pattern paper on the table, find the center of the paper and draw a vertical line through it. This represents the center of the sleeve.

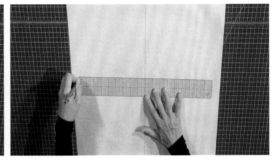

Step 2B
Measure down by 9" (23cm) from the top of the paper and then square a line across off the centerline. This represents the bicep line.

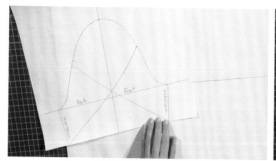

Step 3
Place the sleeve draft over the new paper. Line up the front underarm seam with the left side of the center vertical line of the paper, matching the corner bicep line of the sleeve with the bicep line of the paper.

Step 4
Use tape on the top and the bottom to secure the sleeve draft to the paper.

Step 5
Using your tracing wheel, trace the front of the sleeve only, beginning at the front sleeve cap, continuing along the cap to the back cap. Then trace the front petal style line to the underarm. Trace the notches—back, center, and front.

Step 6
Loosen the tape and remove the draft from the paper.

Step 7
Now position the back sleeve on the paper, lining up the back underarm seam of the sleeve with the right side of the center vertical line of the paper. Be sure to match the corner bicep line of the sleeve with the bicep line of the paper. Use the same piece of tape to hold the sleeve down.

Step 8
Trace the back of the sleeve beginning at the front sleeve cap, continuing around the cap to the back, moving along the back petal style line to the underarm. Trace the center and back notches. Remove the draft from the paper.

Step 9
The next step is to outline the tracing lines with your pencil, but first draw arrows indicating the grainline at the center of the underarm.

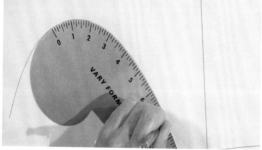

Step 10
Next, with your styling curve, true the back cap, then turn the curve and true the other side of the cap and underarm.

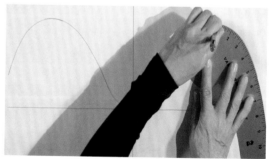

Step 11
Flip the curve and true the front underarm and cap.

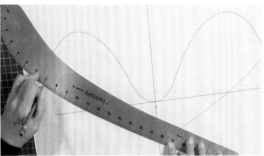

Step 12
Use your hip curve and mark the front petal style line from cap to underarm. Flip the curve over and mark the back petal style line from cap to underarm.

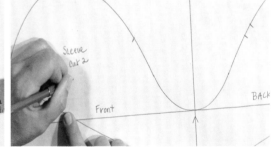

Step 13
You will need to blend the line of the underarm at the hem so that it is not a point. Use a red pencil and your hip curve to blend a nice smooth curve. Flip the curve to re-blend the line. You will notice that the sleeve inseam will shorten as a result of this step.

Step 14
Pencil in the notches on the front sleeve cap and then the notches on the back sleeve cap. Label the "Back" sleeve and the "Front" sleeve, and annotate the draft with "Sleeve," "Cut 2," and "Size 6," or whatever your particular size may be.

Module 5:
Final Steps

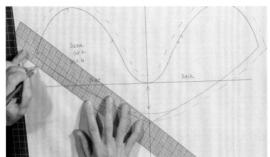

Step 1
Resting your ruler on the stitching line of the sleeve at the ½" (1.3cm) mark, add ½" (1.3cm) seam allowance to the sleeve, beginning at the front cap. Pivot the ruler around the front cap, the underarm, the back petal style line, the new hemline, and the front petal style line.

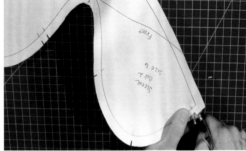

Step 2
This sleeve's hem can either be lined or finished with a bias binding. Once you have finished adding seam allowances all around, cut the pattern out. Using your notcher, make the back sleeve notches, the underarm notch, and the front sleeve notches.

Step 3
Lift the pattern from the table, overlap the sleeve, matching the notches, and check your petal sleeve.

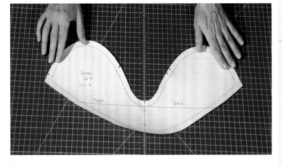

Step 4
You have now finished drafting your Petal Sleeve pattern.

Self-evaluation

☐ Did I draw my petal style line properly?

☐ Have I marked the front and back of the sleeve before tracing the style lines?

☐ Did I blend the underarm hem so it is a smooth curve and not a point?

☐ Are all of my notches properly placed?

2 Skirts

A straight skirt sloper is the foundation of many of your future skirt designs. You will learn how to draft a basic straight skirt from measurements, taken either from a live model or from a dress form. Once you have extracted the key measurements, you will use our straight skirt measurement form to record them, including wearing ease, and then commence on executing the draft. Positioning the front and back waist darts and calculating the dart intake amounts will produce a skirt with two front and back darts.

Next, you will learn how to draft four different types of circle skirt: Full Circle, often seen in evening and special occasion dresses, and the Three Quarter Circle, Half Circle and Quarter Circle, popular in casual sportswear and childrenswear. By using our radius calculations charts and skirt measurement forms to calculate and record your measurements, you will be able to easily draft these skirts. Due to the amount of fullness inherent in these types of skirts, you will be guided as to how to finalize the hems and given advice on both grainline positioning and seaming.

Straight Skirt Sloper

Learning objectives

- ☐ Establish measurements using a dress form or live figure to take and record key measurements

- ☐ Draft the skirt—preparing paper block with guidelines, adding ease, shaping the side seam and planning the darts

- ☐ Add final marks—cutting out the skirt sloper, trueing the waistline, marking zipper and dart notches and annotating and adding grainlines

- ☐ Check the fit—cutting the sloper in muslin, with appropriate seam allowance, pinning it together and adjusting the draft as necessary

Tools and supplies:

- Shoulder Dart Bodice Sloper (see Lesson 3.1) or Side Bust Dart Bodice Sloper (see Lesson 3.2)
- Style tape
- White unlined pattern paper—28 x 23¼" (71 x 59cm)
- Muslin (calico) for fit-testing

Straight Skirt Measurement Form

Body Measurements			Total		Wearing Ease		Total	
	Inches	CM	Inches	CM	Inches	CM	Inches	CM
Desired skirt length								
Front waist measurement								
Front hip measurement								
Back waist measurement								
Back hip measurement								
Dart Measurements							**Total**	
							Inches	CM
Front-waist draft measurement								
Front-waist body measurement (including ease ¼"/6mm)								
Front dart intake								
Front dart intake ÷ 2								
Back-waist draft measurement								
Back-waist body measurement (including ease ¼"/6mm)								
Back dart intake								
Back dart intake ÷ 2								

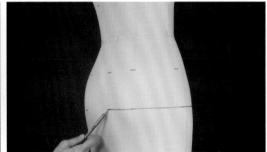

Step 1A

In preparation for drafting the straight skirt sloper, you will first establish the hip level on your dress form using style tape at 7" (18cm) down from the waistline. Style-tape the right side of the dress form, from center front ...

... to center back, parallel to the floor.

Step 1B

The easiest way to do this is by resting your L square on the table as you turn the dress form, making sure that your hip level style tape aligns with the ruler at the 7" (18cm) mark, from front to back.

Step 2

You will be recording your measurements on our Straight Skirt Measurement Form.

Step 3A

Start by establishing your desired skirt length. Our skirt will measure 24" (61cm). You will then record your desired skirt length on the Skirt Measurement Form. Place your tape measure at the waist tape.

Measure down to your desired hemline.

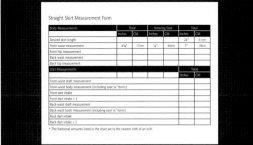

Step 3B

Measure from side seam to center front in the middle of the waist tape. This is your front waist measurement.

Step 3C

Our front waist measures 6¾" (17.2cm) so we will record that on our Straight Skirt Measurement Form. We will add ¼" (6mm) wearing ease to that and record the total front waist measurement as 7" (rounded to 18cm).

Step 3D

Next, measure from side seam to center front at the hip level to establish your front hip measurement. Record this measurement.

Step 3E
Our front hip measures 8½" (21.5cm). We will add ½" (1.3cm) wearing ease to that measurement and record the total front hip measurement of 9" (rounded to 23cm) on the form.

Step 4A
Next, measure from center back to the side seam in the middle of the waist tape to establish your back waist measurement, then record this on the form.

Step 4B
Our back waist measures 6" (15.2cm). We will add ¼" (6mm) wearing ease to that measurement and record the total back waist measurement of 6¼" (rounded to 16cm) on the form.

Step 4C
Measure your back hip next, from center back to side seam, and record that measurement.

Step 4D
Our back hip measures 9¾" (24.7cm). We will add ½" (1.3cm) wearing ease to that measurement and record a total back hip measurement of 10¼" (26cm).

Module 2:

Drafting the Skirt

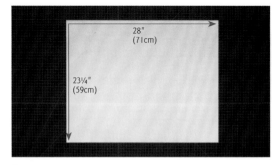

Step 1
Prepare a piece of unlined white pattern paper measuring your desired skirt length plus 4" (10cm), by your front and back hip measurement, plus 4" (10cm). For a US size 6 (UK size 10), we cut our paper at 28" (71cm) long by 23¼" (59cm) wide.

Step 2A
Come in 2" (5cm) from both ends of the length edge of the pattern paper and draw a line indicating center front.

Step 2B
Write "CF" in the middle of the paper.

Step 3A
Measure along 2" (5cm) on the center front line from the right side of the pattern paper and place a mark.

Step 3B
Square a line off center front at this mark across the width of the paper. This represents the waistline.

Step 3C
Write "WL" in the middle of the line close to the paper's edge.

Step 4A
Measure from the waistline, your desired skirt length, and make a mark.

Now square a line across the width of the paper. This is the hemline of the skirt.

Step 4B
Write "HL" above the hemline.

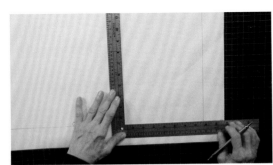

Step 5A
Measure down from the waistline by 7" (18cm) and square a line off center front. This represents the hipline.

Step 5B
Write "HL" next to the line.

Step 6A
At the center front/hipline intersection, measure your total front hip measurement, including wearing ease, and place a mark. This represents the side seam.

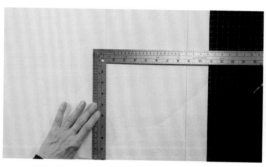
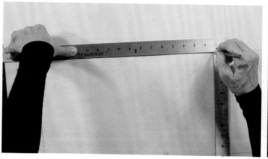

Step 6B

To create the side seam, use your L square to square a line off the hipline from the side seam mark, above the hipline.

Then square a line off the hipline at the side seam mark, but below the hipline, down to the edge of the paper.

Step 6C

Write "SS" below the hipline along the side seam.

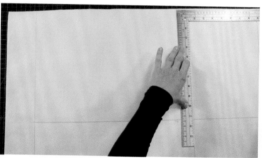

Step 7A

At the side seam/hipline intersection, measure over by your total back hip measurement, including wearing ease, and place a mark. This represents center back.

Step 7B

Square a line off the hipline at the center back mark, above the hipline, to create the upper part of the skirt's center back.

Square a line off the hipline at the center back mark, below the hipline, to continue the lower part of the center back.

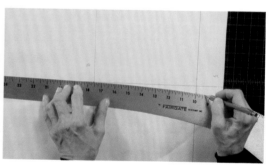

Step 7C

Label the center back with "CB" in the middle of the line.

Step 8A

Now at the side seam/waistline intersection, measure over ½" (1.3cm) on both sides of the side seam line and place a mark. This is will be the new shaped front and back side seam.

Step 8B

Using your hip curve, draw a line to shape the front side seam from about ¾" (2cm) above the waist to the hip.

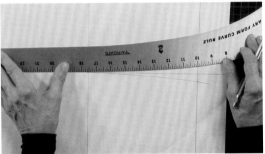

Step 8C
Now flip the hip curve over at the same position on the hip curve to shape the back side seam, from waist to hip. Be sure that your line extends above the waistline.

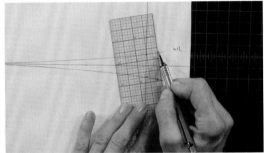

Step 9A
At the new shaped side seam/waist intersection, raise the waistline by ½" (1.3cm) and place a mark, first on the front, and then repeat this step on the back waistline.

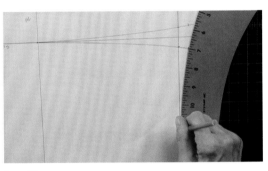

Step 9B
To shape the front waistline, use your hip curve and red pencil to blend from the front raised side seam down to nothing at center front.

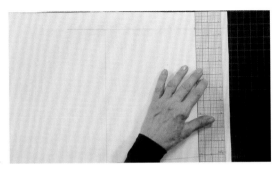

Step 9C
Before you can shape the back waist, you must first lower the center back waist by ½" (1.3cm) and place a ¼" (6mm) mark that is squared off from center back.

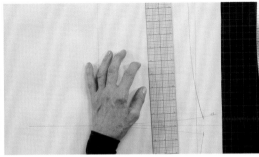

Step 9D
Now blend a curved line from the lowered center back mark to the raised waistline at the side seam to form the back waistline.

Module 3:

Marking the Front Waist Darts

Step 1A
To plan the front waist darts, you must first measure your front waist draft from center front to the side seam.

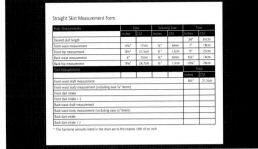

Step 1B
Record your front waist draft measurement on the Straight Skirt Measurement Form in the space provided, under Dart Measurements. Our measurement is 8½" (21.5cm).

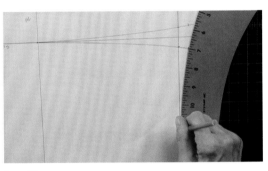

Step 2
Now take your front waist measurement, including ease, and record that total—in our case, 7" (18cm)—in the space provided for the front waist body measurement, in the Dart Measurements section.

Straight Skirt Measurement Form

Body Measurements	Total		Wearing Ease		Total	
	Inches	CM	Inches	CM	Inches	CM
Desired skirt length					24"	61cm
Front waist measurement	6¾"	17cm	¼"	6mm	7"	18cm
Front hip measurement	8½"	21.5cm	½"	1.3cm	9"	23cm
Back waist measurement	6"	15cm	¼"	6mm	6¼"	16cm
Back hip measurement	9¾"	24.7	½"	1.3cm	10¼"	26cm

Dart Measurements					Total	
					Inches	CM
Front-waist draft measurement					8½"	21.5cm
Front-waist body measurement (including ease ¼"/6mm)					7"	18cm
Front dart intake					1½"	3.8cm
Front dart intake ÷ 2						
Back-waist draft measurement						
Back-waist body measurement (including ease ¼"/6mm)						
Back dart intake						
Back dart intake ÷ 2						

* The fractional amounts listed in the chart are to the nearest 16th of an inch

Step 3A

Now subtract your front waist draft measurement from your front waist body measurement and record that number in the space provided on the form for the front dart intake. In our case, the dart intake is 1½" (3.8cm).

Straight Skirt Measurement Form

Body Measurements	Total		Wearing Ease		Total	
	Inches	CM	Inches	CM	Inches	CM
Desired skirt length					24"	61cm
Front waist measurement	6¾"	17cm	¼"	6mm	7"	18cm
Front hip measurement	8½"	21.5cm	½"	1.3cm	9"	23cm
Back waist measurement	6"	15cm	¼"	6mm	6¼"	16cm
Back hip measurement	9¾"	24.7	½"	1.3cm	10¼"	26cm

Dart Measurements					Total	
					Inches	CM
Front-waist draft measurement					8½"	21.5cm
Front-waist body measurement (including ease ¼"/6mm)					7"	18cm
Front dart intake					1½"	3.8cm
Front dart intake ÷ 2					¾"	2cm
Back-waist draft measurement						
Back-waist body measurement (including ease ¼"/6mm)						
Back dart intake						
Back dart intake ÷ 2						

* The fractional amounts listed in the chart are to the nearest 16th of an inch

Step 3B

Because we will be drafting two front darts for this skirt sloper, you will divide your dart intake measurement in half, and record that measurement on the form—front dart intake (÷2). Our dart intake for each front dart will be ¾" (2cm).

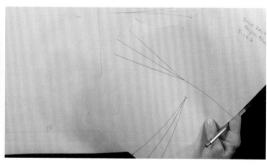

Step 4A

The placement of the first front-waist dart will align with the waist dart of your Side Bust Dart Bodice Sloper, or your Front Shoulder Dart Bodice Sloper, or with the princess seam of your dress form.

Step 4B

Turn the front bodice sloper to the wrong side and align its center front/waist intersection with that on the skirt. Place a mark on the skirt waistline to indicate the dart notch closest to center front. Then remove the front bodice sloper from the draft.

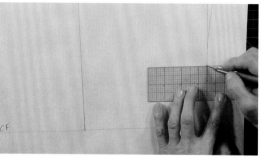

Step 4C

Next, measure over your front dart intake (÷ 2) amount—in our case, ¾" (2cm)—and place a mark to form the first dart.

Step 5A

Now find the midway point of the first dart and place a mark. A quick and easy way to do this is to measure the full span and then fold your tape measure over to locate the halfway point.

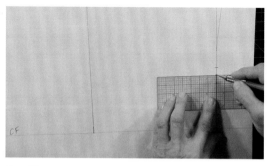

Step 5B

Square a line down from the waist at the first dart's center mark for 3½" (9cm). This is the dart's vanishing point.

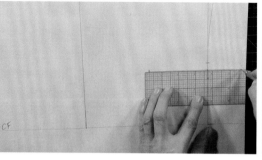

Step 5C

Draw the center dart line so that it extends beyond the waistline.

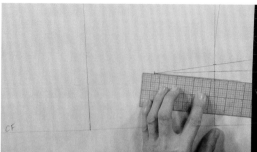

Step 5D

Complete the dart by connecting the vanishing point of the dart to the waist dart intake marks, extending the lines beyond the waistline.

Step 6A
To locate the position of the second front dart, measure the distance between the side seam to the first dart with your tape measure in order to establish the midway point.

Step 6B
Again, you can do this by folding your tape measure in half, as demonstrated. Place a mark at this point. This is the center of the second dart.

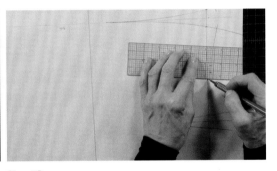

Step 6C
Use your ruler to measure and mark the second dart's pickup. Since our dart intake (÷ 2) amount is ¾" (2cm) we will measure half that amount on both sides of the dart's centerline. Complete the dart by connecting its vanishing point to the waist dart intake marks, extending the lines beyond the waistline.

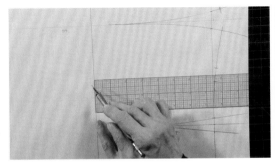

Step 6D
Squaring off from the hipline, establish the centerline of the second dart.

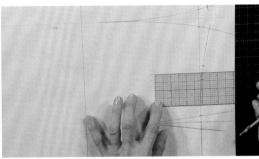

Step 6E
This dart will measure 3" (7.5cm) down from the waistline. Extend the centerline up, through the waist, to the paper's edge.

Complete the dart legs from the vanishing point to the waist.

Module 4:

Marking the Back Waist Darts

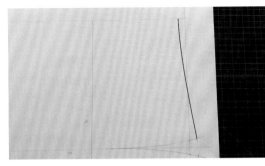

Step 1A
To plan the back darts, you must first measure your back waist draft from center back to the side seam along the back waistline.

Step 1B
Record your back waist draft measurement on the Straight Skirt Measurement Form in the space provided, under Dart Measurements. Our measurement is 8½" (21.5cm).

Step 2
Now take your back waist measurement, including ease, and record that total—in our case, 6¼" (16cm)—in the space provided for the back waist body measurement, in the Dart Measurements section.

Step 3A

Now, subtract your back waist draft measurement from your back waist body measurement, and record that number in the space provided on the form for the back dart intake. In our case, the dart intake is 2¼" (5.7cm).

Step 3B

We will be drafting two back darts for this skirt sloper, so just as you did for the front, divide your back dart intake measurement in half, and record that measurement on the form—back dart intake (÷2). Here, each back dart is 1⅛" (2.8cm).

Step 4A

The placement of the first back dart, the one closest to center back, will align with the waist dart of the back bust dart bodice sloper from Lesson 3.1. Or, it can sit approximately 2¾" (7cm) from center back for a US size 6 (UK size 10) dress form, and farther away for larger sizes.

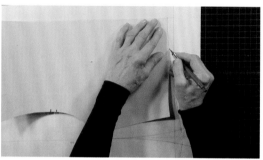

Step 4B

Turn the back bodice sloper to the wrong side, and align the center back/waist intersection of the bodice to that on the skirt. Place a mark on the skirt waistline to indicate the dart notch closest to center back.

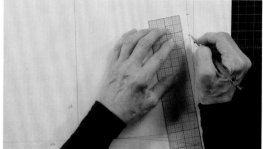

Step 4C

Next, measure over by your back dart intake (÷ 2) amount—in our case, 1⅛" (2.8cm)—and place a mark for the first dart.

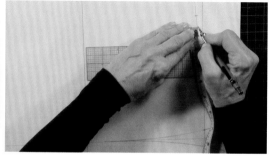

Step 5A

Now find the midway point of the first back dart and place another mark. As in the previous module, a quick and easy way to do this is to fold your tape measure, as demonstrated. Place a mark at the first dart's center.

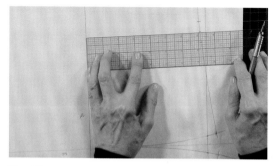

Step 5B

Squaring off from the hipline, use your ruler to establish the centerline of the dart.

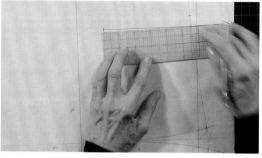

Draw in the midway line of the dart. Extend the line above the waist, and end the dart at 5½" (14cm) below the waist. Place a mark to indicate the dart's vanishing point.

Step 6A

To find the position of the second back dart, use your tape measure to find the midway point between the first dart leg line and the back side seam.

Step 6B

Fold the tape measure in half and place a mark on the waistline. This is the centerline of the second back dart.

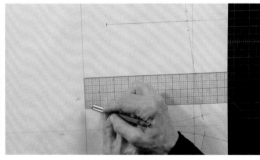

Step 6C

Now align your ruler with the dart centerline, squaring off from the hipline.

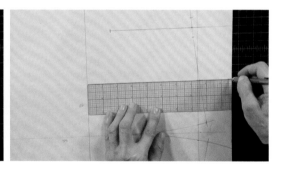

Draw a line that extends beyond the waist, and end the dart 5" (12.5cm) below the waist.

Place a mark to indicate the dart's vanishing point. Back darts should always end at least 1" (2.5cm) above the hipline and sometimes higher, depending on the fullness of the derrière.

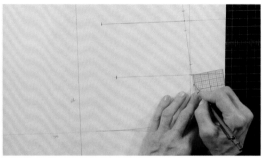

Step 6D

Mark your divided dart intake measurement on both sides of the second dart's centerline. In our case, this is ⁵⁄₁₆" (8mm).

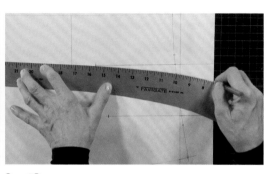

Step 7A

Now you will begin shaping the center back darts using your hip curve. Connect the vanishing point to the dart leg mark at the waistline.

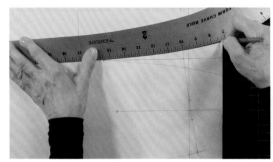

Step 7B

Flip the hip curve over at the same mark on the ruler and then draw the dart leg on the other side.

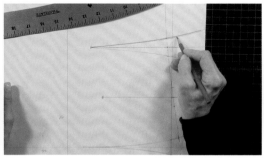

Step 7C

If you find that a correction is necessary, re-mark the line using hatch marks or a different colored pencil.

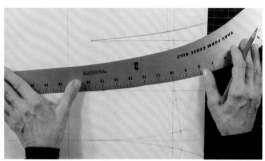

Step 7D

Now move to the second back dart. Use your hip curve to draw the dart leg, first on one side and then the other.

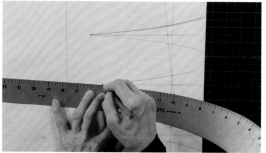

Tip

The first dart, closest to center front and center back, is positioned midway between center front and center back. The second dart is midway between the first dart and the side seam.

Remember to use the same number on the hip curve so that both dart legs have the same shape.

Module 5:

Trueing the Waistline

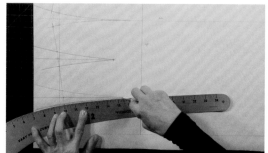

Step 1A

Begin by scoring the legs of the dart closest to center back using your hip curve and awl, from waist to vanishing point.

Step 1B

Repeat this step for the second dart.

Step 2A

Now move to the front dart and repeat this process. This time score the dart leg closest to center front using a ruler.

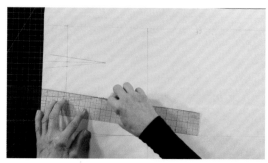

Step 2B

Complete the process by scoring the second front dart.

Step 3A

Now cut the skirt draft out along the hemline.

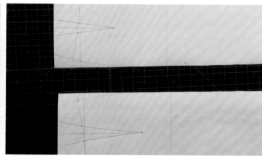

Step 3B

Cut along the original side seam to separate the front and back skirt. Do not cut away the excess paper at the waist, the center back, or the center front.

Step 4A
Now close and flatten the center back dart, with the dart excess going in the direction of center back. Note how the waistline does not match up exactly. Secure the dart with tape just below the waistline.

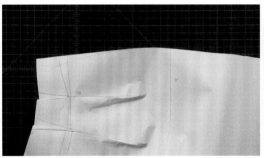

Step 4B
Repeat the process for the second front dart, creasing the dart along the scored edge and flattening it so that you can tape it down below the waist. Again, note that the waistline of the dart does not match exactly.

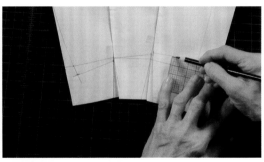

Step 5A
Use your ruler and blue pencil to square a line off the center back of the skirt for about 1½" (3.8cm).

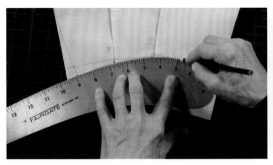

Step 5B
Use your hip curve to blend the back waistline from the side seam to the squared back waistline.

Step 5C
Trace the new back waistline along the darts to capture the direction of the dart intake.

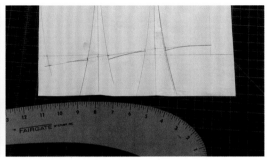

Step 5D
Remove the tape from the darts. Open the draft so that it lies flat on the table.

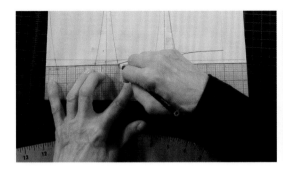

Step 5E
Following the tracing marks, use your ruler and blue pencil to mark the dart intake at the waistline.

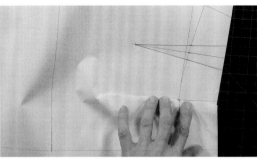

Step 6A
Now move to the front darts and repeat the process of folding and closing the dart closest to the center, with the dart intake going in the direction of center front. Secure the dart with tape below the waist.

Step 6B
Close the second dart, again with the dart intake going in the direction of center front. Secure it with tape below the waist. Note that the front darts may also not align at the waistline.

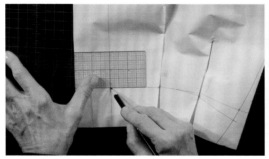

Step 6C

Just as you did on the back skirt, square a line off center front at the waistline.

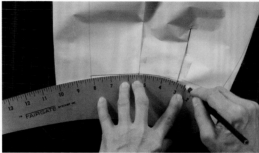

Step 6D

Position your hip curve to create a nice smooth curve along the front waistline with your blue pencil.

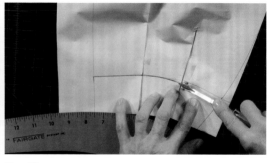

Step 6E

Trace the new front waistline along the darts to capture the direction of the dart intake.

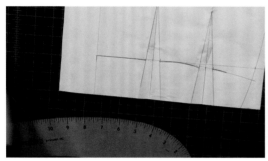

Step 6F

Remove the tape from the darts and open the draft, so that it lies flat on the table.

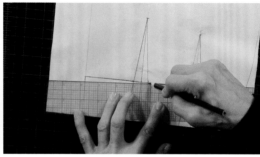

Step 6G

Following the tracing marks, use your ruler and blue pencil to mark the front dart intake at the waistline.

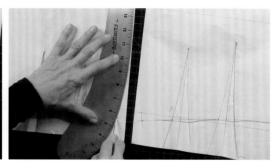

Step 7A

Next, you will score the front side seam above the hip, using your hip curve and awl.

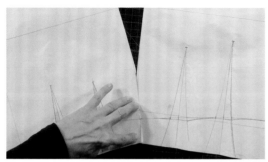

Step 7B

Fold the excess paper over at the front side seam and align the front and back waistline. Secure this with tape slightly below the waistline.

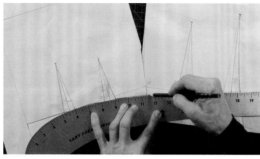

Step 7C

Using your hip curve, true the waistline at the side seam with your blue pencil to form a nice smooth curve. Then remove the tape.

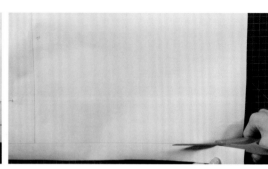

Step 8A

Cut out the back and front skirt from the draft along the center front and back of the skirt.

Be sure to cut along the blue lines at the waistline.

Step 8B
Trim away the excess paper at the back and front side seams.

Step 9
Measure down 7" (18cm) from the center back waistline and place a mark. Add a second mark ½" (1.3cm) away from the first. This designates the zipper notches.

Step 10A
Annotate the back sloper with "Back Straight Skirt Sloper," "Size 6," or whatever your size happens to be.

Step 10B
Annotate the front with "Front Straight Skirt Sloper," and your particular size.

Step 10C
Label the center back "CB."

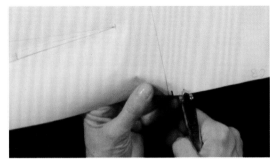

Step 11A
Next, double-notch the center back zipper position.

Step 11B
Notch the back darts and the front darts.

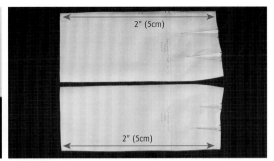

Step 11C
Add the front and back grainlines, 2" (5cm) away from the center front and center back of the skirt slopers.

Step 11D
Cut the skirt sloper out in muslin (calico), pin the pieces together, and check the fit. Make any necessary changes to the draft before transferring it to oaktag (card).

You have now finished drafting your Straight Skirt Sloper.

Skirts

Tip
Be sure to add seam allowances to your muslin sloper— 1" (2.5cm) on the side seams and waistline and 1 ½" (3.8cm) hem allowance.

Self-evaluation

☐ Have I extracted and recorded all of the necessary skirt measurements properly?

☐ Did I use the same number on the hip curve to draft my side seams and darts?

☐ Have I calculated the correct placement for my front and back darts?

☐ Were my darts positioned in the correct direction before trueing the waistline?

☐ Have I added all of my notches?

A dress from the Delpozo Fall 2015 collection with an embellished quarter circle skirt.

Quarter Circle Skirt

Learning objectives

☐ Establish and record key measurements, prepare a paper block

☐ Draft the skirt—marking the center back, establishing the waistline radius using the chart, establishing the hip circumference, drafting the waistline, marking the center front, adding ease, marking the hem, adding the side seams

☐ Add the final marks—adding the seam allowances, marking zipper notches, drafting the hem, cutting out the pattern, establishing the grainline to achieve the desired look, annotating the pattern

Tools and supplies:

- White unlined pattern paper—19 x 40" (48 x 102cm)
- Fractions to Decimals and the Metric Conversion Table
- Quarter Circle Radius Measurement Chart and Form

Step 1A

For this lesson you will be using our Quarter Circle Skirt
Measurement Form and Quarter Circle Skirt Radius Calculation
Chart, provided below and opposite.

Quarter Circle Skirt Measurement Form

Body Measurements	Total	
	Inches	Centimeters
Desired skirt length		
Waist circumference		
Waist circumference minus ½" (1.3cm)		
Radius		
Hip circumference (7"/18cm from waistline)		

* The fractional amounts listed in the charts are to the nearest 16th of an inch

Quarter Circle Skirt Radius Calculation Chart

Circumference		Radius		Circumference		Radius		Circumference		Radius	
inches	cm	inches	cm	inches	cm	inches	cm	inches	cm	inches	cm
10	25.4	6 3/8"	16.2	24	61.0	15 1/4"	38.8	38	96.5	24 1/4"	61.4
10 1/2	26.7	6 5/8"	17.0	24 1/2	62.2	15 5/8"	39.6	38 1/2	97.8	24 1/2"	62.3
11	27.9	7"	17.8	25	63.5	15 7/8"	40.4	39	99.1	24 7/8"	63.1
11 1/2	29.2	7 3/8"	18.6	25 1/2	64.8	16 1/4"	41.2	39 1/2	100.3	25 1/8"	63.9
12	30.5	7 5/8"	19.4	26	66.0	16 1/2"	42.0	40	101.6	25 1/2"	64.7
12 1/2	31.8	8"	20.2	26 1/2	67.3	16 1/2"	42.0	40 1/2	102.9	25 3/4"	65.5
13	33.0	8 1/4"	21.0	27	68.6	17 1/4"	43.7	41	104.1	26 1/8"	66.3
13 1/2	34.3	8 5/8"	21.8	27 1/2	69.9	17 1/2"	44.5	41 1/2	105.4	26 3/8"	67.1
14	35.6	8 7/8"	22.6	28	71.1	17 7/8"	45.3	42	106.7	26 3/4"	67.9
14 1/2	36.8	9 1/4"	23.4	28 1/2	72.4	18 1/8"	46.1	42 1/2	108.0	27"	68.7
15	38.1	9 1/2"	24.3	29	73.7	18 1/2"	46.9	43	109.2	27 3/8"	69.5
15 1/2	39.4	9 7/8"	25.1	29 1/2	74.9	18 3/4"	47.7	43 1/2	110.5	27 3/4"	70.3
16	40.6	10 1/8"	25.9	30	76.2	19 1/8"	48.5	44	111.8	28"	71.1
16 1/2	41.9	10 1/2"	26.7	30 1/2	77.5	19 3/8"	49.3	44 1/2	113.0	28 3/8"	72.0
17	43.2	10 7/8"	27.5	31	78.7	19 3/4"	50.1	45	114.3	28 5/8"	72.8
17 1/2	44.5	11 1/8"	28.3	31 1/2	80.0	20"	50.9	45 1/2	115.6	29"	73.6
18	45.7	11 1/2"	29.1	32	81.3	20 3/8"	51.7	46	116.8	29 1/4"	74.4
18 1/2	47.0	11 3/4"	29.9	32 1/2	82.6	20 3/4"	52.6	46 1/2	118.1	29 5/8"	75.2
19	48.3	12 1/8"	30.7	33	83.8	21"	53.4	47	119.4	29 7/8"	76.0
19 1/2	49.5	12 3/8"	31.5	33 1/2	85.1	21 3/8"	54.2	47 1/2	120.7	30 1/4"	76.8
20	50.8	12 3/4"	32.3	34	86.4	21 5/8"	55.0	48	121.9	30 1/2"	77.6
20 1/2	52.1	13"	33.1	34 1/2	87.6	22"	55.8	48 1/2	123.2	30 7/8"	78.4
21	53.3	13 3/8"	34.0	35	88.9	22 1/4"	56.6	49	124.5	31 1/4"	79.2
21 1/2	54.6	13 5/8"	34.8	35 1/2	90.2	22 5/8"	57.4	49 1/2	125.7	31 1/2"	80.0
22	55.9	14"	35.6	36	91.4	22 7/8"	58.2	50	127.0	31 7/8"	80.9
22 1/2	57.2	14 3/8"	36.4	36 1/2	92.7	23 1/4"	59.0	50 1/2	128.3	32 1/8"	81.7
23	58.4	14 5/8"	37.2	37	94.0	23 1/2"	59.8	51	129.5	32 1/2"	82.5
23 1/2	59.7	15"	38.0	37 1/2	95.3	23 7/8"	60.6	51 1/2	130.8	32 3/4"	83.3

Fractions to Decimals

$1/64$	0.0156	0.0	$33/64$	0.5156	0.5
$1/32$	0.0312	0.0	$17/32$	0.5312	0.5
$3/64$	0.0469	0.0	$35/64$	0.5469	0.5
$1/16$	0.0625	0.1	$9/16$	0.5625	0.6
$5/64$	0.0781	0.1	$37/64$	0.5781	0.6
$3/32$	0.0938	0.1	$19/32$	0.5938	0.6
$7/64$	0.1094	0.1	$39/64$	0.6094	0.6
$1/8$	0.1250	0.1	$5/8$	0.6250	0.6
$9/64$	0.1406	0.1	$41/64$	0.6406	0.6
$5/32$	0.1562	0.2	$21/32$	0.6562	0.7
$11/64$	0.1719	0.2	$43/64$	0.6719	0.7
$3/16$	0.1875	0.2	$11/16$	0.6875	0.7
$13/64$	0.2031	0.2	$45/64$	0.7031	0.7
$7/32$	0.2188	0.2	$23/32$	0.7188	0.7
$15/64$	0.2344	0.2	$47/64$	0.7344	0.7
$1/4$	0.2500	0.2	$3/4$	0.7500	0.8
$17/64$	0.2656	0.3	$49/64$	0.7656	0.8
$9/32$	0.2812	0.3	$25/32$	0.7812	0.8
$19/64$	0.2969	0.3	$51/64$	0.7969	0.8
$5/16$	0.3125	0.3	$13/16$	0.8125	0.8
$21/64$	0.3281	0.3	$53/64$	0.8281	0.8
$11/32$	0.3438	0.3	$27/32$	0.8438	0.8
$23/64$	0.3594	0.4	$55/64$	0.8594	0.9
$3/8$	0.3750	0.4	$7/8$	0.8750	0.9
$25/64$	0.3906	0.4	$57/64$	0.8906	0.9
$13/32$	0.4062	0.4	$29/32$	0.9062	0.9
$27/64$	0.4219	0.4	$59/64$	0.9219	0.9
$7/16$	0.4375	0.4	$15/16$	0.9375	0.9
$29/64$	0.4531	0.5	$61/64$	0.9531	1.0
$15/32$	0.4688	0.5	$31/32$	0.9688	1.0
$31/64$	0.4844	0.5	$63/64$	0.9844	1.0
$1/2$	0.5000	0.5	1	1.0000	1.0

Metric Conversion Table

inches	1/64	1/8	1/4	3/8	1/2	5/8	3/4	7/8
	0.16	0.32	0.64	0.95	1.27	1.59	1.91	2.22
1	2.54	2.70	2.86	3.18	3.49	3.81	4.13	4.45	4.76
2	5.08	5.24	5.40	5.72	6.03	6.35	6.67	6.99	7.30
3	7.62	7.78	7.94	8.26	8.57	8.89	9.21	9.53	9.84
4	10.16	10.32	10.48	10.80	11.11	11.43	11.75	12.07	12.38
5	12.70	12.86	13.02	13.34	13.65	13.97	14.29	14.61	14.92
6	15.24	15.40	15.56	15.88	16.19	16.51	16.83	17.15	17.46
7	18	17.94	18.10	18.42	18.73	19.05	19.37	19.69	20.00
8	20.32	20.48	20.64	20.96	21.27	21.59	21.91	22.23	22.54
9	22.86	23.02	23.18	23.50	23.81	24.13	24.45	24.77	25.08
10	25.40	25.56	25.72	26.04	26.35	26.67	26.99	27.31	27.62
11	27.94	27.94	28.10	28.26	28.58	28.89	29.21	29.53	29.85
12	30.48	30.64	30.80	31.12	31.43	31.75	32.02	32.39	32.70
13	33.02	33.18	33.34	33.66	33.97	34.29	34.61	34.93	35.24
14	35.56	35.72	35.88	36.20	36.51	36.83	37.15	37.47	37.78
15	38.10	38.26	38.42	38.74	39.05	39.37	36.69	40.01	40.32
16	40.64	40.80	40.96	41.28	41.59	41.92	42.23	42.55	42.86
17	43.18	43.34	43.50	43.82	44.13	44.45	44.77	45.09	45.40
18	45.72	45.88	46.04	46.36	46.67	46.99	47.31	47.63	47.94
19	48.26	48.42	48.58	48.90	49.21	49.53	49.85	50.17	50.48
20	50.80	50.96	51.12	51.44	51.75	52.07	52.39	52.71	53.02
21	53.34	53.50	53.66	53.98	54.29	54.61	54.93	55.25	55.56
22	55.88	56.04	56.20	56.52	56.83	57.15	57.47	57.79	58.10
23	58.42	58.58	58.74	59.06	59.37	59.69	60.01	60.33	60.64
24	60.96	61.12	61.28	61.60	61.91	62.23	62.55	62.87	63.18
25	63.50	63.66	63.82	64.14	64.45	64.77	65.09	65.41	65.72
26	66.04	66.20	66.36	66.68	66.90	67.31	67.63	67.95	68.26
27	68.58	68.74	68.90	69.22	69.53	69.85	70.17	70.49	70.80
28	71.12	71.28	71.44	71.76	72.07	72.39	72.71	73.03	73.34
29	73.66	73.82	73.98	74.30	74.61	74.93	75.25	75.57	75.88
30	76.20	76.36	76.52	76.84	77.15	77.47	77.79	78.11	78.42

inches	1/16	1/8	1/4	3/8	1/2	5/8	3/4	7/8
	0.16	0.32	0.64	0.95	1.27	1.59	1.91	2.22
31	78.74	78.90	79.06	79.38	79.69	80.01	80.33	80.65	80.96
32	81.28	81.44	81.60	81.92	82.23	82.55	82.87	83.19	83.50
33	83.82	83.98	94.14	84.46	84.77	85.09	85.41	85.73	86.04
34	86.36	86.52	86.68	87.00	87.31	87.63	87.95	88.27	88.58
35	88.90	89.06	89.22	89.54	89.85	90.17	90.49	90.81	91.12
36	91.44	91.60	91.76	92.08	92.39	92.71	93.03	93.35	93.66
37	93.98	94.14	94.30	94.602	94.93	95.25	95.57	95.89	96.20
38	96.52	96.68	96.84	97.16	97.47	97.79	98.11	98.43	98.74
39	99.06	99.22	99.38	99.70	100.01	100.33	100.65	100.97	101.28
40	101.60	101.76	101.92	102.24	102.55	102.87	103.19	103.51	103.82
41	104.14	104.30	104.46	104.78	105.09	105.41	105.73	106.05	106.36
42	106.68	106.84	107.00	107.32	107.63	107.95	108.27	108.59	108.90
43	109.22	109.38	109.54	109.86	110.17	110.49	110.81	111.13	111.44
44	111.76	111.92	112.08	112.40	112.71	113.03	113.35	113.67	113.98
45	114.30	114.46	114.62	114.94	115.25	115.57	115.89	116.21	116.52
46	116.84	117.00	117.16	117.48	117.79	118.11	118.43	118.75	119.06
47	119.38	119.54	119.70	120.02	120.33	120.65	120.97	121.29	121.60
48	121.92	122.08	122.24	122.56	122.87	123.19	123.51	123.83	124.14
49	124.46	124.62	124.78	125.10	125.41	125.73	126.05	126.37	126.68
50	127.00	127.16	127.32	127.64	127.95	128.27	128.59	128.91	129.22
51	129.54	129.70	129.86	130.18	130.49	130.81	131.13	131.45	131.76
52	132.08	132.24	132.40	132.72	133.03	133.35	133.67	133.99	134.30
53	134.62	134.78	134.94	135.26	135.57	135.89	136.21	136.53	136.84
54	137.16	137.32	137.48	137.80	138.11	138.43	138.75	139.07	139.38
55	139.70	139.86	140.02	140.34	140.65	140.97	141.29	141.61	141.92
56	142.24	142.40	142.56	142.88	143.19	143.51	143.83	144.15	144.46
57	144.78	144.94	145.10	145.42	145.73	146.05	146.37	146.69	147.00
58	147.32	147.48	147.64	147.96	148.27	148.59	148.91	149.23	149.54
59	149.86	150.02	150.18	150.50	150.81	151.13	151.45	151.77	152.08
60	152.40	152.56	152.72	153.04	153.35	153.67	153.99	154.31	154.62

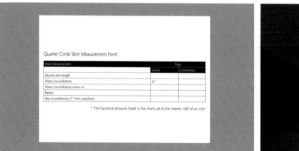  

Step 2A

On your Quarter Circle Skirt Measurement Form, record your waist circumference measurement in the space provided. For our US size 6 (UK size 10) dress form this is 27" (68.5cm).

Step 2B

Next, decide on the desired length of your skirt. Here we are measuring from the middle of the front waist tape of the dress form, but you could also take a body measurement.

Step 2C

Our skirt length will be 19" (48cm) so we will record this on the form in the space provided.

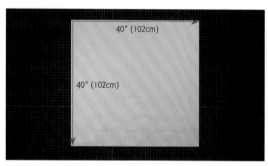 

Step 3A

For a desired skirt length of 19" (48cm), prepare a piece of white unlined pattern paper measuring 40" (102cm) square. Adjust these dimensions if you choose a shorter or longer skirt.

Step 3B

If your pattern paper is not wide enough for your desired skirt length then you will need to tape an extra length of paper onto the paper block, as demonstrated here.

Module 2:

Drafting the Skirt

 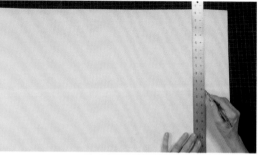 

Step 1A

Measure and mark 3" (7.5cm) in from the right-side vertical edge of the paper, as demonstrated. Make several marks down the papaer at the same distance in from the edge.

Step 1B

Connect the 3" (7.5cm) vertical marks with your metal ruler. This line represents the center back on one side of the skirt.

Step 1C

Now place marks along the bottom horizontal edge of the paper, 3" (7.5cm) up from the bottom edge.

Step 1D

Connect the horizontal marks with your metal ruler. This line represents the center back on the other side of the skirt.

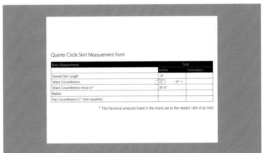

Step 2A

Now refer to the Quarter Circle Skirt Measurement Form. Take your waist circumference measurement and subtract ½" (1.3cm) for bias stretch. Record that measurement on the form in the space provided. Our waist circumference is 27" (68.6cm)—minus ½" (1.3cm) equals 26½" (67.3cm).

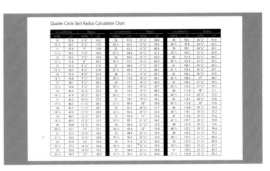

Step 2B

Now refer to the Quarter Circle Skirt Radius Calculation Chart to find the radius of your skirt's subtracted waist measurement to the closest ½" (1.3cm). Our subtracted waist measurement is 26½" (67.3cm), and therefore our corresponding radius measurement is 16½" (42cm).

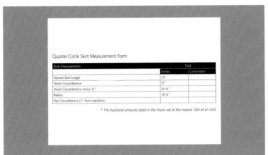

Step 2C

Now record your radius measurement in the space provided on the Quarter Circle Skirt Measurement Form. We have recorded 16½" (42cm).

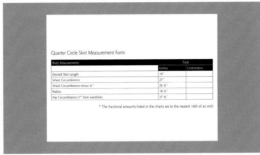

Step 2D

You will also need to record your hip circumference, measured at 7" (18cm) down from the waist, and record that measurement on your Quarter Circle Skirt Measurement Form. Our hip circumference measures 37½" (95cm).

Step 3A

At the intersection of the 3" (7.62cm) lines, which we will refer to as the center point, measure over your radius measurement and place a mark on the horizontal center back line.

Step 3B

Now measure your radius from center point on the vertical center back line and place a mark.

Step 3C

To draft the waistline, insert a pushpin (drawing pin) into the radius measurement on your tape measure and anchor it to the cutting mat at the center point.

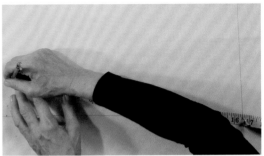

Step 3D

Now pivot the tape measure as you mark the shape of the waistline using small dashes.

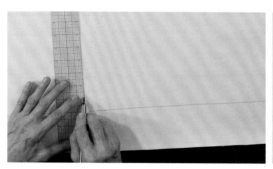

Step 4A
Now square a line off the horizontal center back line for about 1" (2.5cm).

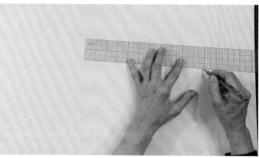

Step 4B
Then square another line for 1" (2.5cm) off the vertical center back line.

Step 4C
Use your styling curve or hip curve to shape the waist by connecting the waistline markings.

Step 5A
Now walk your tape measure along the waistline to find the halfway point of the waistline, which will become the center front of the skirt. Place a notch mark here.

Step 5B
Continue to walk the tape measure to the vertical center back, to check that your drafted waistline equals your subtracted waistline measurement.

Step 5C
Label the center front of the skirt with "CF," and both sides of the center back of the skirt with "CB."

Step 6A
Measure down 7½" (19cm) from the skirt waist, starting from the horizontal center back seam. Place marks at approximately 2 to 3" (5–7.5cm) intervals, until you reach the vertical center back seam. This represents the hipline.

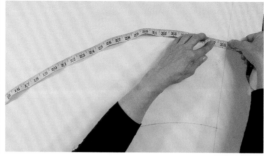

Step 6B
Now walk your tape measure along the hipline from center back to center back. Our hip draft measures 38⅜" (97.5cm).

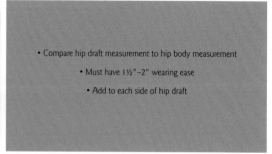

- Compare hip draft measurement to hip body measurement
- Must have 1½"–2" wearing ease
- Add to each side of hip draft

Step 6C
Compare your pattern hip draft measurement to your hip body measurement. You must have between 1½" (3.8cm) and 2" (5cm) worth of wearing ease on the hip of your skirt.

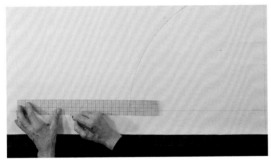

Step 7A

Our hip draft measures 38⅜" (97.5cm), but our actual hip measures 37½" (95.3cm), so we will be adding ½" (1.3cm) to each side of the hip using a red pencil and our metal ruler.

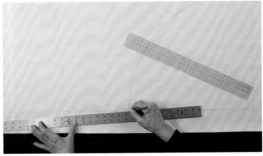

Step 7B

Connect the center back/waist intersection to the extended hip mark and create a new center back seam.

Step 7C

Label this "New Center Back" in red pencil.

Step 7D

Repeat this process on the other side, adding ½" (1.3cm) at the hip mark and then connecting a line from the waist to the ½" (1.3cm) hip mark and then down to the hem.

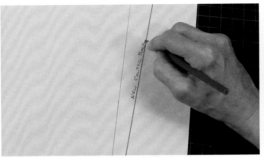

Step 7E

Label this "New Center Back."

Step 8

To mark the hem, rest your metal ruler on the center back waist at the desired skirt length measurement. Then slide the ruler along the waistline as you place hem marks at 2 to 3" (5–7.5cm) intervals from center back to center back.

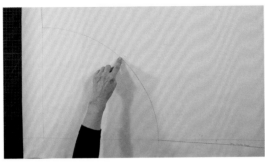

Step 9A

Next, find the side seam, which is positioned halfway between the center front and the center back stitching line.

Step 9B

Rest your ruler along the waistline, find the midway point, and place a mark.

Step 9C

Repeat this process on the other side, measuring along the waistline from the center front to the center back stitching line. Place a mark to indicate the side seam.

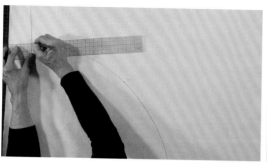

Step 10A
Since the back waistline dips lower than the front, you need to lower the center back waist by ¼" (6mm), using your red pencil. Lower the back waist first on one side and then on the other. Make sure that your lowered back waistlines are squared off the center back stitching line for about ½" (1.3cm).

Step 10B
Now use your styling curve to shape the new lowered back waistline, blending the waistline to the side seam. Label the side seam with "SS."

Step 10C
Repeat this process on the other side of the back waistline. Label the side seam with "SS."

Module 3:

Seam Allowances &
Final Steps

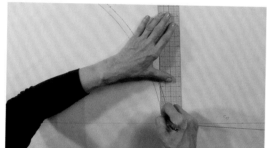

Step 1
Next you will add ½" (1.3cm) seam allowance to the waistline, beginning at the lowered center back stitching line on one side and continuing to the center back stitching line on the other side. (In the industry, and depending on the company, this seam allowance could also be ⅜"/1cm.)

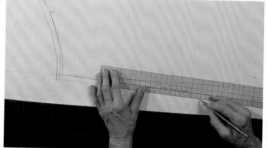

Step 2A
Now add ½" (1.3cm) seam allowance to one of the center back seams.

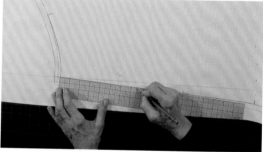

Step 2B
Place two zipper notches, ½" (1.3cm) apart, at 7" (18cm) down from the lowered waistline.

Tip
* Trueing the hem, however, will be temporary since circle skirts have a certain amount of bias. It is recommended that they be cut in the desired fabric, left to hang for several hours, and then the pattern adjusted to compensate for the bias stretch.

Step 2C
Repeat the process of adding seam allowance and zipper notches on the other center back seam.

Step 3A
Now use your tracing wheel to connect the hem marks to shape the curve of the hem. You could also use your hip curve, and pencil in the curve of the hem.

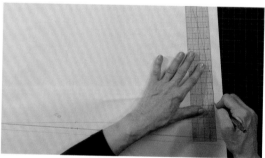

Step 3B
Add ½" (1.3cm) hem allowance to the skirt hem, following the tracing marks, but again, this will be adjusted later for the bias stretch in the final pattern.

Step 4
Trim away the excess paper at the hem.

Step 5A
Trim away the excess paper at the center back seam.

Step 5B
Then trim away the excess seam allowance at the waistline.

Step 5C
And finally, trim away the excess paper from the other center back seam.

Step 6A
Fold the skirt in half along center front, matching the center back seam layers.

Step 6B
Crease the center front with your fingers.

Step 7
Open the skirt again and lay it flat on the table.

Step 8
Choose the grainline next. For a flatter front, choose to place your center front on straight grain with a bias back.

Step 9A
Or, for a flared look at center front, choose to put the center front on bias. To do this, create a 2 x 2" (5 x 5cm) square on the center front.

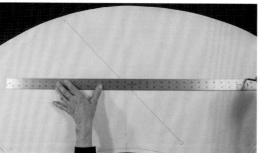

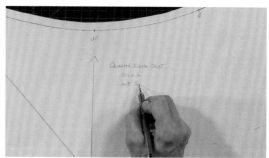

Step 9B
Connect the diagonal corners of the 2 x 2" (5 x 5cm) square with your metal ruler, and mark this line in red pencil. Be sure that your fabric width is wide enough for a bias grain front.

Step 10
Another option, which will also produce a flat center front look, is to place your grainline in the length grain, by squaring a line off center front at a right angle to the centerline.

Step 11
Once you have marked your desired grainline, annotate your draft with "Quarter Circle skirt," "Size 6," or whatever size your skirt happens to be, and "Cut 1."

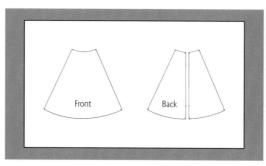

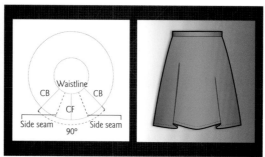

Step 12A
Other options for this draft are a quarter circle skirt with side seams and a center back seam.

Step 12B
You have now finished your Quarter Circle Skirt pattern.

Self-evaluation

☐ Did I accurately calculate my skirt's radius?

☐ Did I check that my drafted waistline equals my subtracted waistline measurement?

☐ Have I compared my hip draft measurement to my hip body measurement and adjusted my pattern?

☐ Did I choose and mark my skirt's grainline?

Half Circle Skirt

Learning objectives

☐ Establish and record key measurements, and prepare a paper block folded in half

☐ Draft the waistline radius using the chart, marking the side seam and skirt length, marking zipper notches

☐ Add the final marks—tracing the marks onto the lower layer of the paper block, trueing and adding seam allowances, cutting out the pattern, establishing the grainline, annotating the pattern

Tools and supplies:

- White unlined pattern paper—27 x 54" (68.6 x 137cm)
- Drawing compass
- Fractions to Decimals and the Metric Conversion Table (see pages 88–89)

Step 1A

For this lesson you will be using our Half Circle Skirt
Measurement Form and Half Circle Skirt Radius Calculation
Chart, provided below.

Half Circle Skirt Measurement Form

Body Measurements	Total	
	Inches	Centimeters
Desired skirt length		
Waist circumference		
Waist circumference minus ½" (1.3cm)		
Radius		

* The fractional amounts listed in the charts are to the nearest 16th of an inch

Half Circle Skirt Radius Calculation Chart

Circumference inches	cm	Radius inches	cm
10	25.4	3 1/8"	8.1
10 1/2	26.7	3 3/8"	8.5
11	27.9	3 1/2"	8.9
11 1/2	29.2	3 5/8"	9.3
12	30.5	3 7/8"	9.7
12 1/2	31.8	4"	10.1
13	33.0	4 1/8"	10.5
13 1/2	34.3	4 1/4"	10.9
14	35.6	4 1/2"	11.3
14 1/2	36.8	4 5/8"	11.7
15	38.1	4 3/4"	12.1
15 1/2	39.4	4 7/8"	12.5
16	40.6	5 1/8"	12.9
16 1/2	41.9	5 1/4"	13.3
17	43.2	5 3/8"	13.7
17 1/2	44.5	5 5/8"	14.1
18	45.7	5 3/4"	14.6
18 1/2	47.0	5 7/8"	15.0
19	48.3	6"	15.4
19 1/2	49.5	6 1/4"	15.8
20	50.8	6 3/8"	16.2
20 1/2	52.1	6 1/2"	16.6
21	53.3	6 5/8"	17.0
21 1/2	54.6	6 7/8"	17.4
22	55.9	7"	17.8
22 1/2	57.2	7 1/8"	18.2
23	58.4	7 3/8"	18.6
23 1/2	59.7	7 1/2"	19.0
24	61.0	7 5/8"	19.4
24 1/2	62.2	7 3/4"	19.8
25	63.5	8"	20.2
25 1/2	64.8	8 1/8"	20.6
26	66.0	8 1/4"	21.0
26 1/2	67.3	8 1/4"	21.0
27	68.6	8 5/8"	21.8
27 1/2	69.9	8 3/4"	22.2
28	71.1	8 7/8"	22.6
28 1/2	72.4	9 1/8"	23.0
29	73.7	9 1/4"	23.4
29 1/2	74.9	9 3/8"	23.9
30	76.2	9 1/2"	24.3
30 1/2	77.5	9 3/4"	24.7
31	78.7	9 7/8"	25.1
31 1/2	80.0	10"	25.5
32	81.3	10 1/8"	25.9
32 1/2	82.6	10 3/8"	26.3
33	83.8	10 1/2"	26.7
33 1/2	85.1	10 5/8"	27.1
34	86.4	10 7/8"	27.5
34 1/2	87.6	11"	27.9
35	88.9	11 1/8"	28.3
35 1/2	90.2	11 1/4"	28.7
36	91.4	11 1/2"	29.1
36 1/2	92.7	11 5/8"	29.5
37	94.0	11 3/4"	29.9
37 1/2	95.3	11 7/8"	30.3
38	96.5	12 1/8"	30.7
38 1/2	97.8	12 1/4"	31.1
39	99.1	12 3/8"	31.5
39 1/2	100.3	12 5/8"	31.9
40	101.6	12 3/4"	32.3
40 1/2	102.9	12 7/8"	32.7
41	104.1	13"	33.1
41 1/2	105.4	13 1/4"	33.6
42	106.7	13 3/8"	34.0
42 1/2	108.0	13 1/2"	34.4
43	109.2	13 5/8"	34.8
43 1/2	110.5	13 7/8"	35.2
44	111.8	14"	35.6
44 1/2	113.0	14 1/8"	36.0
45	114.3	14 3/8"	36.4
45 1/2	115.6	14 1/2"	36.8
46	116.8	14 5/8"	37.2
46 1/2	118.1	14 3/4"	37.6
47	119.4	15"	38.0
47 1/2	120.7	15 1/8"	38.4
48	121.9	15 1/4"	38.8
48 1/2	123.2	15 1/2"	39.2
49	124.5	15 5/8"	39.6
49 1/2	125.7	15 3/4"	40.0
50	127.0	15 7/8"	40.4
50 1/2	128.3	16 1/8"	40.8
51	129.5	16 1/4"	41.2
51 1/2	130.8	16 3/8"	41.6

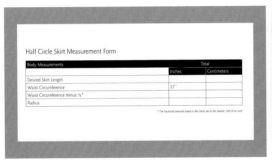

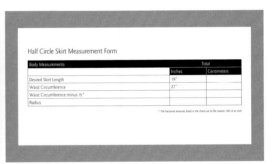

Step 2A

On your Half Circle Skirt Measurement Form, record your waist circumference measurement in the space provided. The waist circumference for our US size 6 (UK size 10) dress form is 27" (68.5cm).

Step 2B

Next, decide on the desired length of your skirt. Here we are measuring down from the middle of the front waist tape of the dress form, but you could also take a body measurement.

Step 2C

Record that measurement on your Half Circle Skirt Measurement Form. Our desired skirt length is 19" (48cm).

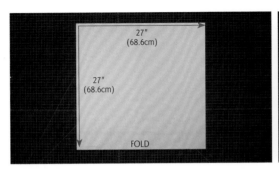

Step 3

Now prepare a piece of white unlined pattern paper measuring 27" (68.6cm) wide by 54" (137cm) long, for a 19" (48cm)-long skirt. Adjust these dimensions for a shorter or longer skirt.

Step 4

Fold the paper in half in the length direction, with the fold facing you. The fold represents the center front of the skirt.

Step 5A

Use your clear plastic ruler to draw a vertical line ½" (1.3cm) away from the right-hand edge of the paper. This represents the skirt's center back seam.

Step 5B

Label the center back seam with "CB."

Step 6

Secure the paper layers together with pins, as demonstrated.

Opposite: A tweed half circle skirt from the Karen Walker collection of Fall 2015.

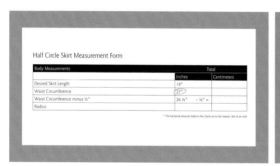

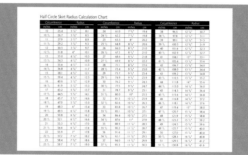

Step I

Take your waist circumference measurement and subtract ½" (1.3cm) for bias stretch. Then record that measurement on the Half Circle Skirt Measurement Form. Our waist circumference is 27" (68.6cm)—minus ½" (1.3cm) equals 26½" (67.3cm).

Step 2

Next, you need to find the radius of your waistline using our Half Circle Skirt Radius Calculation Chart. Locate your skirt's subtracted waist measurement to the closest ½" (1.3cm). See the corresponding radius measurement for that waist size. Our subtracted waist is 26½" (67.3cm), so our radius is 8¼" (21cm).

Step 3A

The next step is to measure your radius amount from the intersection of the fold and center-back stitching line, which we will call the center point. Measure along the fold edge your radius amount and place a mark.

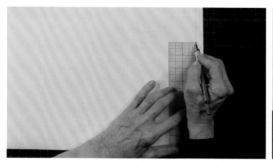

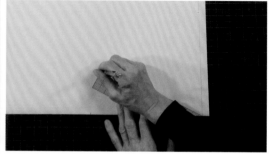

Step 3B

Then measure your radius amount from the fold, along the center back stitching line, and place a mark.

Step 4

To mark the waistline, you have several choices. You can use a compass, providing it can open to your radius amount. To do this, set the compass to the radius amount, anchor its pointed end at center point, then mark the waistline as you swing the compass from the fold to the center back stitching line.

Step 5

Or you can mark the radius using a ruler by pivoting the ruler at your radius amount from the center point, marking from center front to center back.

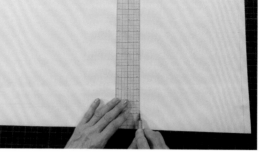

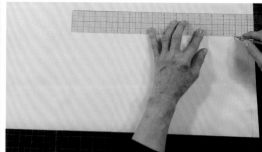

Step 6

The most convenient way to mark the radius is with a tape measure and pushpin (drawing pin). Insert the pin into the tape measure at the radius measurement, then anchor the pin into the cutting mat at center point. Mark the radius as you pivot the tape measure from center front to center back.

Step 7A

Use your ruler to square a line off the center front at the center front waist mark.

Step 7B

Square a line off the center back at the center back waist mark.

Step 7C
Now blend the front and back waistline with your styling curve, following your radius waist markings.

Step 7D
If you do not use a compass to mark the waistline, you will need to blend it so that it forms a nice smooth curve.

Step 8A
Use your clear plastic ruler to check that the waistline from the center back stitching line to center front, when doubled, equals your reduced waist circumference measurement.

Tip
* Trueing the hem, however, will be temporary since circle skirts have a certain amount of bias. It is recommended that they be cut in the desired fabric, left to hang for several hours, and then the pattern adjusted to compensate for the bias stretch.

Step 8B
Place a mark midway on the waistline to denote the side seam. Label it "SS."

Step 9
Use your metal ruler to mark the skirt length by sliding the ruler along the waistline. Mark the skirt length with a series of dashes, approximately 2 to 3" (5 to 7.5cm) apart. Be sure that the hemline is at a right angle at center front and center back.*

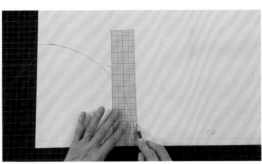

Step 10A
Because the back of the waist dips lower than the front, you will need to lower the center back of the skirt by ¼" (6mm) using your red pencil. Be sure to square a line off center back for about 1" (2.5cm).

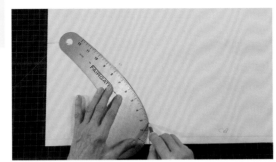

Step 10B
Use your styling curve to true the lowered back waist, blending to the side seam mark.

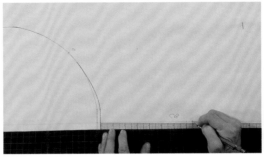

Step 11
Now place two zipper notch marks, ½" (1.3cm) apart, 7" (18cm) down from the lowered back waistline.

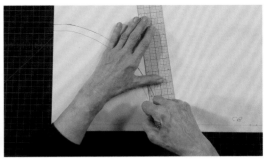

Step 12
Add ½" (1.3cm) seam allowance to the waistline, from center front to the lowered center back.

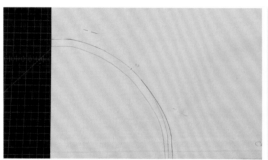

Step 13A
Pin the skirt layers together below the waistline to hold them in place.

Step 13B
Trim away the excess paper above the waistline.

Step 14
For clarification purposes, write "CF" along the center front of the skirt pattern.

Module 3:

Final Steps

Step 1A
Use your tracing wheel to trace the waistline onto the underside of the skirt.

Step 1B
Trace the side seam notch onto the other side of the skirt.

Step 1C
Trace both zipper notches onto the other side next.

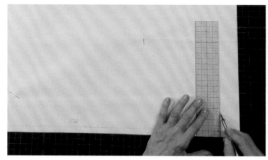

Step 2A
Square a 2" (5cm) line off the center back hem.

Step 2B
Do the same for the center front, squaring off a line for about 2" (5cm).

Step 2C
Next, you will true the hemline. You can do this by using a hip curve and connecting the hem marks.

Step 2D
Or you can use your tracing wheel to connect the marks. Remember, you will need to adjust the hem of this pattern once it is cut in fabric and has had a chance to hang.

Step 3
Add ½" (1.3cm) seam allowance to the hemline following the tracing marks, or if you elected to mark your hem with a hip curve, then add the ½" (1.3cm) seam allowance from the penciled hem marking.

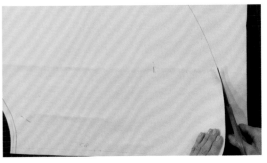

Step 4
Cutting along the hem edge, trim away the excess paper at the hem.

Step 5
Remove the pins holding the skirt layers together.

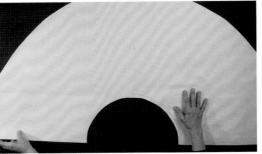

Step 6
Unfold the skirt pattern layers, and then lay the pattern flat on the table.

Step 7A
Pencil in the center front waist and the waist stitching line onto the other side of the skirt pattern from center front to center back. Here, we are using our ruler but you could also use your styling curve.

Step 7B
Now mark your side seam notch.

Step 8A
Pencil in the center back stitching line at ½" (1.3cm) away from the edge of the paper.

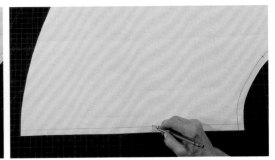

Step 8B
Mark the zipper notches.

Step 9
Next, you will add your grainline. Grainline is based on the fabric width, the skirt length, and the desired look of the skirt. Placing your grainline along center front, as demonstrated, will produce a flat-looking skirt front.

Step 10A
Or you could choose bias grain for a flared look at center front, although you must check whether your fabric is wide enough. For bias grain on center, create a 2 x 2" (5 x 5cm) box on the center front line with your clear plastic ruler. Then, mark the opposite corners of the box.

Step 10B
Use a red pencil and metal ruler to connect the corners of the box. Be sure your fabric is wide enough for bias grain. If not, you may have to extend the skirt by adding a piece on one side of the skirt bottom.

Step 11
Another option is to place your skirt front on the length grain of the fabric. This will produce a look similar to straight grain on center. Here, we demonstrate this grain option with blue pencil, squaring off center front.

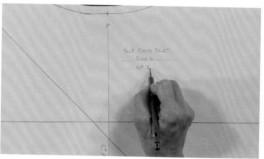

Step 12A
Once you have marked your desired grainline, annotate your draft with "Half Circle Skirt," "Size 6," or whatever size your skirt happens to be, and "Cut 1."

Step 12B
You have now finished your Half Circle Skirt pattern.

Self-evaluation

☐ Did I accurately calculate my skirt's radius?

☐ Does my drafted waistline equal my reduced waistline measurement?

☐ Did I lower my back waistline?

☐ Have I marked all of my notches properly?

Three Quarter Circle Skirt

Learning objectives

☐ Establish and record key measurements, prepare a double-folded paper block

☐ Drafting the waistline using the chart, adding seam allowances, marking the center front and back and the hemline, marking the hem allowance

☐ Adding final marks and tracing them onto the lower layer of the paper block, trueing, adding seam allowances and cutting out the pattern, establishing the grainline, annotating the pattern

Tools and supplies:

- Three Quarter Circle Skirt Measurement Form
- Three Quarter Circle Skirt Radius Calculations Chart
- Women's Dress Form
- Fractions to Decimals and the Metric Conversion Table (see pages 88–89)

Step 1A

For this lesson you will be using our Three Quarter Circle Skirt
Measurement Form and Three Quarter Circle Skirt Radius
Calculation Chart, provided below.

Three Quarter Circle Skirt Measurement Form

Body Measurements	Total	
	Inches	Centimeters
Desired skirt length		
Waist circumference		
Waist circumference minus 1″ (2.5cm)		
Radius		

* The fractional amounts listed in the charts are to the nearest 16th of an inch

Three Quarter Circle Skirt Radius Calculation Chart

Circumference		Radius		Circumference		Radius		Circumference		Radius	
inches	cm	inches	cm	inches	cm	inches	cm	inches	cm	inches	cm
10	25.4	2 $\frac{1}{8}$"	5.4	24	61.0	5 $\frac{1}{8}$"	12.9	38	96.5	8 $\frac{1}{8}$"	20.5
10 $\frac{1}{2}$	26.7	2 $\frac{1}{4}$"	5.7	24 $\frac{1}{2}$	62.2	5 $\frac{1}{4}$"	13.2	38 $\frac{1}{2}$	97.8	8 $\frac{1}{8}$"	20.8
11	27.9	2 $\frac{3}{8}$"	5.9	25	63.5	5 $\frac{1}{4}$"	13.5	39	99.1	8 $\frac{1}{4}$"	21.0
11 $\frac{1}{2}$	29.2	2 $\frac{1}{2}$"	6.2	25 $\frac{1}{2}$	64.8	5 $\frac{3}{8}$"	13.7	39 $\frac{1}{2}$	100.3	8 $\frac{3}{8}$"	21.3
12	30.5	2 $\frac{1}{2}$"	6.5	26	66.0	5 $\frac{1}{2}$"	14.0	40	101.6	8 $\frac{1}{2}$"	21.6
12 $\frac{1}{2}$	31.8	2 $\frac{5}{8}$"	6.7	26 $\frac{1}{2}$	67.3	5 $\frac{5}{8}$"	14.3	40 $\frac{1}{2}$	102.9	8 $\frac{5}{8}$"	21.8
13	33.0	2 $\frac{3}{4}$"	7.0	27	68.6	5 $\frac{3}{4}$"	14.6	41	104.1	8 $\frac{3}{4}$"	22.1
13 $\frac{1}{2}$	34.3	2 $\frac{7}{8}$"	7.3	27 $\frac{1}{2}$	69.9	5 $\frac{7}{8}$"	14.8	41 $\frac{1}{2}$	105.4	8 $\frac{3}{4}$"	22.4
14	35.6	3"	7.5	28	71.1	6"	15.1	42	106.7	8 $\frac{7}{8}$"	22.6
14 $\frac{1}{2}$	36.8	3 $\frac{1}{8}$"	7.8	28 $\frac{1}{2}$	72.4	6"	15.4	42 $\frac{1}{2}$	108.0	9"	22.9
15	38.1	3 $\frac{1}{8}$"	8.1	29	73.7	6 $\frac{1}{8}$"	15.6	43	109.2	9 $\frac{1}{8}$"	23.2
15 $\frac{1}{2}$	39.4	3 $\frac{1}{4}$"	8.4	29 $\frac{1}{2}$	74.9	6 $\frac{1}{4}$"	15.9	43 $\frac{1}{2}$	110.5	9 $\frac{1}{4}$"	23.4
16	40.6	3 $\frac{3}{8}$"	8.6	30	76.2	6 $\frac{3}{8}$"	16.2	44	111.8	9 $\frac{3}{8}$"	23.7
16 $\frac{1}{2}$	41.9	3 $\frac{1}{2}$"	8.9	30 $\frac{1}{2}$	77.5	6 $\frac{1}{2}$"	16.4	44 $\frac{1}{2}$	113.0	9 $\frac{1}{2}$"	24.0
17	43.2	3 $\frac{5}{8}$"	9.2	31	78.7	6 $\frac{5}{8}$"	16.7	45	114.3	9 $\frac{1}{2}$"	24.3
17 $\frac{1}{2}$	44.5	3 $\frac{3}{4}$"	9.4	31 $\frac{1}{2}$	80.0	6 $\frac{5}{8}$"	17.0	45 $\frac{1}{2}$	115.6	9 $\frac{5}{8}$"	24.5
18	45.7	3 $\frac{7}{8}$"	9.7	32	81.3	6 $\frac{3}{4}$"	17.2	46	116.8	9 $\frac{3}{4}$"	24.8
18 $\frac{1}{2}$	47.0	3 $\frac{7}{8}$"	10.0	32 $\frac{1}{2}$	82.6	6 $\frac{7}{8}$"	17.5	46 $\frac{1}{2}$	118.1	9 $\frac{7}{8}$"	25.1
19	48.3	4"	10.2	33	83.8	7"	17.8	47	119.4	10"	25.3
19 $\frac{1}{2}$	49.5	4 $\frac{1}{8}$"	10.5	33 $\frac{1}{2}$	85.1	7 $\frac{1}{8}$"	18.1	47 $\frac{1}{2}$	120.7	10 $\frac{1}{8}$"	25.6
20	50.8	4 $\frac{1}{4}$"	10.8	34	86.4	7 $\frac{1}{4}$"	18.3	48	121.9	10 $\frac{1}{8}$"	25.9
20 $\frac{1}{2}$	52.1	4 $\frac{3}{8}$"	11.0	34 $\frac{1}{2}$	87.6	7 $\frac{3}{8}$"	18.6	48 $\frac{1}{2}$	123.2	10 $\frac{1}{4}$"	26.1
21	53.3	4 $\frac{1}{2}$"	11.3	35	88.9	7 $\frac{3}{8}$"	18.9	49	124.5	10 $\frac{3}{8}$"	26.4
21 $\frac{1}{2}$	54.6	4 $\frac{1}{2}$"	11.6	35 $\frac{1}{2}$	90.2	7 $\frac{1}{2}$"	19.1	49 $\frac{1}{2}$	125.7	10 $\frac{1}{2}$"	26.7
22	55.9	4 $\frac{5}{8}$"	11.9	36	91.4	7 $\frac{5}{8}$"	19.4	50	127.0	10 $\frac{5}{8}$"	27.0
22 $\frac{1}{2}$	57.2	4 $\frac{3}{4}$"	12.1	36 $\frac{1}{2}$	92.7	7 $\frac{3}{4}$"	19.7	50 $\frac{1}{2}$	128.3	10 $\frac{3}{4}$"	27.2
23	58.4	4 $\frac{7}{8}$"	12.4	37	94.0	7 $\frac{7}{8}$"	19.9	51	129.5	10 $\frac{7}{8}$"	27.5
23 $\frac{1}{2}$	59.7	5"	12.7	37 $\frac{1}{2}$	95.3	8"	20.2	51 $\frac{1}{2}$	130.8	10 $\frac{7}{8}$"	27.8

Step 2A

On your Three Quarter Circle Skirt Measurement Form, record your waist circumference measurement in the space provided. The waist circumference for our US size 6 (UK size 10) dress form is 27" (68.5cm).

Step 2B

Next, decide on the desired length of your skirt. Here we are measuring from the middle of the front waist tape of the dress form, but you could also use a body measurement to find the desired length.

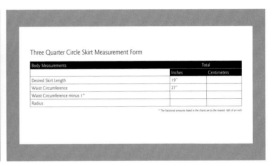

Step 2C

Record your desired skirt length measurement on your Three Quarter Circle Skirt Measurement Form. Our desired skirt length is 19" (48cm).

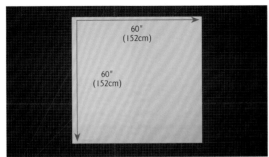

Step 3A

Prepare a piece of white unlined pattern paper measuring 60" (152cm) square for a 19" (48cm)-long skirt. Adjust the paper accordingly for a shorter or longer skirt.

Step 3B

Fold the paper in half and in half again so that the two folded edges align, and with the one paper fold positioned to your right.

Step 3C

Depending on the width of your pattern paper, you might need to extend the length of the paper with tape, as demonstrated.

Module 2:

Drafting the Waistline

Step 1

Secure the pattern paper layers with weights.

Opposite: A three quarter satin skirt from Madame Adassa, shown at LA Fashion Week for Fall/Winter 2018.

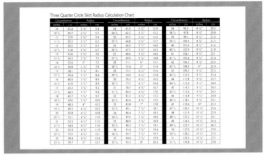

Step 2

Take your waist circumference measurement and subtract 1" (2.5cm), then record that measurement on the Three Quarter Circle Skirt Measurement Form. Our waist circumference is 27" (68.5cm)—minus 1" (2.5cm) equals 26" (66cm).

Step 3A

Next, you need to find the radius of your waistline. To do this, refer to our Three Quarter Circle Skirt Radius Calculation Chart and locate the your skirt's subtracted waist measurement, to the closest ½" (1.3cm). See the corresponding radius measurement for that waist amount. Our subtracted waist is 26" (66cm) so our radius is 5½" (14cm).

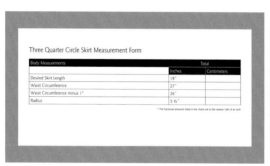

Step 3B

Record your radius measurement on the Three Quarter Circle Skirt Measurement Form. We will record our radius measurement as 5½" (14cm).

Step 4A

You may find it helpful to use our Fractions to Decimal Chart on page 88.

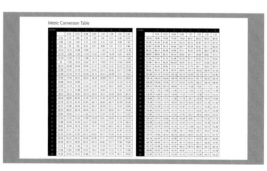

Step 4B

And, if you prefer working in centimeters, use our Metric Conversion Table on page 89.

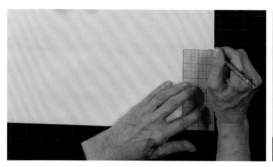

Step 5

At the intersection of the folded edges of the paper, which we will call the center point, measure down your radius measurement and place a ¼" (6mm)-long mark on each of the folded edge. We will measure down 5½" (14cm) for our skirt.

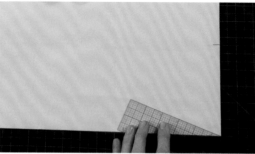

Step 6A

From the center point, we will form the radius of the inner circle, which will become the waistline.

Step 6B

Rest you ruler on your radius measurement at the center point and then pivot the ruler from that point as you mark the waistline, from one folded edge of the paper to the other.

Step 7

Another method of marking the waistline radius is by using a tape measure and pushpin (drawing pin). Insert the pin into the tape measure at the radius measurement, then anchor the pin into the cutting mat at center point. Mark the radius as you pivot at center point from folded edge to folded edge.

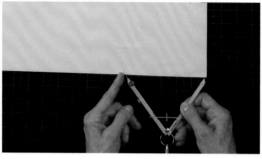

Step 8

Or you can use a pencil compass by setting the compass to your radius measurement. This particular compass does not open wide enough to be able to use it, but if it were wide enough, we would place the pointed end of the compass into the center point, and swing the compass from fold to fold to mark the shape of the waistline.

Step 9A

Since we used the tape measure method to mark the waist radius, we will now true the waistline using our styling curve and following the marks.

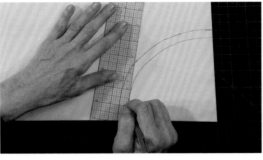

Step 9B

Add ½" (1.3cm) seam allowance to the waist next. We are using ½" (1.3cm) seam allowance, however you may wish to use ⅜" (1cm), the industry standard.

Step 9C

Cut away the excess paper from the waist.

Step 10

Remove the weights. Then unfold one layer of the skirt draft and lay it flat on the table.

Module 3:

Adding Seam &
Hem Allowances

Step 1A

You will now add seam allowance to the skirt panels. Begin by drawing a line down the center of both panels along the foldline. This represents one of the center back seams.

Step 1B

Add ½" (1.3cm) seam allowance to this center back seam and write "½" (1.3cm)" within the seam allowance.

Step 1C

Now move to the right skirt panel and add ½" (1.3cm) seam allowance to the fold edge of that section. This is your other center back seam.

Step 1D

Write "½" (1.3cm)" within the seam allowance of this center back seam.

Step 2A

Now extract the right side panel from the draft by cutting along the center back seam allowance from waist to hem.

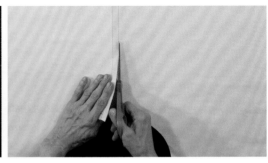

Step 2B

Move to the other center back seam and cut away the excess paper along that seam. Make sure that you are only cutting a single layer of paper.

Step 2C
Remove the extracted right-side skirt panel from the draft.

Step 3A
Next, you will be matching the center back seams.

Step 3B
Position the draft so that the center back seams align. Be sure that they align at the waist and at the hem.

Step 3C
Pin the two center back seams together in the seam allowance from waist to hem.

Step 3D
Smooth the paper so that it lies flat on the table and so that you can crease the fold edge, which will now become the center front of the skirt.

Step 4
Once you have pinned the paper layers together below the waistline, use your scissors to trim any excess paper at the waistline seam allowance, so that the edges align.

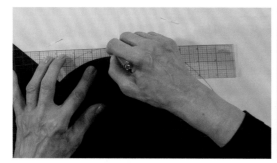

Step 5A
Use your ruler to square a line off the center front/waist intersection, then continue to pencil in the waist stitching line by measuring in ½" (1.3cm) from the cut edge.

Step 5B
Now use your tracing wheel to transfer the waist stitching line to the underside of the skirt waist.

Step 6A
Write "CF" along the center front fold of the skirt.

Step 6B
Write "CB" along the center back seam of the skirt.

Step 7A
Use your clear plastic ruler to measure the waist from center front to the stitching line at center back.

Step 7B
Find the halfway point of the waistline and indicate it with a notch mark and the letters "SS."

Tip
* These marks will be temporary since a full skirt such as this must hang for several hours after it is cut in fabric so that the bias has a chance to relax. Once the skirt has had a chance to hang, the hem can be marked and the pattern adjusted accordingly.

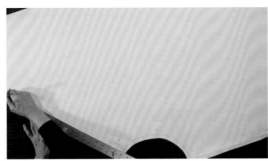

Step 8A
Next, you will mark the hemline using your metal ruler, starting at center front. Resting the ruler at the waist stitching line, at your desired skirt length measurement, place a mark to indicate the hem.

Step 8B
Now pivot the ruler along the waistline as you mark the hem from center front to center back. Place your marks approximately 4" (10cm) apart.*

Step 8C
Now square a line off the center back seam, for approximately 3" (7.5cm).

Step 8D
Reposition the paper, and then square a line off the center front at the hem, for about 2" (5cm).

Step 8E
You can use your hip curve and a pencil to shape the hem by connecting the hem marks that you created earlier.

Step 8F
Or, a faster method to mark the skirt's hemline is to use your tracing wheel to connect the marks, as demonstrated, from center back to center front.

Tip

The amount of bias stretch on a circle skirt depends upon the fabric type and weight. Lightweight fabrics may have more bias stretch than mediumweight fabrics.

Step 8G

Add ½" (1.3cm) seam allowance to the hemline from the tracing mark. And remember that you will need to test the pattern first in fabric to let the bias grain settle before you can adjust the final hem of this pattern.

Module 4:

Final Steps

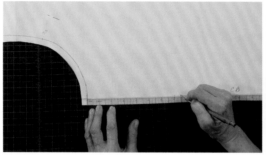

Step 1

At 7" (18cm) down from the stitching line of the center back waistline, place two notches, ½" (1.3cm) apart, for the zipper.

Step 2

Transfer-trace the zipper notches to the underside of the center back skirt with your tracing wheel.

Step 3

Then transfer-trace the side seam notch to the underside of the skirt waist.

Step 4

Now cut away the excess paper at the hemline.

Step 5

Remove the holding pins, unfold the pattern draft, and lay it flat on the table.

Step 6

Mark the zipper notches and the center back seam.

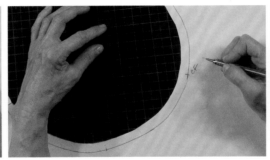

Step 7

Mark the stitching line of the skirt on the other side of the pattern, following your waist tracing line. Any adjustments to the seam allowance width can be made later, along with the hem adjustments.

Step 8

Now add a center front waist notch mark and write "CF" under the notch.

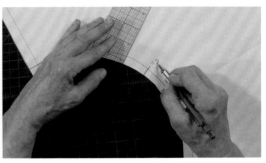

Step 9

Mark your side seam notch at the waist and add "SS" under it.

Step 10A

Now you will add your grainline. This is based on the fabric width and the desired look of the skirt. For a flat front look, you can have the straight grain along the center front, as here. However, a 60" (152cm)-wide fabric is necessary, otherwise the skirt will require an added pieced seam at the bottom of the skirt.

Step 10B

Or, you could choose bias grain for a flared look at center front. For this, create a 2 x 2" (5 x 5cm) box on the center front line with your clear plastic ruler. Then, mark the opposite corners of the box.

Step 10C

We will use red pencil and our metal ruler to connect the corners of the box. However, be sure that your fabric is wide enough for this grain choice.

Step 10D

Or you can choose to have your center front skirt cut along the length grain of the fabric. This will produce a flat front look similar to that of straight grain. For this you will square a line off center front, as demonstrated. Here we are marking the grainline in blue pencil.

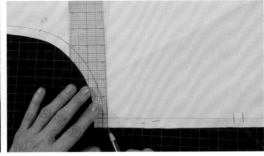

Step 11A

Because the back waist of the body dips lower than the front, you will lower the center back waist by ¼" (6mm). Use your red pencil and square a line off center back, ¼" (6mm) below the back waist.

Step 11B

Now blend the lowered waistline to the side seam using your styling curve.

Step 11C
Trace the new lowered waistline onto the underside of the skirt.

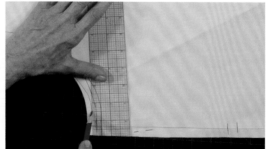

Step 11D
Then add ½" (1.3cm) seam allowance to the new back-waist stitching line.

Step 11E
Trim away the excess paper at the back waist.

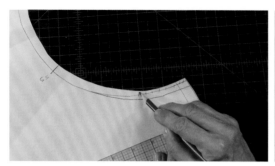

Step 11F
Mark the stitching line of the back waist on the underside, following the new lowered-waist tracing line. Mark the old waistline with red pencil hatch marks.

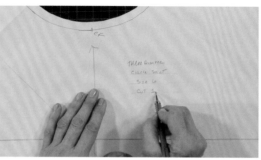

Step 12
Once you have chosen your grainline—either straight grain, bias, or cross grain—annotate the pattern with "Three Quarter Circle Skirt," "Size 6," or whatever your particular size happens to be, and "Cut 1."

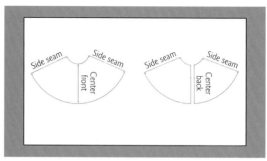

Step 13A
If you choose to add side seams to the skirt, separate the skirt at the side seams, add ½" (1.3cm) seam allowance, and draw the back grainline so that it corresponds to the center-front grainline.

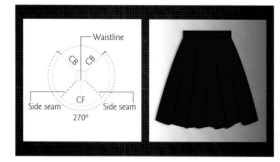

Step 13B
You have now finished drafting your Three Quarter Circle Skirt.

Self-evaluation

☐ Did I accurately calculate my skirt's radius?

☐ Did I have to add extra paper to accommodate a longer length skirt?

☐ Have I marked my waistline radius properly?

☐ Did I lower my back waistline?

☐ Did I add my notches and grainline?

Full Circle Skirt

Learning objectives

☐ Establish and record key measurements, prepare the paper blocks

☐ Draft the skirt front—establishing the waistline using the waistline radius chart, adding seam allowances, trueing the hem, adding the hem allowance, cutting out the pattern

☐ Draft the skirt back—tracing the front onto the second paper block

☐ Adding final notches and stitching lines, establishing the grainline, annotating the pattern

☐ Design options—adding a center back seam, or center front and back seams, creating a handkerchief hem

Tools and supplies:

- White unlined pattern paper—24 x 48" (61 x 122cm)
- Drawing compass
- Fractions to Decimals and the Metric Conversion Table (see pages 88–89)

Step 1A

For this lesson you will be using our Full Circle Skirt
Measurement Form, as well as our Full Circle Skirt Radius
Calculation Chart, provided below.

Full Circle Skirt Measurement Form

Body Measurements	Total	
	Inches	Centimeters
Desired skirt length		
Waist circumference		
Waist circumference minus 1" (2.5cm)		
Radius		

* The fractional amounts listed in the charts are to the nearest 16th of an inch

Full Circle Skirt Radius Calculation Chart

Circumference		Radius		Circumference		Radius		Circumference		Radius	
inches	cm	inches	cm	inches	cm	inches	cm	inches	cm	inches	cm
10	25.4	1 $^5/_8$"	4.0	24	61.0	3 $^7/_8$"	9.7	38	96.5	6"	15.4
10 $^1/_2$	26.7	1 $^5/_8$"	4.2	24 $^1/_2$	62.2	3 $^7/_8$"	9.9	38 $^1/_2$	97.8	6 $^1/_8$"	15.6
11	27.9	1 $^3/_4$"	4.4	25	63.5	4"	10.1	39	99.1	6 $^1/_4$"	15.8
11 $^1/_2$	29.2	1 $^7/_8$"	4.6	25 $^1/_2$	64.8	4"	10.3	39 $^1/_2$	100.3	6 $^1/_4$"	16.0
12	30.5	1 $^7/_8$"	4.9	26	66.0	4 $^1/_8$"	10.5	40	101.6	6 $^3/_8$"	16.2
12 $^1/_2$	31.8	2"	5.1	26 $^1/_2$	67.3	4 $^1/_4$"	10.7	40 $^1/_2$	102.9	6 $^1/_2$"	16.4
13	33.0	2 $^1/_8$"	5.3	27	68.6	4 $^1/_4$"	10.9	41	104.1	6 $^1/_2$"	16.6
13 $^1/_2$	34.3	2 $^1/_8$"	5.5	27 $^1/_2$	69.9	4 $^3/_8$"	11.1	41 $^1/_2$	105.4	6 $^5/_8$"	16.8
14	35.6	2 $^1/_4$"	5.7	28	71.1	4 $^1/_2$"	11.3	42	106.7	6 $^5/_8$"	17.0
14 $^1/_2$	36.8	2 $^1/_4$"	5.9	28 $^1/_2$	72.4	4 $^1/_2$"	11.5	42 $^1/_2$	108.0	6 $^3/_4$"	17.2
15	38.1	2 $^3/_8$"	6.1	29	73.7	4 $^5/_8$"	11.7	43	109.2	6 $^7/_8$"	17.4
15 $^1/_2$	39.4	2 $^1/_2$"	6.3	29 $^1/_2$	74.9	4 $^3/_4$"	11.9	43 $^1/_2$	110.5	6 $^7/_8$"	17.6
16	40.6	2 $^1/_2$"	6.5	30	76.2	4 $^3/_4$"	12.1	44	111.8	7"	17.8
16 $^1/_2$	41.9	2 $^5/_8$"	6.7	30 $^1/_2$	77.5	4 $^7/_8$"	12.3	44 $^1/_2$	113.0	7 $^1/_8$"	18.0
17	43.2	2 $^3/_4$"	6.9	31	78.74	4 $^7/_8$"	12.5	45	114.3	7 $^1/_8$"	18.2
17 $^1/_2$	44.5	2 $^3/_4$"	7.1	31 $^1/_2$	80.01	5"	12.7	45 $^1/_2$	115.6	7 $^1/_4$"	18.4
18	45.7	2 $^7/_8$"	7.3	32	81.28	5 $^1/_8$"	12.9	46	116.8	7 $^3/_8$"	18.6
18 $^1/_2$	47.0	3"	7.5	32 $^1/_2$	82.55	5 $^1/_8$"	13.1	46 $^1/_2$	118.1	7 $^3/_8$"	18.8
19	48.3	3"	7.7	33	83.82	5 $^1/_4$"	13.3	47	119.4	7 $^1/_2$"	19.0
19 $^1/_2$	49.5	3 $^1/_8$"	7.9	33 $^1/_2$	85.09	5 $^3/_8$"	13.5	47 $^1/_2$	120.7	7 $^1/_2$"	19.2
20	50.8	3 $^1/_8$"	8.1	34	86.36	5 $^3/_8$"	13.7	48	121.9	7 $^5/_8$"	19.4
20 $^1/_2$	52.1	3 $^1/_4$"	8.3	34 $^1/_2$	87.63	5 $^1/_2$"	13.9	48 $^1/_2$	123.2	7 $^3/_4$"	19.6
21	53.3	3 $^3/_8$"	8.5	35	88.9	5 $^5/_8$"	14.1	49	124.5	7 $^3/_4$"	19.8
21 $^1/_2$	54.6	3 $^3/_8$"	8.7	35 $^1/_2$	90.17	5 $^5/_8$"	14.4	49 $^1/_2$	125.7	7 $^7/_8$"	20.0
22	55.9	3 $^1/_2$"	8.9	36	91.44	5 $^3/_4$"	14.6	50	127.0	8"	20.2
22 $^1/_2$	57.2	3 $^5/_8$"	9.1	36 $^1/_2$	92.71	5 $^3/_4$"	14.8	50 $^1/_2$	128.3	8"	20.4
23	58.4	3 $^5/_8$"	9.3	37	93.98	5 $^7/_8$"	15.0	51	129.5	8 $^1/_8$"	20.6
23 $^1/_2$	59.7	3 $^3/_4$"	9.5	37 $^1/_2$	95.25	6"	15.2	51 $^1/_2$	130.8	8 $^1/_4$"	20.8

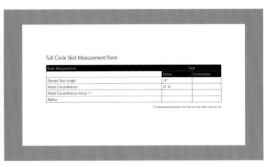

Step 2A

On your Full Circle Skirt Measurement Form, record your waist circumference in the space provided. The waist circumference for our US size 6 (UK size 10) dress form is 27½" (70cm).

Step 2B

Next, decide on the desired skirt length. Here we are measuring from the middle of the front waist tape of the dress form, but you could also take a body measurement.

Step 2C

Record that measurement on your Full Circle Skirt Measurement Form. Our desired skirt length is 19" (48cm).

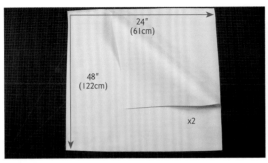

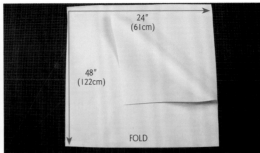

Step 3

For our size 6, we prepared two pieces of white unlined pattern paper measuring 24" (61cm) wide by 48" (122 cm) long. Adjust your measurements accordingly for a shorter or longer skirt.

Step 4

Fold the first paper piece in half in the lengthwise direction, with the fold closest to you.

Module 2:

Drafting the Skirt Front

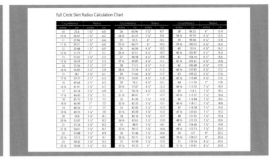

Step 1

With the fold of the first pattern paper block facing you, measure in ½" (1.3 cm) from the right-side edge and draw a line from the edge of the paper to the fold. This represents the skirt's side seam. Write "SS" along the line.

Opposite: Derya Acikgoz presented a red full skirt paired with a faux leather top at Istanbul Fashion Week for Fall/Winter 2016.

Step 2

Now refer to your Full Circle Skirt Measurement Form. Take your total waist circumference measurement (measured from center front to center front) and subtract 1" (2.5 cm). Record that measurement on the form in the space provided. Our waist circumference is 27½" (70cm)—minus 1" (2.5cm) equals 26½" (67.5cm)

Step 3

Now refer to our Full Circle Skirt Radius Calculation Chart to find the radius of your skirt's subtracted waist measurement to the closest ½" (1.3cm). Our subtracted waist measurement is 26½" (67.5cm) and therefore our radius is 4¼" (11cm).

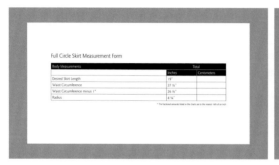

Step 4

Record your radius measurement in the space provided on the Full Circle Skirt Measurement Form. We will record 4¼" (11cm).

Step 5A

You may find it helpful to use our Fractions to Decimal Chart on page 88.

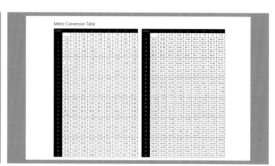

Step 5B

And, if you prefer working in centimeters, use our Metric Conversion Table on page 89.

Step 6A

The intersection of the fold, which is the center front of the skirt, and the ½" (1.3cm) side seam mark will be referred to as the center point.

Step 6B

We will be measuring down our calculated radius measurement from this center point.

Step 6C

There are several ways to mark the radius. One way is to use a tape measure and pushpin (drawing pin). Insert the pin at the radius measurement on your tape measure, then anchor the pushpin into the cutting mat at the center point. Mark the radius as you pivot at center point from the fold to the side seam line.

Step 6D

Or you can use a clear plastic ruler, pivoting from the center point as you mark from the fold to the side seam. To use this method, you must continually check that your ruler is placed at the correct radius measurement from the center point.

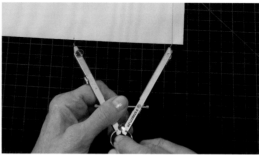

Step 6E

Or you can use a pencil compass. Set the compass to your radius measurement. Refer to page 102, Step 4, to see how to use the compass.

Step 6F

Place the pointed end of the compass into the center point and swing the compass from the fold to the side seam, marking the shape of the front waistline as you go.

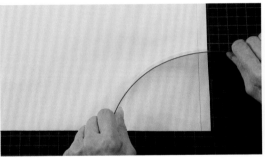

Step 6G

Use your ruler to check that your front waist measurement is accurate, by measuring from the center front fold to the side seam. The measurement should be one fourth of your total waist circumference measurement, less the 1" (2.5cm). In our case it is 26½" (67cm) divided by 4, or 6⅝" (17cm).

Step 7

Label the center front by writing "CF" on the fold.

Step 8

Label the front waistline by writing "Front" above the waist, close to the fold.

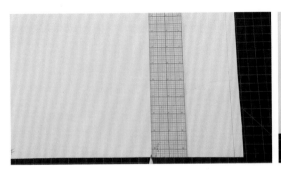

Step 9A

Use your ruler and red pencil to square a line off center front at ¼" (6mm) below the center front waist intersection. This will become the center back skirt waistline since the back waistline is lower than the front.

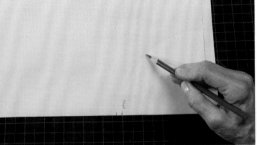

Step 9B

Find the halfway point between the fold and the side seam.

Step 9C

Next, using a styling curve, blend the back waistline curve from the center back to the midway point.

Step 9D

Above the red back waistline, write "Back."

Step 10

Use your tracing wheel to trace the front waistline, from the center front to the side seam.

Step 11A

Use your ruler to check that your center front waist is at a right angle to center front for about ½" (1.3cm).

Tip

* Trueing the hem, however, will be temporary since circle skirts have a certain amount of bias. It is recommended that they be cut in the desired fabric, left to hang for several hours, and then the pattern adjusted to compensate for the bias stretch.

Step 11B
You will use your yardstick to mark the skirt length. Measure your desired skirt length from the waist at center front and place a mark to indicate the hem. Here we are measuring at the 19" (48cm) mark.

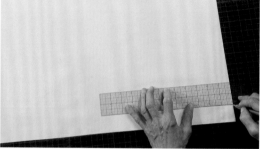

Step 11C
Slide the yardstick along the waistline at the skirt length measurement on the ruler from center front to the side seam. Mark the hem with a series of dashes, keeping the hemline at a right angle both at center front and at the side seam.*

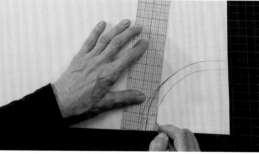

Step 12
Now add ½" (1.3cm) seam allowance to the front waistline. However, in the industry, and depending on the company, the seam allowance might be ⅜" (1cm).

Step 13
Using paper scissors, cut away the excess paper from the front waistline.

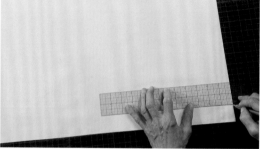

Step 14A
Next, reposition the skirt so that you can work on the hemline. Start by squaring a line off the center front/hem mark for about 1½" (3.8cm).

Step 14B
You must also square off at the side seam/hem intersection for about 1½" (3.8cm).

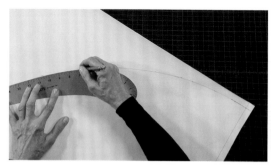

Step 14C
Use your hip curve to lightly connect the hem markings from center front to the side seam. As mentioned earlier, you must let the skirt hang before you can firmly establish the hem of the pattern.

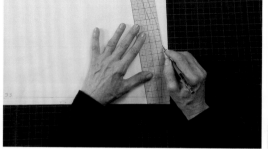

Step 14D
Add ½" (1.3cm) seam allowance to the hem next.

Step 15A
Place weights on the front pattern to secure the layers.

Step 15B
Cut away the excess paper at the hem.

Tip
The width of your fabric will help determine the full circle skirt's grainline.

Module 3:

Drafting the Skirt Back

Step 1
Position your second pattern paper block, which will become the back skirt, with the folded edge facing you.

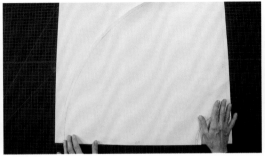

Step 2
Line up the center front and the side seam edge of your front skirt to the back skirt paper block below, as demonstrated.

Step 3
Secure the pattern with weights.

Step 4A
Now trace the back waistline onto the paper below.

Step 4B
Remove the weights and the skirt front from the paper below.

Step 5
Add the side seam line to the back skirt pattern at ½" (1.3cm) away from the right-side edge. Annotate the side seam with the letters "SS."

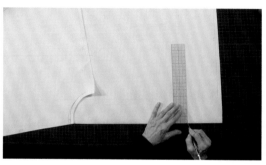

Step 6A
Square a line off the center back waist for about ½" (1.3cm).

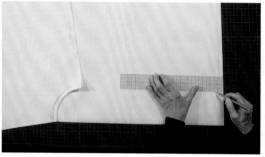

Step 6B
Then square another line off the side seam/waist intersection for about ½" (1.3cm).

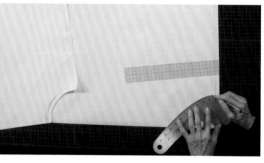

Step 7
Use your styling curve and, following your tracing marks, pencil in the back waistline.

Step 8
Write "CB" on the center back skirt fold.

Step 9
Now add ½"(1.3cm) seam allowance to the back waistline.

Step 10A
You will now repeat the steps for marking the back skirt hem as you did for the front skirt hem, by resting the ruler at the back waist stitching line.

Step 10B
Connect the hem marks with your hip curve.

Step 10C
Then add the ½" (1.3cm) hem allowance. Since you will most likely need to adjust the hem after the skirt hangs anyway, you could just copy the skirt front hem onto the back.

Step 10D
Secure the back skirt layers with weights.

Step 10E
Trim away the excess paper at the hem and at the waistline.

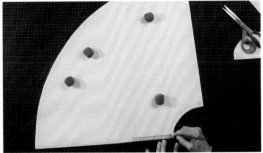

Step 11
So that you can differentiate the skirt back from the front, place a notch at the waistline, ½" (1.3cm) away from center back, using a red pencil.

Step 12
On the skirt front waist, for clarification purposes, draw lines through the back waist to avoid confusion.

Module 4:

Final Steps

Step 1
Open the front skirt pattern and flatten the pattern on the table. Add a center front notch mark with your red pencil.

Step 2
Add the side seam stitching line to the other side of the pattern.

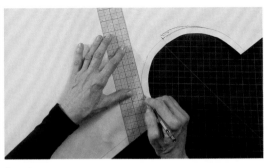

Step 3
Now add the waist stitching line to the other side of the front skirt pattern.

Step 4
Next, you will decide on the skirt's grainline. For a smooth looking front, you would place the straight grain along the center front, as demonstrated.

Step 5A
For the maximum amount of flare at center front you would place the center front on bias. For this, draw a 2 x 2" (5 x 5cm) box centered along center front with your clear plastic ruler, as demonstrated.

Step 5B
Use your metal yardstick and red pencil to connect the corners of the box, and draw a line to create the bias grainline.

Step 6A

Or you could place the straight grain horizontally on the skirt which would again, produce a flatter, smoother skirt front.

Step 6B

Place the yardstick at a right angle off center front and draw a line across the width of the skirt. This option is great for a stripe fabric or for fabric that is narrow in width. Whichever grain option you choose, you must do the same for the back skirt.

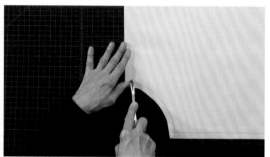

Step 7A

Now move to the skirt back. With your tracing wheel, trace the back waist notch onto the other side of the waist.

Step 7B

Draw in the stitching line of the side seam with your ruler.

Step 7C

Draw in the other side of the back waistline, following your tracing lines.

Step 8

For this skirt we decided to choose center front on bias. Following the steps for bias grain as we did on the front skirt, mark your bias grainline.

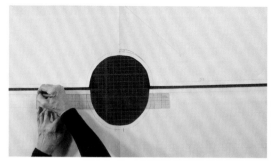

Step 9A

With the front and back side seam matched up on the table, measure down 7" (18cm) from the waist stitching line of the skirt. This will be your zipper notch opening.

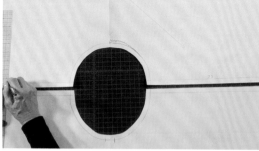

Step 9B

Place a corresponding zipper notch on the back side seam.

Step 10A

Annotate the back skirt with "Full Circle skirt," "Back," "Size 6," or whatever your size happens to be, and "Cut 1."

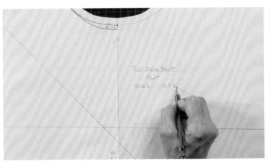

Step 10B
Now annotate the front skirt with " Full Circle Skirt," "Front," your size, and "Cut 1."

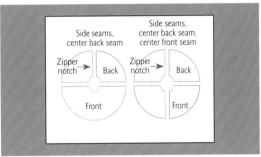

Step 10C
Although we have drafted this skirt with side seams, you could also choose to add a center back seam or a center front *and* center back seam.

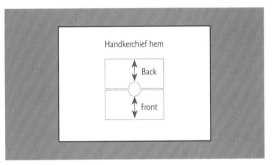

Step 10D
If you want to create a handkerchief hem instead of a circular hem, as demonstrated in these images, then omit the front and back pattern hem steps where you shaped your hem.

Step 10E
You have now finished your Full Circle Skirt pattern.

Self-evaluation

☐ Did I accurately calculate my skirt's radius?

☐ After drafting the skirt's radius, did I check it against my front waist measurement?

☐ Have I lowered my back waistline?

☐ Did I consider the width of my fabric when choosing my skirt's grainline?

3 Bodices

A tight-fitting bodice, known as a 'moulage' or mold, is the foundation for many of your future dress, blouse, and jacket designs. We will teach you how to draft this bodice, (consisting of a shoulder and waist dart), from actual body measurements or from our women's global size chart. You will learn how to convert the moulage to a sleeveless bodice oaktag sloper and one with a sleeve. From there you will explore variations on how to pivot the front shoulder dart to other areas, including to the side seam, the armhole, or as a single dart at the waist and also how to pivot a back-shoulder dart to the neckline.

In addition, we will teach you a two-dart pivoting technique, whereby you will be able to create multiple dart combinations. Next, you will draft a fitted torso sloper, adapted from your Shoulder Dart Bodice sloper. This chapter concludes with instructions for drafting two types of sleeves—a raglan sleeve (with one- and two-piece variations) and a kimono sleeve. These lessons employ slopers drafted previously in this chapter, as well as the straight sleeve sloper that you will have drafted at the very start of the book.

Drafting a Shoulder Dart Bodice Sloper from Measurements

Learning objectives

☐ Extract body measurements from either a live model, dress form or the size range chart

☐ Prepare paper pieces, marking the paper to establish the front and back bodice block widths

☐ Plan the front and neckline, shoulder, armhole

☐ Draft the apex, bustline and front and back darts

☐ Finish the draft—trueing the shoulder and waistline

☐ Transfer the draft to muslin, add seam allowances, fit the bodice and copy the finished bodice to oaktag

Tools and supplies:

- Notcher
- Women's Body Measuring Points Diagram
- Women's Body Measuring Points Chart (see Appendix, p.332)
- Women's Global Size Range Bodice Chart (see Appendix, p.338)
- Bodice Sloper Worksheet
- Fractions to Decimals Chart
- Metric Conversion Table
- Muslin (calico) for fit-testing
- Dress Form

Christopher Kane applies a satin zig-zag appliqué to this basic bodice and skirt for London Fashion Week. (Fall/Winter 2015/2016)

Step 1

For this lesson, you will need to refer to the following diagrams and charts: Women's Body Measuring Points Diagram, Moulage Measurement Worksheet, Fractions to Decimals Chart, and Metric Conversion Table. You will also need Women's Body Measuring Points Chart and Women's Global Size Range Bodice Chart, both of which can be found in the Appendix.

Step 2

You can view our video lesson entitled 'Measuring the Female Body' for help on how to measure an actual person. Or, you can refer to our Women's Body Measuring Points Diagram, below, which illustrates the measuring points that you will need for this lesson and is color-coded to work with our Women's Body Measuring Points Chart, which is on pages 332–336.

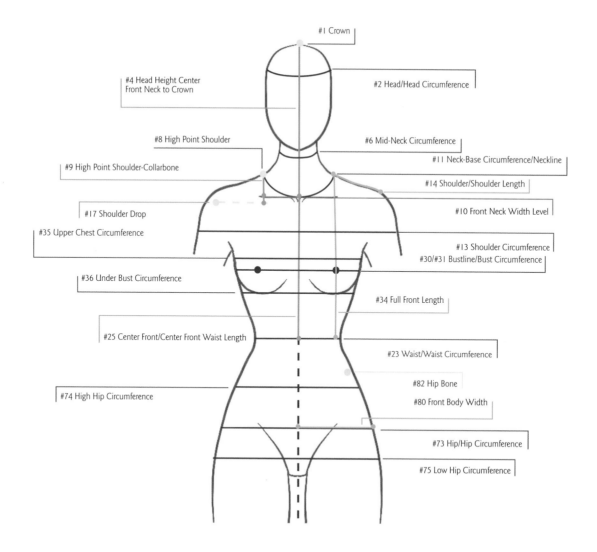

#1 Crown

#4 Head Height Center Front Neck to Crown

#2 Head/Head Circumference

#8 High Point Shoulder

#6 Mid-Neck Circumference

#9 High Point Shoulder-Collarbone

#11 Neck-Base Circumference/Neckline

#14 Shoulder/Shoulder Length

#17 Shoulder Drop

#10 Front Neck Width Level

#35 Upper Chest Circumference

#13 Shoulder Circumference

#30/#31 Bustline/Bust Circumference

#36 Under Bust Circumference

#34 Full Front Length

#25 Center Front/Center Front Waist Length

#23 Waist/Waist Circumference

#82 Hip Bone

#74 High Hip Circumference

#80 Front Body Width

#73 Hip/Hip Circumference

#75 Low Hip Circumference

Horizontal measurements
Vertical measurements
Circumference measurements
Body contour measurements
Point

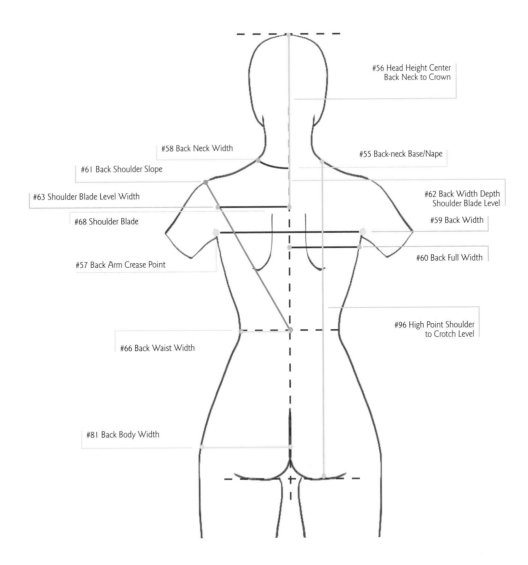

#56 Head Height Center
Back Neck to Crown

#58 Back Neck Width

#55 Back-neck Base/Nape

#61 Back Shoulder Slope

#63 Shoulder Blade Level Width

#62 Back Width Depth
Shoulder Blade Level

#68 Shoulder Blade

#59 Back Width

#57 Back Arm Crease Point

#60 Back Full Width

#96 High Point Shoulder
to Crotch Level

#66 Back Waist Width

#81 Back Body Width

Horizontal measurements
Vertical measurements
Circumference measurements
Body contour measurements
Point

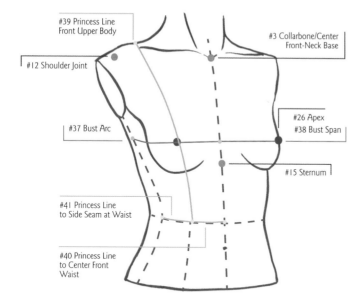

#39 Princess Line Front Upper Body

#3 Collarbone/Center Front-Neck Base

#12 Shoulder Joint

#26 Apex
#38 Bust Span

#37 Bust Arc

#15 Sternum

#41 Princess Line to Side Seam at Waist

#40 Princess Line to Center Front Waist

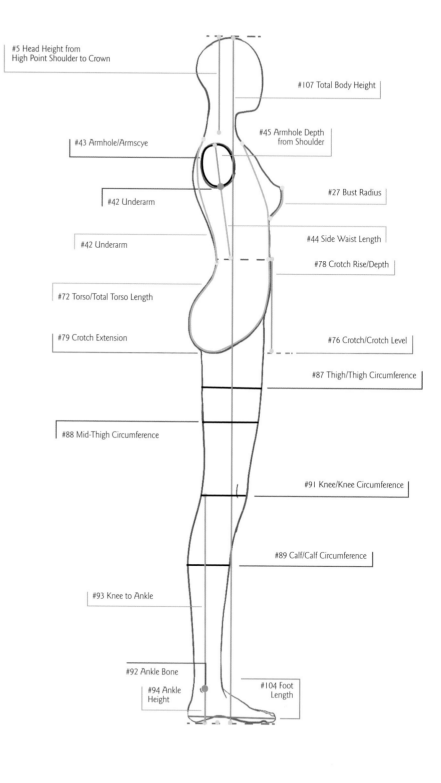

#5 Head Height from High Point Shoulder to Crown

#107 Total Body Height

#43 Armhole/Armscye

#45 Armhole Depth from Shoulder

#27 Bust Radius

#42 Underarm

#44 Side Waist Length

#42 Underarm

#78 Crotch Rise/Depth

#72 Torso/Total Torso Length

#79 Crotch Extension

#76 Crotch/Crotch Level

#87 Thigh/Thigh Circumference

#88 Mid-Thigh Circumference

#91 Knee/Knee Circumference

#89 Calf/Calf Circumference

#93 Knee to Ankle

#92 Ankle Bone

#94 Ankle Height

#104 Foot Length

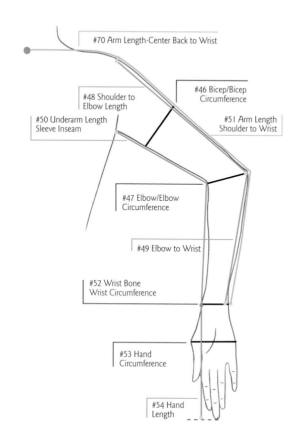

#70 Arm Length-Center Back to Wrist

#48 Shoulder to Elbow Length

#46 Bicep/Bicep Circumference

#50 Underarm Length Sleeve Inseam

#51 Arm Length Shoulder to Wrist

#47 Elbow/Elbow Circumference

#49 Elbow to Wrist

#52 Wrist Bone Wrist Circumference

#53 Hand Circumference

#54 Hand Length

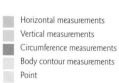

Horizontal measurements
Vertical measurements
Circumference measurements
Body contour measurements
Point

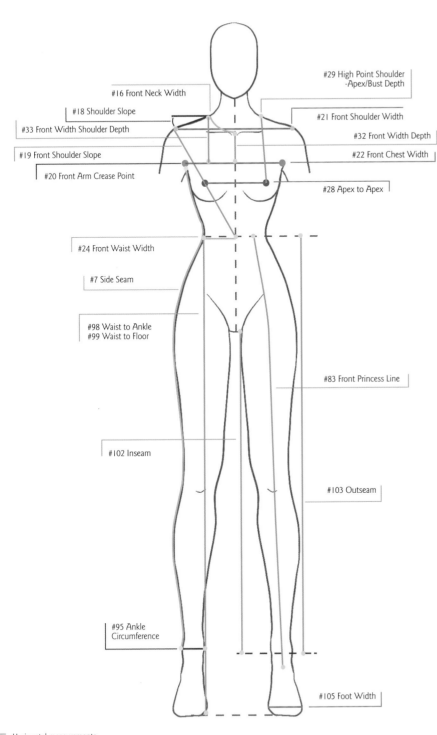

#29 High Point Shoulder -Apex/Bust Depth

#16 Front Neck Width

#18 Shoulder Slope

#21 Front Shoulder Width

#33 Front Width Shoulder Depth

#32 Front Width Depth

#19 Front Shoulder Slope

#22 Front Chest Width

#20 Front Arm Crease Point

#28 Apex to Apex

#24 Front Waist Width

#7 Side Seam

#98 Waist to Ankle
#99 Waist to Floor

#83 Front Princess Line

#102 Inseam

#103 Outseam

#95 Ankle Circumference

#105 Foot Width

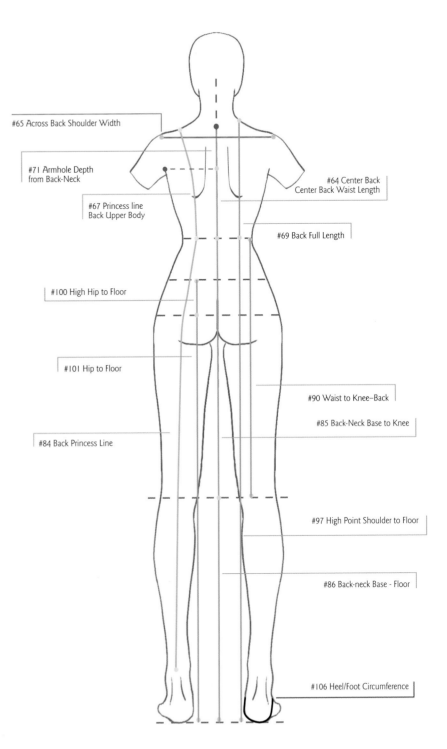

#65 Across Back Shoulder Width

#71 Armhole Depth from Back-Neck

#64 Center Back Center Back Waist Length

#67 Princess line Back Upper Body

#69 Back Full Length

#100 High Hip to Floor

#101 Hip to Floor

#90 Waist to Knee–Back

#85 Back-Neck Base to Knee

#84 Back Princess Line

#97 High Point Shoulder to Floor

#86 Back-neck Base - Floor

#106 Heel/Foot Circumference

Horizontal measurements
Vertical measurements
Circumference measurements
Body contour measurements
Point

Drafting a Shoulder Dart Bodice Sloper from Measurements

Step 3A

You will need to extract and record the following front body measurements on the Moulage Measurement Worksheet.

Moulage Measurement Worksheet– Front

#34   Full Front Length 17 ³⁄₈"

#37   Bust Arc 9 ³⁄₈" plus ½" ease (1.3cm) = 9⁷⁄₈"

#10   Front Neck Width Level 2 ³⁄₈" plus ⅛" ease (3mm) = 2 ½"

#9   High Point Shoulder to Collarbone 2 ½" plus ⅛" ease (3mm) = 2 ⁵⁄₈"

#29   High Point Shoulder to Apex 10 ½"

#38   Bust Span 3 ¾"

#24   Front Waist Width 7 ⅛" plus ¼" (6mm) ease = 7 ³⁄₈" total Front Waist Width

J to C   Measurement 8 ⁷⁄₈" minus total #24 Front Waist Width Measurement 7 ³⁄₈" = 1 ½" dart intake, divided by 2 = ¾"

#44   Side Waist Length 8 ½"

#45   Armhole Depth from Shoulder 5 ½"

#14   Shoulder Length Measurement 5" plus ⅛" (3mm) ease = 5 ⅛"

M to E Measurement 7 ⁵⁄₈" minus # 14 total Shoulder Length Measurement 5 ⅛" = 2 ½" dart intake, divided by 2 = 1 ¼"

#32   Front Width Depth 4 ⅛"

#22   Front Chest Width Measurement 13 ½" divided by 2 = 6 ¾"

Step 3B
And you will extract and record the following back body
measurements on the Moulage Measurement Worksheet.

Moulage Measurement Worksheet – Back

#60   Back Full Width 8 ⅝" plus ½" (1.3cm) ease = 9 ⅛"

#64   Center Back Waist Length 16 ⅜"

#66   Back Waist Width 6" plus ¼" (6mm) ease = 6 ¼" total Back Waist Width

P to Q Measurement 8 ⅛" minus total Back Waist Width Measurement 6 ¼" = ⅞" dart intake,
        divided by 2 = 1"

#10   Front Neck Width Level 2 ⅜" plus ¼" (6mm) ease = 2 ⅝"

#69   Back Full Length 17 ¼"

#14   Shoulder Length 5" plus ¼ = 5 ¼" divided by 2 = 2 ⅝"

#62   Back Width Depth 4 1/16"

#63   Shoulder Blade Level Width 7" plus ⅜" (1cm) = 7 ⅛"

---

*Fractions are rounded up to the nearest 1/16 th of an inch

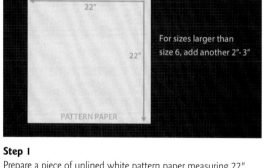

Step 1

Prepare a piece of unlined white pattern paper measuring 22" (55.9 cm) square [for sizes larger than size 6, add another 2" (5 cm) – 3" (7.2 cm)].

Step 2

Download the Moulage Measurement Worksheet to assist you when calculating and recording measurements as you draft.

Step 3A

Position the paper folded, with the fold away from you.

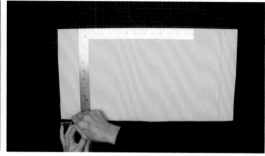

Step 3A

Then, using your L square at 2" (5.1cm) down from the top, square a line across the paper. Label this point A.

Step 3B

Measure down from A, along the fold, your #34 Full Front Length measurement, and square a line across the paper. [Our #34 measures 17 3/8" (44.1cm)]. Label that intersection B.

Step 3C

Then square a line off B, the width of the paper. This is your front waistline. Mark it "WL," as demonstrated.

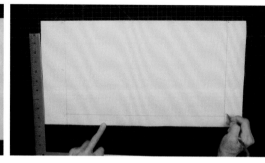

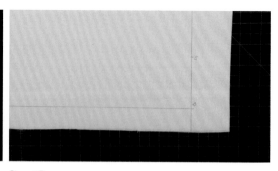

Step 4A

Now we will determine the width of the moulage block. Measure over from B by your #37 Bust Arc measurement. Add ½" (1.3 cm) ease and label that C. Use your Moulage Measurement Worksheet to record these measurements. Ours measures 9⅜" (23.8 cm) plus ½" (1.3 cm), which equals 9⅞" (25.1 cm).

Step 4B

Square a line over from the B/C line to the A line and label this new line "CF" (center front). Label the intersection D.

Step 5A

To draft the neckline, take your #10 Front Neck Width Level measurement, add ⅛" (3 mm) worth of ease, and record these measurements on your worksheet. Then measure that amount, from D along the A/D line and label this point E. Ours measures 2 ⅜" (6 cm) plus ⅛" (3 mm), which equals 2½" (6.4 cm).

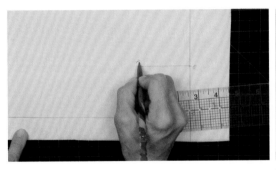

Step 5B

Next, on your worksheet, record your **#9 High Point Shoulder to Collarbone** measurement, plus ⅛" (3 mm). Then square down that amount from E and mark this point as F. Ours measures 2½" (6.4 cm) plus ⅛" (3 mm), which equals 2⅝" (6.7 cm).

Step 5C

Then square a line off to center front and mark that point G.

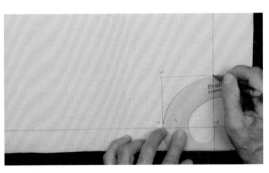

Step 5D

Place a mark ¼" (6 mm) in from G and mark this point H. Then, using your French curve, connect E to H to form the front neckline.

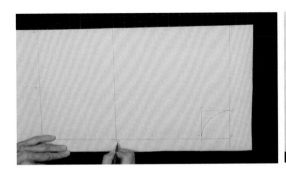

Step 6

Next you will draw the bust level by measuring down from D by your **#29 High Point Shoulder to Apex** measurement. Ours measures 10½" (26.7 cm). Then square a line. Mark this as I and label it "BL." This is the bust level.

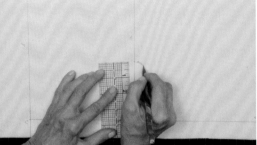

Step 7A

Measure over from I by your **#38 Bust Span** measurement and label this point "apex." Ours measures 3¾" (9.6 cm).

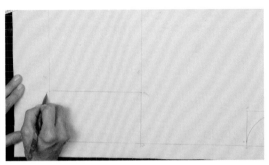

Step 7B

Square a line off the bustline at the apex to the waistline, and mark that as point I. This is the centerline of the front waist dart.

Step 8

Measure over 1" (2.5 cm) from point B, at the fold, and label this J.

Step 9A

Next you will plan your waist dart. To do this, take your **#24 Front Waist Width** measurement, add ¼" (6 mm), and record these measurements on the worksheet. Our front waist width measures 7⅛" (18.1 cm) plus ¼" (6 mm), which equals 7⅜" (18.7 cm).

Step 9B

Now measure from J to C and record that measurement on the worksheet. Subtract your **#24 Front Waist Width** measurement (including ease) from your J to C measurement and the difference will become your total dart-intake amount. Our J to C measures 8⅞" (22.6 cm), minus 7⅜" (18.7 cm), which is 1½" (3.8 cm). Then divide that amount by 2 to determine the dart amount on each side of the dart centerline. Our dart intake measures ¾" (2 cm).

Bodices

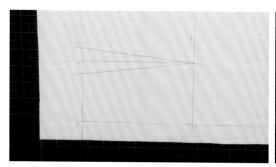

Step 9C

Mark that amount on each side of point #1, and then connect the dart-intake points to the apex, which is the dart's vanishing point.

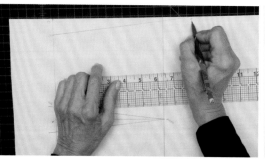

Step 10A

Now you will mark the side seam, by taking your **#44 Side Waist Length** measurement—in our case, 8½" (21.6 cm)—and pivoting the ruler from point J by that amount until the ruler hits the fold of the paper. Label that point K.

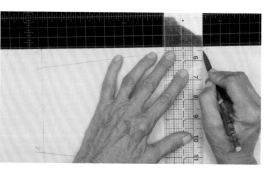

Step 10B

Square off a ¼" (6 mm) line from the fold at K.

Step 11A

Measure up from K by your **#45 Armhole Depth from Shoulder** measurement and label this L. Refer to our Women's Global Size Range Bodice Chart in the Appendix for the armhole depth for your size. Ours is 5½" (14 cm) for a US size 6.

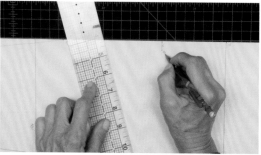

Step 11B

Measure in ½" (1.3 cm) from L, place a mark, and label this M.

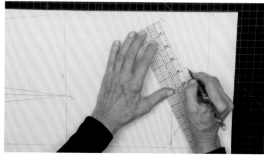

Step 12A

To form the shoulder, connect M to E. Then, place a mark at the midway point of M/E and mark it as #2. This is the centerline of the front shoulder dart. Our midway point is 3⅞" (9.9 cm).

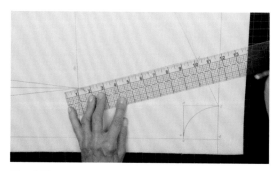

Step 12B

Now, connect #2 to the apex.

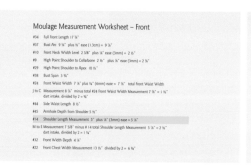

Step 12C

To calculate the shoulder dart intake, record your **#14 Shoulder Length** measurement on the worksheet, add ⅛" (3 mm) ease, and record the total front shoulder length measurement. Our shoulder length measurement is 5" (12.7 cm) plus ⅛" (3 mm). which equals 5⅛" (13 cm).

Step 12D

Now, record the M to E measurement, then subtract the total #14 Shoulder Length measurement; the difference is your front shoulder dart-intake amount. Our M to E of 7⅝" (19.4 cm), minus our total shoulder length of 5⅛" (13 cm), means that our total dart intake will be 2½" (6.4 cm).

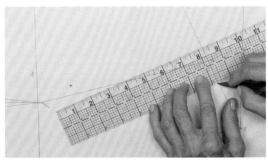

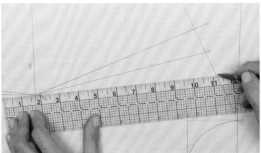

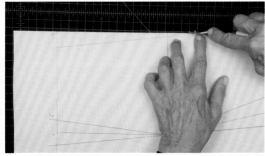

Step 12E

Divide that total dart-intake amount in half and then mark that amount on either side of the dart centerline. Our dart intake is 1¼" (3.2 cm).

Step 12F

Connect the dart-intake marks to the apex. Extend the dart lines past the shoulder seam.

Step 13

With a tracing wheel, trace the side seam onto the underside from J to K. Trace the waist at J for about ¼" (6 mm), and also at K. Unfold the paper to check that the tracing marks have transferred.

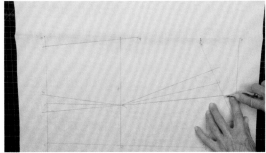

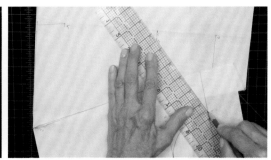

Step 14

Open the draft, and using the tracing wheel, trace the front shoulder dart leg line closest to center front.

Step 15A

Fold the paper at the bustline and close the dart, with the dart excess going in the direction of center front, then secure it with tape.

Step 15B

Using a red pencil, reconnect the shoulder points M to E.

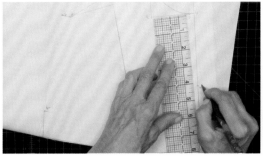

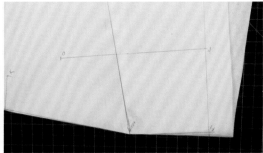

Step 15C

Trace the new shoulder line at the dart intake with the tracing wheel.

Step 16A

Measure down from G by your **#32 Front Width Depth** measurement. And mark this as N. Ours measures 4⅛" (10.5 cm).

Step 16B

Calculate half the distance of your **#22 Front Chest Width** measurement on the worksheet. Then square off from center front at N by that amount and mark that point as O. Ours measures 6¾" (17.2 cm). Make sure that your dart is securely taped down before measuring and drawing this line.

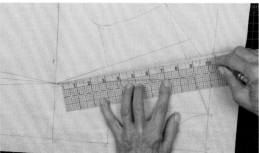

Step 17

Now use your French curve to draft the armhole, connecting points M, O, and K. You will need to draw this in two stages and blend the lines to achieve a nice smooth curve. Use your red pencil to mark corrections.

Step 18

Open the draft, remove the tape from the shoulder dart, and true the new shoulder seam. Then extend the dart intake lines past the shoulder seam.

Module 3:

Drafting the Back

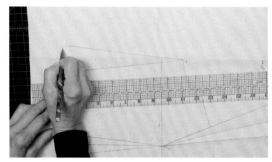

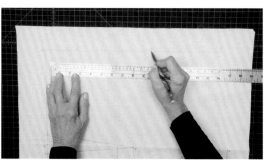

Step 1

Pencil in your traced back side-seam line and label the back waist/side-seam intersection point P.

Step 2

Now record your **#60 Back Full Width** measurement, plus ½" (1.3 cm) ease on the worksheet. Then square off from the fold, across the paper from B through P, your full back-width measurement and label this point Q. Our measurement is 8⅝" (20.3 cm) plus ½" (1.3 cm), making a total of 9⅛" (21.3 cm).

Step 3

Square a line up from Q, your **#64 Center Back Waist Length** measurement and label this point R. Our measurement is 16⅜" (41.6 cm). Label it "CB" (center back).

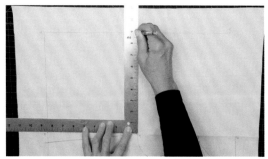

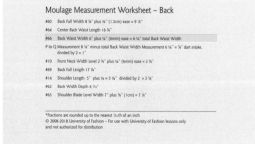

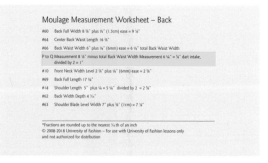

Step 4

Then square off the fold at K, across the back, and label that S.

Step 5A

Next, you will plan your back waist dart. To do this, on your worksheet, record your **#66 Back Waist Width** measurement and add ¼" (6 mm). Our back waist width measures 6" (15.2 cm), plus ¼" (6 mm), which equals 6¼" (15.9 cm).

Step 5B

Now measure waist points P to Q and record that measurement on the worksheet. Subtract the total Back Waist Width measurement (including ease) from P to the Q measurement; the difference will become the total back waist-dart intake. Our P/Q measures 8⅛" (20.3 cm), minus 6¼" (15.2 cm), so our total dart intake is 1⅞" (4.8 cm); divided by 2, this is rounded to 1" (2.5 cm).

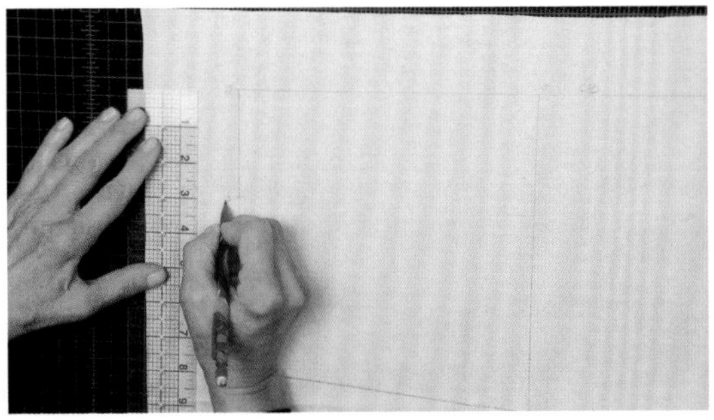

Step 5C
The position of the back waist dart is the same distance from center back as the front waist dart is from center front. In our case, that amount is 3" (7.6 cm). Place a mark 3" (7.6 cm) away from center back and label it #3.

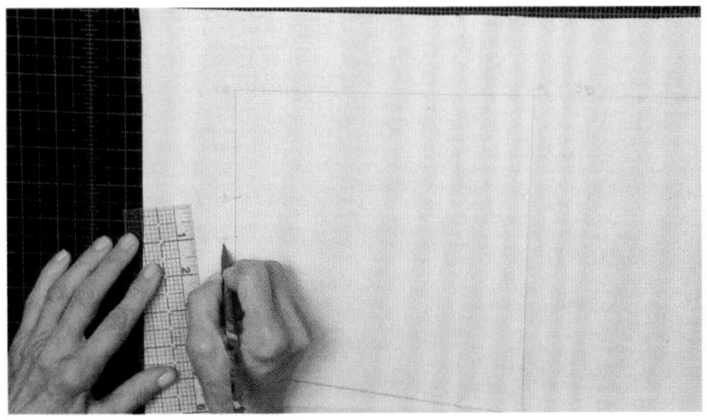

Step 5D
Then measure over by the divided dart-intake amount—in our case, 1" (2.5cm)—and mark that as point #4. This is the centerline of the waist dart.

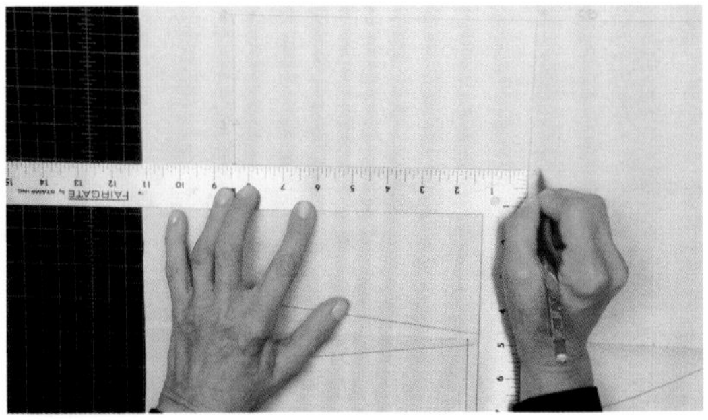

Step 5E
Then square a line up from point #4 to the S/K line. Label this point #5. This is the vanishing point of the back waist dart.

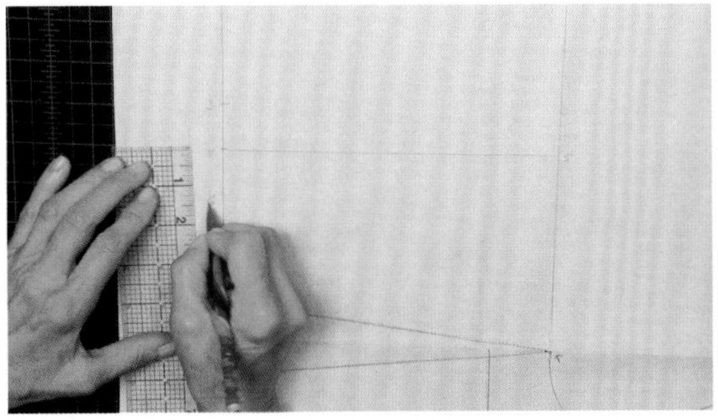

Step 5F
Measure over from point #4 by the divided dart-intake amount and label it #6.

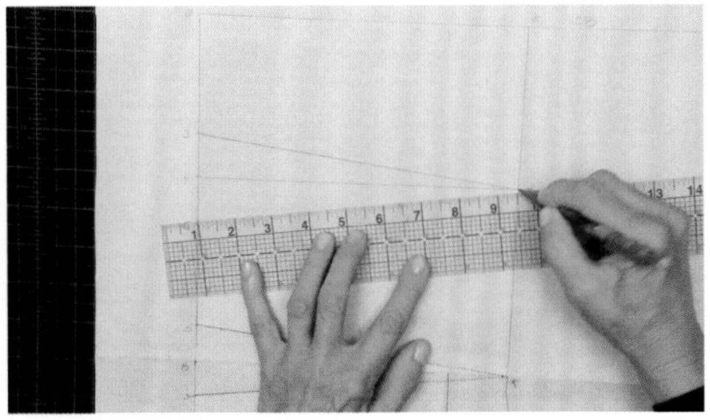

Step 5G
Then connect the dart-intake marks #3 and #6 to the waist dart's vanishing point #5.

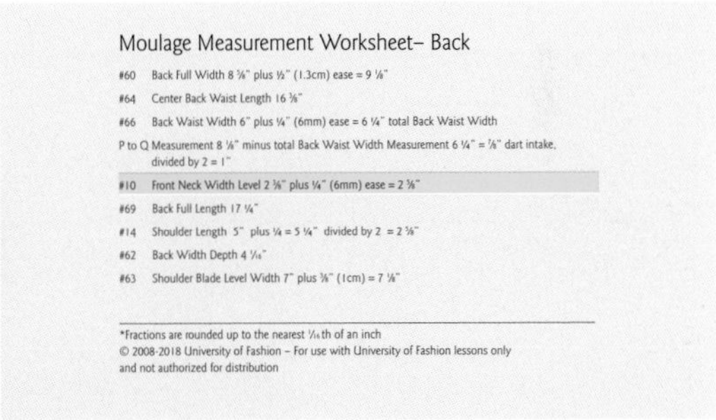

Moulage Measurement Worksheet– Back

#60 Back Full Width 8 5/8" plus 1/2" (1.3cm) ease = 9 1/8"
#64 Center Back Waist Length 16 3/8"
#66 Back Waist Width 6" plus 1/4" (6mm) ease = 6 1/4" total Back Waist Width
P to Q Measurement 8 1/8" minus total Back Waist Width Measurement 6 1/4" = 7/8" dart intake, divided by 2 = 1"
#10 Front Neck Width Level 2 3/8" plus 1/4" (6mm) ease = 2 5/8"
#69 Back Full Length 17 1/4"
#14 Shoulder Length 5" plus 1/4 = 5 1/4" divided by 2 = 2 5/8"
#62 Back Width Depth 4 1/16"
#63 Shoulder Blade Level Width 7" plus 3/8" (1cm) = 7 3/8"

*Fractions are rounded up to the nearest 1/16th of an inch
© 2008-2018 University of Fashion – For use with University of Fashion lessons only and not authorized for distribution

Step 6A
To find your back neck width, take your **#10 Front Neck Width Level** measurement, add ¼" (6 mm), and then record these measurements on your worksheet. Ours measures 2⅜" (6.7 cm), plus ¼" (6 mm), which equals 2⅝" (6.7 cm).

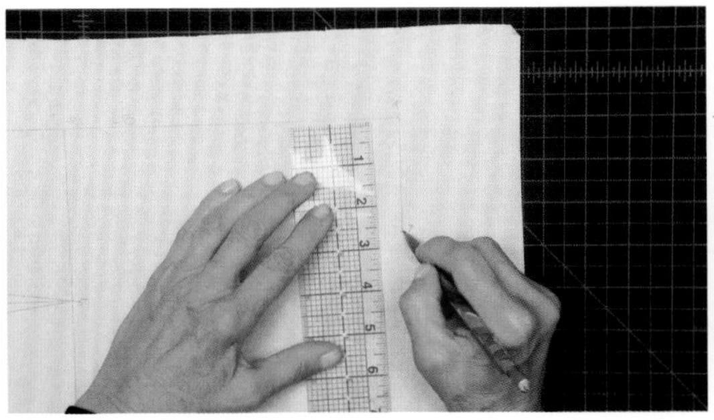

Step 6B
Now square a line off R by that amount and label this point T.

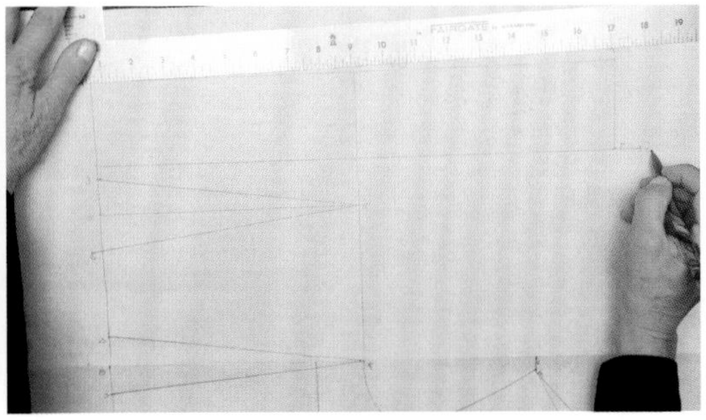

Step 6C
Square a line up from the Q/P to T by your **#69 Back Full Length** measurement and mark this as point U. Ours measures 17¼" (43.9 cm).

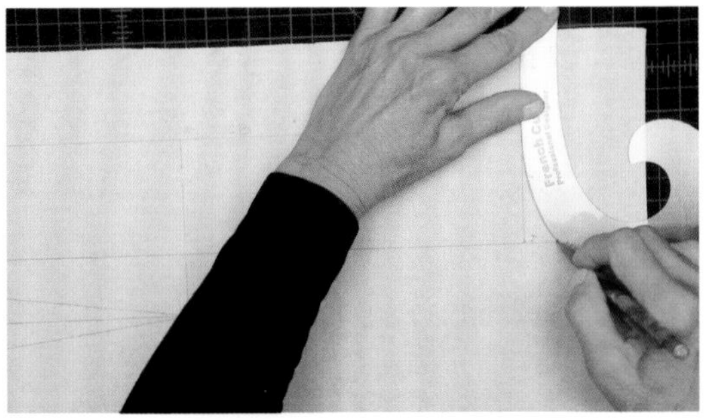

Step 6D
Use your French curve to shape the back neckline from R to U. Your line will rest about ¾" (2 cm) away from the center-back line.

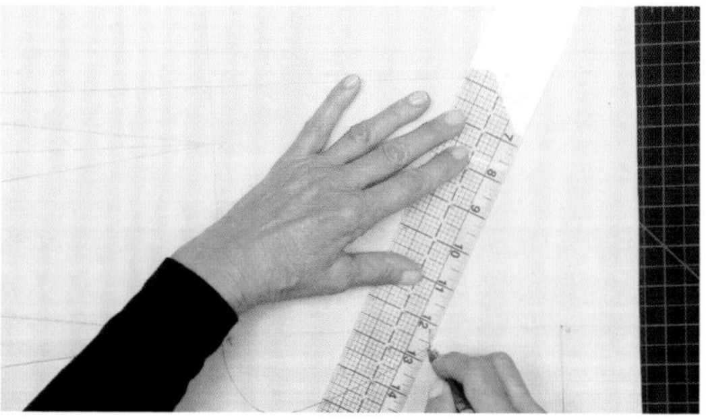

Step 7

Draw a light line connecting U to M to form the back shoulder.

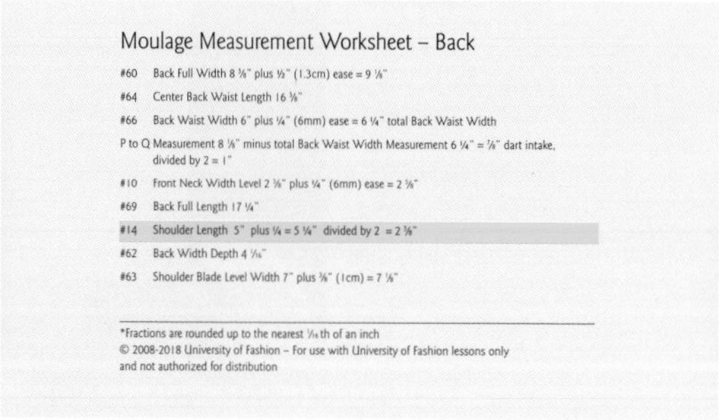

Moulage Measurement Worksheet – Back

#60 Back Full Width 8⅝" plus ½" (1.3cm) ease = 9⅛"

#64 Center Back Waist Length 16⅜"

#66 Back Waist Width 6" plus ¼" (6mm) ease = 6¼" total Back Waist Width

P to Q Measurement 8⅛" minus total Back Waist Width Measurement 6¼" = ⅞" dart intake, divided by 2 = 1"

#10 Front Neck Width Level 2⅜" plus ¼" (6mm) ease = 2⅝"

#69 Back Full Length 17¼"

#14 Shoulder Length 5" plus ¼ = 5¼" divided by 2 = 2⅝"

#62 Back Width Depth 4 1/16"

#63 Shoulder Blade Level Width 7" plus ⅜" (1cm) = 7⅜"

*Fractions are rounded up to the nearest 1/16th of an inch

© 2008-2018 University of Fashion – For use with University of Fashion lessons only and not authorized for distribution

Step 8A

Now take your **#14 Shoulder Length** measurement, add ¼" (6 mm), and divide that number by 2. Record those measurements on your worksheet. Ours measures 5" (12.7 cm) plus ¼" (6 mm), which equals 5¼" (13.4 cm). Divided by 2, the final figure is 2⅝" (6.7 cm).

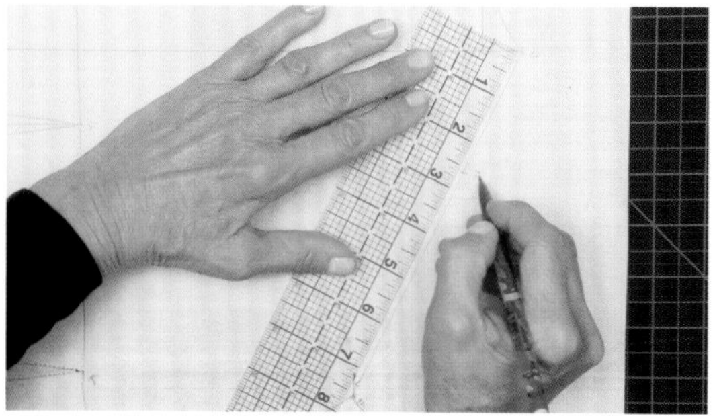

Step 8B

Measure over from U by that amount, place a mark, and label it #7. This is your first leg dart line.

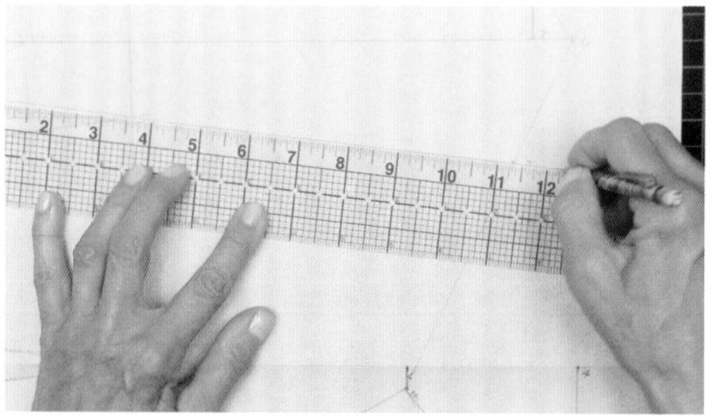

Step 8C

Now connect point #7 with point #5.

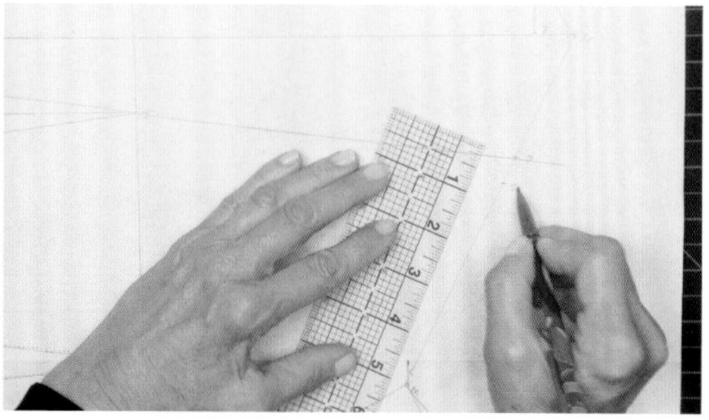

Step 8D

Measure over ½" (1.3 cm) from #7 along the U/M line and label this #8. This is your back shoulder dart-intake amount.

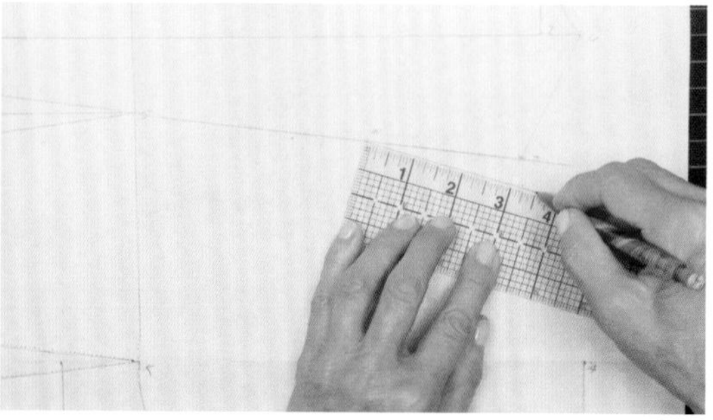

Step 8E

Then measure down 3" (7.6 cm) from point #7, and label that point #9. Then connect point #9 to #8 to complete the back shoulder dart.

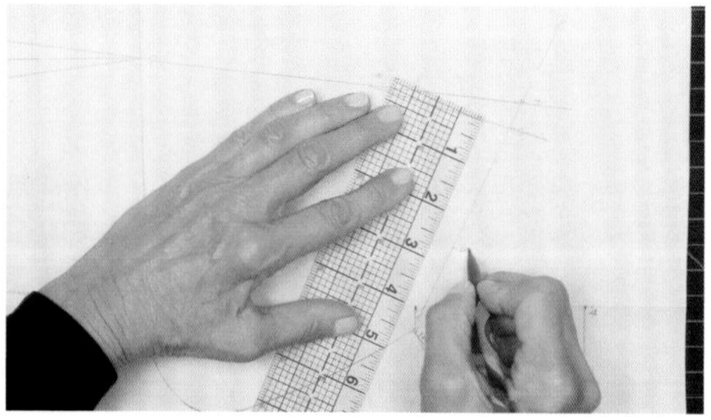

Step 9

Complete the shoulder seam by measuring over from #8 to M by your divided shoulder measurement. Ours measures 2⅝" (6.7 cm). Label this V.

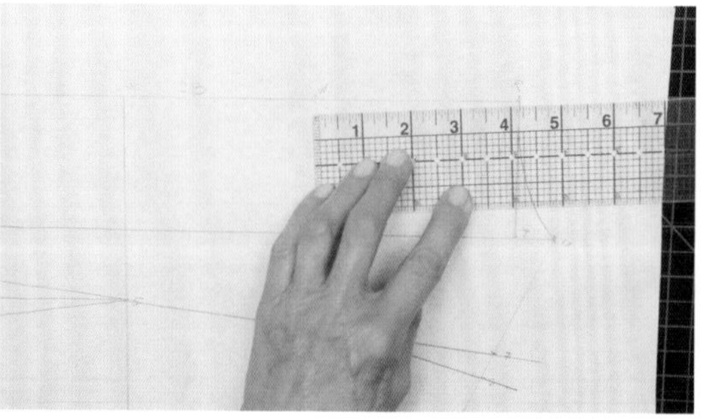

Step 10A

Measure down from R by your #62 Back Width Depth and label it W. Our measurement is 4 1/16" (10.4 cm).

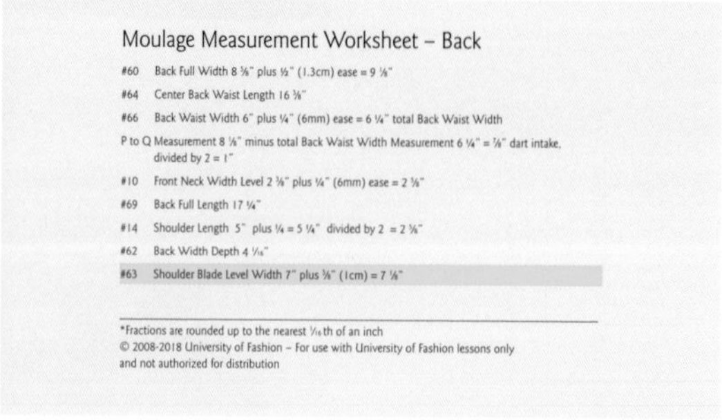

Moulage Measurement Worksheet – Back

#60 Back Full Width 8⅝" plus ½" (1.3cm) ease = 9⅛"

#64 Center Back Waist Length 16⅜"

#66 Back Waist Width 6" plus ¼" (6mm) ease = 6¼" total Back Waist Width

P to Q Measurement 8⅛" minus total Back Waist Width Measurement 6¼" = ⅞" dart intake, divided by 2 = 1"

#10 Front Neck Width Level 2⅜" plus ¼" (6mm) ease = 2⅝"

#69 Back Full Length 17¼"

#14 Shoulder Length 5" plus ¼ = 5¼" divided by 2 = 2⅝"

#62 Back Width Depth 4 1/16"

#63 Shoulder Blade Level Width 7" plus ⅜" (1cm) = 7⅜"

*Fractions are rounded up to the nearest 1/16th of an inch

© 2008-2018 University of Fashion – For use with University of Fashion lessons only and not authorized for distribution

Step 10B

Now take your #63 Shoulder Blade Level Width measurement, add ⅜" (6 mm), and record those measurements. Ours measures 7 (17.8 cm), plus ⅜" (1 cm), which equals 7⅜" (18.8 cm).

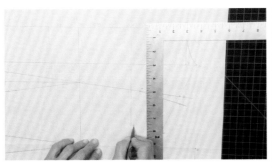

Step 10C
Measure over from W by that measurement and label it X.

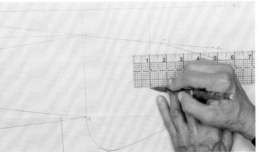

Step 11A
Square a guideline down from X for 1" (2.5 cm).

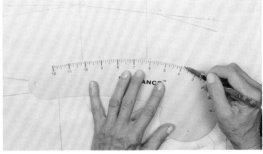

Step 11B
Square off for ¼" (6 mm) from K, then use your styling curve to draft the back armhole, connecting V, X, and K. The back armhole is done in two steps. First mark the upper portion.

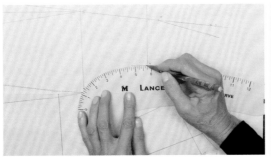

Step 11C
Then flip the curve over to mark the lower half. Be sure that your tool rests on the guideline. Re-blend your lines with red pencil if necessary.

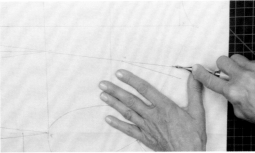

Step 12A
Use your tracing wheel to trace the back shoulder dart line closest to center back.

Step 12B
Fold the paper at the vanishing point of the back shoulder dart and close the dart, with the dart intake going in the direction of center back. Secure the closed dart with tape.

Step 13A
Using a styling curve and red pencil, re-mark the shoulder seam. This is done in two steps since the back shoulder is curved. Mark from neck to dart with a slight curve.

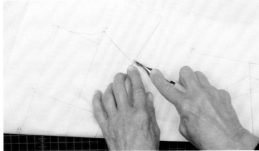

Step 13B
Trace the dart-intake area with a tracing wheel.

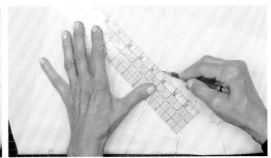

Step 13C
Then open the dart and re-mark.

Bodices

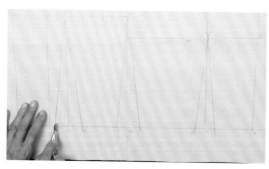

Step 1

Trace the front waist-dart leg line closest to center front and the back waist-dart leg line closest to center back. Then separate the front and back draft.

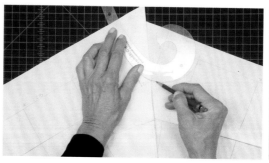

Step 2

Close the front and back shoulder darts and secure them with tape. Match up the front and back shoulder intersections by folding the back over the front, and then blend the neckline with your red pencil and French curve, eliminating any points.

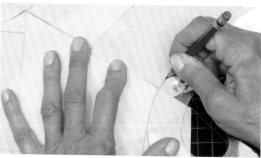

Step 3

Now do the same for the front and back shoulder/armhole intersection.

Step 4

Remove the shoulder dart tape and move to the side seams. Fold and tape the back side seam over the front side seam and make any adjustments to the side-seam/armhole intersection in red pencil.

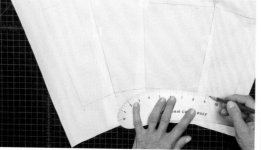

Step 5A

Now close the front and back waist darts and secure them with tape. Then use your hip curve and red pencil to blend the waistline along the dart and side-seam areas so that the waistline is a nice smooth curve.

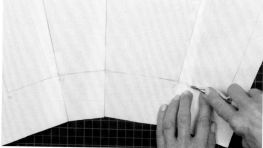

Step 5B

Use your tracing wheel to trace the waist dart-intake area.

Step 5C

Re-mark the dart intake at the waistline with red pencil.

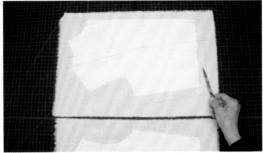

Step 1
Press your front and back moulage draft flat with an iron, set on a light heat setting with no steam.

Step 2
Trace off the front and back onto muslin (calico), adding a 1" (2.5 cm) seam allowance at the side seam and waistline, and ½" (1.3 cm) at the shoulder, armhole, and neckline. Be sure to trace along your new lines.

Step 3
Pin the bodice muslin together, then fit it on a dress form or real body. Make any necessary corrections to the muslin, then transfer these to the draft.

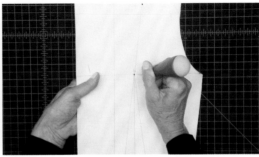

Step 4
Once any corrections have been made, you are ready to staple your paper sloper draft to oaktag and to cut the pieces out along the stitching lines.

Step 5
Use an awl to punch holes in all of the dart vanishing points.

Step 6
Use your notcher to mark the dart-intake points of each of the darts.

Step 7A
Remove the drafts from the oaktag and annotate your slopers: "Front Moulage," and "Size 6," or whatever your size happens to be. Do the same for the back.

Step 7B
You have now successfully drafted a shoulder dart moulage from measurements.

Module 6:
Converting a Moulage to a Bodice Sloper with Ease

Step 1
To convert your moulage to a bodice sloper with ease, begin by transferring your front and back moulage to white unlined pattern paper.

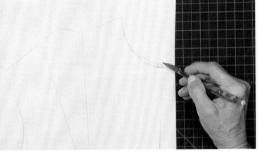

Step 2
Drop the neckline at the center front by ¼" (6 mm) and re-blend the neckline to nothing at the shoulder.

Step 3A
Lower the back waist dart by 1" (2.5 cm) and re-true the dart leg closest to the side seam.

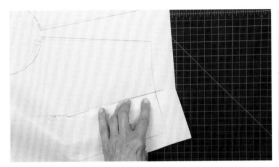

Step 3B
Fold the back waist dart, with the dart excess going in the direction of center back, then tape it closed.

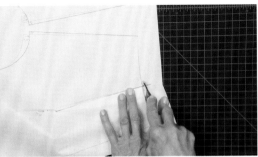

Step 3C
Trace the dart at the waist with a tracing wheel.

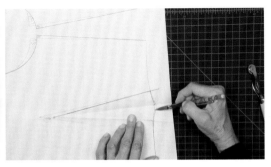

Step 3D
Open the dart and re-mark the waist.

Step 4
For a sleeveless bodice sloper, you must drop the front and back side seam by ½" (1.3 cm) and extend out at the underarm by ¼" (6 mm) to nothing at the waist.

Opposite: A basic bodice attached to a flare skirt from the collection of Carla Ruiz, Barcelona Bridal Week 2018.

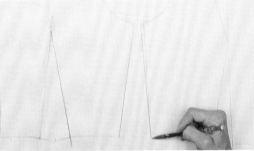

Step 5
For a bodice sloper with a sleeve, you must to drop the armhole by 1" (2.5 cm), both front and back (at the side-seam/armhole intersection), and extend out by ½" (1.3 cm) to nothing at the waist.

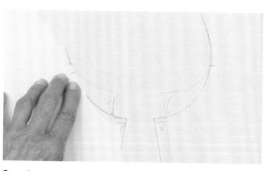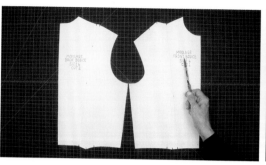

Step 6
Now use your sleeve sloper to mark the bodice armhole notches, walking the sleeve into the front and the back.

Step 7A
Then transfer the draft of the bodice with sleeve ease to oaktag.

Step 7B
You have now converted a moulage to a bodice sloper with ease

Self-evaluation

☐ Have I calculated and recorded all of the necessary measurements accurately?

☐ Did I square-off all of my intersections at a 90-degree angle?

☐ Are all of my front and back darts trued in the proper direction?

☐ Did I press my paper draft with a dry iron before transferring to oaktag?

☐ Did I add my sleeve notches to my Bodice Sloper with a Sleeve?

Pivoting a Front Shoulder Dart to the Side Seam

Learning objectives

☐ Prepare the pieces—punching a hole at the dart vanishing point and apex point on the front bodice sloper, marking the side seam bust dart

☐ Trace the bodice sloper—copying the sloper onto the paper, pivoting on the apex point to reposition the width of the shoulder dart to the side seam

☐ True the pattern—joining the dart vanishing point to dart notches, straightening the shoulder line, closing the side seam dart and blending the side seam

Tools and supplies:

- Front Shoulder Dart Bodice (see Lesson 3.1)
- White unlined pattern paper—3" (7.5cm) bigger than your sloper on all sides

Step 1

For this lesson, you will need to use your front bodice sloper with a shoulder dart and waist dart (see Lesson 3.1).

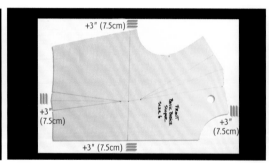

Step 2

You will also need a piece of white unlined pattern paper that measures 3" (7.5cm) larger than your front bodice sloper on all four sides.

Step 3

Before you begin, use your awl to punch a hole into the dart vanishing points and the apex point on your front bodice sloper.

Step 4

You will be transferring the shoulder dart to the desired point at the side seam. In this case you will mark your side seam bust dart at 2" (5cm) below the armhole.

Step 5A

Begin tracing the bodice, starting at the shoulder dart notch closest to center front, as you hold the sloper down with your other hand.

Step 5B

Continue tracing along the edge of the sloper, including the waist dart notches.

Step 5C

Be sure to mark the waist dart's vanishing point.

Step 5D

Continue tracing the bodice until you reach your new side bust dart pencil mark and place a mark on the paper at that point.

Step 6

Even though you are going to be moving the shoulder dart to the side seam, you will be pivoting the shoulder dart from the apex point on the bustline, and not from the shoulder dart's vanishing point.

Step 7A

Place the tip of your pencil into the apex point in preparation for closing the shoulder dart out, as you pivot the sloper to transfer the shoulder dart intake to create the side bust dart.

Step 7B

Once the shoulder dart is closed, continue to trace the bodice from the shoulder dart notch closest to the armhole. Be sure to trace off your armhole notch as you go.

Step 8

Stop tracing when you reach your new side bust dart mark on your sloper, and place a mark on the paper at this point. Be sure that you have captured all of your markings before you remove the sloper from the paper.

Module 2:

Trueing the Darts

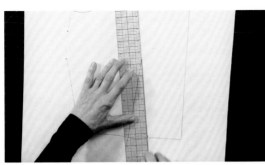

Step 1

First, you will true the waist dart. Connect the vanishing point of the dart to the dart intake notch at the waist, first on one side and then on the other side of the dart.

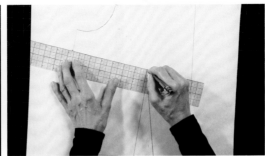

Step 2A

Next, connect the apex point to the side bust dart intake marking closest to the armhole.

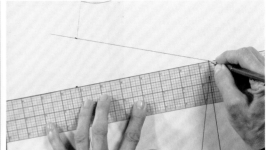

Step 2B

Now pivot your ruler at the apex to complete the lower dart leg.

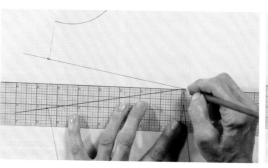

Step 3A
Since bust darts never vanish at the apex, you will reduce the vanishing point of the side bust dart by 1" (2.5cm) using your red pencil.

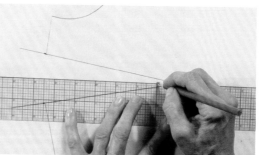

Step 3B
Place a mark 1" (2.5cm) away from the apex in the middle of the dart intake.

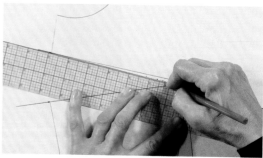

Step 3C
Connect the upper leg of the side bust dart from the vanishing point to the side seam.

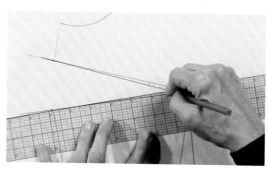

Step 3D
Pivot the ruler at the vanishing point and true the lower dart intake to the side seam.

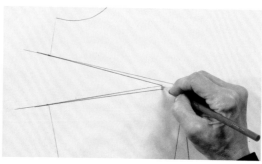

Step 3E
Place a mark at the vanishing point of the side bust dart.

Module 3:

Trueing the Bodice

Step 1
Next, you will true the shoulder, since this line has changed after having moved the dart. To do this, use your red pencil.

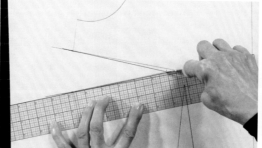

Step 2
Use your awl to score the lower dart intake line from side seam to vanishing point.

Step 3
Crease the lower dart intake with your fingers, and then close the dart, with the dart excess going in the direction of the waistline.

Step 4
Tape the dart closed along the dart leg and just outside of the side seam, as demonstrated.

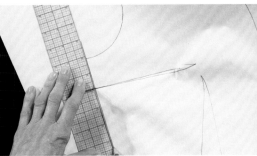

Step 5A
True the side seam using your red pencil and ruler. True from the underarm to the waistline.

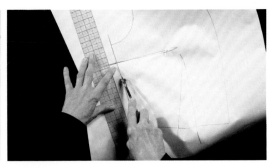

Step 5B
Then use your tracing wheel to trace the new side seam in the dart area.

Step 6A
Remove the tape and open the side bust dart so that it is flat on the table.

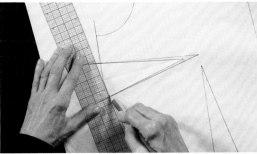

Step 6B
True the tracing marks at the side bust dart with your ruler and red pencil.

Step 7A
Annotate the draft with the words: "Side Seam Bodice Dart, Size 6", or whatever your size happens to be. You have now finished pivoting the bodice's shoulder dart to a side seam bust dart.

Self-evaluation

- [ ] Did I copy my Shoulder Dart Bodice accurately?
- [ ] Did I pivot the bust dart from the apex when moving it to the side seam?
- [ ] Have I closed the side bust dart properly before trueing the side seam?
- [ ] Did I adjust the vanishing points of my side bust and waist darts?

Pivoting a Front Shoulder Dart to a Waist Dart

Learning objectives

☐ Punching a hole at dart vanishing points and apex point on the front bodice sloper

☐ Copying the sloper onto paper, pivoting on the apex point to reposition the width of the shoulder dart to the waistline

☐ True the pattern—drafting dart legs, straightening the shoulder line, closing the waistline dart and blending the waistline

Tools and supplies:

- Front Shoulder Dart Bodice (see Lesson 3.1)
- White unlined pattern paper—3" (7.5cm) bigger than your sloper on all sides

Step 1

For this lesson, you will need to use your front bodice sloper with a shoulder dart and waist dart (see Lesson 3.1).

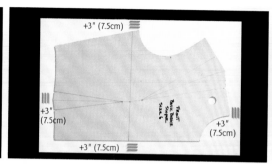

Step 2

You will also need a piece of white unlined pattern paper that measures 3" (7.5cm) larger than your front bodice sloper on all four sides.

Step 3

For this lesson, you will transfer the shoulder dart into the waist dart. Before you start, make sure that you have made small holes at the dart vanishing points and at the apex point. Use your awl to punch the holes.

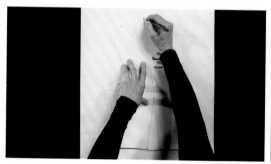

Step 4A

Begin tracing the bodice, starting at the shoulder dart notch closest to center front, as you firmly hold the sloper down with your other hand.

Step 4B

Continue tracing along the edge of the sloper, until you reach the waist dart notch closest to center front.

Step 5A

Place a mark at the apex, since you will be pivoting from the apex and not from either of the dart vanishing points.

Step 5B

Place the tip of your pencil into the apex point, in preparation for closing the shoulder dart.

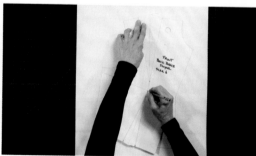

Step 5C

Then, as you pivot the sloper to close the shoulder dart, the dart excess will transfer to the waist dart.

Step 6A

Once the shoulder dart is closed, continue to trace the bodice from the shoulder dart notch closest to the armhole. Be sure to trace off your armhole notch as you go.

Step 6B
Continue tracing the bodice until you reach the waist notch closest to the side seam and place a mark. Be sure that you have captured all of your markings before you remove the sloper from the paper.

Self-evaluation

- [ ] Did I punch holes in my sloper at the apex and dart vanishing points?
- [ ] Have I marked the shoulder and waist dart closest to center front before pivoting the shoulder dart?
- [ ] Did I pivot from the apex and not the dart vanishing point when closing the shoulder dart?
- [ ] Did I adjust the waist dart's vanishing point?
- [ ] Is my waist dart closed in the correct direction before I true the waistline?

Module 2:
Trueing the Waist Dart

Step 1
To true the waist dart, connect the vanishing point of the dart to the dart intake notch, first on one side and then on the other side of the dart.

Step 2A
Since bust darts never vanish at the apex, you will reduce the vanishing point of the waist dart by 1" (2.5cm), using your ruler and pencil.

Step 2B
Place a mark 1" (2.5cm) away from the apex in the middle of the dart intake.

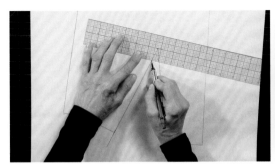

Step 2C
Find the midway point of the dart intake at 1" (2.5cm) below the apex.

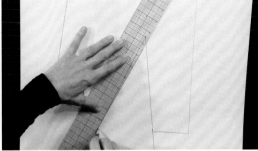

Step 2D
With your red pencil, connect the new 1" (2.5cm) lowered vanishing point of the dart to the waistline notch.

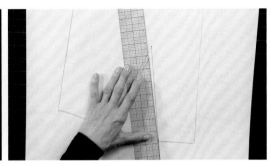

Step 2E
Pivot the ruler at the dart vanishing point and true the other side of the waist dart.

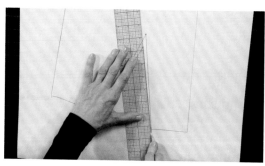

Step 1

Use your awl to score the dart leg closest to center front, from the vanishing point to the waist.

Step 2

Reposition the bodice and then fold it along the scored dart leg line so that you can close the dart, with the dart excess going in the direction of center front.

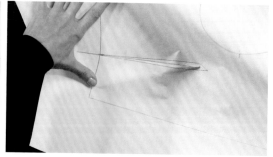

Step 3

Tape the dart closed along the dart leg and just outside of the waist seam, as demonstrated.

Step 4

Use your styling curve and red pencil to blend the waist along the dart area.

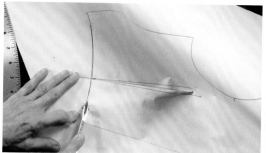

Step 5

Now use your tracing wheel to trace the waistline from the center front to the waist dart.

Step 6

Remove the tape and open the waist dart, so that it is flat on the table.

Step 7

Now, following the tracing marks, true the waist dart intake stitching line.

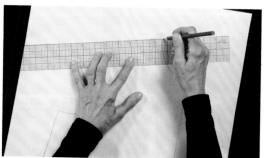

Step 8

Then re-true the shoulder line of the bodice, using the red pencil.

Step 9

Annotate the draft with "Front One Waist Dart Bodice, Size 6," or whatever your size happens to be. You have now finished transferring the bodice's shoulder dart to waist dart.

You have now finished transferring the bodice's shoulder dart to a waist dart.

Pivoting a Front Shoulder Dart to an Armhole Dart

Learning objectives

☐ Punching a hole at dart vanishing points and apex point on the front bodice sloper, marking the armhole dart position

☐ Copying the sloper onto paper, pivoting on the apex point to reposition the width of the shoulder dart to the armhole dart position

☐ True the pattern—joining the dart vanishing point to dart notches, straightening the shoulder line, closing the armhole dart and blending the armhole line

Tools and supplies:

- Front Shoulder Dart Bodice Sloper (see Lesson 3.1)
- White unlined pattern paper—3" (7.5cm) bigger than your sloper on all sides

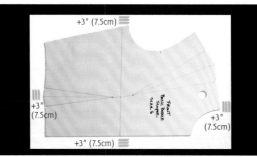

Step 1
For this lesson, you will need to use your front bodice sloper with a shoulder dart and waist dart (see Lesson 3.1).

Step 2
You will also need a piece of white unlined pattern paper that measures 3" (7.5cm) larger than your front bodice sloper on all four sides.

Step 3
Before you start, make sure that you have made small holes at the dart vanishing points and at the apex point of your sloper. Use your awl to punch the holes.

Step 4
You will be transferring the shoulder dart to the armhole, positioned at approximately 1" (2.5cm) below the mid armhole notch. Place a mark on your bodice sloper at this point.

Step 5A
Begin tracing the bodice, starting at the shoulder dart notch closest to center front, as you firmly hold the sloper down with your other hand.

Step 5B
Continue tracing along the edge of the sloper. Be sure to transfer the waist notches to the paper below.

Step 5C
Continue to trace the bodice, but stop when you reach the armhole dart mark. Place a corresponding mark on the paper at this point.

Step 6
Mark the vanishing point of the waist dart.

Step 7
Then mark the apex point, since we will be pivoting the shoulder dart to the armhole from this point and not from the waist dart.

Step 8A
Be sure that you have captured all of your marks. Next, with the point of the pencil in the apex, you will close the shoulder dart so that you can transfer the dart excess into the armhole.

Step 8B
Once you have closed the shoulder dart, so that the shoulder dart notches align, you can trace the balance of the bodice.

Step 8C
Trace the balance of the shoulder, the armhole, and the armhole notch. Stop when you reach your bodice armhole dart mark. Place a mark on the paper at this position. Remember to mark the armhole notch. Be sure that you have captured all of your markings before you remove the sloper from the paper.

Module 2:

Trueing the Darts

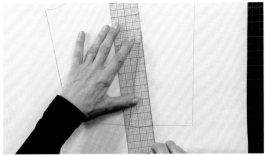

Step 1
True the waist dart by connecting the vanishing point of the dart to the dart intake notch at the waist. True one dart leg, and then pivot the ruler at the vanishing point to true the other.

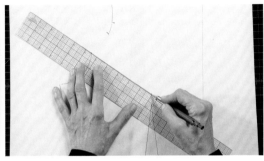

Step 2A
Next, you will true the lower leg of the armhole dart. True from the apex point to the armhole dart intake mark.

Step 2B
Pivot the ruler from the apex and complete trueing the dart to the upper armhole dart intake mark.

Step 3A
Since bust darts never vanish at the apex, you will reduce the vanishing point of the armhole dart by 1" (2.5cm) using your ruler and red pencil.

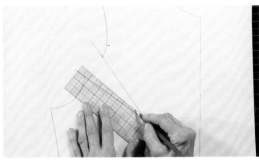

Step 3B
Place a mark 1" (2.5cm) away from the apex in the middle of the dart intake.

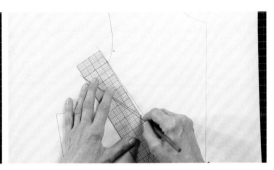

Step 3C
With your red pencil, connect the new vanishing point to the lower dart intake mark at the armhole. Then pivot your ruler from the vanishing point to draw in the upper leg of the dart to the armhole.

Step 3D
Place a mark at the armhole dart's vanishing point.

Module 3:

Trueing the Bodice

Step 1
Re-true the shoulder line of the bodice using a red pencil.

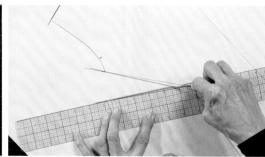

Step 2
Now use your awl to score the dart leg closest to center front.

Step 3A
Fold along the scored dart leg line and close the armhole dart, with the dart excess going in a downward direction.

Step 3B
Close the dart, matching the armhole dart legs. Tape the dart in place along the dart leg line, and just outside of the armhole line, as demonstrated.

Step 4
Use your styling curve and red pencil to true the dart area, blending it to the armhole.

Step 5A
Use your tracing wheel to trace the dart area of the armhole.

Opposite: By pivoting the bust dart to the armhole, Mari Axel is able to create contrast insets at the shoulder. (Spring/Summer 2013)

Step 5B
Remove the tape and open the armhole dart so that it is flat on the table.

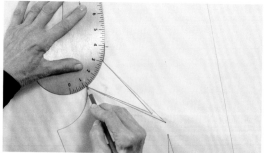

Step 5C
True the armhole dart intake lines with your styling curve, following the tracing marks.

Step 6
Annotate the draft with "Armhole Dart Bodice" and "Size 6," or whatever your size happens to be. You have now finished transferring the bodice's shoulder dart to an armhole dart.

Self-evaluation

☐ Have I determined the best position for my armhole dart so that it is neither too high nor too low?

☐ Did I mark the correct start and end points, prior to pivoting the shoulder dart?

☐ Did I pivot the shoulder dart from the apex and not from the dart's vanishing point?

☐ Once I closed the armhole dart did I re-true the armhole and shoulder seam?

Pivoting darts, such as this dress with a French dart, opens up numerous design possibilities as demonstrated by Fei Gallery & Boutique Sun Xuefei Collection. (Spring/Summer 2016)

Pivoting a 2 Dart Bodice Variation (Neck & French Dart)

Learning objectives

☐ Prepare the pieces—preparing paper blocks, tracing the bodice sloper onto paper, marking the apex, trueing the waist and shoulder darts

☐ Plan the new darts—marking the positions of the neck and French dart, drafting the new darts

☐ Manipulate the darts—cutting the dart lines, securing the paper pattern to the second paper block, closing existing darts to move their width to the new darts

☐ True the bodice—drafting dart legs, closing the French dart and blending the side seam, closing the neck dart and blending the neckline, trueing the waistline and armhole

Tools and supplies:

- Front Shoulder Dart Bodice (see Lesson 3.1)
- Two blocks of white unlined pattern paper— 3" (7.5cm) bigger than your sloper on all sides

Step 1
For this lesson, you will need to use your front bodice sloper with a shoulder dart and waist dart (see Lesson 3.1).

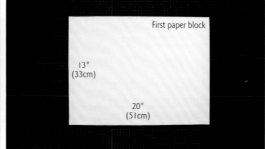

Step 2
You will also need two pieces of white unlined pattern paper. The first piece will measure slightly larger than your bodice. Our block measures 13" (33cm) wide by 20" (51cm) long.

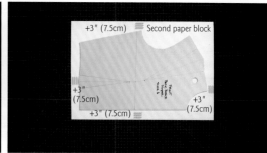

The second paper block will measure 3" (7.5cm) larger than your bodice on all four sides.

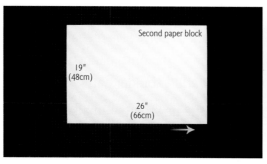

Our block measures 19" (48cm) wide by 26" (66cm) long.

Step 3A
Trace off the entire bodice, including the notches, onto the smaller paper block.

Step 3B
Mark the apex on the paper below, and then complete the bodice tracing.

Step 3C
It is not necessary for you to mark the dart vanishing points, only mark the apex point.

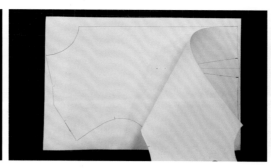

Step 4
Holding the bodice down with one hand, turn the sloper over and check that you have captured all of your markings, then remove the bodice sloper from the table.

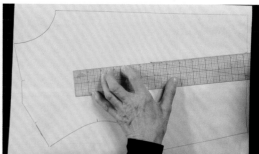

Step 5
True in the waist dart from the apex point to the waist dart intake marks on both sides.

Step 6
Now true the shoulder dart from the apex point to the shoulder dart intake marks on both sides.

Step 7
Cut away the excess paper around the entire bodice.

Module 2:

Planning the Neck &
French Darts

Step 1
On our paper sloper you will mark the desired position of your neck dart. We are placing a mark on the neckline about 1½" (3.8cm) from center front.

Step 2
Next, plan the position of your French dart. We will mark ours at 1½" (3.8cm) up from the waist, at the side seam.

Step 3A
You will be moving your waist dart to the position of the French dart mark.

Step 3B
You will move your shoulder dart to the position of the neck dart mark.

Step 4
You will begin by drawing a line from your neck dart mark to the apex using a red pencil and ruler.

Step 5
Now draw a line from the apex to the French dart mark, again in red pencil.

Step 1

Center your paper bodice on the larger block of pattern paper.

Step 2A

The next step will be to cut along specific dart lines. You will cut along the waist dart line closest to center front.

Step 2B

You will also cut along the French dart line ...

Step 2C

... and the shoulder dart line closest to center front.

Step 2D

You will also cut along the neck dart line.

Step 3A

Begin by cutting the waist dart line. For this, and all the lines that you will be cutting into, you will be stopping ⅛" (3mm) before you reach the apex.

Step 3B

Reposition the paper and cut along the French dart line next. Again, stopping within ⅛" (3mm) of the apex.

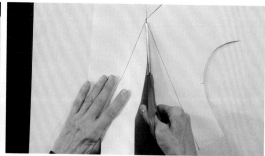

Step 3C

Reposition the paper again and cut along the shoulder dart line closest to center front, stopping within ⅛" (3mm) of the apex.

Step 3D

And finally, cut along the neck dart line, stopping within ⅛" (3mm) of the apex.

Step 3E
It is important that the remaining paper at the apex point holds the dart lines together.

Should the joint break, use a very small piece of tape to secure the point.

Step 4
Secure the bodice to the paper below with two strips of tape along center front.

Step 5A
Now close the shoulder dart, as demonstrated. Note that the shoulder dart intake opens up to create the neck dart.

Step 5B
Tape the shoulder dart closed at the shoulder seam, and secure the bodice to the paper. Then tape the neck dart to the paper.

Step 6A
Close the waist dart next, as demonstrated. This action opens up and creates the side seam French dart.

You may need to reposition your center front tape so that the waist area of the bodice lies flat.

Step 6B
Smooth the paper flat, and then secure the closed waist dart with tape.

Step 6C
Now tape the bodice to the paper at the neck dart.

Step 6D
Smooth the bodice flat with your hands, and tape the underarm at the side seam.

Step 6E
Add another piece of tape to secure the side seam and the upper French dart leg.

Step 6F
Then finish by placing a last piece of tape at the side seam/ waistline intersection.

Module 4:
Trueing the Darts & Bodice

Step 1A
Switch to a blue pencil so that you can mark the vanishing points of the darts, since bust darts should never vanish exactly at the apex.

Step 1B
On the neck dart, measure up 1″ (2.5cm) from the apex and place a mark in the middle of this dart.

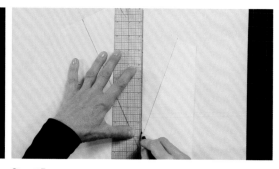

Step 2A
Connect the new neck dart vanishing point to the dart intake mark on one side of the neck dart.

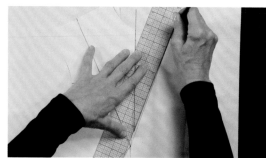

Step 2B
Then mark the other side of the neck dart.

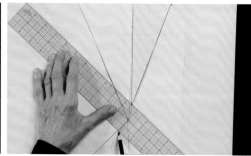

Step 3A
Now move to the French dart and measure down 1″ (2.5cm) from the apex and place a mark in the middle of this dart.

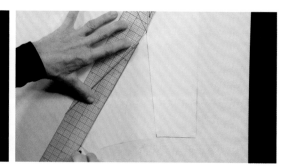

Step 3B
Connect the vanishing point of the French dart to the intake mark, first on one side and then on the other.

Step 4A
Before you can true the darts, you must add more tape to them to hold them in place.

Step 4B
Tape along both sides of each dart.

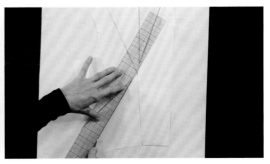

Step 5A
With your awl, score the lower dart leg of the French dart from the vanishing point to the dart intake mark.

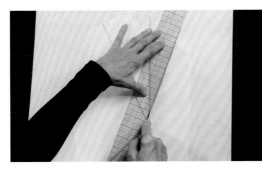

Step 5B
Now score the neck dart leg closest to center front, from the neck dart intake mark to the vanishing point.

Step 6A
Crease the dart leg with your fingers and close the French dart, matching the side seam line, with the dart excess going in a downward direction.

Step 6B
Secure the dart with two small pieces of tape along the dart leg line.

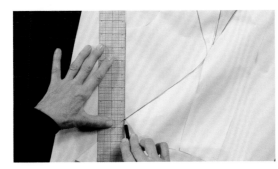

Step 6C
Re-true the side seam using your ruler and blue pencil.

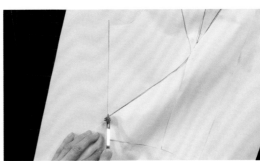

Step 6D
Now use your tracing wheel to true the French dart area of the side seam.

Step 6E
Remove the tape from the French dart and flatten the dart on the table.

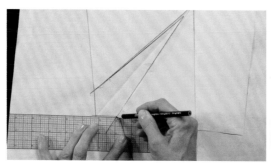

Step 6F
Following the tracing lines, true the French dart intake stitching line with blue pencil.

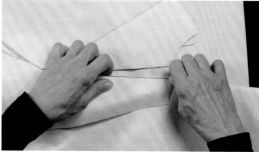

Step 7A
Now crease and close the neckline dart, with the dart excess going in the direction of center front.

Step 7B
Tape the neckline dart along the dart leg line.

Step 7C
Use your French curve or styling curve to re-true the dart area at the neckline.

Step 7D
Now use your tracing wheel to trace the neckline from center front to the neck dart.

Step 7E
Remove the tape and open the neck dart so that it lies flat on the table. Then true the dart intake line following the tracing marks.

Module 5:

Finishing the Draft

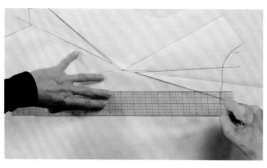

Step 1
Next, you will true your lines using blue pencil, starting with the center front of the bodice.

Step 2A
Now square a line off the center front waistline.

Step 2B
Use your styling curve to true the waistline.

Step 3A

Next true your armhole, repositioning your styling curve to blend a nice smooth curve.

Step 3B

Be sure to square a line off the armhole/side seam intersection.

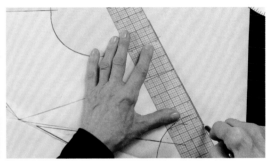

Step 4

True the shoulder seam next, making sure that the shoulder/armhole intersection is a right angle.

Step 5A

Fold back the shoulder/neckline section of the bodice and trim away a portion of the dart intake so that you will be able to true the neckline.

Step 5B

True the neckline with your styling curve along the shoulder/armhole section.

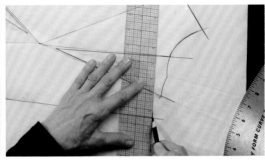

Step 5C

Square a line off the center front/neckline intersection with your ruler for about ¼" (6mm).

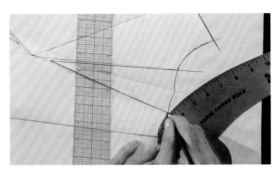

Step 5D

Then finish trueing the neckline by blending a line to the ¼" (6mm) mark.

Step 6

Mark the armhole notch next.

Step 7

Once you have made all of the necessary markings, remove the draft from the paper below.

Step 8
Go back in and true any broken lines using your blue pencil and ruler.

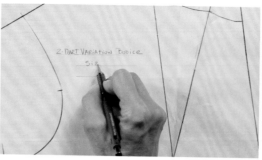

Step 9A
Annotate the bodice with "2 Dart Variation Bodice" and whatever your size happens to be.

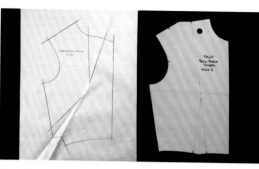

Step 9B
You have now finished transferring the bodice's shoulder and waist darts into a neckline and French dart.

Self-evaluation

☐ As I copied my oaktag sloper, did I mark the apex point and not the dart vanishing points?

☐ Did I mark my new dart positions so that they meet at the apex?

☐ Have I slashed my new dart lines no closer than $1/16$" (2mm) of the apex?

☐ Did I adjust the new darts' vanishing point?

☐ After I closed my new darts, did I re-true the neckline and side seam?

Upper back darts are either at the shoulder or the neck. Here is an example of the same dress with the darts moved from the shoulder to the neck.

Pivoting a Back Shoulder Dart to a Back Neck Dart

Learning objectives

- ☐ Preparing the paper block, marking the new back dart position on the back bodice sloper, punching a hole at the waist dart vanishing point

- ☐ Copying the sloper onto paper, pivoting on the waist dart point to reposition the width of the shoulder dart to the back neck dart position

- ☐ True the bodice—trueing the waist dart, drafting the back neck dart, straightening the shoulder and back neckline

Tools and supplies:

- Back Shoulder Dart Bodice (see Lesson 3.1)
- White unlined pattern paper—3" (7.5cm) bigger than your sloper on all sides

Step 1

For this lesson, you will need to use your Back Shoulder Dart Bodice (see Lesson 3.1).

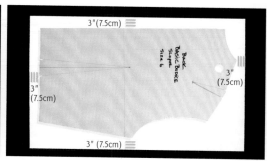

Step 2

You will also need one piece of white unlined pattern paper that measures 3" (7.5cm) larger than your back sloper on all sides.

Step 3

You will be moving the back shoulder dart to the neckline. Begin by placing a mark on the back neckline of the oaktag sloper, 1" (2.5cm) away from the center back/neck intersection. This will be the back neck dart's new position.

Step 4

Use your awl to punch a small hole in the vanishing point of the back waist dart.

Step 5A

Next, trace your back bodice onto the paper below. Begin tracing from the dart intake notch closest to the armhole.

Step 5B

Continue tracing around the bodice, including the notches.

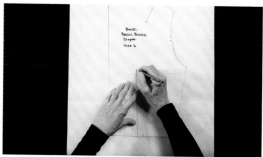

Step 5C

Mark the vanishing point of the back waist dart.

Step 5D

Continue tracing the back bodice onto the paper until you reach your back neck dart mark on the bodice's neckline. Mark the position of the neck dart on the paper.

Step 6A

With your pencil in position at the waist dart's vanishing point, use your other hand to pivot the bodice sloper.

Step 6B
Pivot the sloper from the vanishing point to the right, as you close the shoulder dart. This action will transfer the shoulder dart excess to the neck.

Step 6C
Now continue to trace the bodice from the shoulder dart notch closest to center back, to your bodice's neck dart mark.

Step 6D
Place a mark on the paper that aligns with the new back neck dart mark.

Step 7
Check that you have captured all of your markings, then remove the back bodice sloper from the table.

Tip
Remember that when transferring the back shoulder dart to the back neck, always pivot from the waist dart vanishing point, never from the shoulder dart vanishing point.

Module 2:

Marking the Darts

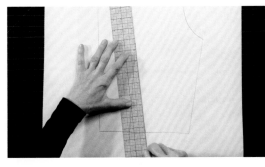

Step 1
First, you will mark the waist dart. Mark from the vanishing point to the dart intake notch at the waist, first on one side and then on the other.

Step 2A
Now you will connect the vanishing point of the waist dart to the back neck dart closest to center back.

Step 2B
Use your ruler to draw a line from the vanishing point to slightly beyond the back neck mark.

Step 3A

Reposition your ruler and place a mark at 3″ (7.5cm) down from the shoulder, along the dart line. This is the vanishing point of the back neck dart.

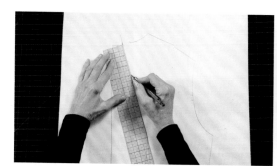

Step 3B

Complete the back neck dart on the other side.

Module 3:

Trueing the Back Bodice

Step 1A

As a result of shifting the back shoulder dart to the neck, you will need to re-true the shoulder seam. Use your red pencil and styling curve to blend the seam from neck to mid shoulder.

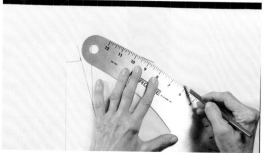

Step 1B

Flip the curve over to blend from the armhole to mid shoulder.

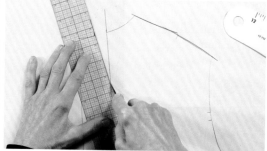

Step 2A

Now use your awl to score the neck dart leg line closest to center back.

Step 2B

Crease the scored dart leg line and close the dart, with the dart excess going in the direction of center back.

Step 2C

Secure the dart with a small piece of tape along the dart leg line.

Step 3A

Re-true the back neckline with your red pencil and styling curve.

Left: Thom Browne repositions the back shoulder dart into the princess seam on a jacket from his Paris Fashion Week Collection. (Fall/Winter 2018/2019)

Step 3B
Use your tracing wheel to true the dart area of the back neckline.

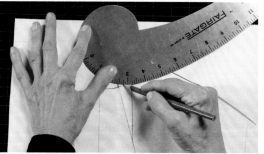

Step 3C
Remove the tape, lay the dart flat on the table, and true the neck dart intake with your red pencil and styling curve.

Step 4A
Annotate the bodice with "Back Neck Dart Bodice" and whatever your size happens to be.

Bodices

Step 4B
You have now finished transferring the bodice sloper's back shoulder dart to a back neck dart.

Self-evaluation

☐ Did I mark the correct position for my back neck dart?

☐ Have I made a punch hole at the vanishing point of my back waist dart?

☐ Did I accurately trace the start and end point for pivoting the shoulder dart?

☐ Did I pivot and connect the new back neck dart from the waist dart's vanishing point?

☐ Is my neck dart and neckline trued properly?

Converting a Bodice Sloper into a Fitted Torso Sloper

Learning objectives

☐ Prepare the pieces—preparing the paper block, tracing the sloper onto the paper, marking guidelines and dart vanishing points

☐ Plan the torso dart—drafting existing darts, squaring off and measuring to establish the new dart position

☐ Finish the paper pattern—trueing side seams, drafting and balancing new darts, adding grainlines, cutting out the pattern

☐ Transfer to muslin—adding seam allowances, tracing the pattern onto muslin, pinning the pieces, snipping into darts, checking the fit on the dress form

Tools and supplies:

- Front/Back Shoulder Dart Bodice (see Lesson 3.1)
- White unlined pattern paper—22 x 28" (56 x 71cm)
- Muslin (calico) for fit-testing
- Dress form

Step 1

For this lesson, you will need to use the Front/Back Shoulder Dart Bodice Sloper, drafted in Lesson 3.1.

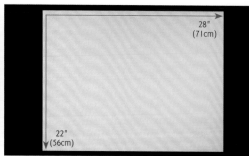

Step 2

Prepare a block of white unlined pattern paper measuring 22" (56cm) wide by 28" (71cm) long.

Step 3

With the length side of the paper facing you, draw a line 1" (2.5cm) in from the edge of the paper.

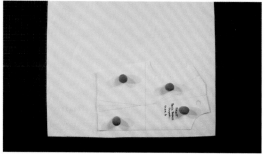

Step 4A

Align your front bodice sloper along the 1" (2.5cm) line, at 1" (2.5cm) in from the short right side of the paper. Use weights to secure the sloper to the paper.

Step 4B

Trace your front bodice sloper onto the paper below. Be sure to trace all of your darts and dart notches.

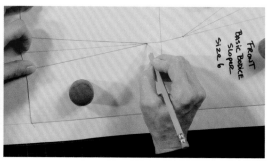

Make sure you also transfer your dart vanishing points.

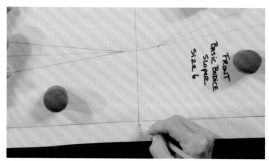

Step 4C

Mark your bust guideline. Then remove the front bodice sloper from the draft.

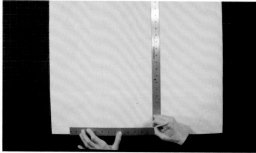

Step 5A

Next, rest your L square on the center front bustline mark and make a mark.

Step 5B

Then square a line off across the width of the paper.

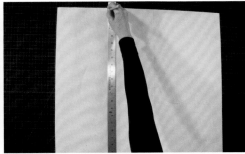

Step 5C
Next, rest your L square on the bustline at the center front/waistline intersection.

Step 5D
Then square a line across the width of the paper, just as you did for the bustline. This is the new waist guideline.

Step 6
Measure down 7" (18cm) from the front waistline and square a line across the paper to form the torso sloper's hipline.

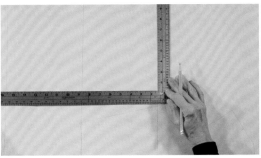

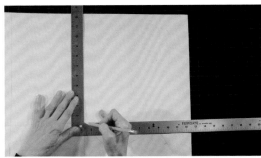

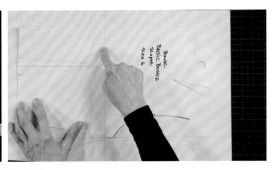

Step 7A
Now square a line down from the front side seam/armhole intersection to the hip by resting the L square on the bustline. Draw a guideline from the side seam/armhole intersection to the hipline. This is your side seam guideline.

Step 7B
Flip the L square over, rest it on the bust guideline, and extend the side seam guideline to the top of the paper.

Step 7C
Now align your back sloper with the front sloper's armhole and align the back bust guideline with the bust guideline of the paper, as demonstrated.

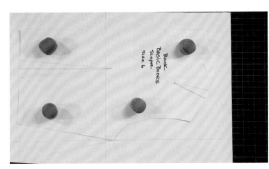

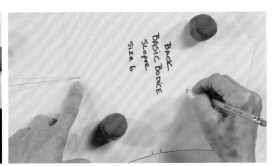

Step 7D
Secure the back sloper to the paper with weights.

Step 7E
Trace your back bodice sloper onto the paper. Make sure you transfer your armhole and dart notches.

Step 7F
Make sure that you also transfer the vanishing points of your back darts. Then remove the weights and the back bodice sloper from the table.

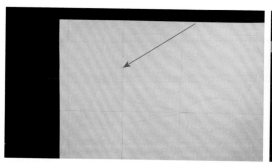

Step 7F

Do not be concerned that the waistline of your front and back slopers are lower than the waist guideline of the paper.

Step 8A

Now you will square a line off the bustline, and continue your center back line to the hipline of the paper.

Step 8B

Flip the L square over on the bustline, and extend the center back line to the top of the paper. Write "CB" on the center back line of the draft.

Module 2:

Planning the Torso Dart

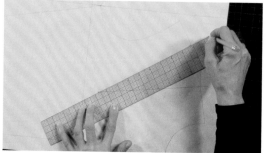

Step 1A

Begin by drawing in your front shoulder dart.

Step 1B

Then draw in your front waist dart.

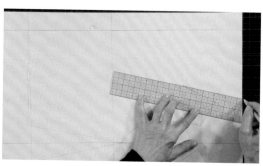

Step 2A

Move to the back and draw in your back shoulder dart.

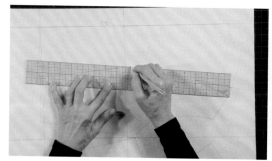

Step2B

Then draw in your back waist dart.

Step 3A

Reposition the draft so that the hip and waistline are facing you. Square a line off the bustline through the center of the front waist dart.

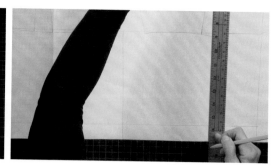

Step 3B

Take this line to the end of the paper.

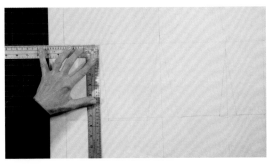

Step 4A

Now repeat the process on the back, squaring off the bustline and through the center of the back waist dart.

Step 4B

Draw a line down to the end of the paper.

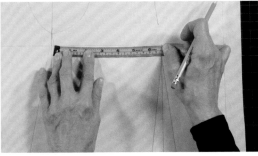

Step 5A

Measure between the apex and the side seam along the front bustline with your tape measure.

Find the midway point between the apex and the side seam on the bustline by folding your tape measure in half. Place a mark. This is the position of the front side dart.

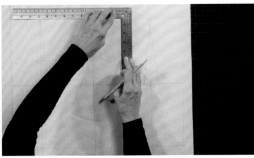

Step 5B

Square a line off the bustline, at the front side dart mark, to the end of the torso.

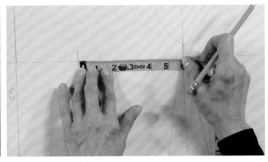

Step 6A

Repeat this step on the back. Measure between the center back dart and the side seam with your tape measure.

Tip

The fitted torso sloper is drafted with two front and two back waist darts, and shaping at the side seam/waist. For a non-fitted torso sloper silhouette, however, simply ignore the waist darts, eliminate the waist shaping steps, and use the side seam guideline as the side seam. The result is a boxy torso sloper.

Step 6B
Find the midway point between the center back dart and the side seam by folding the tape measure. Place a mark. This is the position of the back side dart.

Step 6C
Square a line off the back guideline, at the back side dart mark, to the end of the torso.

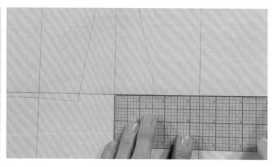

Step 7A
Measuring at the waistline, find the amount of space between the front bodice side seam and the side seam guideline. Record that measurement.

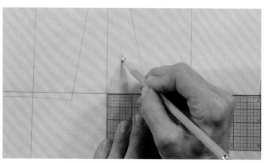

Ours measures 1⅝" (4cm).

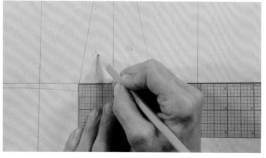

Step 7B
Now measure the amount of space between the back waist and the side seam guideline and record that measurement. Ours measures 1½" (3.8cm).

Step 7C
Take the smaller of the front and back side seam numbers and divide that by 3. In our case that would be 1½" (3.8cm) divided by 3, or ½" (1.3cm). This will be the amount that you will use to shape your front and back side seam.

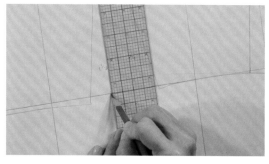

Step 7D
Use your red pencil to measure and mark your one-third measurement from both sides of the side seam guideline at the waistline. Here we are measuring out ½" (1.3cm) on each side of the side seam guideline. This will become our new front and back side seam.

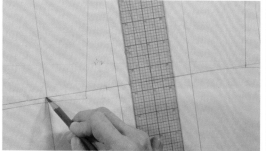

Step 7E
Move to the back side dart line. Measure and mark your one-third measurement on both sides of that line at the waistline.

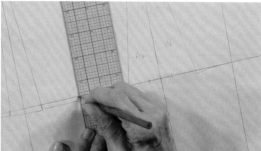

Again, in our case we are placing ½" (1.3cm) marks on both sides of the back side dart line.

Step 7F
For the front side dart, take your total front side seam space measurement (here 1⅝"/4cm) and subtract your one-third divided back dart measurement (here ½"/1.3cm). Our total is 1⅛" (2.7cm). Divide that measurement to get the dart intake amount to mark on both sides of the front side dart centerline. Our measurement is ⁹⁄₁₆" (1.4cm). For demonstration purposes we will measure using ⅝" (1.5cm).

Step 7G
On both sides of the centerline of the front side dart, measure over and mark your front side dart intake on the waistline.

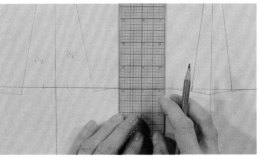

We will measure over ⅝" (1.5cm).

Module 3:
Trueing the Torso Side Seam & Darts

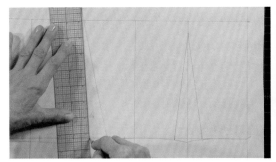

Step 1A
With your red pencil, connect the front side seam/armhole intersection to the new front side seam mark at the waist.

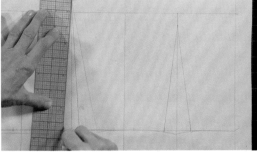

Step 1B
Repeat this step for the back side seam/armhole intersection to the new back side seam/waistline mark.

Step 1C
Annotate the new back side seam, both front and back, with "Cutting Line."

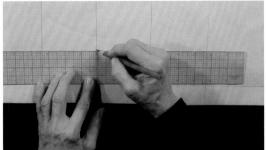

Step 2A
In preparation for shaping the side seam, place a mark at 2" (5cm) up from the hem on the side seam guideline.

Step 2B
Using a red pencil and your hip curve, connect the front waist/side seam intersection with the 2" (5cm) mark. Note the exact number on the hip curve. In our case, 10" (25.4cm).

Step 2C
Flip the hip curve over at the exact same number on the curve, and then connect the back waist/side seam mark to the 2" (5cm) mark. It is important that the front and back side seams are symmetrical, since this will become the sloper's side seam.

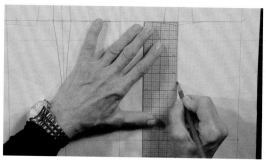

Step 3A

Measure down 3½" (9cm) from the waist on the centerline of the front center waist dart and place a mark.

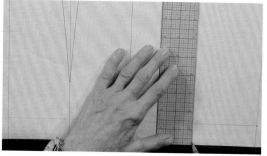

Step 3B

Now measure over by ¼" (6mm) from that mark, to one side of the centerline, and draw a line down to the hem.

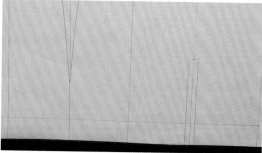

Do the same on the other side of the centerline.

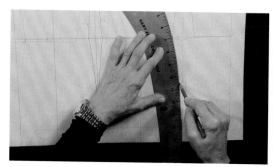

Step 3C

Next, you will shape and mark the front center dart from the waist marks to the 3½" (9cm) marks. Connect the two marks with your hip curve and red pencil. Once again, note the number on the hip curve at the waist. In our case, 7" (18cm).

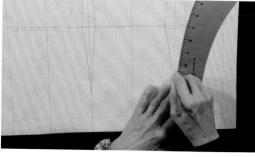

Step 3D

Flip the hip curve over to the exact same number on the curve, and then connect the other side of the front center waist dart, from waist to the 3½" (9cm) mark.

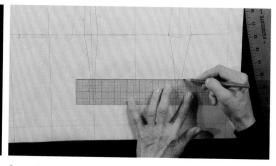

Step 3E

Next, square a line off the front center waist dart at the 3½" (9cm) mark.

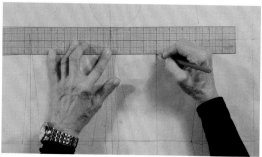

Step 4A

Now move to the front side waist dart. Place a mark 1" (2.5cm) down, on the dart's centerline, from the bust guideline. This is the dart's vanishing point.

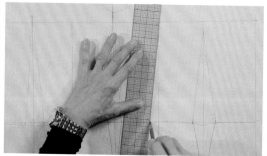

Step 4B

Connect the vanishing point of the front side waist dart to the waist mark.

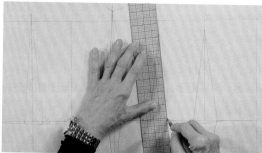

Step 4C

Then pivot the ruler at the vanishing point and mark the other side of the dart to the waist.

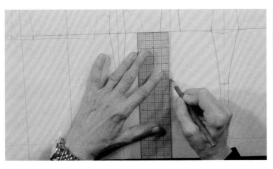

Step 4D
Measure down from the waist 3" (7.5cm) along the centerline of the front side waist dart and mark the vanishing point.

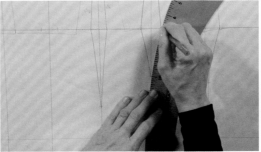

Step 4E
Now finish by shaping the front side waist dart, below the waist. Connect the waist mark to the vanishing point of the dart. Remember to use the same number on the hip curve to curve both sides of the dart. Note that the markings for the front center dart above the waist remain the same.

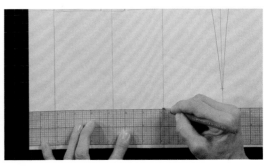

Step 5A
Next, you will form the lower section of the back waist darts. Start by marking the vanishing point of each dart on the dart's centerline.

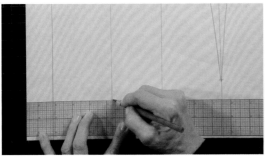

This will be at 1" (2.5cm) up from the hipline.

Step 5B
Shape the lower center back dart with your hip curve from the waist to the 1" (2.5cm) mark. Make sure that you flip the curve at the same number, just as you did for the front waist dart, so that the dart's shape is symmetrical.

Step 5C
Now shape the lower back side dart, repeating the process of connecting the waist marks to the vanishing point.

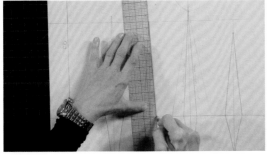

Step 5D
Move to the back side dart above the waist, and connect the vanishing point to each side of the dart at the waist. Note that the markings for the front center dart above the waist remain the same.

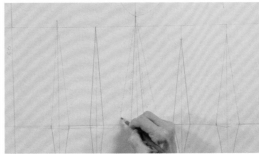

Step 6
For clarification purposes and to avoid confusion, draw red hatch marks along the pencil lines at the side seam of the lower torso, first on one side and then on the other.

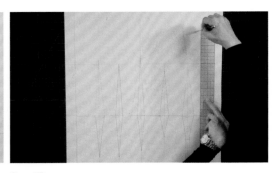

Step 7A
Add the grainline to the front torso sloper with arrows at 2" (5cm) in from center front.

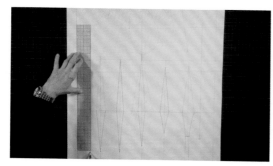

Step 7B
Add the grainline to the back torso sloper, again at 2" (5cm) in from center back.

Step 8A
Annotate the front sloper with "Front Torso Sloper" and "Size 6," or whatever your size happens to be.

Step 8B
Then annotate the back sloper with "Back Torso Sloper" and your particular size.

Step 9A
Carefully cut your front torso sloper out of the pattern draft.

Step 9B
When you reach the front side seam be sure you cut along the red line, which is the new side seam.

Step 9C
Continue cutting out the front sloper, along the hipline and along the center front.

Step 10A
Move to the back sloper and, again, be sure to cut along the new back side seam cutting line.

Step 10B
Continue to cut the back sloper along the cutting lines.

Step 11
This is your finished front and back torso sloper.

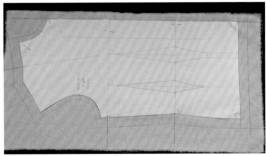

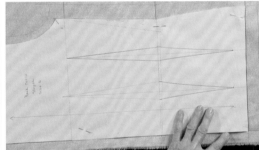

Step 1A

You will now transfer your torso sloper to muslin. For fitting purposes we have added 1" (2.5cm) seam allowances to the shoulder, the center front, and the side seam, and we added a 1" (2.5cm) hem allowance. We added ½" (1.3cm) seam allowance at the neckline and at the armhole.

Step 1B

For the back torso sloper, we added the same seam and hem allowances.

Step 2A

Trace all of your darts onto the muslin by sandwiching tracing paper face down between the paper sloper and the muslin.

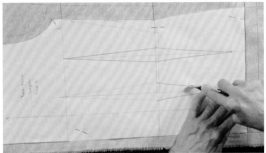

Step 2B

Use your tracing wheel to transfer your dart markings and vanishing points onto the muslin below.

Check that all of your markings have been transferred.

Step 3

Cut your back and front sloper out of the muslin.

Step 4A

Pin your front and back torso sloper together, as demonstrated, in preparation for fitting it on your dress form (tailor's dummy).

Step 4B

Be sure to snip all of the darts at the waist.

Step 4C

And snip the waist at the side seam.

Tip
You are now ready to move on to the next lesson, which will show you how to true your pattern, and then how to transfer it from muslin to oaktag.

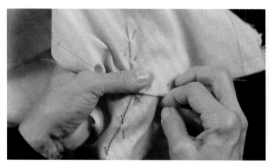

Step 4D
Pin the shoulder seam closed, pinning the back over the front, matching the armhole and neckline seams.

Step 5A
Place your torso sloper on the dress form to check the fit, and to confirm that you have the correct amount of ease at the bust and at the hip.

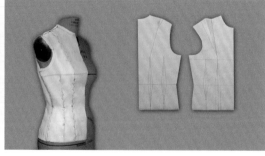

Step 5B
You are now ready to move on to the next lesson, which will show you how to true the pattern, and then how to transfer your torso sloper from muslin to oaktag.

Self-evaluation

☐ Have I traced my front shoulder dart bodice and back shoulder dart bodice slopers accurately?

☐ Do my bodice slopers align with my guideline markings?

☐ Have I transferred all of my notches and dart vanishing points?

☐ Have I calculated my waist darts accurately and positioned them properly?

☐ Did I use my hip curve correctly so that my darts, and my front and back side seams are shaped symmetrically?

☐ Have I cut and fit my torso sloper in muslin and made any necessary corrections?

Transferring the Torso Sloper to Oaktag

Learning objectives

☐ Prepare the pieces—preparing and marking the paper blocks and oaktag, pressing the muslin bodice pieces, marking the waistline

☐ Transfer the bodice onto the paper—tracing all the lines and markings onto the paper, trueing the paper patterns

☐ Transfer the paper patterns onto oaktag—tracing all the lines and markings onto oaktag, punching a hole at dart vanishing points, cutting out the patterns, trueing the oaktag sloper, transferring notches and marks

Tools and supplies:

- Fitted Torso Sloper in muslin (calico) (see Lesson 3.7)
- Fitted Sleeve Sloper (see Lesson 1.3)
- White unlined pattern paper—32″ (81cm) square
- Oaktag (card)—32″ (81cm) square

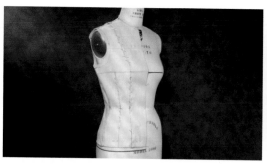

Step 1

For this lesson you will need the torso sloper that you prepared in muslin and fitted on the dress form in the previous lesson.

Step 2

You will also need to prepare a piece of white unlined pattern paper measuring 32" (81cm) square.

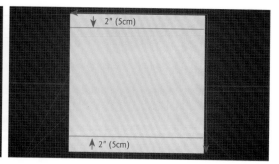

Step 3

Draw a line 2" (5cm) away from the edge of the paper on two sides.

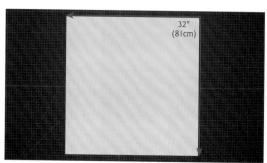

Step 4

You will also need a 32" (81cm) square block of oaktag.

Step 5

Once you have unpinned your muslin sloper, press the muslin pieces with your iron. Use steam to help flatten the fabric folds, and always press in the direction of the grainlines.

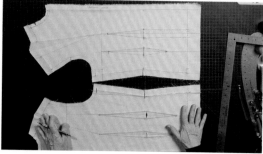

Step 6

Place your front and back muslin pieces on the table, with the back piece closest to you. Position them side by side, aligning at the underarm, waist, and hem.

Step 7

Now rest one side of your L square along center front. Align the other side with the waistline of the front and the back muslin.

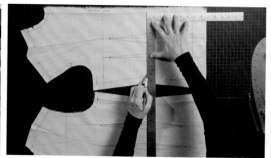

Step 8

Draw a line across the waistline of both front and back pieces, from center front to center back.

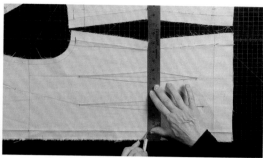

Make sure that your waistline on the back is at a right angle to center back.

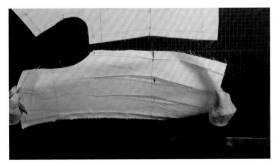

Step 9
Remove the front and back muslin pieces from the table.

Module 2:
Tracing the Front Sloper

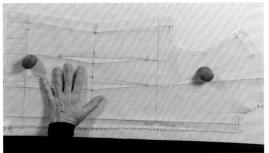

Step 1
With your torso front on top of the 32″ (81cm) square piece of pattern paper, align the center front of the sloper to the 2″ (5cm) line of the paper, which is a right angle to the waistline. Use weights to hold the muslin in place.

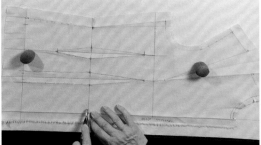

Step 2
Trace off 1″ (2.5cm) of the center front waistline onto the paper below, using your tracing wheel. Then put the muslin aside.

Step 3A
Rest your L square on center front at the waistline, then square off a line.

Step 3B
Draw the line across the width of the paper to the 2″ (5cm) line on the other side.

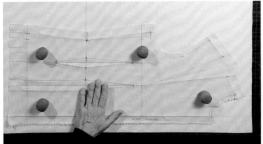

Step 4
Now align the sloper with the 2″ (5cm) line and the waistline. Hold the sloper down with several weights.

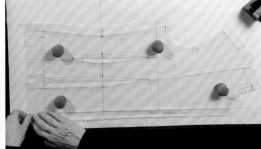

Step 5
For extra stability, tape the sloper down along the shoulder, the side seam at the underarm and at the hem, and at the center front hem.

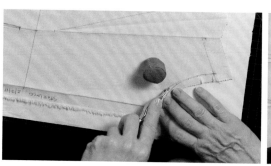

Step 6

You will now trace the stitching line of the sloper, beginning at the center front neck.

Step 7

Note how we are holding down the fabric with the other hand as we trace, so that the muslin does not stretch. Trace the shoulder, the first dart leg, the dart's vanishing point, and the other dart leg.

Step 8

Continue to trace the shoulder, the armhole, and the side seam. Press down hard on the tracing wheel as you trace, to be sure that you leave enough of an impression on the paper below, since you will be using these lines for trueing.

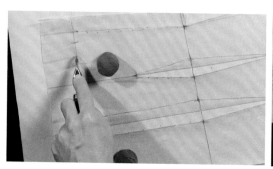

Step 9

Trace the front hem from center front to the side seam.

Step 10A

Trace one side of the bust dart, from the hem all the way up past the bustline to the vanishing point of the shoulder dart.

Step 10B

Then trace the vanishing point of both darts.

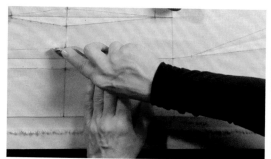

Step 10C

Finish tracing the other side of the bust dart, from vanishing point to hem.

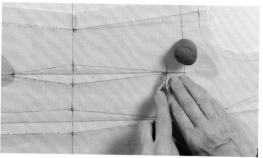

Step 11A

Next, you will trace one side of the front guideline dart, from hem to vanishing point, then continue the line to the bustline.

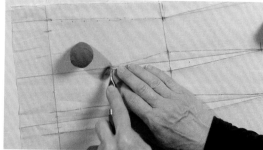

Step 11B

Finish tracing the other side of the guideline dart, from vanishing point to hem. Then trace the vanishing point.

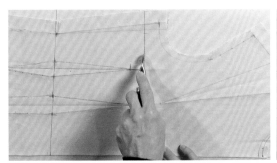

Step 11C
Trace the bustline from center front to the side seam ...

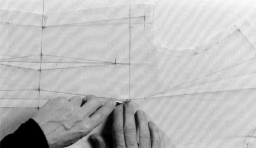

... and the dart placement on the bustline for both darts.

Step 12
Now reposition the paper with the 2" (5cm) guideline facing you. Lay the back muslin sloper along the 2" guideline, and aligned with the waist guideline on the paper.

Module 3:

Trueing the Front Sloper

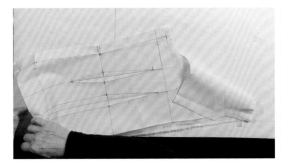

Step 1
Remove the weights and tape, then remove your front muslin piece from the table.

Step 2A
Looking at the tracing marks, you will begin trueing the front torso sloper using your styling curve.

Step 2B
Begin penciling in at the neckline.

Step 3
Use your ruler to true one side of the shoulder and shoulder dart, then pivot the ruler and true the other side of the dart and shoulder.

Step 4
Switch back to your styling curve to true the front armhole. Make sure that you are connecting all of the tracing marks.

Step 5A
Use your ruler to true the straighter portion of the armhole, then pivot the ruler to true the side seam, stopping at the waist.

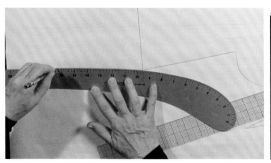

Step 5B
Change to your hip curve and true the front hipline.

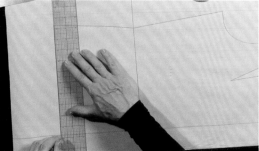

Step 6
With your ruler, true the bottom edge of the sloper, making sure that the line is at a right angle to the center front.

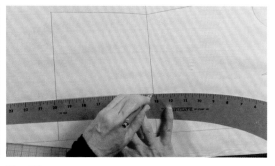

Step 7A
Now you will true the darts, starting with the bust dart. Use your hip curve and true one side of the dart from hem to waist, noting what number on the curve you have positioned the curve at the waist.

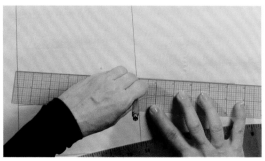

Step 7B
Switch to the ruler and true from the waist to the vanishing point. Pivot the ruler and continue the other side of the dart to the waist.

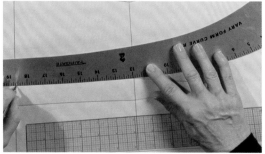

Step 7C
Place the hip curve at the same position as you trued the other side of this dart, and true from waist to hem.

Step 8A
Move next to the guideline dart. True one side of the dart with the hip curve, from waist to dart vanishing point.

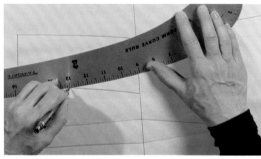

Step 8B
Note the position and number on the curve as you flip it to true the other side of the dart, from waist to vanishing point.

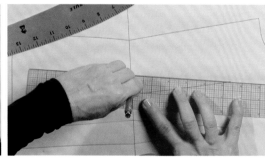

Step 8C
Position your ruler at the waist to vanishing point, and true one side of the dart. Then pivot your ruler at the vanishing point.

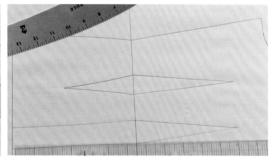

Step 8D
True the other side of the dart, from vanishing point to waist.

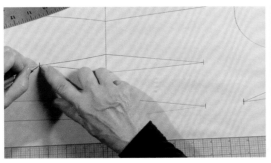

Step 9
Mark all of the vanishing points on the front darts.

Step 10A
Separate the front sloper from the back with your paper scissors.

Step 10B
Cut out the trued front torso sloper from the paper. Hold the paper down with your free hand, and reposition the paper as you cut.

Step 11A
Once you have finished cutting the neckline area, you will need to close out the shoulder dart to true that dart. Finger press the dart leg closest to the neckline.

Step 11B
Now close the dart from the vanishing point to the shoulder, cupping the paper at the vanishing point so that it will flatten.

Step 11C
Once you have closed the dart, place a piece of tape just below the shoulder to hold it in place.

Note that the dart legs do not align at the shoulder, so you will need to true the shoulder with your ruler.

Step 11D
Redraw the shoulder using your red pencil and ruler, from the neck to the armhole.

Step 11E
Then cut the shoulder out on the new shoulder line.

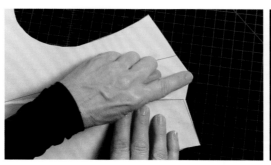

Step 11F
Remove the tape, open the dart, and note the new direction of the dart material at the shoulder.

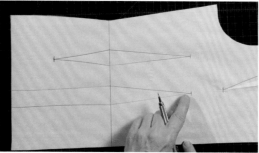

Step 12A
Now you will draw a line down the center of the bust dart. Start by measuring from the center front to the dart's vanishing point.

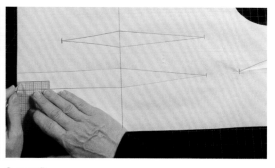

Step 12B
Next, move the ruler down the center front to the hem at that same measurement and place a mark.

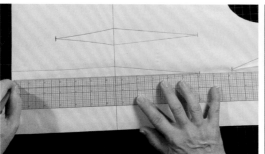

Step 12C
Draw in the dart's centerline up to the dart's vanishing point.

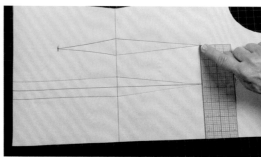

Step 13A
To create the centerline for the guideline dart, repeat this process, beginning by measuring from the center front to the upper dart vanishing point.

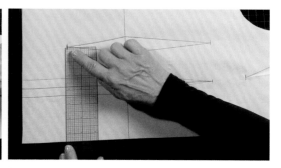

Step 13B
Now move the ruler down center front to the lower vanishing point at that same measurement, and check that this vanishing point is at the same measurement from the center front.

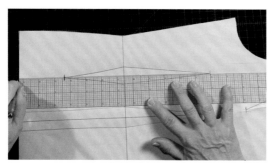

Step 13C
Then draw a line from the upper vanishing point through the lower vanishing point, ending at the hem.

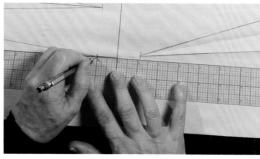

Step 13D
Now connect the bust dart's vanishing point to the bustline.

Step 13E
Then pivot the ruler and continue the line though the shoulder dart's vanishing point, and along the dart leg closest to the neck, ending at the shoulder.

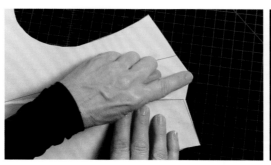

Step 13F
Continue the guideline dart's centerline from the vanishing point up to the bustline.

Module 4:

Tracing & Trueing the Back Sloper

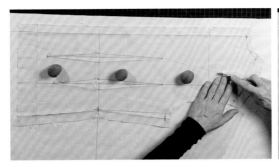

Step 1
Next, you will trace all of the stitching lines from the back sloper onto the paper below with your tracing wheel.

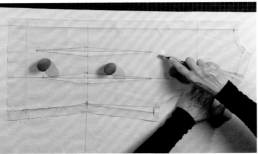

Step 2
Be sure to include the line that connects the shoulder dart to the waist dart.

Step 3
You will start the trueing process at the center back neck of the back sloper, by squaring a line off center back for ¼" (6mm) with your ruler.

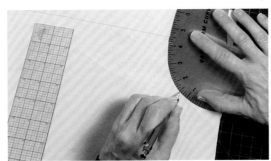

Step 4
Switch to your styling curve, and true in the back neck to the end of the squared line.

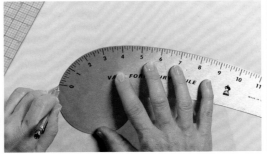

Step 5
Then position the styling curve into the back armhole, aligning the curve with the tracing marks, and true the armhole.

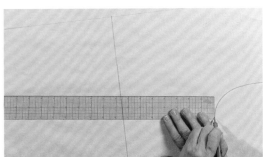

Step 6A
Align the end of the ruler at the underarm/side seam intersection and square off for ¼" (6mm).

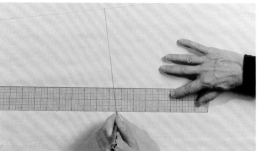

Step 6B
Then true the side seam to the waist.

Step 7
Use your hip curve to true the side seam from waist to the bottom of the sloper, following the tracing marks.

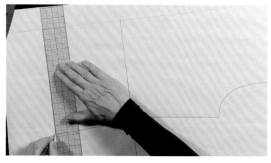

Step 8
With your ruler, square a line off the center back and true in the bottom of the back sloper, from center back to the side seam.

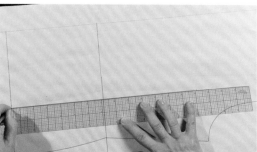

Step 9
You will now true the center of the back waist guideline dart, whose vanishing points are equidistant from center back and at a right angle to the waistline. Draw the centerline from the top vanishing point through the bottom vanishing point, ending the line at the hem.

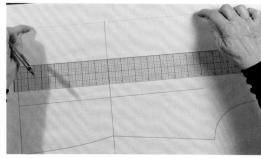

Step 10A
You will true the center waist dart next. This dart's centerline is also equidistant from center back.

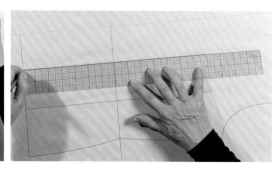

Step 10B
Place your ruler in the center of the dart at a right angle to the waistline. True in the dart's center, from the vanishing point to the hem.

Step 11A
Next, you will true the stitching lines of the darts, beginning with the guideline dart.

Step 11B
Mark the end point of that dart.

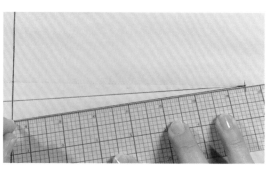

Step 11C
True from the top end point of one side of the dart to the waist.

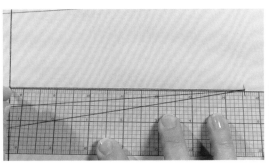

Step 11D
Pivot the ruler and true the other side of the dart, from the top end point to the waist.

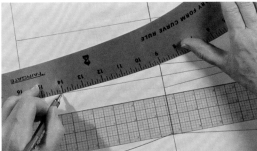

Step 11E
Mark the bottom end point of the dart, then switch to your hip curve and true one side of the dart from waist to end point, following your tracing marks, and noting the position of the curve at the waist.

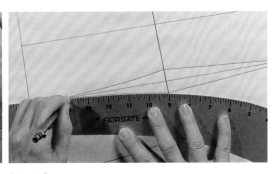

Step 11F
Flip the hip curve to the same measurement on the curve at the waist, and true the other side of the dart.

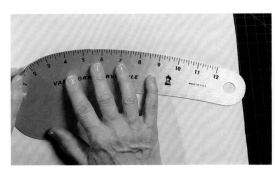

Step 12A
Now switch to your styling curve and true the back underarm, following the tracing marks.

Step 12B
Flip the curve over and true the upper armhole from shoulder to notch, creating a nice smooth line.

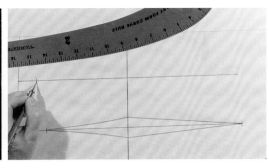

Step 13A
Mark the vanishing point of the lower waist dart.

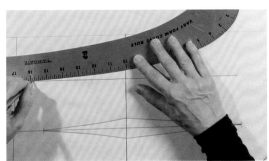

Step 13B
Position the hip curve on one side of the dart, following your tracing marks, and true from the waist to the dart's vanishing point. Note the position of the hip curve at the waist.

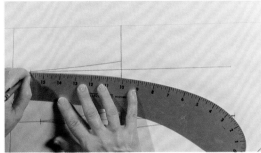

Step 13C
Now flip the curve at the same point, then true the other side of the dart, from the waist to the dart's vanishing point.

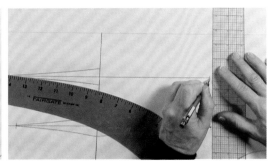

Step 13D
Mark the dart's upper vanishing point.

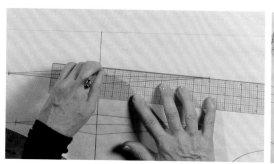

Step 13E

Use your ruler to connect one side of the dart from the waist to the vanishing point. Then pivot the ruler and true the other side of the dart, from vanishing point to waist.

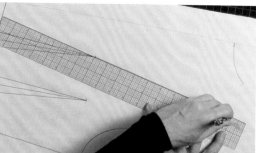

Step 13F

Reposition the ruler while the pencil is still at the vanishing point of the center waist dart, and connect from this dart's vanishing point to the back shoulder dart line closest to the neck, ending at the shoulder.

Step 13G

Mark the vanishing point of the back shoulder dart.

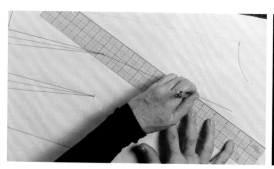

Step 13H

Now true the other side of the shoulder dart, closest to the armhole, from vanishing point to shoulder.

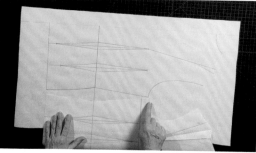

Step 14

You must now check that your front and back side seams match.

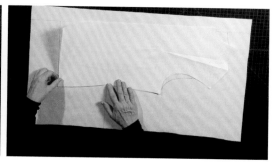

Do this by taking your front sloper draft and placing it wrong side up on top of the back paper sloper. Align the waistlines and side seams and check that they match. If they do not, you should make any necessary corrections now.

Step 15

Cut the back sloper out of the paper along the stitching line, beginning at the armhole. Hold the paper down with your other hand as you continue to cut the side seam, the hem, and along the center back from hem to neckline.

Step 16A

Before cutting the shoulder, you must first close the back shoulder dart. Finger press the dart leg closest to the neckline, then close the dart from shoulder to vanishing point.

Step 16B

Tape the dart closed, then true the shoulder using your styling curve. True from neck to dart, following your tracing lines.

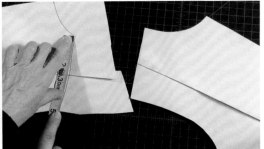

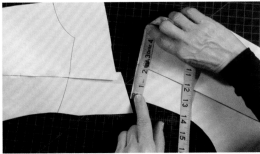

Step 16C

Then flip the curve and true from dart to armhole.

Step 17A

Now use your tape measure to measure the width of the back shoulder.

Step 17B

Then measure the width of the front shoulder. Check that your back shoulder is no more than ¼" (6mm) wider, due to ease, than your front shoulder.

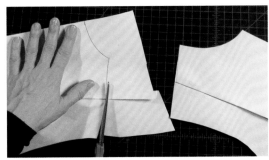

Step 18A

Cut along the back shoulder, from armhole to neck, with the dart closed. Then cut along the stitching line at the neck.

Step 18B

Slash into the tape holding down the shoulder dart, then open the dart.

Step 18C

Then slash into the tape holding down the front shoulder dart and open that dart, in preparation for transferring the sloper to oaktag.

Module 5:

Transferring the Paper
Sloper to Oaktag

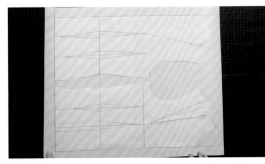

Step 1A

On your 32" (81cm) oaktag block, rest your front torso sloper along a line drawn at 2" (5cm) away from one edge.

Step 1B

Rest the hem of the front and back torso slopers on a line drawn at 2" (5cm) in from the left edge of the oaktag.

Step 1C

Then rest the back torso sloper on a line drawn at 2" (5cm) away from the top edge of the oaktag.

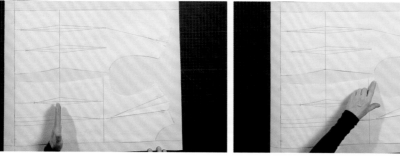

Step 1D
The waist of the front and back torso sloper rests on a line drawn across the oaktag at the waist level.

Step 2
Once you have aligned the front and back torso slopers along the oaktag guidelines, tape both front and back down on the oaktag in the corners and along the centerlines, in preparation for tracing.

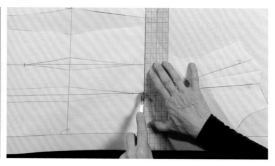

Step 3A
Use your tracing wheel to trace all of your front and back paper sloper guidelines, darts, and dart stitching lines. The pointed tracing wheel tool makes it easier to see the lines on the oaktag.

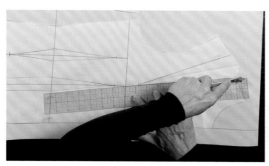

Step 3B
Use a ruler to true all of the straight lines on the front and back.

Step 4
Once you have traced all of your lines, use your awl to punch holes on the dart vanishing points—the front shoulder dart, and the bust and guideline's upper and lower darts—then move to the back sloper. Punch the vanishing points of the lower waist darts, the upper waist darts, and the back shoulder dart.

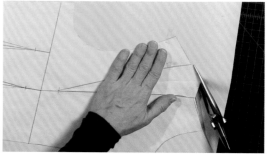

Step 5A
Using your paper shears, start cutting out the front sloper along the stitching line at the neck/shoulder intersection.

Step 5B
As you cut, you will need to hold the paper down with your other hand, and when cutting along curves you will need to fold the paper back to make the cutting process easier.

Step 6
Once you have finished tracing and cutting out the oaktag front and back torso sloper, remove the paper pattern from the oaktag.

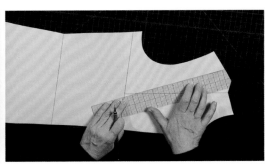

Step 1

Next, you will true the front and back of the oaktag sloper. Start by drawing in the front bustline with your ruler. Make sure that your line is at a right angle to center front.

Step 2A

Draw in one leg of the front shoulder dart, from the apex/bustline intersection, through the dart's vanishing point, to the shoulder mark nearest the neckline. Mark the vanishing point of the dart.

Step 2B

Draw in the other leg of the front shoulder dart, from the vanishing point to the shoulder mark.

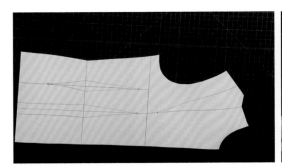

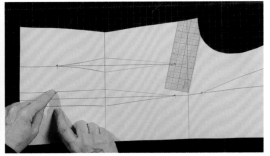

Step 3

Once you have trued all of your darts and guidelines, exactly as you did when you traced the muslin sloper to the pattern paper, you are ready to finish marking and trueing the front sloper.

Step 4

Mark the bust dart on both sides of the dart leg at the level of the front guideline dart. Your ruler should be placed at a right angle to center front.

Step 5A

With your awl, punch holes into both sides of the bust dart at the new marks and on the waistline.

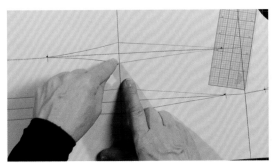

Step 5B

Punch holes into the guideline dart's waist dart marks, and continue to punch holes into the vanishing points of all three front darts, and all three darts on the back sloper.

Step 6A

Using your fitted sleeve sloper, you will now transfer the armhole notches to the torso's armhole.

Step 6B

With the wrong side of the front sleeve face up, walk the sleeve into the front torso's armhole, beginning at the side seam/underarm intersection. Pivot the sleeve with your free hand and transfer the position of the front notch onto the armhole of the oaktag sloper below.

Step 6C
Next, you will transfer the back sleeve notches. Flip the back sleeve to the wrong side, and walk the sleeve into the armhole of the back torso's armhole, just as you did for the front. Mark the position of both back notches on the armhole of the oaktag sloper below.

Step 7A
Use your notcher to notch the front armhole, both sides of the front shoulder dart, and the waist at the side seam. Note how the notcher is placed right in the center of the notch mark.

Step 7B
You will also notch the placement on the front hem of the guideline dart, both legs of the bust dart, and the waist at center front.

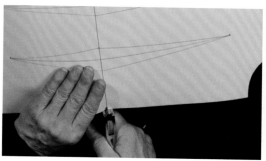

Step 7C
On the back torso sloper, notch the back armhole notches, both legs of the back shoulder dart, the waist at center back, and the waist at the side seam. If you are not careful and your notch is not centered on the mark, your sloper will not be trued properly.

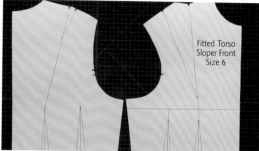

Step 8A
Annotate the front sloper with "Fitted Torso Sloper," "Front," and "Size 6," or whatever your size happens to be.

Fitted Torso
Sloper Front
Size 6

Step 8B
Annotate the back sloper with "Fitted Torso Sloper," "Back," and "Size 6," or your particular size.

Fitted Torso
Sloper Back
Size 6

Fitted Torso
Sloper Front
Size 6

Step 8C
You have now finished transferring your muslin Fitted Torso Sloper to oaktag.

Self-evaluation

☐ Did I press my torso sloper fitting muslin first, before transferring it to paper?

☐ Does my muslin torso sloper align with my paper guidelines?

☐ Have I accurately traced all of my muslin markings onto the paper?

☐ Did I re-true all of my darts?

☐ Are my front and back side seams and shoulder seams aligned?

☐ Are all of my intersections at right angles and my curves smooth before I transfer my sloper from paper to oaktag?

Raglan Sleeve Sloper

Learning objectives

☐ Preparing the paper blocks and marking guidelines, tracing the sleeve and front and back bodice into one unit, transferring notches, trueing darts

☐ Draft the raglan sleeve—measuring and marking the raglan style lines, trueing the lines, adding notches

☐ Extract a one-piece raglan sleeve—copying the sleeve pattern onto a paper block, redrafting the armhole, trueing lines, checking the fit into the bodice

☐ Extract a two-piece raglan sleeve—copying the front and back sleeves onto a paper block, trueing lines, adding notches

☐ Extract the bodice—copying the front and back bodice onto paper blocks, trueing the seams, adding notches

Tools and supplies:

- Front One Waist Dart Bodice Sloper (see Lesson 3.3)
- Back Neck Dart Bodice Sloper (see Lesson 3.6)
- Straight Sleeve Sloper (see Lesson 1.1)
- Five blocks of white unlined pattern paper (see overleaf)

Step 1

For this lesson you will need your front one waist dart bodice sloper (transferred to oaktag) ...

... your back neck dart bodice sloper (transferred to oaktag) ...

... and your straight sleeve sloper.

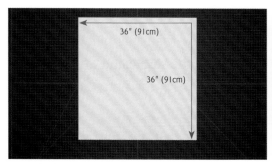 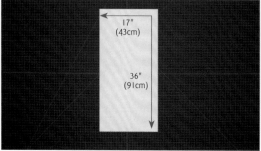 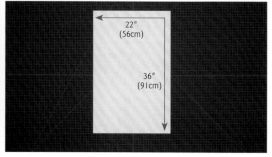

Step 2A

To begin this lesson, prepare five pieces of white unlined pattern paper. The first piece of pattern paper will measure 36" (91cm) square. (For sizes larger than a US size 6 / UK size 10, adjust the paper sizes accordingly.)

Step 2B

The next piece of pattern paper measures 17" (43cm) wide by 36" (91cm) long.

Step 2C

The third piece of pattern paper measures 22" (56cm) wide by 36" (91cm) long.

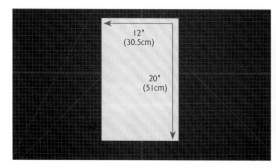  

Step 2D

The last two pieces of pattern paper each measure 12" (30.5cm) wide by 20" (51cm) long.

Step 3

With the 36" (91cm) square pattern paper on the table, find the midway point and square a vertical line from one end of the paper to the other. This is the centerline of the sleeve.

Step 4A

Measure down 10" (25.5cm) from the top of the paper and place a mark.

Step 4B
Then square a line across on both sides of the centerline.

This is the sleeve cap guideline.

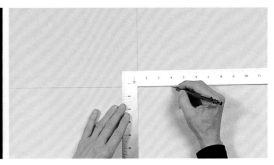

Step 4C
Place a mark at 4" (10cm) from the centerline on both sides of the sleeve cap guideline.

Step 5A
Position the centerline of your sleeve sloper with the sleeve centerline on the paper, and align the sleeve cap with the sleeve cap guideline on the paper.

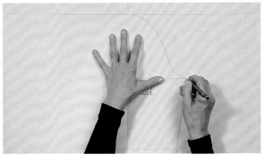

Step 5B
Now trace the sleeve off onto the paper below. Hold the sleeve sloper down firmly with your other hand as you trace. Be sure to copy all of the notches.

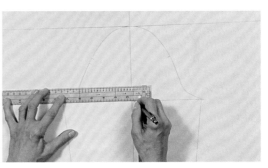

Step 5C
Use your L square to square off the centerline to mark your sleeve bicep guideline.

Step 5D
Now mark your elbow line, by squaring off from both sides of the centerline at the elbow notches.

Step 6A
The next step is to position your front bodice sloper so that the bodice's front armhole notch aligns with the front sleeve notch, and the bodice's upper armhole is resting on the upper front sleeve cap.

Step 6B
Hold the front bodice sloper down on the draft with weights.

Step 6C

Now repeat this process for the back bodice sloper. Align the bodice's back armhole notch with the back sleeve notch, and make sure the back bodice's armhole rests on the upper cap of the back sleeve.

Step 6D

Hold the sloper down with weights.

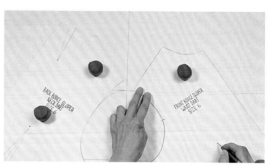

Step 7A

Next, you will trace the front bodice sloper onto the paper below, beginning at the front shoulder/neck intersection.
Be sure to trace all of your notches and the dart vanishing point.

Step 7B

Now trace off the back bodice sloper onto the paper below.

Step 7C

Remember to transfer the notches and the waist and neck dart markings.

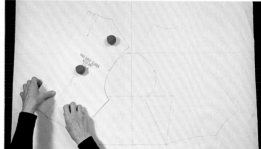

Step 8

Then remove the slopers from the table.

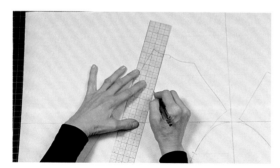

Step 9

And finally, connect your darts. Start with the front waist dart, then mark your back neck dart and your back waist dart.

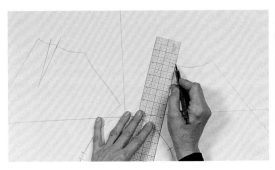

Step 1A
At the front bodice neck/shoulder intersection, measure over
1" (2.5cm) and place a mark on the front neckline.

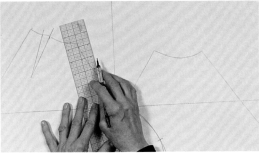

Step 1B
Now measure over and place a mark on the back neckline
1" (2.5cm) away from the back shoulder/neck intersection.

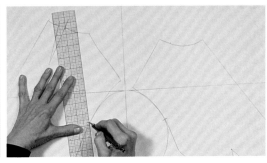

Step 1C
Draw light dashes connecting the back neck mark to the top
back armhole notch.

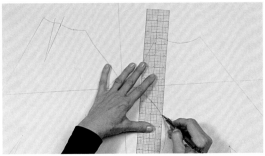

Step 1D
Repeat this step on the front bodice. Draw light dashes
connecting the neck mark to the front armhole notch.

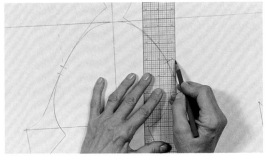

Step 2A
Switch to your red pencil and place a mark on the front bodice
½" (1.3cm) away from the front armhole notch.

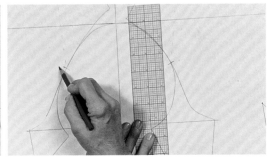

Step 2B
Repeat this step on the back. Measure ½" (1.3cm) from the
top back armhole notch and then place a mark on the bodice at
that point.

Step 2C
Use your hip curve to blend the front neck mark to the
½" (1.3cm) mark alongside the front armhole notch, creating
a gentle curve with your red pencil.

Step 2D
Flip the hip curve over and complete the style line of the front
raglan sleeve by drawing in the lower section of the armhole,
from the front notch to the side seam of the front bodice.

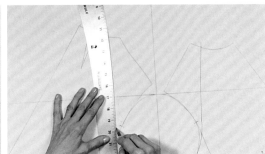

Step 2E
Repeat this process on the back. Blend from the back neckline
mark to the ½" (1.3cm) mark alongside the top back notch to
create the style line of the back raglan sleeve.

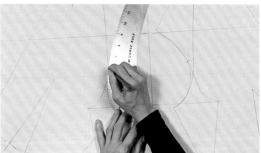

Step 2F

Flip the hip curve and blend the lower section of the back armhole, from the back notch down to the side seam of the back bodice.

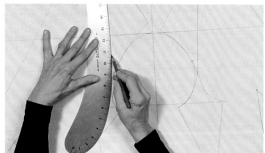

Step 2G

Go back and re-blend the curve if necessary.

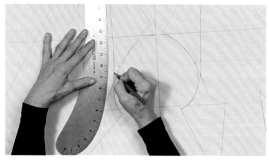

Step 2H

To avoid confusion, draw hatch marks on the original line with your red pencil once the line has been re-blended.

Step 3A

The next step is to blend the lower section of the front raglan sleeve, from the front ½" (1.3cm) notch mark to the front sleeve's underarm seam. Switch to a blue pencil to draft this portion of this lesson.

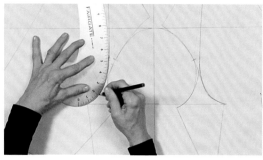

Step 3B

Repeat this step on the back sleeve. Blend the lower section of the back raglan sleeve, from the back ½" (1.3cm) notch mark to the back sleeve's underarm seam.

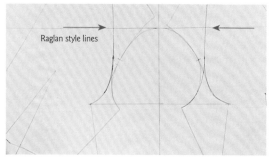

Step 3C

Note that the red lines you drew will become the raglan style lines for the bodice...

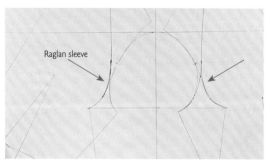

...while the blue lines belong to the raglan sleeve.

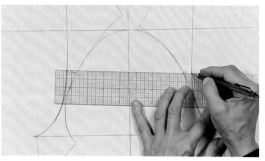

Step 4A

Transfer the front notch onto the front raglan line, level with the existing notch.

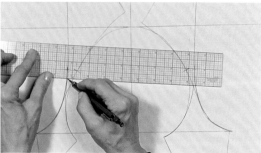

Step 4B

Then transfer both notches on the back raglan line.

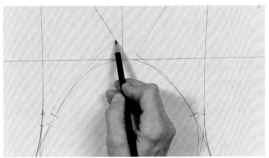

Step 5A

Now you need to equalize the distance between the back ...

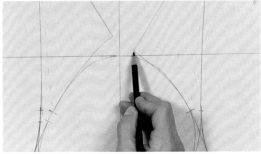

... and front shoulder from the sleeve centerline.

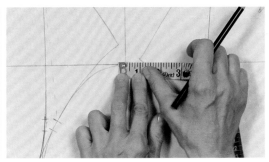

Step 5B

First, measure the distance with your tape measure.

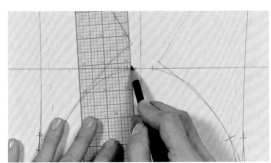

Step 5C

Then fold the tape measure in half, as demonstrated. Our measurement is ½" (1.3cm).

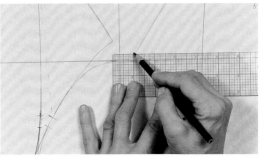

Step 5D

Or, you can use a ruler and measure along the sleeve cap line from the back to the front shoulder point and divide that number in half.

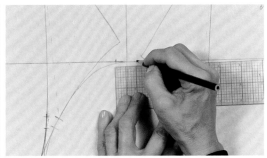

Step 5E

Then mark your divided measurement along the sleeve cap guideline, measured from both sides of the sleeve centerline. This is the new shoulder point. In our case this is ½" (1.3cm) from each side of the sleeve centerline.

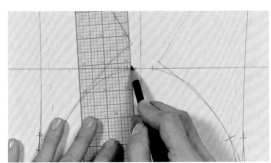

Step 5F

Now you need to add ⅛" (3mm) of ease to both sides of the new shoulder point.

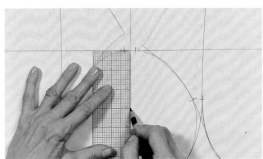

Step 6A

Then measure down 3" (7.5cm) from the intersection of the sleeve center/sleeve cap guideline and place a mark. This represents the vanishing point of the dart for the one-piece raglan sleeve.

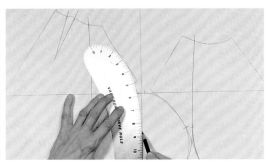

Step 6B

The next step is to shape the back shoulder by blending the new back shoulder marks with your hip curve. Note that the curve is blended from the mid back shoulder and not from the back shoulder point.

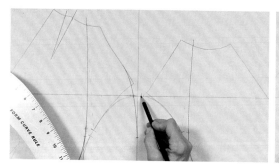

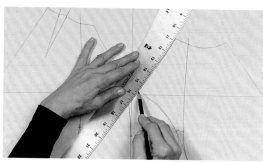

Step 6C

You will now repeat this step on the front shoulder. However, for the front, shaping will start at the front neck, then down to the shoulder, and on to the 3" (7.5cm) mark.

Step 6D

For extra shoulder height you can blend to the raised front shoulder mark, or you can blend to the original mark, depending on the desired look.

Step 6E

Here we are lightly blending to the original shoulder mark.

Step 6F

Flip your curve and blend from the shoulder mark to the 3" (7.5cm) mark. Then go back in and refine the line.

Module 3:

Extracting the
Raglan Sleeve

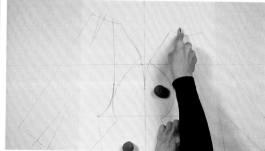

Step 1

Slip your 17" (43cm) by 36" (91cm) piece of unlined pattern paper under the sleeve portion of the draft, in preparation for the next step, which is to extract the raglan sleeve from the draft.

Step 2A

Place weights on top of the draft to hold the paper layers in place. Using your tracing wheel, begin tracing the front underarm of the sleeve, following the blue pencil line first.

Step 2B

Then continue along the red line, up to the front neckline. Be sure to trace the front sleeve notch.

Step 2C
Trace the 3″ (7.5cm) mark, and then the front shoulder, from the 3″ (7.5cm) mark up to the front neckline, following the blue pencil line.

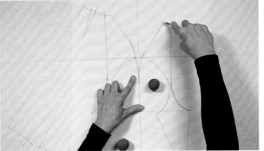

Step 2D
Also trace the front neckline of the sleeve.

Step 2E
Now trace the back sleeve, following the blue pencil lines from the 3″ (7.5cm) mark, to the back neck, and along the back neckline of the raglan sleeve.

Step 2F
Finish tracing the back raglan sleeve line from the blue pencil line, up along the red line, ending at the back neckline.

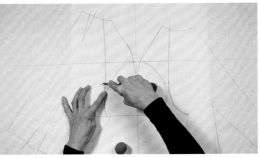

Step 2G
Be sure to trace both notches on the back sleeve.

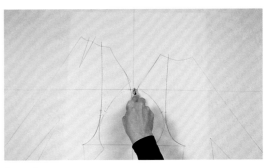

Step 3A
Trace the sleeve centerline at the sleeve cap intersection.

Step 3B
Trace the sleeve centerline at the sleeve hem.

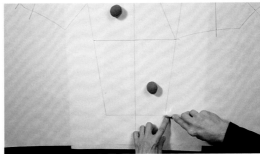

Step 3C
Then make a cross-mark with the tracing wheel at the intersection of the front and back sleeve underarm seam and hem.

Step 3D
Move to the elbow line and trace a cross-mark at the intersection of the back and front underarm seam and elbow line.

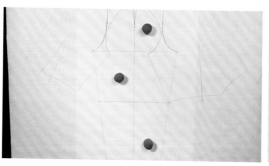

Step 4

Check to be sure that you have captured all of the tracing marks. Then remove the weights and separate the top draft from the sleeve draft below, in preparation for trueing the sleeve portion of the draft.

Step 5A

The next step is to pencil in all of your sleeve tracing marks.

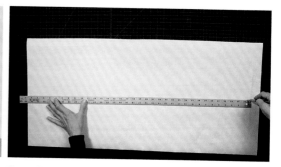

Step 5B

Reposition the sleeve horizontally, with the sleeve hem to your right, and begin by connecting the top and bottom sleeve centerline tracing marks.

Step 5C

Connect the sleeve elbow line marks, front to back.

Step 5D

And connect the sleeve hem marks, front to back.

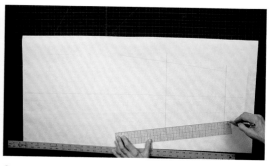

Step 5E

Connect the sleeve underarm seam marks on the front sleeve, from armhole to hem. Then connect the back underarm seam.

Step 5F

Switch to your hip curve to mark the back armhole, following the tracing marks, from the underarm to the back neckline.

Step 5G

Now mark the back sleeve dart and shoulder seam following the tracing marks. Start from the 3" (7.5cm) mark and blend to the neckline.

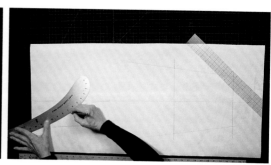

You will have to reposition the hip curve in order to blend a nice smooth line.

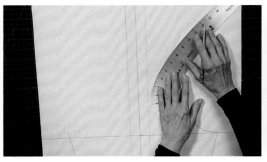

Step 5I
Repeat this step to mark the front sleeve dart and shoulder seam. Find the best position on the hip curve to make your line.

Step 5J
Flip the hip curve over and complete the marking of your front dart/shoulder line. Refine the curve if needed.

Step 5K
Mark the front armhole from the underarm to the neckline. Be sure to mark the sleeve notch.

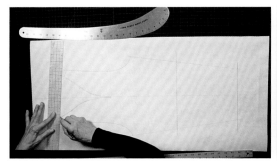

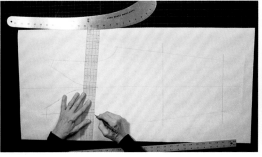

Step 5L
Use your clear plastic ruler to mark the front and back neckline.

Step 5M
Mark the dart's vanishing point and both back sleeve notches.

Step 6A
The next step is to raise the front and back sleeve at the underarm to add additional lift to the sleeve. Start by measuring up 1" (2.5cm) from the front sleeve underarm and place a mark with your red pencil.

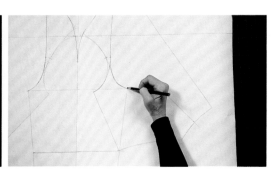

Step 6B
Repeat this step for the back sleeve. Place a mark 1" (2.5cm) from the back underarm.

Step 7A
Now you will be blending the front and back raglan sleeve armhole to this new raised underarm mark, from the neck to the underarm, and then from the underarm to the sleeve hem.

Step 7B
To do this, you will be taking the shape of the front underarm of the original draft.

Raglan Sleeve Sloper

Step 7C
You will then align the front underarm shape of the original draft with that of the sleeve draft, matching them up at the front notches.

Step 7D
You will also match the two draft layers at the sleeve armhole/ underarm seam intersection.

Step 7E
With the two layers matched up at the front notch, secure them with a pushpin.

Step 7F
Now, as you look through the paper, pivot the top sleeve layer so that the 1" (2.5cm) raised mark of the sleeve draft hits the intersection of the armhole/underarm seam on the paper draft below, as demonstrated.

Step 7G
Looking through the paper, dot the shape of the armhole below onto the sleeve draft.

Step 7H
Repeat these steps for the back armhole by lining up the sleeve's back top notch with the back top notch below.

Step 7I
Repeat the process you used for the front sleeve. Look through the paper and pivot the back sleeve draft until the 1" (2.5cm) mark rests on the intersection of the back armhole and sleeve underarm below.

Step 7J
Mark this with broken lines, using your blue pencil. Remove the pushpin and separate the sleeve from the draft below.

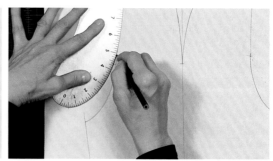

Step 7K
Use your styling curve to true the new armhole of the back sleeve, from the top notch to the armhole/underarm intersection.

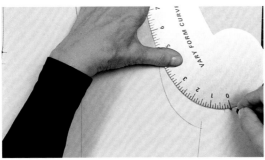

Step 7L

Then true the new armhole of the front sleeve, from the notch to the armhole/underarm intersection.

Step 8A

Next, you will true the sleeve underarm seams. Position your hip curve and blend the back underarm seam from the new underarm intersection toward the hem. Note the number on the hip curve at the armhole.

Step 8B

Then position the hip curve at the same number on the front new underarm and blend this seam, from the new underarm intersection toward the hem.

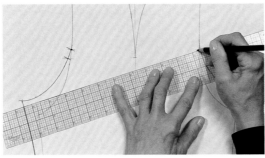

Step 9

Use your ruler to mark the back and front sleeve notches onto the new underarm seamlines.

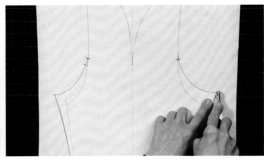

Step 10A

Use your tracing wheel to trace the new front underarm seam, starting at ½" (1.3cm) below the underarm, and then continuing up to the front sleeve notch.

Step 10B

Repeat the process of tracing the new back armhole onto the back sleeve.

Step 11A

To test that your sleeve's front and back armhole fits into the armhole of your raglan bodice, flip the sleeve draft over to the wrong side and, looking through the paper, mark the sleeve's back and front armhole. Mark from the neck to the sleeve's underarm seam.

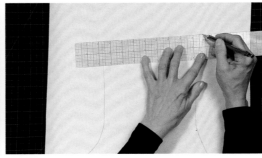

Step 11B

Mark the neck/armhole intersections of both the front and the back sleeve.

Step 12A

Now you are going to walk the front raglan sleeve's armhole into the front bodice's armhole, starting at the neckline.

Step 12B
First match up the neckline of the front sleeve to the front bodice's neckline.

Step 12C
Then walk the sleeve's armhole into the bodice's armhole, pivoting the sleeve draft as you go.

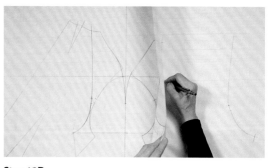

Step 12D
Continue to check that your seamlines align by folding back the paper as you walk the sleeve into the bodice's armhole.

Bodices

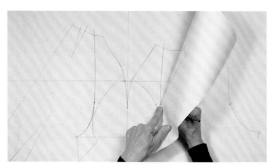

Step 12E
Make sure that your notches align. Adjust the sleeve if necessary.

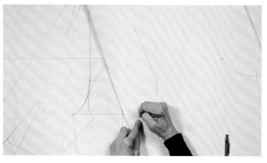

Step 12F
Continue to pivot and walk the front sleeve seam into the front bodice armhole until you reach the underarm seam. Use your red pencil to make any necessary adjustments.

Step 12G
Repeat these steps for the back sleeve by walking the back sleeve into the armhole of the back bodice, making sure that the back sleeve fits perfectly into the back armhole.

Step 12H
Looking through the paper, align the back necklines and then walk the sleeve into the bodice's armhole, pivoting with the tip of your pencil as you go until you reach the underarm seam.

Step 13A
Transfer any adjustments to the right side of the sleeve that you made while walking your armhole seams.

Step 13B
To do this, transfer the correction to the right side of the sleeve in red pencil.

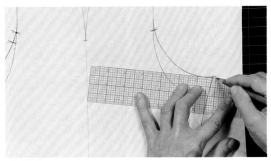

Step 13C
Then re-true the underarm/armhole intersection, as shown.

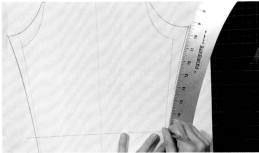

Step 13D
Now re-blend the underarm seam of the sleeve using your hip curve.

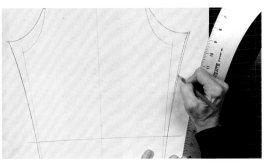

Step 13E
Cross out the original line to avoid confusion.

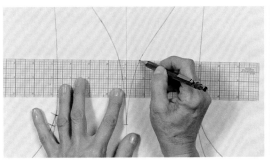

Step 14A
At the curviest part of the shoulder, place corresponding notches on both the front and back dart.

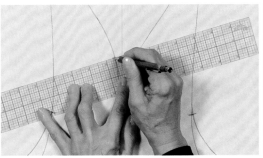

Step 14B
Then re-mark them so that they are at right angles to the seam.

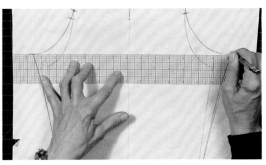

Step 15
Draw a new bicep line, squared off from the sleeve centerline, connecting the new front and back underarm seams.

Step 1

To create a two-piece raglan sleeve with a shoulder seam, lay the 22" (56cm) by 36" (91cm) pattern paper flat on the table, with the shorter side of the paper facing you. Find the midway point and place a mark. Then square a line off the bottom edge at the midway mark in the length direction of the paper.

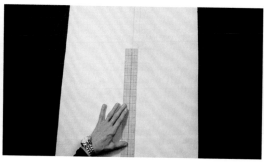

Step 2

Draw a line 1" (2.5cm) away from the centerline of the paper, first on one side and then on the other. This is the front and back shoulder seam.

Step 3A

Measure down 15" (38cm) along the centerline from the top of the paper.

Step 3B

Then square a line across the paper. This represents the sleeve's bicep line.

Step 4A

Next you will position the one-piece raglan sleeve draft so that the intersection of the centerline and front sleeve bicep line matches up with ...

... the shoulder/bicep line intersection on the right side of the block's centerline.

Step 4B

Looking through the paper, make sure that all of the points align. Then add weights to hold the layers in place.

Step 5A

Next, trace the front sleeve onto the paper below, starting at the sleeve hem/centerline intersection, working up to the underarm.

Step 5B

Trace the elbow with a notch.

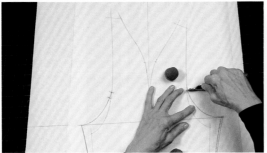

Step 5C
Trace the front armhole to the neck, and mark the front sleeve notch.

Step 5D
Trace the dart vanishing point. Trace along the shoulder seam above the dart to the neckline. And then trace along the front sleeve neckline.

Step 5E
Make sure that you have traced all of the front sleeve notches, including the shoulder notch above the dart.

Step 5F
Trace a cross-mark at the front elbow/centerline intersection.

Step 6A
Now remove the weights and reposition the one-piece sleeve draft to repeat the process, this time aligning the back sleeve's bicep/centerline intersection with the paper block's bicep/shoulder intersection.

Step 6B
Once the bicep and centerlines have been lined up, secure the layers with weights.

Step 7A
Trace the back sleeve onto the paper below, starting with a cross-mark at the underarm/hem intersection. Then continue to trace the underarm seam to the armhole.

Step 7B
Trace the back armhole and the back notches.

Step 7C
Trace the dart vanishing point.

Step 7D
Trace the back shoulder above the dart, and the back neckline.

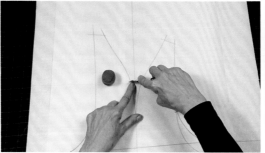

Step 7E
Make sure you remember to trace the shoulder notch above the dart vanishing point.

Step 7F
Trace a cross-mark at the elbow/centerline intersection.

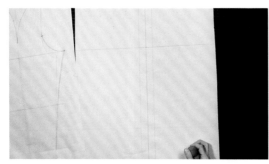

Step 7G
Now remove the weights and separate the sleeve from the draft below, in preparation for trueing the two-piece sleeve.

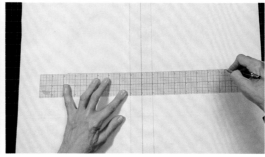

Step 8A
Start by connecting the elbow marks at the underarm seam, front to back, making sure the line is at a right angle to the centerline.

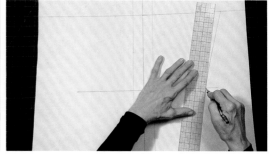

Step 8B
Mark the front underarm seam, following the tracing marks, from armhole to hem. We are using a ruler and pivoting as we draw the curve, but you could also use a hip curve.

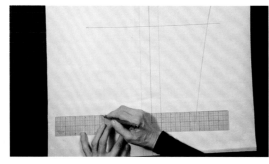

Step 8C
Mark the hem next.

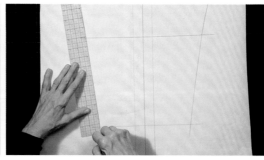

Step 8D
Now mark the back underarm seam, from armhole to hem.

Step 8E
Move to the top of the front sleeve next and mark the front armhole from the neck to the underarm, following your tracing marks. Again, we are using a ruler and pivoting as we mark, but you could also use your curve tools.

Step 8F
Use your hip curve to mark the front shoulder from the neck to the dart's vanishing point. Flip the curve as required to follow the tracing marks.

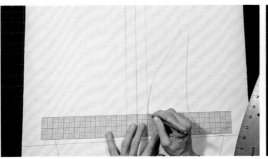

Step 8G
Mark the vanishing point of the front dart.

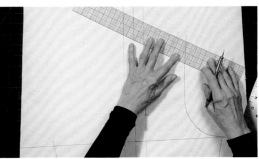

Step 8H
Then mark the front shoulder seam.

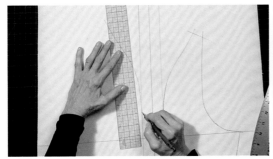

Step 9A
Move to the back sleeve and, following the tracing marks, mark the back shoulder, from the neck to the dart vanishing point.

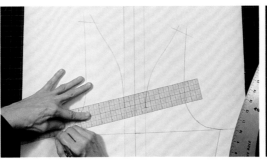

Step 9B
Mark the back neckline and the back armhole from the neckline to the underarm seam.

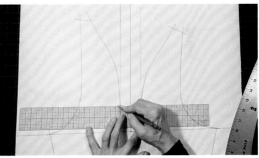

Step 9C
Mark the vanishing point of the dart on the back sleeve.

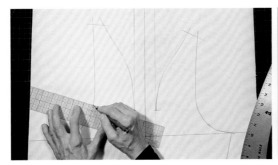

Step 9D
Mark both back armhole notches.

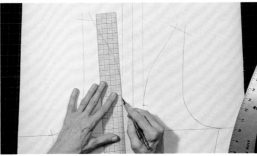

Step 10
Erase and redraw any of your lines so that they are smooth and clean.

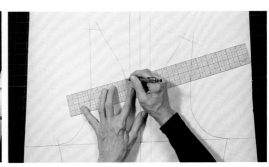

Step 11
Mark the shoulder notches above the dart vanishing point, both front and back.

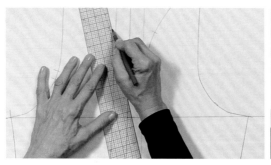

Step 12A
Place a mark ⅛" (3mm) up from both the back and front shoulder mark for wearing ease.

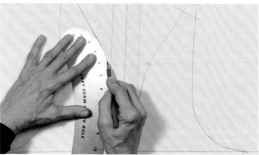

Step 12B
Now blend the shoulder from the back neckline to the new raised shoulder mark.

Step 12C
Repeat this process on the front shoulder, blending from the front neckline to the new ⅛" (3mm) raised shoulder mark. Flip your hip curve to complete the process.

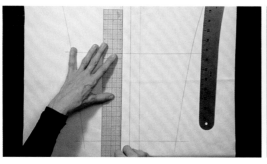

Step 13A
Move to the back shoulder seam and blend a curved line from the raised shoulder notch mark, all the way down to the back sleeve hem. This is the new outer seam of the raglan sleeve.

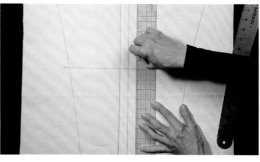

Step 13B
Repeat this step on the front shoulder seam, blending the shoulder from the newly raised shoulder notch mark to the front sleeve hem, to form the new outer sleeve seam.

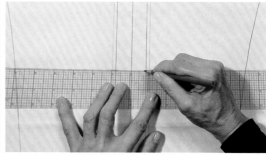

Step 14
Mark the elbow at the back and front outer sleeve seam.

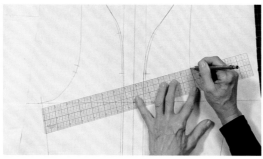

Step 15
Mark the front armhole notch.

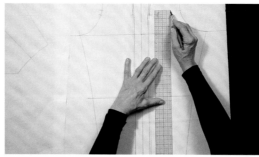

Step 16A
Draw in a grainline on the front sleeve by squaring a line off the bicep line, with arrows at both ends.

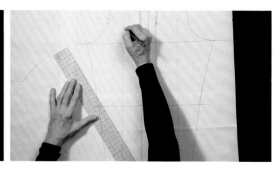

Step 16B
Repeat this process on the back sleeve by squaring a line off the bicep on the back sleeve. Then mark the ends with arrows.

Step 1
Next, you will extract the front and back bodice from the draft. Slip your 12" (30.5cm) by 20" (51cm) paper block under the front bodice portion of the original draft.

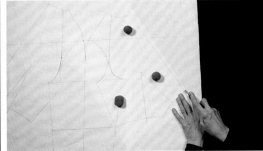

Step 2A
Secure the layers together with weights, in preparation for tracing the front onto the paper block below. Trace a cross-mark at the center front/waist intersection and then continue around the bodice to the armhole.

Step 2B
Trace the front bodice's armhole, following the red pencil line, to the shoulder. Be sure to trace the front armhole notch.

Step 2C
Cross-mark the vanishing point of the front waist dart.

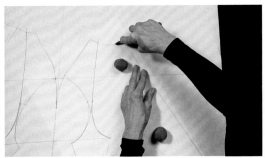

Step 2D
Trace the center front/neckline intersection and the neckline.

Step 2E
Trace the dart intake notches at the waistline. Be sure that you have traced all of the key points, then remove the weights and separate the bodice from the original draft.

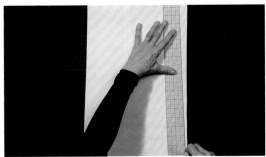

Step 3A
Now mark the tracings on the front bodice. Begin by connecting the center front cross-marks.

Step 3B
Then mark the waist dart.

Step 3C
Square a line off center front at the waistline.

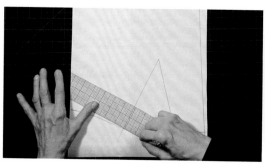

Step 3D

Then mark the waistline with your ruler, pivoting the ruler as you follow the tracing marks. You can also do this with a hip curve.

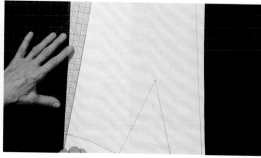

Step 3E

Mark the dart vanishing point and connect the cross-marks at the side seam.

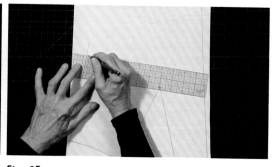

Step 3F

Square off at the side seam/armhole intersection, then reposition the paper to continue marking the bodice.

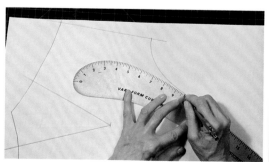

Step 3G

Mark the armhole next. Here we are using our hip curve to mark from the side seam to the notch, following the tracing lines.

Step 3H

Flip the curve over to complete the armhole to the neckline, and then mark the front notch.

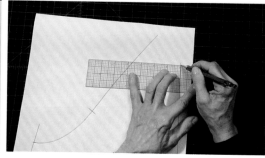

Step 3I

Finish transferring the front bodice by squaring a line off the center front neck.

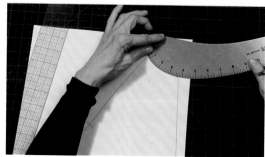

Step 3J

Then mark the neckline.

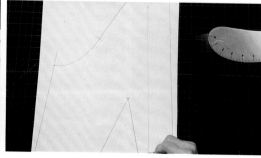

Step 3K

Now add the grainline with arrows at either end, drawn 2" (5cm) away from center front.

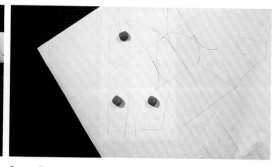

Step 4A

Now repeat the transferring process for the back, by slipping your 12" (30.5cm) by 20" (51cm) paper block under the back bodice portion of the original draft and securing the layers together with weights.

Step 4B

Now you will transfer all of the key points. Begin by cross-marking the center back/waistline intersection and tracing your waistline and waist dart.

Step 4C

Trace the back armhole following your red pencil bodice markings, from the side seam to the neckline. Remember to trace the back notches.

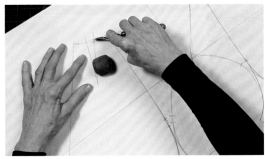

Step 4D

Trace the back neck, cross-mark the center back/neck intersection, then trace the back neck dart. Check that you have captured all of your markings, then remove the weights and separate the back bodice from the original draft.

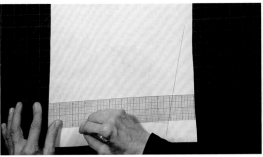

Step 5A

Repeat the process of marking the back bodice just as you did for the front. Be sure to square off at all of the key areas, such as the intersections between center front/back and the waistline, and center front/back and the neckline.

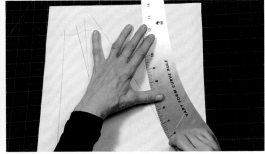

Step 5B

Use a combination of your ruler and hip curve to mark the tracing lines, and be sure to mark all of the notches.

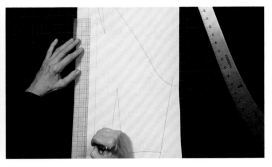

Step 5C

Add your back grainline at 1" (2.5cm) away from center back, drawing arrows at either end of it.

Module 6:

Trueing the Bodice & the One- and Two-piece Raglan Sleeve

Step 1A

Next, you will score your back bodice's raglan armhole, from the neck to the top back notch, with your awl and ruler.

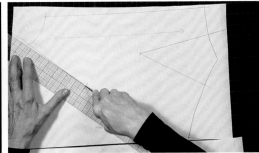

Step 1B

Repeat this step on the front bodice's raglan armhole.

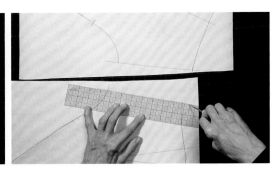

Step 1C

Score the back side seam as well, from armhole to waist.

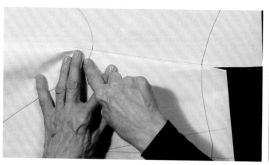

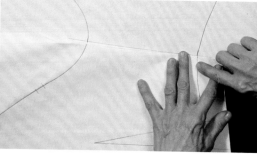

Step 2A

Now fold the back side seam allowance under and match the back side seam with the front at the armhole and at the waist. Make sure that you have a nice smooth curve at the armhole, as demonstrated here.

Step 2B

Check the curve at the waist/side seam intersection.

Make any adjustments necessary using your red pencil.

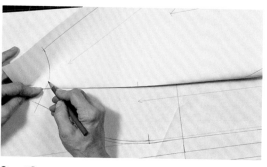

Step 3A

Next, you will walk your front bodice's armhole into the armhole of your two-piece front sleeve.

Step 3B

To do this, fold along the scored seam line of the front armhole, matching the notches as you walk the front bodice into the sleeve's armhole, from notch to neck.

Step 3C

If you find that the seam does not match up exactly, then make any necessary adjustments using your hip curve and red pencil.

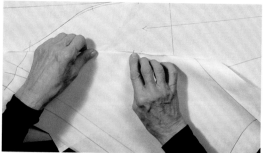

Step 3D

Repeat this step for the two-piece back sleeve. Match up the top back notch of the bodice with the back of the two-piece sleeve's top notch. Then walk the back bodice armhole into the sleeve armhole. Be sure that you walk the seam correctly, pivoting at small intervals.

Step 3E

If you find a difference when you reach the neck, then make any necessary adjustments using a red pencil.

Step 3F

Again, make your correction using your hip curve and red pencil.

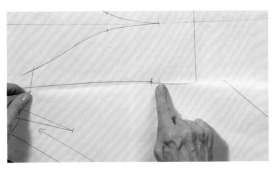

Step 4A

Now you will repeat the process, but this time you will walk the back bodice armhole into the armhole of the one-piece back sleeve from top notch to neck. Make any adjustments if necessary.

Step 4B

Then walk the front bodice armhole into the armhole of the front one-piece sleeve, making any adjustments in red.

Step 5A

Annotate your front bodice with "Front Raglan Sloper" and "Size 6," or whatever your size happens to be.

Step 5B

Annotate your back bodice with "Back Raglan Sloper" and "Size 6," or whatever your size happens to be.

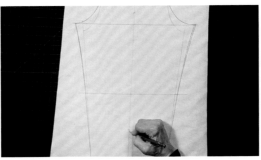

Step 6A

Now draw arrows on the centerline of your one-piece raglan sleeve. This is the sleeve's grainline.

Step 6B

Annotate the one-piece sleeve with "One Piece Raglan Sleeve Sloper" and your size.

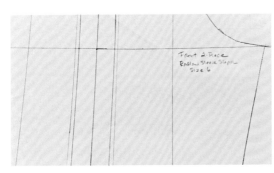

Step 7A

Now annotate the two-piece raglan sleeve in the same way, starting with the front sleeve.

Step 7B

Then annotate the two-piece back sleeve.

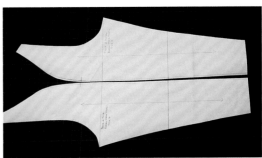

Step 8

Once your drafts are completed, the next step is to cut out each of the pieces. Be sure to cut along the correct lines.

Step 9
Now cut out the one-piece sleeve.

Step 10
And finally, cut out the back and the front raglan bodice.

Step 11
Use your notcher to indicate all of the bodice darts and the armhole notches.

Step 12
Create the notches on your one-piece sleeve at the elbow, the armhole, at the centerline, and on the shoulder.

Step 13A
Then notch your two-piece sleeve at the armhole and along the shoulder and elbow.

Step 13B
You have now finished drafting a Raglan Sleeve Sloper with a one-piece and two-piece sleeve.

Self-evaluation

☐ Have I used my front bodice one-waist dart sloper, my back neck dart sloper and my straight sleeve sloper for this lesson?

☐ Have a placed my slopers properly along the guidelines?

☐ Did I place my sleeve notches in the correct position?

☐ Have I equalized the sleeve centerline accurately?

☐ Are my sleeve and shoulder notches placed properly?

Kimono Sleeve Sloper

Learning objectives

☐ Preparing the paper blocks and marking guidelines

☐ Trace the sloper pieces—tracing the back bodice and moving the back neck dart to the armhole, drafting the kimono sleeve line, tracing the front bodice and moving part of the waist dart to the armhole

☐ Add marks—annotating the pieces, drafting lines, notching key points

☐ Extract the pattern pieces—copying the back and front pieces onto fresh paper blocks, trueing lines, adding notches, cutting out the pieces

Using the kimono sleeve sloper as a foundation, many variations can be created such as this piece by Jotaro Saito. (Fall/Winter 2015)

Tools and supplies:

- Front One Waist Dart Bodice Sloper (see Lesson 3.3)
- Back Neck Dart Bodice Sloper (see Lesson 3.6)
- Straight Sleeve Sloper (see Lesson 1.1)
- Five blocks of white unlined pattern paper

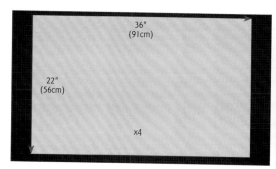

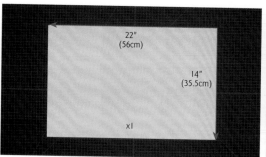

Step IA

To begin this lesson, prepare four pieces of white unlined pattern paper, measuring 36" wide x 22" long (91x 56cm).

Step IB

Prepare another piece of white unlined pattern paper measuring 14" wide by 22" long (35.5 x 56cm).

Step 2

You will also need your Front One Waist Dart Bodice Sloper and your Back Neck Dart Bodice Sloper, both transferred to oaktag (see Lesson 3.1).

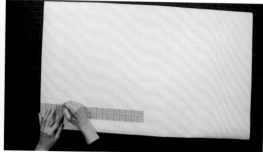

Step 3

And you will need the Straight Sleeve Sloper you prepared in Lesson 1.1.

Step 4A

Take the first piece of 36 x 22" (91 x 56cm) paper and lay it down with the long edge facing you. On the left side, measure in 4" (10cm) and place a mark, both top and bottom.

Step 4B

Connect the 4" (10cm) marks with your metal ruler. This represents center back.

Step 5A

Align the center back of your bodice sloper with the center back line of the paper, 2" (5cm) from the top.

Step 5B

Trace the back neck, from the dart notch closest to center back, across to the center back line.

Step 5C

Then trace the waist, from the center back line to the dart waist notch closest to center back.

Step 5D
Trace the vanishing point of the waist dart next.

Step 5E
Continue to trace the waist, the side seam, and the armhole, stopping at the armhole notch closest to the shoulder.

Step 6A
Now you will close out the back neck dart and move the neck dart to the armhole. Do this by pivoting the bodice from the vanishing point of the back waist dart.

Step 6B
As you close the back neck dart, the dart excess is repositioned to the armhole.

Step 6C
With the back neck dart now closed, trace from the back neck dart, along the shoulder, stopping at the first armhole notch.

Step 6D
Remove the back sloper and note how the dart excess has been transferred to the armhole.

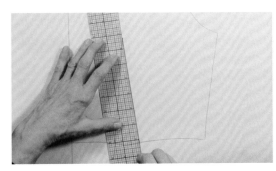

Step 7
Use your clear plastic ruler to draw in the waist dart.

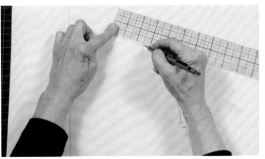

Step 8
Find the midway point of the back shoulder and place a mark.

Step 9A
Next, you will raise the shoulder/armhole intersection. Raise it by ¼" (6mm) and place a mark.

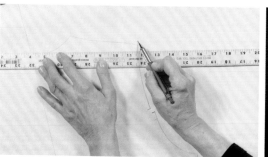

Step 9B
To create the back shoulder and sleeve line for the kimono sleeve, you will connect the midway shoulder point to the ¼" (6mm) raised mark, using your metal ruler.

Step 9C
Draw the shoulder line from the midway shoulder mark, intersecting the ¼" (6mm) mark, across to the right side of the paper.

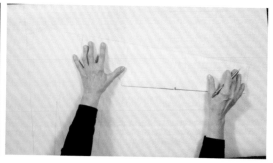

Step 10A
Align the fold of your sleeve sloper with the kimono sleeve line, matching the cap of the sleeve with the shoulder/armhole intersection of the bodice.

Step 10B
Trace the wrist and the sleeve inseam, and be sure to trace the elbow notch.

Step 10C
Continue to trace the sleeve inseam, but stop when you reach the sleeve underarm/inseam intersection.

Step 10D
Place a mark to designate the elbow at the kimono sleeve line. Then remove the sleeve from the draft.

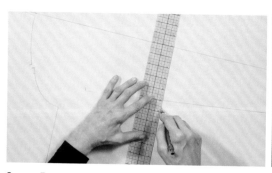

Step 10E
Next, you will connect the elbow line markings by squaring off from the kimono sleeve line.

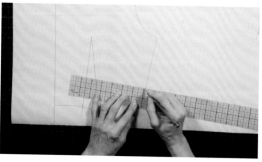

Step 11A
In preparation for shaping the kimono side seam, measure up 2" (5cm) from the back bodice waist and place a mark.

Step 11B
The next step is to create the underarm shape of the kimono sleeve sloper, from the elbow line to your 2" (5cm) mark. You can use a hip curve, although you may find it easier to draw it freehand. You can always erase and refine the curve if necessary.

Step 1A
Begin the kimono front draft by copying your Front One Waist Dart Bodice Sloper onto the 14 x by 22" (35.5 x 56cm) pattern paper.

Step 1B
Be sure to trace the entire sloper, including the dart vanishing point, the apex point, and all of the notches. Then remove the sloper from the paper.

Step 2A
Then connect the apex point to the front armhole notch.

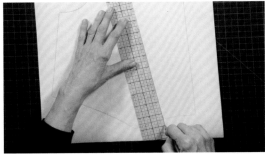

Step 2B
Connect the apex point to the waist notch that is closest to center front.

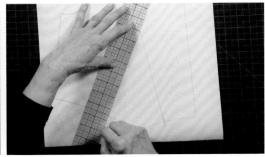

Step 2C
Pivot the ruler and connect the apex point to the dart notch closest to the side seam.

Step 3
Now use your paper scissors to cut out the front bodice.

Step 4A
Cut along the waist dart leg closest to the center front, up to the apex point.

Step 4B
Reposition the bodice and then cut along the armhole line, but stop right before you reach the apex point.

Step 4C
Cutting up to, but not into, the apex point will allow you to pivot the waist dart closed. However, if you should mistakenly cut through, then simply reconnect this point using a very small piece of tape.

Step 5A
Turn the front bodice over and align the front shoulder seam with the shoulder seam of the back kimono draft. Use a pushpin (drawing pin) to secure the front and back shoulder/neckline intersections, as demonstrated.

Step 5B
Now line up the front side seam with the back side seam markings of the draft. Be sure that the front and back waist intersections align.

Step 5C
You may need to clip a little bit closer to the apex point so that your front side seam will lie flat.

Step 5D
Reposition the front side seam, again matching up the front side seam to the back side seam and the waist intersections.

Step 5E
Secure the front to the back with tape at the side seam intersections of the armhole and waist.

Step 6A
Once you secure the side seam, you will notice that the front waist dart will start to overlap, which is fine.

Step 6B
The reason for the overlap is that you will be shifting some of the front waist dart excess into the front armhole.

Step 6C
Secure the front bodice to the back paper draft with tape. Tape down the front armhole, the front shoulder, and the waist dart.

Step 6D
Then tape down the center front of the bodice, at the bottom …

... and at the top.

Step 7A
Using your red pencil, mark the front shoulder/neck intersection, along the front neckline and the center front/neckline intersection, on the paper below.

Step 7B
Now mark the center front/waist intersection on the paper below.

Step 7C
Continue to mark the front waistline on the paper below, indicating the dart intake line closest to center front with a dash.

Step 7D
Locate the front dart intake line closest to the side seam by turning back the paper at the waist.

Step 7E
Place a dash on the paper below, to indicate that front dart intake line.

Step 7F
Now complete marking the front waistline, from the dart intake line to the side seam.

Step 8
Use your awl to transfer the apex point of the front bodice to the paper below.

Step 9
Now carefully remove the front bodice from the draft.

Step 1A
Since you have prepared your front kimono draft over your back draft, you should annotate the back and front draft for clarification purposes. In pencil, write "Back Neck" along the back draft's neckline.

Step 1B
Indicate the center back with "CB."

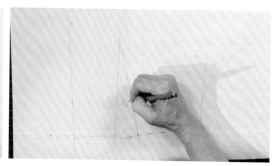

Step 1C
Then write "Back Dart" inside the back dart intake.

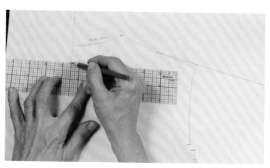

Step 2A
Switch to a red pencil to mark the front kimono draft. Begin at the neckline by marking the center front neck for ½" (1.3cm).

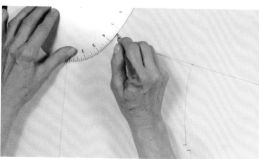

Step 2B
Use your styling curve to connect the marks.

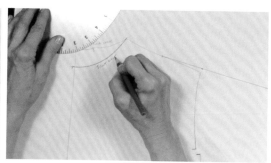

Step 2C
Annotate the front neckline, as demonstrated.

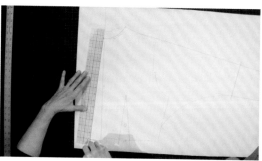

Step 3A
The next step is to draw your center front line, following the red markings. Connect the red mark at the neck to the red mark at the waist with your plastic ruler.

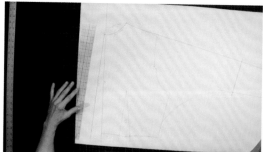

Step 3B
Label the center front with "CF," using your red pencil.

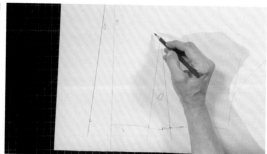

Step 4A
To draw the front dart, you will be connecting the red waist dart intake marks to the punch hole mark.

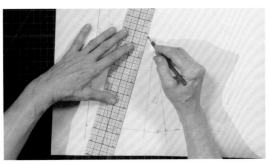

Step 4B
Draw a line connecting the apex mark to the dart intake mark closest to the center front.

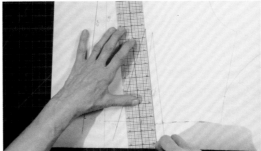

Step 4C
Then pivot the ruler to connect the apex mark to the red dart intake mark closest to the side seam.

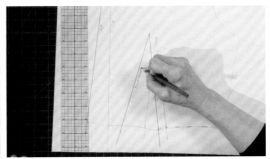

Step 4D
Label this dart "Front Dart," using your red pencil.

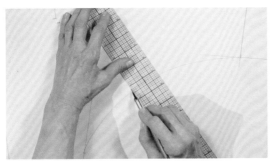

Step 5
At the curviest portion of the underarm seam, draw three notches ½" (1.3cm) apart.

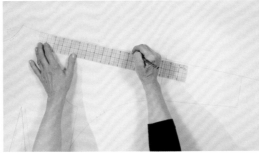

Step 6A
Locate the halfway point between the mid-shoulder mark and the wrist.

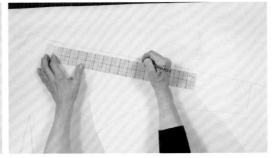

Step 6B
Place a notch on the shoulder line at that point.

Module 4:

Extracting the Front & Back Draft

Step 1A
Place the second sheet of 36 x 22 by 22" (91 x 56cm) white unlined pattern paper on the table, in preparation for extracting the back kimono draft from the front.

Step 1B
Place your kimono draft face-up on top of the paper. Align the edges of the paper layers and secure them with weights.

Step 2A
Now begin the process of transfer-tracing the back draft onto the paper below, starting at the back waistline. Begin at the red front dart intake line and trace across toward center back.

Step 2B
Since you will be using a ruler to draw the center back, you need only trace the center back at the waist intersection ...

... and at the back/neck intersection.

Step 2C
Trace the back neckline from shoulder to center back.

Step 2D
Trace the pencil line at the back waist, from the dart intake line to the center back.

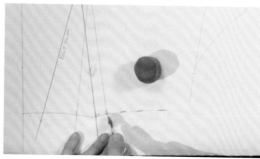

Step 2E
You will also trace the back dart intake at the waist, and the dart intake notches.

Step 2F
Be sure to trace the vanishing point of the back dart and not the front apex point.

Step 2G
Finish tracing the back waist, from the side seam to the dart intake notch.

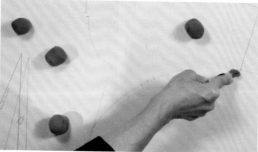

Step 3A
Now trace the side seam, from the waist, along the curve to the elbow line.

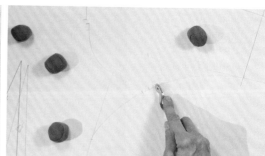

Step 3B
Be sure to transfer the three side seam notches.

Step 3C
Now continue tracing the underarm seam, from the wrist to the elbow line.

Step 3D
Be sure to trace the elbow notch.

Step 4A
Continue tracing along the wrist. As you trace, hold the paper down, as demonstrated, to keep the layers from slipping.

Step 4B
Next, trace the intersection of the wrist and shoulder seam.

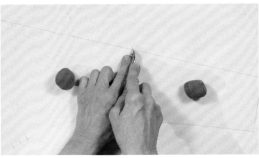

Step 5A
Then trace the elbow line intersection.

Step 5B
Trace the midway notch.

Step 5C
Then trace the shoulder line from that notch to the neckline.

Step 5D
You must also trace the midway shoulder notch. Once you have finished tracing, remove the weights and the draft from the table.

Module 5:

Marking & Trueing the
Back Draft

Step 1
The next step is to mark and true the back kimono pattern.
Start by connecting the back neck and waist markings.

Step 2A
Using your ruler, square a line off center back at the neckline,
for about 1" (2.5cm).

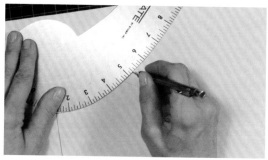

Step 2B
Mark the back neckline using your styling curve, following the
tracing marks.

Step 3
Move to the back shoulder and mark the shoulder to the midway
notch with your styling curve, following your tracing marks.

Step 4
Now use your metal yardstick to true the balance of the
shoulder, from the wrist to the midway shoulder notch.

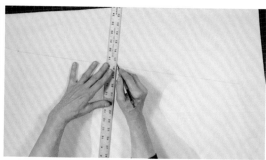

Step 5
Mark the midway notch ...

... and the elbow line.

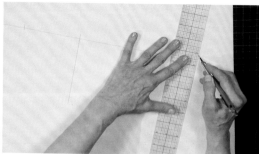

Step 6
Now mark the wrist, from the shoulderline to the underarm.

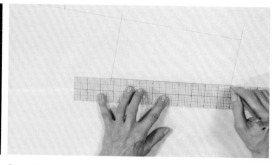

Step 7
Since the underarm seam from wrist to elbow is a straight line,
complete this with your ruler.

Step 8A
Switch to your styling curve to mark the tracing lines along the underarm curve. Be sure to mark the three underarm notches.

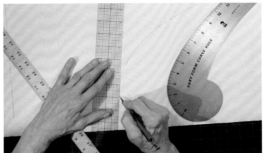

Step 8B
Now flip the curve over, mark the balance of the underarm to the 2" (5cm) mark, following the tracing marks, and complete the side seam to the waist, using a ruler.

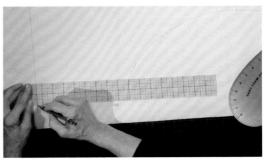

Step 9A
Move to the waist next and square a line off center back to the dart intake notch.

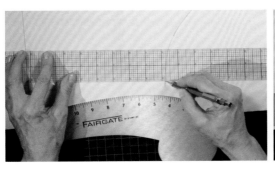

Step 9B
Use your ruler to square a line off the side seam/waistline intersection for approximately 1" (2.5cm).

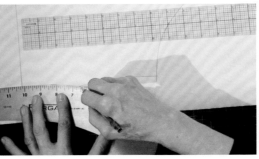

Step 9C
Then use your styling curve to mark the balance of the waistline and the dart intake area, following the tracing marks.

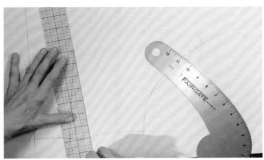

Step 10
Mark the dart notches and then mark the back waist dart, connecting the dart vanishing point to both sides of the dart intake notches at the waist.

Step 11
Annotate the center back with "CB."

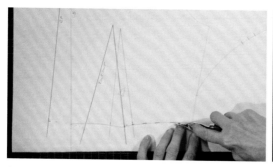

Step 1A

In preparation for marking the front kimono pattern, you must first trace your front lines onto the other side of the paper with your tracing wheel. Trace the front side seam/waist intersection, and along the waist to the front waist dart notch.

Step 1B

Trace both front waist dart notches. The dart intake area will be trued later.

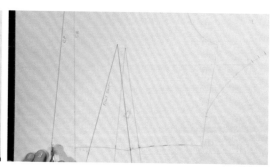

Step 1C

Continue to trace the front waistline to the center front. Then trace the center front/waistline intersection.

Step 2

Now trace the vanishing point of the front waist dart, first horizontally ...

... then vertically.

Step 3

Trace the center front/neckline intersection next.

Step 4

Then trace the neckline from the front shoulder to center front, following the red pencil line.

Step 5A

Place another piece of 36" (91cm) by 22" (56cm) white unlined pattern paper under your pattern draft.

Step 5B

Now flip the draft over, face down, and line up the edges of the paper layers.

Step 6A
The next step will be to transfer the front tracing marks onto the white paper below.

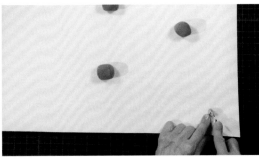

Step 6B
Secure the layers with weights. Then, following the tracing marks, begin the process of tracing the center front/waist intersection onto the paper.

Step 6C
Move to the center front neckline and trace the intersection as well as along the front neckline.

Step 6D
Then continue to trace the shoulder seam, including the shoulder notch.

Because the area between the midway shoulder notch and the elbow is a straight line, you will mark that later with a ruler.

Step 6E
Now trace the elbow line.

Step 6F
Then trace the wrist intersections at the shoulder ...

... and at the sleeve inseam.

Step 6G
Move to the side seam and trace the intersection of the side seam and waist.

Step 6H
Making sure that your other hand is holding down the paper layers firmly, trace the curve of the front side seam and sleeve inseam, all the way to the wrist.

Step 7
Remember to trace the three notches on the underarm curve.

Step 8A
The last step will be to trace the front waistline. Fold the paper over to confirm the placement of the front waist tracing marks.

Step 8B
Now, looking through the paper and following the markings, trace the front waistline.

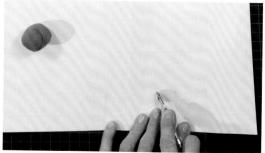

Step 8C
Trace the first dart intake notch and cross-mark the dart vanishing point.

Step 8D
Cross-mark the other dart intake mark, then continue to trace the balance of the waist to the side seam.

Step 8E
Fold back the paper at the waist to check that you have captured all of your markings.

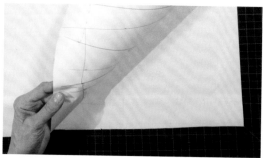

Step 8F
Then remove the weights from the layers.

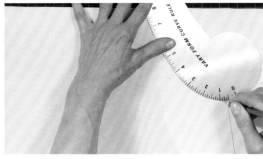

Step 1
Use your metal ruler and draw in the center front of the kimono bodice, connecting the center front/waist intersection to the center front/neck intersection. Label the center front "CF."

Step 2A
Square a line off center front at the neckline for approximately ½" (1.3cm).

Step 2B
True in the front neckline with your styling curve, following your tracing marks.

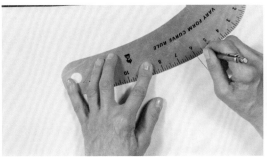

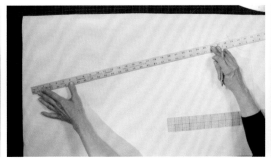

Step 3A
Use your curve to draw the shoulder seam from the shoulder/neck intersection to the mid-shoulder point.

Step 3B
To complete the shoulder seam, use your metal ruler and connect the mid-shoulder notch to the wrist.

Step 3C
Mark the midway shoulder notch.

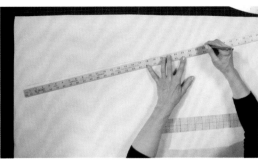

Then mark the elbow notch.

Step 3D
Darken your notches and then go back and re-blend any lines, if you find it necessary.

Step 4A
Mark the wrist and the sleeve inseam to the waist. Here we are using our ruler, pivoting the ruler as we follow our tracing lines. However, for the curvy part of the underarm, you may want to switch to a hip curve.

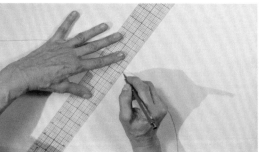

Step 4B
Mark the three underarm notches with your ruler.

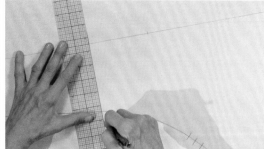

Step 5
Square a line off the shoulder seam to mark the elbow line.

Step 6A
Now you will move to the apex point.

Bodices

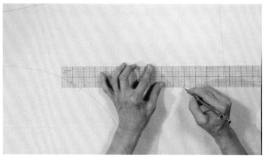

Step 6B
To create the front waist dart, drop 1" (2.5cm) down from the apex point and place a mark. This will be the vanishing point of the front waist dart.

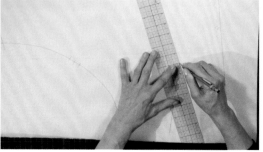

Step 6C
Mark both sides of the front waist dart, pivoting from the lowered dart vanishing point mark.

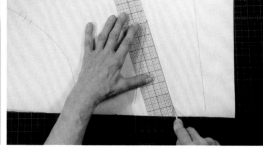

Step 7A
Now you will true the waistline. Start by first scoring the dart line closest to center front with your awl and ruler.

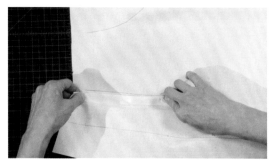

Step 7B
Crease the scored line with your fingers and close the dart, with the dart excess going toward center front. Then secure the dart closed with removable tape.

Step 8A
Reposition the paper in preparation for trueing the front waistline, using a red pencil, from center front to the side seam.

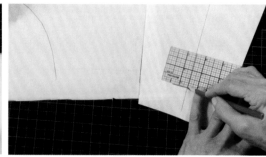

Step 8B
Square a line off the center front for about 1" (2.5cm).

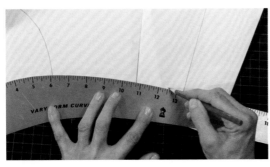

Step 8C

Switch to your hip curve to true the balance of the front waist, from the side seam to the red pencil mark. You will find that your front waistline will change from your original tracing marks.

Step 8D

Mark the new waistline with your red pencil.

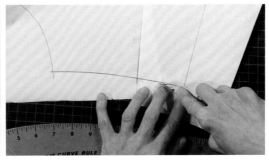

Step 9A

Trace the front waist dart area with your tracing wheel.

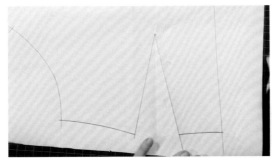

Step 9B

Remove the tape, open the dart, and lay it flat on the table.

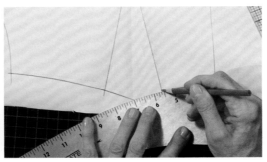

Step 9C

Then true the dart intake stitching line with your styling curve and red pencil.

Module 8:

Cutting Out the Front & Back Draft

Step 1

The next step is to cut out your front kimono sloper draft. Cut along the pencil lines.

Do not cut the excess paper from the front and back waistline, the neckline, or the wrist. We will need to true these areas first.

Step 2

Now cut out the back kimono sloper draft, cutting along the pencil lines, but again, do not cut away the excess paper at the waistline, the neckline, or the wrist.

Step 3A

The next step is to align the front and back shoulder/neckline intersections, as demonstrated.

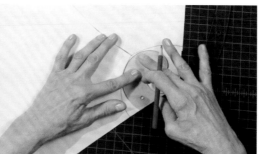

Step 3B

Use your red pencil and French curve to true the shoulder/neckline area so that it is a nice smooth curve.

Step 3C

Now place the front and back waistline side by side at the side seam. Check that the waistline forms a nice continuous curve. Use your hip curve and red pencil to make any adjustments.

Step 3D

Lay the front and back kimono slopers side by side along the shoulder seam next. Match up the necklines, elbows, and wrists.

Step 3E

Use your ruler and red pencil to blend the wrist line, squaring off from the shoulder line, front to back.

Step 4A

Now cut away the excess paper along the back and front wrist.

Step 4B

Cut away the excess paper along the back and front waistline.

Step 4C

Then cut along the front and back neckline.

Step 1
Now you will add your grainlines, beginning with the front kimono sloper. Place a grainline, with end arrows, 2" (5cm) away from center front.

Step 2
Annotate the pattern with "Kimono Sleeve Sloper" and "Size 6," or whatever your size happens to be, and designate it "Front."

Step 3A
Now add the back grainline to the back kimono sloper, 2" (5cm) away from center back. Add the end arrows to the grainline. Now annotate the sloper with "Back Kimono Sleeve Sloper" and "Size 6," or whatever your particular size is.

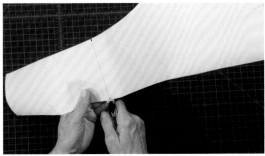

Step 4A
The final step is to notch your slopers with your notcher. Notch the waist darts, the three darts along the curvy part of the underarm seam, and then the elbow notches on both sides of the sleeve.

Step 4B
You should also notch your midway shoulder notch and your shoulder notch.

Step 5A
Then, on your front kimono sleeve sloper, notch all of the same points as on the back.

Step 5B
You have now finished drafting your Kimono Sleeve Sloper.

Self-evaluation

☐ Have I used my front bodice one-waist dart sloper, my back neck dart sloper and my straight sleeve sloper for this lesson?

☐ Did my back neck dart excess move into the back armhole as I closed the dart?

☐ Have I created a nicely curved underarm seam?

☐ Did I slash into the bodice front dart and armhole markings without separating the pieces?

☐ Have I accurately marked and trued my front and back waist darts?

4 Collars

Adding a collar not only finishes a garment's neckline but can also be used as a design detail to frame the face. In this chapter you will learn how to draft the three collar categories: a 'stand' collar, which stands up at the neck, rather than lying flat on the shoulders; a 'convertible' collar, which can be worn open or closed at the neck; and a 'rolled' collar, which rolls along the back neck, conforms to the neckline, cannot be worn open, and rests on the shoulder. The Mandarin and band collars are examples of a stand collar and are the easiest collars to draft. The Mandarin collar sits away from the neck, while the band collar sits closer to the neck.

The convertible collar is a very popular collar due to its versatility, as it can be worn either open or closed at the neck. The Peter Pan collar is an example of a roll collar. In this lesson you will learn how to draft three roll collar variations, each with a different roll and that sit on the shoulder in varying degrees. While this lesson demonstrates a rounded front collar edge, numerous other design ideas using the same principles are possible, such as a pointed collar tip or other stylized versions. The final collar lesson is the sailor collar, which is a roll collar with a stylized wide back.

A traditional mandarin collar is added to a stylized cheongsam by Iris van Herpen. (Fall/Winter 2016/2017)

Mandarin Collar

Learning objectives

☐ Draft the collar—preparing the paper block with marks and guidelines, extracting measurements, drawing the collar

☐ Create the pattern—tracing the collar draft onto pattern paper, adding notches, seamlines and grainline, cutting out the pattern

Tools and supplies:

- Fitted Torso Sloper (see Lesson 3.8)
- White unlined pattern paper—16" (41cm) square

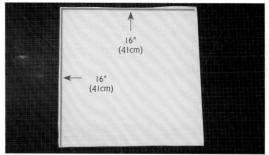

Step 1

For this lesson you will prepare one piece of white unlined pattern paper measuring 16" (41cm) square.

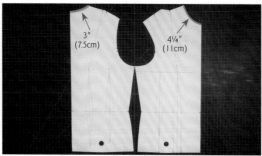

Step 2

You will also need your front and back neck measurement. Here we will refer to our Fitted Torso Sloper (block). Measure the front neck from center front to shoulder, and then measure the back neck from shoulder to center back.

Step 3

Record these measurements in the upper left-hand corner of your paper block. Here, we will record 3" (7.5cm) for our back neck and 4¼" (11cm) for our front neck measurement.

Step 4

Position your L square at approximately 4" (10cm) in from the left edge, which will be center back, and 4" (10cm) up from the bottom of the pattern paper, which represents the neckline. Draw a line either side of the L square for approximately 10" (25.5cm).

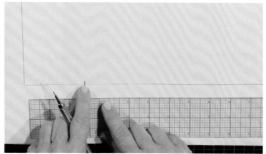

Step 5A

Now use your clear plastic ruler to measure across by your back neck measurement along on your neckline from center back, and place a mark. This represents the shoulder.

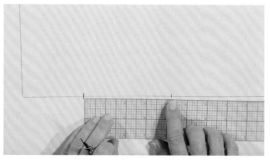

Step 5B

Then measure over, to the right of the shoulder mark, your front neck measurement and place a mark. This represents the center front/neckline.

Step 6A

At the center back, measure up from the neckline 1½" (3.8cm) and place a mark. This represents the collar stand at center back.

Step 6B

We will write "CB" along the center back, and "SH" to indicate the shoulder.

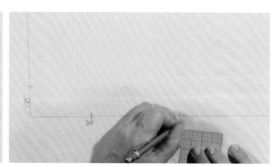

Step 6C

At the center front mark, measure up ½" (1.3cm) and place a dot mark. Write "CF" below the center front neckline.

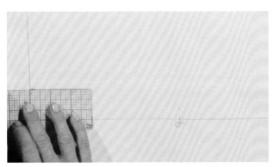

Step 7
Square a line off center back to the shoulder mark.

Step 8A
Now, using your French curve, curve the neckline from the shoulder mark up to the dot that you made ½" (1.3cm) above center front. This is the new neckline. Next we will style the top of the mandarin collar.

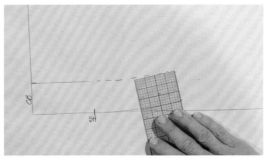

Step 8B
Rest your clear plastic ruler at 1½" (3.8cm) on the new neckline and dot the top line of the collar from shoulder to center front.

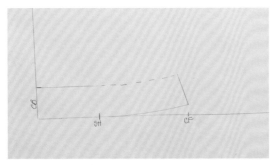

Square a line off the center front neckline to the top of the collar.

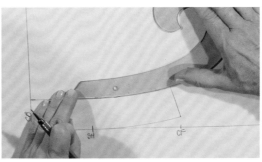

Step 8C
True the dotted top collar with your French curve from center front to the shoulder.

Step 9
Label the draft "Mandarin Collar Draft."

Module 2:

Creating the Pattern

Step 1
We will now cut the pattern paper in half above the collar draft and use the excess to make the collar pattern. To do this, fold the excess pattern paper in half, crease the fold, and flatten the paper with your fingers. The fold will represent center back.

Step 2
Now line up the mandarin collar draft with the folded edge of the pattern paper below.

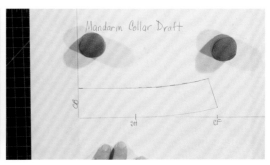

Step 3
Once the mandarin collar draft is aligned with the center back of the second pattern paper block below it, use weights to hold it in place.

Step 4

Using your tracing wheel, trace the collar onto the pattern paper below. Trace the neckline, the center front, and the top edge of the collar, as well as the shoulder notch.

Step 5

Now remove the weights and then separate the draft from the pattern paper.

Step 6

The next step is to pencil in the pattern lines following the tracing lines.

Collars

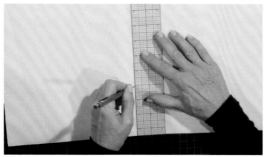

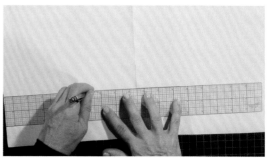

Step 7

Begin by opening up the pattern paper block and laying it out flat on the table.

Step 8

Now mark the center back with your clear plastic ruler.

Step 9A

Reposition the ruler and mark the back neckline, from shoulder to shoulder.

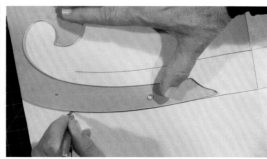

Now mark the top edge of the collar, from shoulder to shoulder.

Step 9B

Using your French curve, follow the tracing marks to draw in the curved lines of the collar's edge ...

... and the neckline, from shoulder to center front.

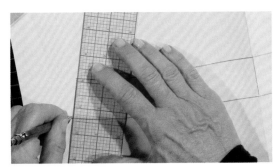

Step 9C
Then mark the center front line.

Step 9D
It may be necessary for you to go back and blend your lines. Here we are using our styling curve and red pencil to blend the collar edge to get a smoother line.

Step 10
Now move to the other side of the collar to repeat the process of marking the lines, beginning with the neckline, then moving on to the top edge, and finally the center front.

Tip
* Depending on the designer's choice, the collar could also be cut in the length grain, in which case the grainline would follow center back.

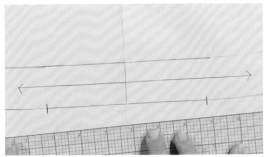

Step 11
The last thing to mark are the shoulder notches.

Step 12
Add the collar's grainline by aligning the clear plastic ruler with center back in the middle of the collar and drawing a line 5" (12.5cm) out from both sides of center back. Place arrows at both ends of the grainline.*

Step 13A
Next, you will add ½" (1.3cm) seam allowance around the entire collar pattern, using a series of dashes. Begin at center front.

Tip
* Although we are using ½" (1.3cm) seam allowances on our collar, production patterns in the fashion industry usually use a ¼" (6mm) seam allowance on collar outer edges, and ⅜" (1cm) at the neckline.

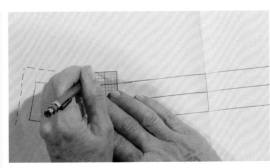
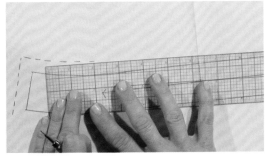

Step 13B
You will find it faster to reposition your ruler and mark the straighter areas of the collar with the long edge of the ruler.

Then pivot the ruler as you get to the curves.*

Step 14
Now annotate the pattern with "Mandarin Collar," "Size 6," and "Cut 2."

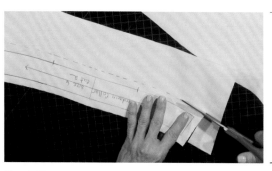

Step 15A
The final step is to cut away the excess paper from the collar pattern, along the top edge of the collar's seam allowance.

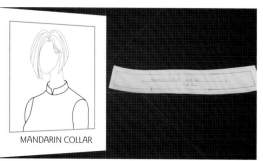

MANDARIN COLLAR

Step 15B
You have now finished drafting your Mandarin Collar.

Collars

Tip
A collar rise for a Mandarin collar (also known as a Mao collar), along the center front neckline, is typically between ¾" (2cm) and 1 ¼" (3.2cm). A rise higher than 2" (5.1cm) will restrict the wearer from lowering their head.

Self-evaluation

- ☐ Have I measured my front and back neckline properly?
- ☐ Did I indicate my shoulder notch?
- ☐ Have I added the appropriate amount of seam allowance?
- ☐ Did I add a grainline?
- ☐ Have I added my seam allowances and annotated my pattern?

Julianna Bass adds a contrast banded collar and yoke to this floor-length evening dress during New York Fashion Week. (Fall 2017)

Band Collar

Learning objectives

☐ Preparing the paper block with marks and guidelines, extracting measurements, drafting the collar

☐ Tracing the collar draft onto pattern paper, adding notches, seamlines and grainline, marking the button position, cutting out the pattern

Tools and supplies:

- Fitted Torso Sloper (see Lesson 3.8)
- White unlined pattern paper—16" (41cm) square

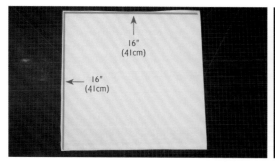

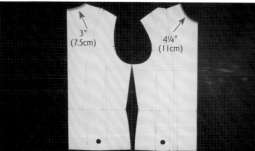

Step 1

For this lesson you will prepare one piece of white unlined pattern paper, measuring 16" (41cm) square.

Step 2

You will also need your front and back neck measurement. Here we will refer to our Fitted Torso Sloper (block). Measure the front neck from center front to shoulder, and then measure the back neck from shoulder to center back.

Step 3

Record these measurements in the upper left-hand corner of your paper block. Here, we will record 3" (7.5cm) for our back neck and 4¼" (11cm) for our front neck measurement.

Step 4

Position your L square about 1" (2.5cm) in from the left edge, which will be center back, and 1" (2.5cm) up from the bottom of the pattern paper, which represents the neckline. Draw a line either side of the L square for approximately 10" (25.5cm).

Step 5A

Now use your clear plastic ruler to measure across by your back neck measurement along on your neckline from center back, and place a mark. This represents the shoulder.

Step 5B

Then measure over, to the right of the shoulder mark, your front neck measurement and place a mark. This represents the center front/neckline.

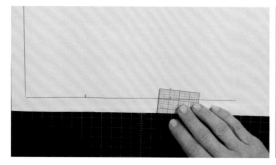

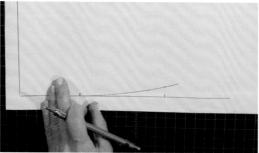

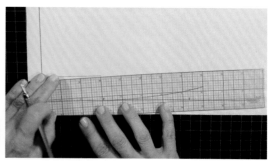

Step 5C

At the center front mark, measure up ½" (1.3cm) and place a dot mark.

Step 5D

Using your styling curve, connect the shoulder to the center front neckline at the mark you just made ½" (1.3cm) up. This is the new neckline. Note how we have extended the line 1" (2.5cm) beyond the center front neck mark.

Step 6A

At the center back, measure up from the neckline 1¼" (3cm) with your clear plastic ruler and draw a line across to the shoulder mark. This represents the top edge of the band collar.

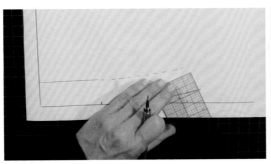

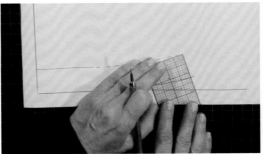

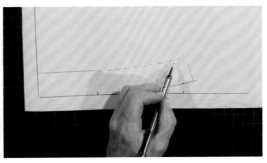

Step 6B

Resting the ruler on the neckline at 1¼" (3cm), pivot the ruler along the new neckline, forming the top edge of the collar, from shoulder to center front.

Step 6C

At ½" (1.3cm) away from the center front mark, draw a partial line along the edge of the collar. This will be the front edge of the collar and the collar extension.

Square a line off to connect the neckline to the top of the collar.

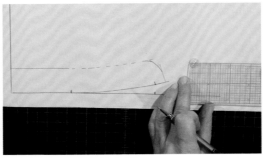

Step 6D

Now position your styling curve and create a nice rounded collar edge. You may have to reposition the curve as you work to blend the curve.

Step 7A

Next, measure the button that you will use so that you can plan for the collar's closure. In this case, we are using a line 20 button (½"/1.3cm wide).

Step 7B

Rest the ruler on the neckline and position it in the middle of the collar width, which for a 1¼" (3cm)-wide collar is ⅝" (1.5cm). Draw a line for ⅝" (1.5cm), starting at the center front mark.

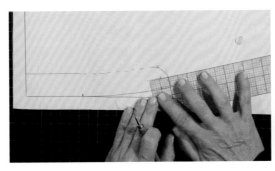

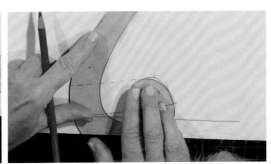

Step 7C

Now measure out ⅛" (3mm) beyond the center front mark and place a cross-mark. This compensates for the buttonhole thread when creating the buttonhole.

Step 7D

Measure back from the center front mark by ½" (1.3cm) and place a cross-mark at the other end of the buttonhole.

Step 8A

Now go back in and perfect the curve of the collar with your French curve and red pencil. Use your eraser to eliminate any unnecessary lines.

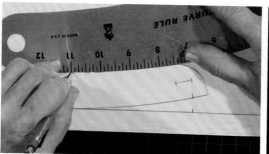

Step 8B
To finish the collar draft, use your styling curve to mark the upper edge of the collar.

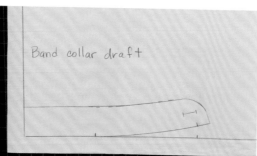

Step 9
Label the draft as "Band Collar Draft."

Module 2:

Creating the Pattern

Step 1
We will now cut the pattern paper in half above the collar draft and use the excess to make the collar pattern. To do this, fold the excess pattern paper in half, crease the fold and flatten the paper with your fingers. The fold represents center back.

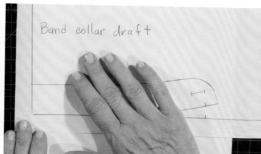

Step 2
Now line up the band collar draft with the folded edge of the pattern paper below.

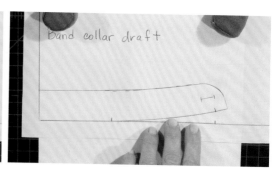

Step 3
Once the band collar draft is aligned with the center back of the second pattern paper block, use weights to hold it in place.

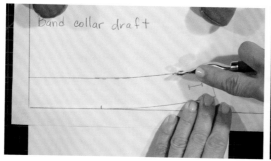

Step 4
Using your tracing wheel, trace the collar onto the pattern paper below. Trace the top edge of the collar, placing pressure on the tracing wheel so that the perforations will be visible on the paper below. Then trace the neckline from front to back, including the center and shoulder notches and the buttonhole.

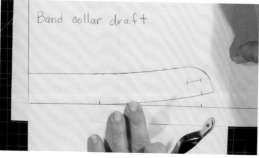

Step 5
Remove the weights and then separate the draft from the pattern paper, in preparation for marking the pattern lines following the tracing lines.

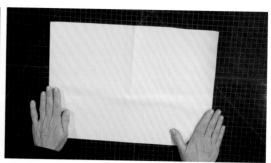

Step 6
Begin by opening up the pattern paper block and laying it flat on the table.

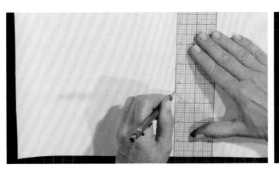

Step 7

Now mark the center back line with your clear plastic ruler.

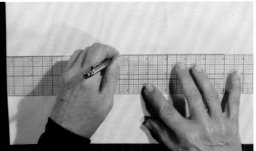

Step 8

Reposition the ruler and mark the back neckline from shoulder to shoulder, and the top edge of the collar from shoulder to shoulder, following the tracing lines.

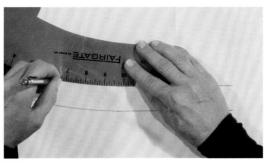

Step 9A

Now, with your styling curve, follow the tracing marks to draw in the curved lines of the neckline from the shoulder to the front edge of the collar. Then draw in the top edge of the collar.

Step 9B

Now mark the rounded edges of the collar. You may have to reposition the curve several times in order to follow the tracing marks and to get a nice smooth curve.

Step 9C

Use your eraser to get rid of any unnecessary lines and to make any corrections on the collar curve and edge. Then re-blend any new lines with your curve or ruler.

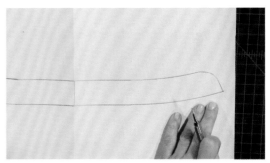

Step 9D

Next, you will repeat the process of marking the neckline of the collar, using your styling curve, following the tracing marks. Mark the top edge of the collar and the rounded front edge of the collar.

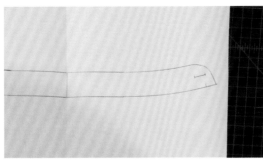

Step 10

Mark the center front notch and the buttonhole, including the end points.

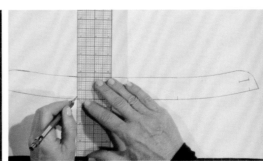

Step 11

Then mark the shoulder notches.

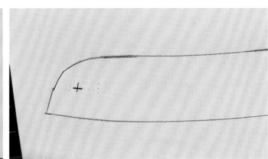

Step 12

Moving to the collar's left side, mark the button placement. This is done with a cross-mark at the end of the button mark that is closest to the edge.

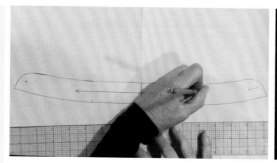

Step 13
Resting the ruler at the neckline at the ⅝" (1.5cm) mark, draw a line for about 4" (10cm) on either side of center back in the middle of the collar. This is the collar's grainline. Add arrows at both ends.*

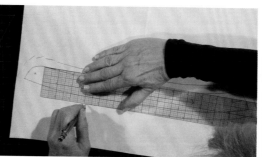

Step 14A
Next, add seam allowances around the entire collar pattern. Start at center front and add ½" (1.3cm) seam allowance using a series of dashes, until you get to the straighter areas of the collar, where you will draw a continuous line.*

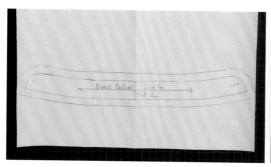

Step 15
Now annotate the pattern with "Band Collar," "Size 6," and "Cut 2."

Step 16A
The final step is to cut away the excess paper from the collar pattern with your paper scissors.

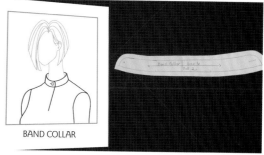

BAND COLLAR

Step 16B
You have now finished your Band Collar draft and pattern.

Self-evaluation

☐ Did I extract my torso sloper's front and back neck measurements correctly?

☐ Does my style line reflect a band collar shape?

☐ Have I indicated my shoulder notch?

☐ Is my collar button/buttonhole positioned properly?

☐ Did I add my collar's grainline?

Convertible Collar

Learning objectives

☐ Preparing the paper blocks with marks and guidelines, extracting measurements, drafting the collar

☐ Create the upper collar pattern—tracing the collar draft onto pattern paper, trueing lines, adding notches, seamlines and grainline, cutting out the pattern

☐ Create the under collar pattern—tracing the collar draft onto pattern paper, trueing and adding markings, cutting out the pattern

Tools and supplies:

- Fitted Torso Sloper (see Lesson 3.8)
- White unlined pattern paper—16" (41cm) square

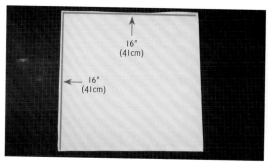

Step 1

For this lesson you will prepare one piece of white unlined pattern paper measuring 16" (41cm) square.

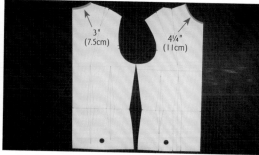

Step 2

You will also need your front and back neck measurement. Here we will refer to our Fitted Torso Sloper (block). Measure the front neck from center front to shoulder, then measure the back neck from shoulder to center back.

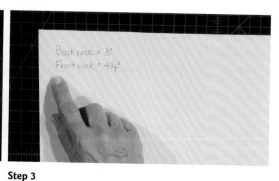

Step 3

Record these measurements in the upper left-hand corner of your paper block. Here, we will record 3" (7.5cm) for our back neck and 4¼" (11cm) for our front neck measurement.

Step 4

Position your L square at approximately 1" (2.5cm) in from the left side edge, which will be center back, and 1" (2.5cm) up from the bottom of the pattern paper, which will represent the neckline. Draw a line on each side of the L square for approximately 9" (23cm).

Step 5A

Now use your clear plastic ruler to measure across by your back neck measurement along on your neckline from center back, and place a mark. This represents the shoulder.

Step 5B

Then measure over, to the right of the shoulder mark, your front neck measurement and place a mark. This represents the center front/neckline.

Step 5C

At the center front mark, measure up ½" (1.3cm) and place a dot mark.

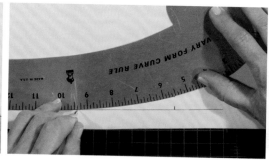

Step 5D

Using your styling curve, connect the shoulder to the center front neckline at the mark you just made ½" (1.3cm) up. This is the new neckline.

Step 6A

At the center back, measure up 3" (7.5cm) from the neckline with your clear plastic ruler and draw a line for approximately 1½" (3.8cm). This represents the top edge of the collar.

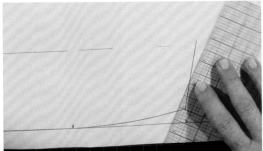

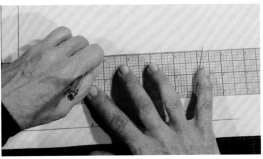

Step 6B
Resting the ruler on the original neckline at 3" (7.5cm), continue to draw a series of short lines from the original neckline, forming the top edge of the collar from shoulder to center front.

Step 6C
At the ½" (1.3cm) dot mark at center front, draw in the desired collar point. This will be the front edge of the collar.

Step 6D
Now use your clear plastic ruler to connect the outer edge of the collar.

Tip
Another collar option could be to round out the collar's edge rather than pointed.

Step 7
Label the draft "Convertible Collar Draft."

Module 2:

Creating the Upper Collar Pattern

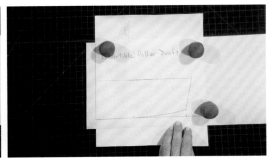

Step 1
We will now cut the pattern paper above the collar draft and use the excess paper to make the upper or top collar pattern. To do this, fold the excess paper in half, crease the fold, and flatten the paper with your fingers. The fold will represent center back.

Step 2
Now line up the center back line of the collar draft with the folded edge of the paper below.

Step 3
Once the folded pattern paper is aligned with the center back of the collar draft, use weights to hold the paper in place.

Step 4

Using your tracing wheel, trace the collar onto the pattern paper below. Trace the top edge of the collar, placing pressure on the tracing wheel so that the perforations reach the paper below. Then trace the neckline from back to front and along the collar point edge, including the shoulder notch.

Step 5

Remove the weights, separate the draft from the pattern paper, and unfold the pattern paper in preparation for marking the traced lines.

Step 6

Using your clear plastic ruler, draw in the center back of the collar.

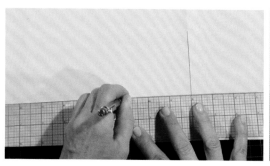

Step 7

Now reposition your ruler along the neckline tracing line, at center back, and then true both sides of the neckline to the shoulder notches.

Step 8

Use your styling curve to true the neckline from the shoulder to the collar point.

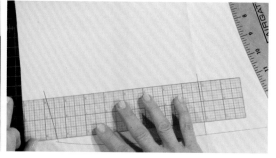

Step 9A

Now trace the collar point with the clear plastic ruler from the neckline to the point.

Step 9B

Mark the edge of the collar next. Here, because the edge of this collar is straight, you will use your ruler. However, when designing a collar with a bit of curve to its edge, you can choose to add this when drafting it.

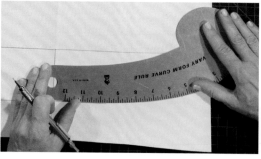

Step 9C

Now repeat the process of trueing on the other side of the collar, starting with the collar's edge, then the collar point, and finally the curve of the neckline.

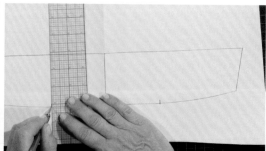

Step 9D

Add the shoulder notch marks, first on one side and then on the other.

Step 10
Now add the collar's grainline in the middle of the collar by squaring a line off center back for 5" (12.5cm) on either side of the center back line. Place an arrow on each side of the grainline.

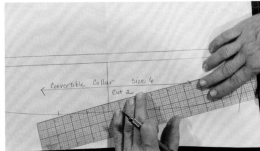

Step 11
Annotate the pattern above the grainline with "Convertible Collar" and "Size 6," and below the grainline write "Cut 2." Finish by adding ½" (1.3cm) seam allowance right round the pattern.*

Step 12
Now cut all around the outer edge of the collar's seam allowance to remove the excess paper.

Module 3:
Creating the Under Collar Pattern

Step 1
To create an under collar for the convertible collar, begin by placing your collar draft face-up on the table.

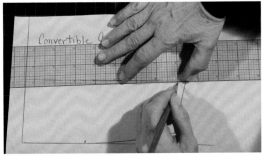

Step 2
Using your red pencil and clear plastic ruler, reduce the collar by drawing a line ⅛" (3mm) away from the edge of the collar, starting at center back, down to nothing at the collar point.*

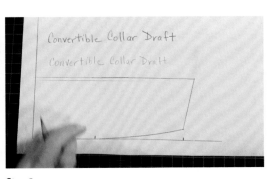

Step 3
Label the under collar draft in red.

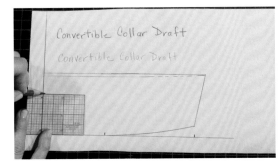

Step 4A
For a better collar roll, the under collar is usually cut on the bias. Mark off a 2 x 2" (5 x 5cm) box at the center back/neckline intersection.

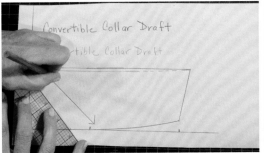

Using the marks as a guide, draw a diagonal bias grainline about 1" (2.5cm) beyond the marks, then add arrows to each end.

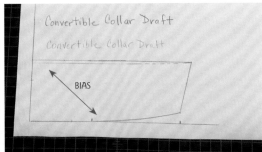

Step 4B
Write the word "Bias" along the top of the grainline.

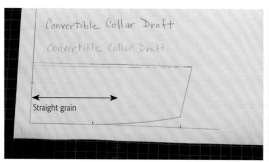

Step 4C

If you choose not to cut your under collar on the bias, then square a line off center back in the middle of the collar and label it "Straight grain."

Step 5

Fold another piece of white unlined pattern paper in half, the same size as your upper collar pattern. Align the center back of your convertible collar draft with the fold on the paper below.

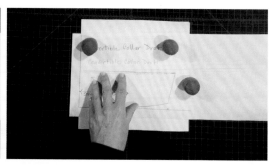

Step 6A

Position weights around the edges of the draft to hold it in place.

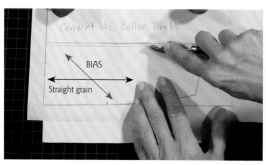

Step 6B

Using your tracing wheel, trace the under collar, beginning at the neckline. Trace the collar point and then along the new (red pencil) reduced outer edge of the collar. Press hard so that all of your tracing marks are transferred to all layers.

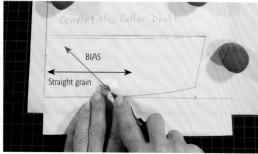

Step 6C

Trace the bias grainline. Then, since we have chosen to cut this collar on the bias, trace the shoulder notches.

Step 6D

Remove the weights and separate the draft from the pattern paper below.

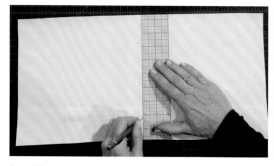

Step 7A

Unfold the under collar pattern paper and draw in the center back line.

Step 7B

Draw in the tracing lines on the neckline, then use your styling curve to draw in the curved portion of the neckline, from shoulder to collar point.

Step 7C

True the reduction of the under collar on the collar's edge to nothing at the point, use your styling curve to true a portion of the outer edge of the collar, and then use your ruler.

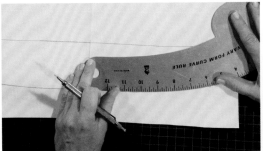

Step 7D
Draw the collar point on the other side of the collar and finish up by switching to your styling curve and drawing the remainder of the neckline.

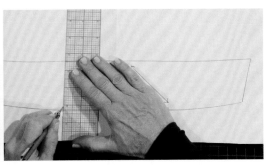

Step 7E
Draw in the shoulder notch, the bias grainline with arrows, and the other shoulder notch.

Another technique is to slide your ruler to true the curve, rather than using your styling curve, as demonstrated here. Just make sure that you follow your tracing marks.

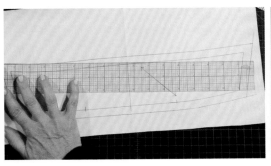

Step 8
Now add your collar seam allowance of ½" (1.3cm), beginning on the under collar's top edge, then working around one side of the collar point to the neckline, then finishing up on the other side of the collar point.

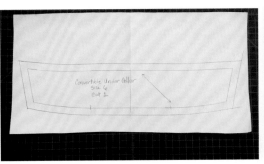

Step 9
Annotate the under collar pattern with "Convertible Under Collar," "Size 6," and "Cut 1."

Step 10A
Cut your under collar pattern out along the outer edge of the pattern and then remove the excess paper.

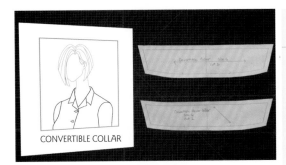

Step 10B
You have now finished your Convertible Collar draft and pattern.

Self-evaluation

☐ Have I measured my front and back neckline properly?

☐ Does my collar style line style reflect a convertible collar shape?

☐ Have I indicated my shoulder notch?

☐ Did I reduce the width of my under collar pattern?

☐ Are my upper and under collar annotated correctly?

Peter Pan Collar— Three Variations

Learning objectives

☐ Preparing paper blocks with marks and guidelines, extracting measurements, drafting a collar with stand

☐ Draft a collar—drawing three collar variations with different-height stands

☐ Create the upper collar pattern—tracing the collar draft onto pattern paper, trueing lines, adding notches, seamlines and grainline, cutting out the pattern

☐ Draft and create the under collar pattern—tracing the collar draft onto pattern paper, trueing and adding markings, cutting out the pattern

Tools and supplies:

- Fitted Torso Sloper (see Lesson 3.8)
- Three blocks of white unlined pattern paper—each 18" (46cm) square

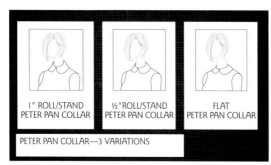

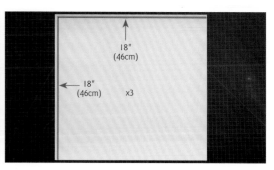

Step 1A

This lesson will teach you how to draft three variations of a Peter Pan collar, beginning with a collar with a 1" (2.5cm) stand, followed by one with a ½" (1.3cm) stand, and lastly, a ⅛" (3mm) stand. Note each collar's position at the neck and how it rests on the body, with the ⅛"-stand collar sitting flat.

Step 1B

We will begin by using our front and back torso slopers, however you could also use your bodice sloper. For this lesson, only use a front sloper with a side seam dart and not a shoulder dart. For the back, only use a sloper with a shoulder dart.

Step 2

To complete a draft and pattern for each of the Peter Pan collars in this lesson, you need to prepare three pieces of white unlined pattern paper, measuring 18" (46cm) square.

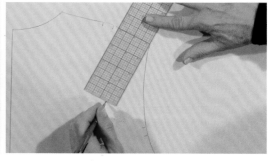

Step 3A

Place your back sloper parallel to the left side of one piece of pattern paper, 1" (2.5cm) away from the edge, with the armhole touching the bottom edge of the paper.

Step 3B

Trace the back sloper onto the pattern paper, starting from the bottom edge of the paper at center back, all around the neckline, shoulder, and down to the armhole. Be sure to trace the notches as you go. Then remove the sloper from the draft.

Step 4

Rest your ruler on the back shoulder at the armhole, measure down 4" (10cm), and place a mark on the back shoulder.

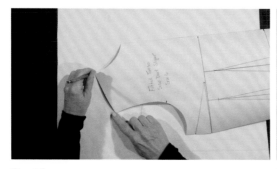

Step 5A

Take your front sloper and match the front neck/shoulder intersection with the back. With your pencil hold down the sloper at the neckline and pivot the front sloper so that the front shoulder meets the 4" (10cm) mark on the back draft.

Step 5B

What we are doing here is overlapping the front shoulder onto the back at the 4" (10cm) mark, which results in creating a less curved neckline and, therefore, a higher collar stand.

Step 6A

Hold the front sloper down with one hand as you trace the front neckline with the other hand, including approximately 3" (7.5cm) of the center front. Then remove the front sloper from the draft.

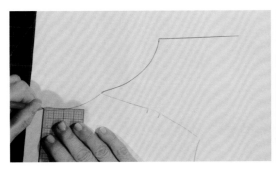

Step 6B

You will notice that the neckline has an odd bump at the shoulder. We will true that a bit later, but first, use your red pencil to square a line off center back, ⅛" (3mm) up from the original neckline, for about ½" (1.3cm).

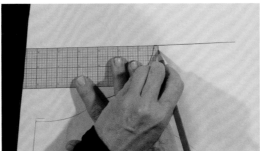

Step 6C

Now lower the front neckline by ¼" (6mm), squaring off at center front.

Step 6D

Use your French curve and red pencil to blend a curve from the new center back neckline, marked in red, to the shoulder.

Step 6E

Then flip the curve over to shape the new lowered front neckline to the shoulder. Mark lightly to establish the curve, and then darken the line with the red pencil once you are satisfied that you have created a nicely shaped neckline curve.

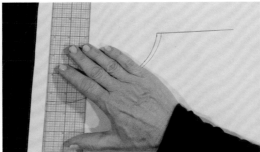

Step 7A

Now form the edge of the back collar by measuring down 2½" (6.3cm) from the new raised center back neckline. Mark the edge of the collar with dashes. Be sure that the collar's center back line is perpendicular to the center back of the draft.

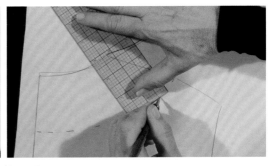

Step 7B

Guide the ruler at the 2½" (6.3cm) mark along the new neckline and fill in the outer edge of the collar with dashes until you reach the shoulder.

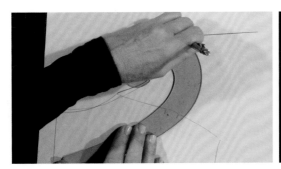

Step 7C

Switch to your French curve to form the edge of the collar from shoulder to center front—or use a ruler if you are looking to create a pointed collar. Position the curve to form the desired shape of the collar edge, making sure that the collar meets the new lowered center front exactly.

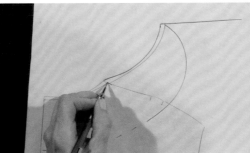

Step 8

Place a notch mark at the shoulder.

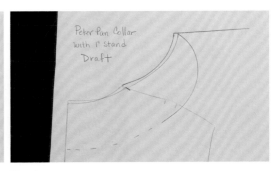

Step 9

In the upper left-hand corner of the paper write "Peter Pan Collar with 1" Stand" and "Draft."

Step 1A

Now we will draft the collar with a ½" (1.3cm) stand. Begin by placing your back sloper parallel to the left side of the pattern paper, 1" (2.5cm) away from the edge, with the armhole touching the bottom edge of the paper.

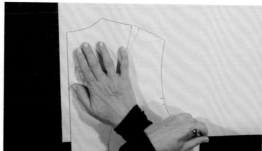

Step 1B

Trace the back sloper onto the pattern paper, starting from the bottom edge of the paper at center back, working all around the neckline, shoulder, and down to the armhole. Be sure to trace the notches as you go. Then remove the sloper from the draft.

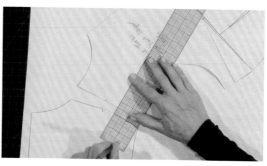

Step 2

Now take your front sloper and position the shoulder next to the back shoulder. Rest your ruler on the back shoulder at the armhole, measure down 2" (5cm), and then place a mark on the back shoulder.

Step 3A

We will now match the front shoulder/armhole intersection with that mark.

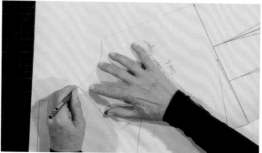

Step 3B

With your pencil hold down the front sloper at the neckline and then pivot the front sloper so that the front shoulder meets the 2" (5cm) mark on the back draft.

Step 3C

By overlapping the front shoulder onto the back at the 2" (5cm) mark, we have created a ½" (1.3cm) stand, which is a slightly lower collar stand than in the previous module.

Step 4A

Hold the front sloper down with one hand as you trace the front neckline with the other hand, including approximately 3" (7.5cm) of the center front. Then remove the front sloper from the draft.

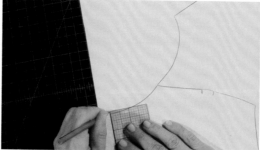

Step 4B

You will notice that the neckline has an odd bump at the shoulder. We will true that a bit later, but first, use your red pencil to square a line off center back, ⅛" (3mm) up from the original neckline, for about ½" (1.3cm).

Step 4C

Now lower the front neckline by ¼" (6mm), squaring off at center front.

Tip

* You need not concern yourself with the back shoulder dart as you mark the collar edge.

Step 4D

Use your French curve and red pencil to blend a curve from the shoulder to the new center back neckline.

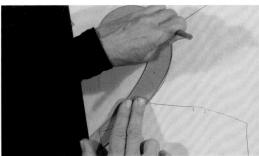

Step 4E

Then reposition the curve to shape the new lowered front neckline from shoulder to center front. Mark lightly to establish the curve and then darken the line with red pencil once you are satisfied that you have created a nicely shaped neckline curve.

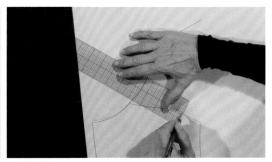

Step 5A

Now mark the edge of the collar with dashes, 3½" (9cm) below the new center back neckline. Keep the collar's center back line perpendicular to the center back of the draft. Mark from center back, along the shoulder, and for approximately 3" (7.5cm) past the shoulder seam.

Step 5B

Use your French curve to complete the collar (or a ruler if you want a pointed collar). Manipulate the curve to find the desired collar shape, but remember to connect to the new lowered neckline at center front. Once you have a shape you like, mark the collar, connecting center front to the collar edge marking.

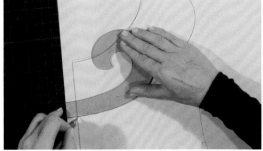

Step 5C

Now you can true the remainder of the collar, repositioning the French curve as you go until you reach center back. Be sure that the center back of the collar is at a right angle to the center back of the torso.

Step 6

Place a notch mark at the shoulder.

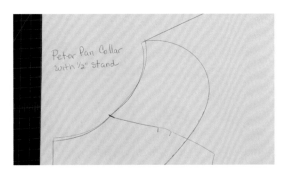

Step 7

In the upper left-hand corner of the paper add the annotation "Peter Pan Collar with ½" stand" and "Draft."

Module 3:

Drafting a Peter Pan collar with a ⅛" (3mm) Stand

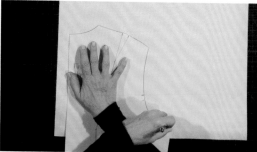

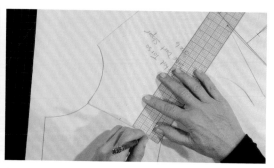

Step 1

Next we will draft the collar with a ⅛" (3mm) stand. This collar sits flat on the body with only a slight roll or stand.

Step 2A

Begin as for the 1" (2.5cm) and ½" (1.3cm) stands, placing your back sloper parallel to the left side of the pattern paper, 1" (2.5cm) away from the edge, with the armhole touching the bottom edge of the paper. Trace the back sloper onto the pattern paper, tracing the notches as you go, then remove the sloper.

Step 2B

Now take your front sloper and position the shoulder next to the back shoulder and repeat the steps for overlapping and pivoting the front shoulder onto the back. But first rest your ruler on the back shoulder at the armhole, measure down ½" (1.3cm), and place a mark on the back shoulder.

Step 2C

With your pencil, hold down the front sloper at the neckline and pivot the sloper so the front shoulder meets the ½" (1.3cm) mark on the back draft. Hold the sloper down with one hand as you trace the front neckline with the other hand, including approximately 3" (7.5cm) of the center front. Remove the sloper.

Step 3A

Using your red pencil and plastic ruler, square a line off center back, ⅛" (3mm) up from the original neckline.

Step 3B

Now lower the front neckline by ½" (1.3cm), squaring off at center front.

Step 3C

Use your French curve and red pencil to blend a curve from the new center back neckline to the shoulder.

Step 4A

Now square a line for approximately ½" (1.3cm) off the lowered neckline with your ruler.

Step 4B

Reposition the French curve and mark the neckline from the shoulder to the new lowered neckline mark.

Step 4C

Mark the shoulder notch next.

Step 4D

Now mark the edge of the collar with dashes, 3½" (9cm) below the new center back neckline. Keep the collar's center back line perpendicular to the center back of the draft. Mark from center back, along the shoulder, for approximately 3" (7.5cm) past the shoulder seam.

Step 4E

Switch to your French curve to complete the collar (or a ruler if you want to create a pointed collar). Manipulate the French curve to find the desired collar shape but remember to connect to the new lowered neckline at center front. Once you have found the shape you like, mark the collar connecting center front to the collar edge marking.

Step 5A

Now true the remainder of the collar, repositioning the French curve as you go until you reach center back. Be sure that the center back of the collar is at a right angle to the center back of the torso.

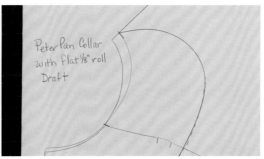

Step 5B

Now notch the shoulder and annotate the draft in the upper left-hand corner of the paper with "Peter Pan Collar with Flat ⅛" roll" and "Draft."

Module 4:

Creating the Upper Collar Pattern

Step 1

Now we will create a pattern for the Peter Pan collar, starting with the upper collar. This process can be used for each of the three collar variations. Fold your second 18" (46cm) square of pattern paper in half and form a crease on the fold.

Step 2

Align the center back of the Peter Pan collar draft with the fold of the pattern paper below. You will be transferring the entire collar draft, so be sure you position the draft on the paper as shown.

Step 3

Once you have aligned the draft on the fold, use weights to hold the draft in place.

Step 4A

Next, trace the collar onto the paper below. Press hard on the tracing wheel so that your markings will permeate through to the layers below. Begin by tracing the new neckline, working from center back to center front.

Step 4B

Now trace the collar's outer edge, from center back to center front. Hold the paper down with your free hand to keep the draft from shifting. Be sure to trace the shoulder notch.

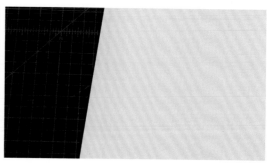

Step 4C

Remove the weights and the draft from the paper below.

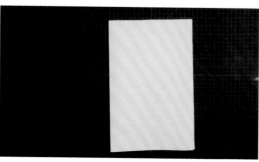

Step 5A

The next step will be to mark the collar pattern following the tracing marks.

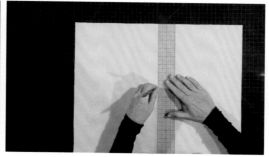

Step 5B

Unfold the pattern paper, flatten the crease, and mark the center back foldline using your clear plastic ruler.

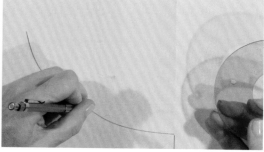

Step 5C

Now switch to your French curve and, following the tracing marks, mark one side of the neckline curve, from center front to shoulder, and from shoulder to center back, repositioning the curve as you go. Mark the shoulder notch.

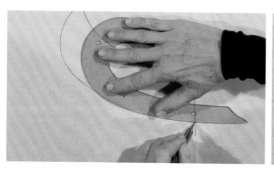

Step 5D

Next, mark one side of the outer edge of the collar, following the tracing marks from center front to center back. You will find that you need to reposition the French curve continually to achieve a smooth line.

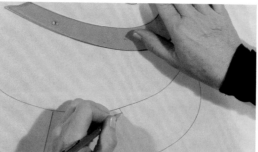

Step 5E

Flip the French curve over and true the other side of the collar in the same way, repositioning the French curve as you follow the tracing markings below. Remember to mark the shoulder notch.

Step 6

Add the grainline arrows to the center back line. Then annotate the pattern with "Peter Pan Collar with 1" Stand," "Size 6," or whatever your size is, and "Cut 1."

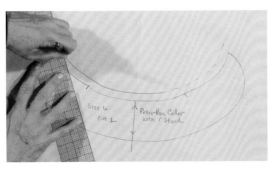

Step 7A

Now add ½" (1.3cm) seam allowance to the entire collar, starting at one end and moving along the neckline. You can mark this in short dashes using the end of your ruler, or you can glide and pivot the long side of the ruler along the collar's stitching line, and mark the seam allowance as a continuous line.

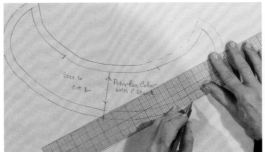

Step 7B

Continue to add ½" (1.3cm) seam allowance to the outer edge of the collar. We are adding ½" (1.3cm) seam allowances here, however seam allowance rules may vary.

Step 8A

Now cut the collar pattern out with your paper scissors along the edge of the seam allowance. You may find it helpful to hold the paper down on the table with your free hand, and let the scissors rest on the table as you cut. Tear away any excess paper as you go to make the cutting process easier.

Step 8B

A tip when cutting is never to lift your pattern off the table. However, you can lift it when you reach the end, or when you are evening out any areas that need trimming.

Tip

For production patterns in the industry, the most common allowance is ⅜" (1cm) at the neckline and ¼" (6mm) around the collar edges.

Module 5:

Drafting the Under Collar

Tip

* Reducing the width of the under collar will prevent the fabric showing on the right side once the collar is sewn. The thicker the fabric, the more you will need to reduce it by.

Step 1

The steps for drafting the Peter Pan under collar are the same for all three variations. Before you begin, you must first true the curved outer edge of the collar draft with your French curve.

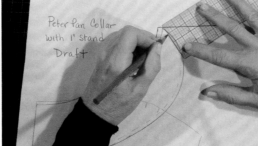

Step 2

Starting at center back, use your ruler and red pencil to mark a broken line ⅛" (3mm) up from the edge of the collar, starting from the center back, all the way around the edge of the collar, and reducing to nothing at center front.*

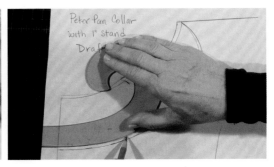

Step 3

Use your French curve to true the broken lines of the outer edge of the collar from center front to center back.

Step 4A
The under collar's grainline will be cut on the bias, for a better roll. To find the bias, rest your plastic ruler along center back and dot both diagonal ends at the 2" (5cm) mark. Then draw a line that is parallel and 1" (2.5cm) away from your diagonal dots.

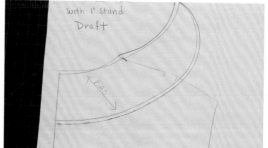

Step 4B
Add the annotation "Bias" above the grainline.

Step 4C
Now write "Peter Pan under collar" and "Draft" below the collar's edge.

Module 6:

Creating the Under
Collar Pattern

Step 1
The steps for creating the Peter Pan under collar are the same for all three variations. Begin by folding your third piece of 18" (46cm) square of white unlined pattern paper in half and form a crease on the fold.

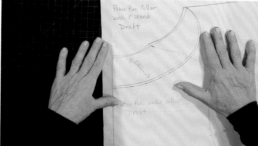

Step 2
Align the center back of the under collar draft with the fold of the paper below, just as you did for the upper collar pattern.

Step 3
Once you have aligned the draft on the fold, use weights to hold the draft in place.

Step 4A
Next, transfer-trace the under collar onto the paper below. Once again, press hard on the tracing wheel since your markings will need to permeate three layers. Begin by tracing the new neckline, working from center back to center front.

Step 4B
Then trace the under collar's outer edge, from center back to center front. Be sure to hold the paper down with your other hand as you trace to keep the draft from shifting.

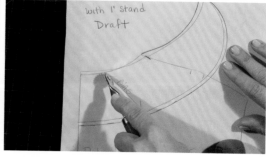

Step 4C
Now trace the shoulder notch and the bias grainline, then remove the weights.

Step 5

Remove the draft from the paper below.

Step 6

The next step will be to mark the under collar pattern following the tracing marks.

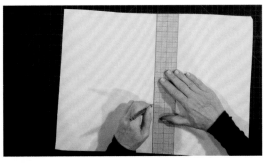

Step 7

Unfold the pattern paper, flatten the crease, and mark the center back foldline using your clear plastic ruler.

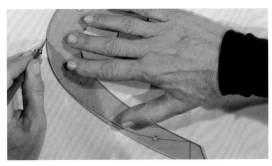

Step 8A

Mark the center back line with your plastic ruler, then switch to your French curve and, following the tracing marks, mark one side of the neckline curve from center back to center front.

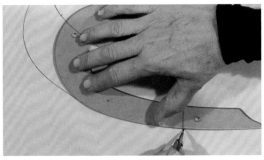

Step 8B

Then mark one side of the outer edge of the collar, following the tracing marks from center front to center back, and repositioning the French curve as required. You can go back later and smooth out the lines for a better curve.

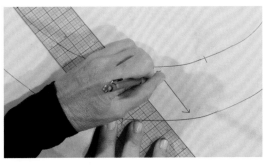

Step 8C

Next, mark the other side of the under collar, starting at center back, moving around the collar to center front, and then mark the neckline. Mark the first shoulder notch, the bias grainline, and then the other shoulder notch.

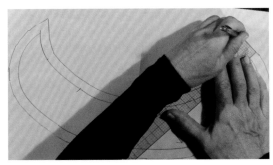

Step 9

Add ½" (1.3cm) seam allowance all around the under collar, just as you did for the upper collar.

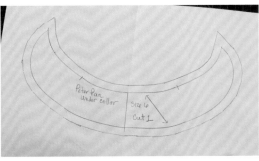

Step 10

Annotate the under collar with "Peter Pan Under Collar," "Size 6," or whatever your size happens to be, and "Cut 1."

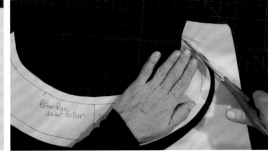

Step 11A

Cut away the excess paper along the edge of the under collar's seam allowance. You have now finished drafting and creating a pattern for three variations of a Peter Pan roll collar.

Self-evaluation

☐ Did I extract my torso sloper's front and back neck measurements correctly?

☐ Was I able to draft each of the three roll collar variations?

☐ Have I indicated my shoulder notches?

☐ Did I reduce the width of each of my under collar patterns?

☐ Have I added the proper seam allowances and annotated my collars patterns?

Lena Hoschek adds a nautical touch to her sailor collar dress shown at Berlin. (Spring/Summer 2017)

Sailor Collar

Learning objectives

☐ Draft the collar—preparing paper blocks with marks and guidelines, choosing the right bodice sloper, tracing the slopers onto paper, drawing the collar

☐ Create the collar pattern—tracing the collar draft onto pattern paper, trueing lines, adding notches, seamlines and grainline, cutting out the pattern

☐ Draft and create the under collar pattern—tracing the collar draft onto pattern paper, trueing and adding markings, cutting out the pattern

Tools and supplies:

- Fitted Torso Sloper (see Lesson 3.8)
- Three blocks of white unlined pattern paper— each 20″ (51cm) square

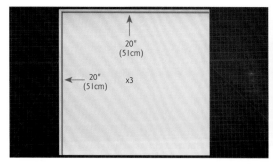

Step 1
For this lesson you will prepare three pieces of white unlined pattern paper, each measuring 20" (51cm) square.

Step 2
For this lesson you can either use your front side bust dart/back shoulder dart bodice sloper, or a fitted torso sloper with a back shoulder dart and a front side bust dart torso sloper. For directions on how to pivot your shoulder dart to the side seam, see Lesson 3.2. Make sure, though, you use a front sloper that has a side seam dart and not one with a shoulder dart.

For the back, use only a sloper with a shoulder dart.

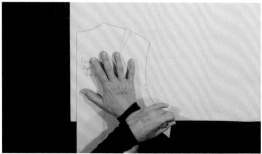

Step 3A
Place your back sloper parallel to and 1" (2.5cm) away from the left edge of the paper, with the armhole touching the paper's bottom edge. Trace the sloper, working from the bottom edge of the paper at center back, around the neckline, shoulder, and down to the armhole, including the notches.

Step 3B
Rest your ruler on the back shoulder at the armhole, measure down ½" (1.3cm), and place a mark on the back shoulder.

Step 3C
Take your front sloper and match the front neck/shoulder intersection with the back. With your pencil, hold down the sloper at the neckline and pivot the sloper so that the front shoulder meets the ½" (1.3cm) mark on the back draft.

Step 3D
Hold the front sloper down with one hand as you trace the front neckline and the center front to the bust level with your other hand.

Step 3E
Now trace the front armhole onto the draft below, from the shoulder to approximately 2" (5cm) past the front armhole notch. Then remove the front sloper from the draft.

Because we are using a back sloper with a shoulder dart, our front and back shoulder do not align. Do not worry about this.

Step 4A

Using your clear plastic ruler and red pencil, square a line for about ½" (1.3cm) off center back, ⅛" (3mm) up from the original neckline.

Step 4B

Now lower the front neckline. Measure 5½" (14cm) down from the center front/neckline intersection and place a mark.

Step 5A

At this mark, connect a line to the shoulder/neckline intersection, creating the sailor collar's front neckline. Then indicate the shoulder notch with your red pencil.

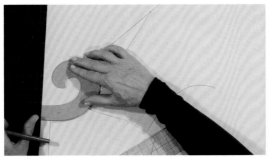

Step 5B

Next, you will true the raised back neckline using your French curve. True from the shoulder seam to the center back. Be sure that center back remains at a right angle.

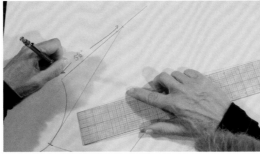

Step 5C

Annotate the draft to indicate that the neckline has been lowered by 5½" (14cm).

Step 6A

Now move to the back and use your ruler to square off 7" (18cm) from the center back/neckline intersection down the center back. Place a mark.

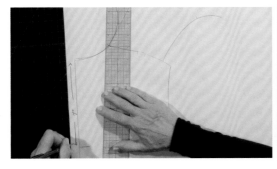

Record this measurement on the draft and add arrows to indicate the depth of the back sailor collar.

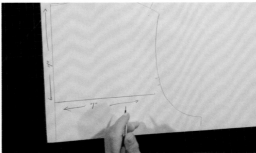

Step 6B

Square a 7" (18cm) line off center back, from the 7" (18cm) mark, and record this measurement below the line with arrows. This is the width of the back sailor collar.

Step 6C

Using your L square, draw a line connecting the outer edge of the back sailor collar, closest to the armhole, to the lowered neckline mark. Note that the collar should be squared at the collar edge and at the center back, as demonstrated here.

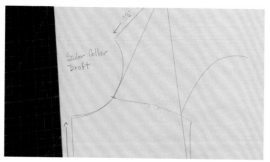

Stylized sailor collars can include a front bow tie, a rounded back collar, a scalloped collar edge or any style variation that you can imagine.

Step 7
In the upper left-hand corner of the paper, add the label "Sailor Collar Draft."

Module 2:
Creating the Collar Pattern

Step 1
Take your second piece of 20" (51cm)-square pattern paper, fold it in half, and crease the folded edge with your fingers.

Step 2A
Align the center back of the sailor collar draft with the foldline of the paper below while also matching the top and bottom edges.

Step 2B
Use weights to help hold the draft in place.

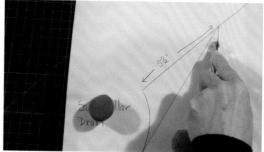

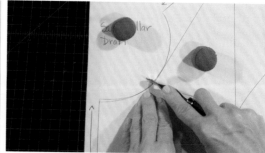

Step 3A
Now, using your tracing wheel, trace the neckline of the collar, from center back down to the lowered neckline at center front. Press hard on the tracing wheel since the impressions you are making will have to go through three paper layers.

Step 3B
Then transfer-trace the collar's edge, starting at center back and working all around the edge until you reach center front.

Trace the shoulder notch and then remove the draft from the paper below.

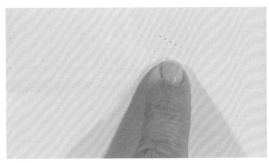

Step 4A

The next step is to draw the pattern lines following your transfer-trace lines.

Step 4B

Using your ruler, and following the tracing lines, draw in the edge of the back collar.

Step 4C

Then move to the outer edge of the collar. Connect the outer edge of the collar to the lowered center front mark, following the tracing lines.

Step 4D

Now move to the back neckline and square a line across for ½" (1.3cm), then draw the curve of the neckline with your French curve, from shoulder to the ½" (1.3cm) center back mark.

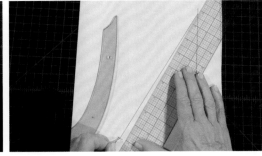

Step 4E

Using your plastic ruler, connect the shoulder to the center front, following the tracing lines. Then mark the shoulder notch.

Step 5A

Once you have drawn in all of your transfer tracing lines, unfold the paper and draw a line along the center back of the sailor collar from top to bottom.

Step 5B

Now you will trace off the other side of the collar, beginning with the outer edge of the back collar.

Step 5C

Draw the side edge of the collar, from the bottom of the collar to the center front.

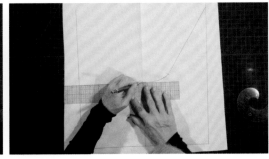

Step 5D

Then move to the back neckline and square a line for ½" (1.3cm) off center back.

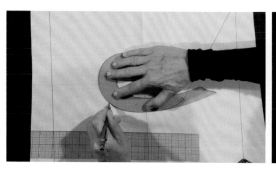

Next, begin the process of using your French curve to draw in the tracing lines from the center back line to the shoulder.

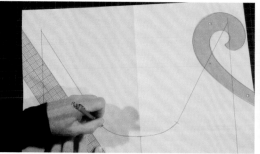

Then switch to your plastic ruler to complete the process of transferring the tracing line from the shoulder to center front. Draw in the shoulder notch.

Step 6A
Add grainline arrows to the center back line.

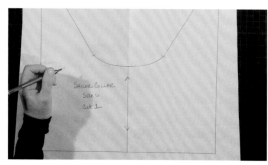

Step 6B
Annotate the pattern on the back collar under the neckline with "Sailor Collar," "Size 6," or whatever your size is, and "Cut 1."

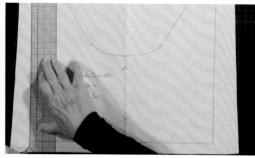

Step 6C
Now add ½" (1.3cm) seam allowance all around the outer edge of the sailor collar using your clear plastic ruler. Start on one side of the collar, adding seam allowance from the center front to the bottom edge.

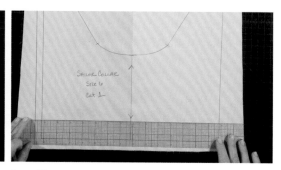

Step 6D
Then add seam allowance across the bottom of the collar.

Step 6E
Add seam allowance to the other side of the collar.

Step 6F
Then begin to add seam allowance to the neckline on one side, at the center front.

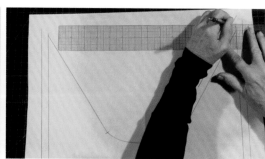

Step 6G
Note how we are squaring off at the neckline point.

Step 6H
Continue working down this side of the front neckline to the center back. Glide the ruler at the ½" (1.3cm) mark along the straight edges, and switch to short dashed lines as you progress from the shoulder to the center back.

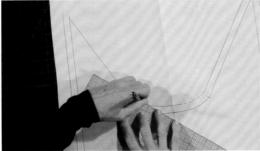

You can also pivot the ruler around curves to make a continuous line rather than dashes.

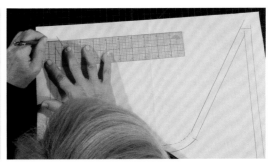

Step 6I
Continue up the other side of the neckline, from shoulder to center front, squaring off the center front point with ½" (1.3cm) seam allowance.

Step 7
Cut out your sailor collar pattern by cutting away the excess paper along the outer edge of your seam allowance line, all around the collar.

Tip
Although we are using ½" (1.3cm) seam allowances on our collar, production patterns in the fashion industry usually use a ¼" (6mm) seam allowance on collar outer edges, and ⅜" (1cm) at the neckline.

Module 3:
Drafting the Under Collar

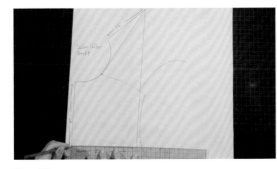

Step 1A
To draft the under collar, you will start by reducing the collar length by ⅛" (3mm) using your red pencil. Place the ruler ⅛" (3mm) up from the bottom of the collar and draw a line.

Step 1B
Then reduce the outer edge of the collar by ⅛" (3mm) to nothing at center front. Start at the bottom collar edge and draw a line that starts at ⅛" (3mm) away from the edge but will end exactly at the center front.

Step 2
Now add the grainline by drawing a line 2" (5cm) away from center back.

Step 3
Label the under collar draft in the upper left-hand corner of the paper with "Sailor Under Collar Draft."

Step 4A
To pattern the under collar you need to trace off all of the red lines onto a separate piece of white unlined pattern paper.

Step 4B
Take your second piece of 20" (51cm)-square pattern paper, fold it in half, and crease the folded edge with your fingers.

Step 5A
Align the center back of the sailor collar draft with the foldline of the paper below, while also matching the top and bottom edges.

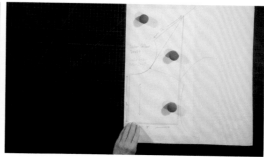

Step 5B
Use weights to help hold the draft in place.

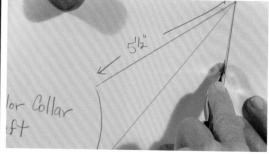

Step 5C
Now, using your tracing wheel, trace the outer edge of the sailor collar, starting at center back and continuing along the outer edge of the collar. Press hard on the tracing wheel since the impressions you are making will have to go through three paper layers. Stop when you reach center front.

Step 5D
Now trace the collar's neckline, from center back to center front.

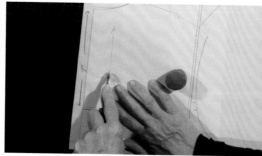

Step 5E
Trace the shoulder notch and the grainline, then remove the weights and the draft from the paper below.

Step 6A
The next step is to draw the pattern lines following your tracing lines. Start by using your French curve to true the neckline from the shoulder to center back, making sure that your center back/neckline intersection remains at a right angle.

Step 6C
Use your ruler and, following the tracing lines, draw in the neckline from shoulder to center front.

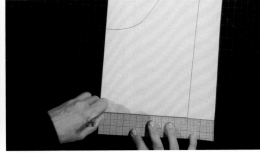

Step 6D
Now, following the tracing lines, connect the collar's outer edge to the bottom edge, then pivot the ruler and mark the bottom of the collar, making sure the center back is at a right angle.

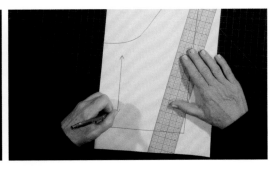

Step 6E
Mark the grainline with arrows top and bottom.

Then mark the shoulder notch.

Step 7
Annotate the pattern with "Sailor Under Collar," "Size 6," or whatever your size happens to be, and "Cut 1."

Step 8A
Next, add ½" (1.3cm) seam allowance all around the pattern, beginning at the bottom of the collar at center back, then down along the outer edge of the collar.

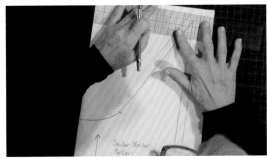

Step 8B
Add ½" (1.3cm) seam allowance to the neckline, to where the center front point meets the neckline.

Continue adding ½" (1.3cm) seam allowance to the neckline until you reach center back.

Step 9
Unfold the under collar pattern and flatten the crease in preparation for marking the lines on the other side of the pattern.

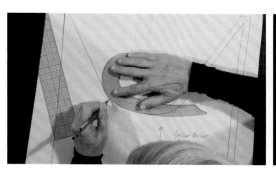

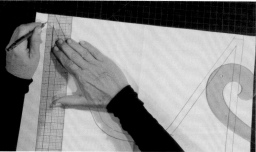

Tip

* Although we are using ½" (1.3cm) seam allowances on our collar, production patterns in the fashion industry usually use a ¼" (6mm) seam allowance on collar outer edges, and ⅜" (1cm) at the neckline.

Step 10

Mark the lines on the other side of the collar, just as you did for the first side. Start with the bottom edge of the collar, following the tracing marks. Mark the outer edge and part of the neckline before switching to the French curve to complete the neckline to center back. Be sure the center back is at a right angle.

Step 11

Add ½" (1.3cm) seam allowance all around the collar, just as you did for the other side. Be sure to add the shoulder notch. We are adding ½" (1.3cm) seam allowances here, however seam allowance rules may vary.*

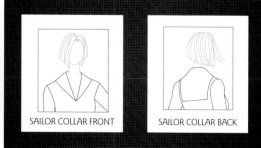

SAILOR COLLAR FRONT   SAILOR COLLAR BACK

Step 12A

Cut out your under collar pattern by cutting away the excess paper along the outer edge of your seam allowance line, all around the collar.

Then pencil in the center back line along the foldline.

Step 12B

You have now finished your Sailor Collar draft and pattern.

Self-evaluation

☐ Have I measured my front and back torso neckline properly?

☐ Does the neckline of my front and back sloper align?

☐ Did I lower my front neckline?

☐ Does the outer edge of my back collar blend smoothly into the center front?

☐ Did I reduce my under collar pattern properly?

Opposite: Laroom added a sailor collar to a sleeveless striped dress for Spring/Summer 2014.

5 Pants

Pants (trousers) that fit well are every women's dream.
In this lesson you will learn how to extract the necessary
measurements, either from a live model or a bifurcated pant
form, and then how to record those measurements on a pant
measurement form in preparation for drafting a basic pants
sloper. We have also supplied a diagram, a plot sheet, and an
illustrated layout, to assist you with this lesson. You will learn
how to plan the waistline, the darts, and the front and back
crotch extensions, also known as the "saddle" of a trouser.
When planning your desired pant hem circumference, we
supply width amounts for both the front and back leg ranging
from a 16" (41cm) to 20" (51cm) ankle width opening.

Once you have finished your pant draft you will cut a fit-
muslin, adding the ½" (1.3cm) seam allowances. Make any
necessary corrections before transferring the sloper to oaktag.
From this pant sloper, you will be able to draft many stylized
pants variations.

Pant Sloper

Learning objectives

- ☐ Extract the measurements—preparing the paper block, style-taping the pant form, taking measurements and recording them on the form

- ☐ Calculate for drafting—using the tables to work out the required measurements

- ☐ Draft the pants—using the measurements to mark guidelines on the paper, drawing the pants pattern, adding waistline darts

- ☐ True the pattern—smoothing lines, adjusting darts, adding notches and annotation, cutting out the pattern

Tools and supplies:

- 48" (122cm) metal ruler
- White unlined pattern paper—36 x 48" (91 x 122cm)
- Style tape
- Pant form (optional)

Step 1

For this pant sloper lesson, you will need to refer to our Pant Measurement Form, and our Plot Sheets 1 and 2.

Pant Measurement Form

Total hem circumference Leg width	
16" (41cm) = Back 4¼" (10.8cm)	Front 3¾" (9.5cm)
17"(43cm) = Back 4½" (11.4cm)	Front 4"(10cm)
18" (46cm) = Back 4¾" (12cm)	Front 4¼" (10.8cm)
19" (48cm) = Back 5" (12.5cm)	Front 4½" (11.4cm)
20" (51cm) = Back 5¼" (13.3cm)	Front 4¾" (12cm)

1. Outseam—waist to ankle = _____

2. Inseam—crotch to ankle = _____

3. Hip circumference = _____

4. Waist circumference = _____

5. Crotch depth = _____ minus 1¼" (3cm) (width of L square) = _____
    plus ¾" (2cm) ease = _____

6. Waist to knee = _____

7. Front princess line = _____

8. Back princess line = _____

9. Waist to hip = _____ (usually 7–9"/18–23cm below the waist)

CALCULATIONS FOR DRAFT

10. Front body width = hip circumference divided by 4 = _____ minus ¼" (6mm)
    = _____ plus ½" (1.3cm) ease = _____ (*1)

11. Back body width = hip circumference divided by 4 = _____ plus ¼" (6mm)
    = _____ plus ½" (1.3cm) ease = _____ (*2)

12. Front waist = waist circumference divided by 4 = _____ plus ¼" (6mm) = _____
    plus 1" (2.5cm) for darts = _____ plus ⅜" (1cm) ease = _____

13. Back waist = waist circumference divided by 4 = _____ minus ¼" (6mm) = _____
    plus 2" (5cm) for darts = _____ plus ⅜" (1cm) ease = _____

14. Front crotch extension = front body width (*1) = _____ divided by 4 = _____

15. Back crotch extension = back body width (*2) = _____ divided by 2 = _____

16. Front grainline/creaseline = front crotch line = _____ divided by 2 = _____ plus ¼" (6mm) = _____

17. Back grainline/creaseline = back crotch line = _____ divided by 2 = _____ plus ¼"(6mm) = _____

PANT FRONT

PANT BACK

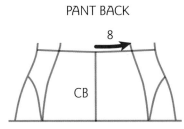

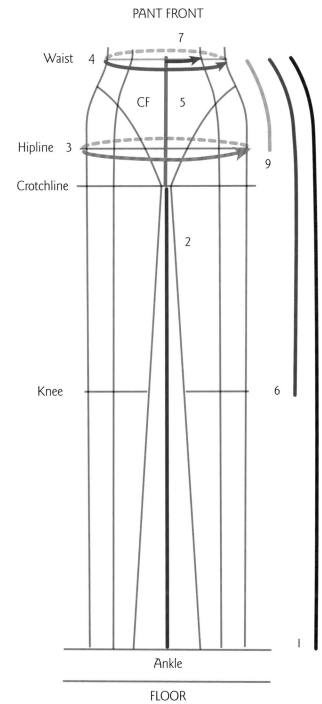

7

Waist   4

CF   5

Hipline   3

9

Crotchline

2

Knee

6

1

Ankle

FLOOR

8

CB

Pant Plot Sheet #1

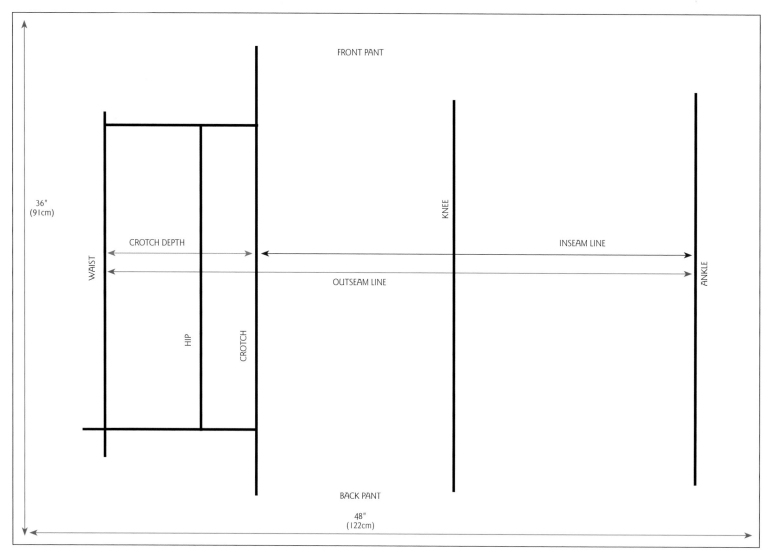

FRONT PANT

KNEE

36"
(91cm)

CROTCH DEPTH

INSEAM LINE

WAIST

OUTSEAM LINE

ANKLE

HIP

CROTCH

BACK PANT

48"
(122cm)

Above: This diagram demonstrates the relationship between key pant lines and intersection variables.

Pant Plot Sheet #2: Pant Sloper Layout

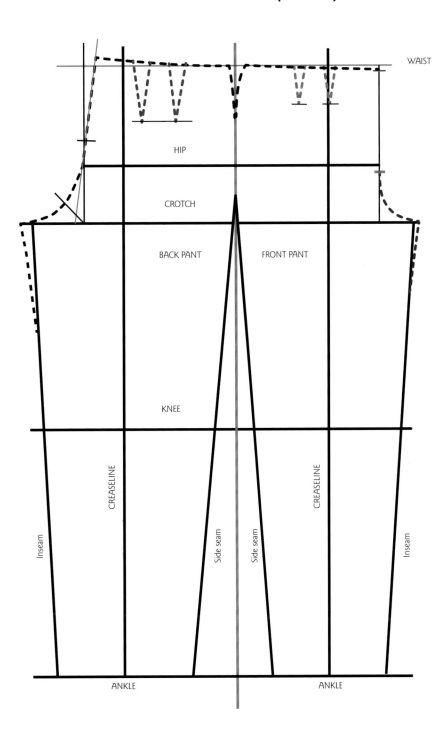

WAIST

HIP

CROTCH

BACK PANT   FRONT PANT

KNEE

CREASELINE

CREASELINE

Inseam

Side seam Side seam

Inseam

ANKLE   ANKLE

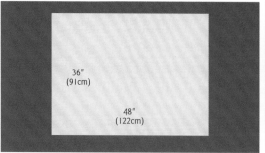

Step 2
You will begin with a piece of white unlined pattern paper, measuring 36" (91cm) wide by 48" (122cm) long.

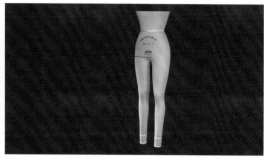

Step 3A
As mentioned previously, we will be using a pant form to extract measurements for drafting our sloper, but you could easily substitute your own body measurements.

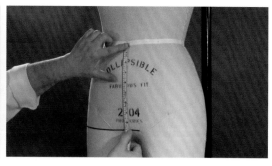

Begin by style-taping the pant form, measuring 9" (23cm) down from the middle of the waist tape on center front. This will be the pant's hipline. The depth of the hipline may vary from 7" (18cm) to 9" (23cm).

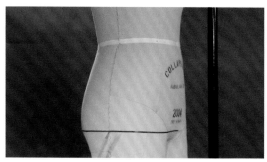

Step 3B
Style-tape the hip parallel to the floor, from the center front to the center back.

Step 3C
You can check the level of the hip tape by resting your L square on the table and turning the dress form to check that the tape is at the same level from front to back.

Step 4
Style-tape the middle of the waist tape from front to back.

Module 2:

Extracting Measurements

Step 1
Next, you will extract measurements from the pant form and record them on the Pant Measurement Form. On the right side seam, use your tape measure to measure the outseam, or side seam, from the middle of the waist tape to the lower twill tape on the pant form.

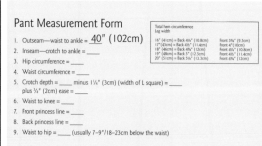

Pant Measurement Form

1. Outseam—waist to ankle = __40"__ (102cm)
2. Inseam—crotch to ankle = ____
3. Hip circumference = ____
4. Waist circumference = ____
5. Crotch depth = ____ minus 1¼" (3cm) (width of L square) = ____ plus ¾" (2cm) ease = ____
6. Waist to knee = ____
7. Front princess line = ____
8. Back princess line = ____
9. Waist to hip = ____ (usually 7–9"/18–23cm below the waist)

Total hem circumference
Leg width

16" (41cm) = Back 4¼" (10.8cm)   Front 3¾"(9.5cm)
17"(43cm) = Back 4½" (11.4cm)   Front 4"(10cm)
18" (46cm) = Back 4¾" (12cm)   Front 4¼" (10.8cm)
19" (48cm) = Back 5" (12.5cm)   Front 4½" (11.4cm)
20" (51cm) = Back 5¼" (13.3cm)   Front 4¾" (12cm)

Record this measurement as #1 on the Pant Measurement Form. The outseam for our US size 6 (UK size 10) pant measures 40" (102cm) long.

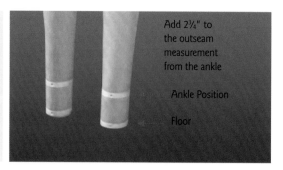

Add 2¾" to the outseam measurement from the ankle

Ankle Position

Floor

You will notice two rows of twill tape at the bottom of the leg. The upper tape serves as the ankle position, and the lower tape, the floor. To draft a pant with the outseam length to the floor, add an additional 2¾" (6.99cm) to the outseam measurement, from the ankle.

Step 2
Measure the inseam of the pant by positioning the tape measure at the center of the crotch and measuring to the ankle. Record this as #2 on the Pant Measurement Form. Our measurement is 30" (76cm).

Step 3
Next, use your tape measure to establish the circumference of the hip. Be sure that the tape measure rests on the hip style tape all the way around the form. Record this measurement as #3 on the chart. Our hip circumference is 37" (94cm).

Step 4
Now measure the circumference of the waist with your tape measure and record this as #4. Our waist circumference measures 27" (68.5cm).

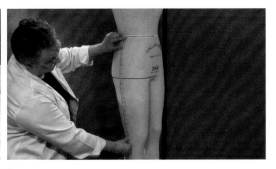

Step 5
Next, position your L square at the crotch to determine the crotch depth. Take the measurement from the bottom edge of the ruler to the middle of the waist tape. This measurement includes the 1¼" (3cm) width of the L square.

Here our crotch depth, including the width of the ruler, is 11½" (29cm). Subtract the 1¼" (3cm) ruler width from that measurement, then add ¾" (2cm) ease, and record this measurement as #5 on the chart. Our total crotch depth measurement, including the ¾" (2cm) ease, equals 11" (27.94cm).

Step 6
Now, at the side seam, measure from the waist to the knee to establish the knee depth.

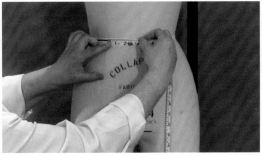

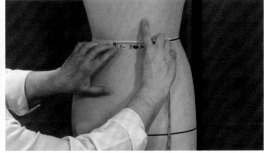

Record this measurement as #6 on the chart. Our knee depth measures 13⅝" (34.5cm).

Step 7
Find the front princess line measurement by measuring on the waistline from the princess seam to center front, and record this measurement as #7 on the chart. Our front princess line measures 3⅜" (8.5cm).

Step 8
Then measure the back princess line from the center back to the princess line at the waistline, and record this measurement as #8 on the chart.

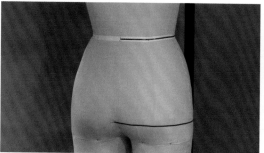

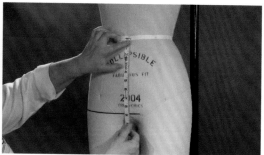

Our back princess line measures 3" (7.5cm).

Step 9
And finally, record your front waist to hip measurement as #9 on the Pant Measurement Form. Our measurement is 9" (23cm).

Module 3:

Calculations for Drafting

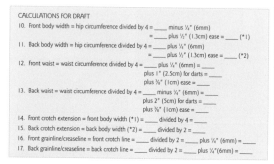

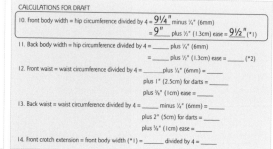

Step 1
Before you start drafting the pant sloper, you need to calculate certain measurements, using the Calculations For Draft section of the Pant Measurement Form.

You may wish to convert your fractions to decimals by using our Fractions to Decimals Chart on p. 88.

Step 2
Our front body width, #10 on the chart, is the hip circumference divided by 4. Ours measures 9¼" (23.4cm). You will subtract ¼" (6mm) from that measurement—which equals 9" (22.8cm)—and then add ½" (1.2cm) for ease, for a total of 9½" (24cm). Add these measurements as #10 on the chart.

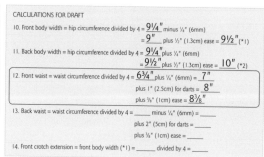

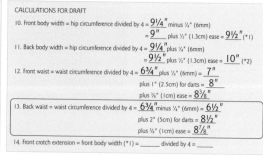

Step 3
Our back body width, at #11, is the hip circumference divided by 4. Ours equals 9¼" (23.5cm). Add ¼" (6mm) to that measurement for a subtotal of 9½" (24.1cm). Then add ½" (1.3cm) ease to that measurement for—in our case—a total of 10" (25.4cm).

Step 4
Next, you will calculate the front waist, #12. Take your total waist circumference and divide it by 4. Here, ours measures 6¾" (17.2cm). Add ¼" (6mm) to that measurement for a total of 7" (17.8cm). Then add 1" (2.5cm) for dart intake and ⅜" (1cm) for ease. Our total front waist measures 8⅜" (21.3cm).

Step 5
Now you will calculate #13, the back waist. Take your total waist circumference and divide it by 4. Ours measures 6¾" (17.1cm). Subtract ¼" (6mm) for a total of 6½" (16.5cm), then add 2" (5cm) for dart intake, to get a total of 8½" (21.5cm). Add ⅜" (1cm) for ease to get a final total of 8⅞" (22.5cm).

13. Back waist = waist circumference divided by 4 = __8"__ minus ¼" (6mm) = __8⅜"__
plus 2" (5cm) for darts = __8½__
plus ⅜" (1cm) ease = __8⅞"__

14. Front crotch extension = front body width (*1) = __9½"__ divided by 4 = __2⅜"__

15. Back crotch extension = back body width (*2) = _____ divided by 2 = _____

16. Front grainline/creaseline = front crotch line = _____ divided by 2 = _____
plus ¼" (6mm) = _____

17. Back grainline/creaseline = back crotch line = _____ divided by 2 = _____
plus ¼"(6mm) = _____

Step 6

To get the front crotch extension (#14), take your front body width measurement—in our case 9½" (24cm)—and divide that number by 4, to get 2⅜" (6cm).

13. Back waist = waist circumference divided by 4 = __8"__ minus ¼" (6mm) = __8⅜"__
plus 2" (5cm) for darts = __8½__
plus ⅜" (1cm) ease = __8⅞"__

14. Front crotch extension = front body width (*1) = __9½"__ divided by 4 = __2⅜"__

15. Back crotch extension = back body width (*2) = __10"__ divided by 2 = __5"__

16. Front grainline/creaseline = front crotch line = _____ divided by 2 = _____
plus ¼" (6mm) = _____

17. Back grainline/creaseline = back crotch line = _____ divided by 2 = _____
plus ¼"(6mm) = _____

Step 7

Next, find #15, the back crotch extension, by taking your back body width measurement—in our case 10" (25.4cm)—and dividing it by 2. Record that measurement. Our measurement is 5" (12.5cm).

13. Back waist = waist circumference divided by 4 = __8"__ minus ¼" (6mm) = __8⅜"__
plus 2" (5cm) for darts = __8½__
plus ⅜" (1cm) ease = __8⅞"__

14. Front crotch extension = front body width (*1) = __9½"__ divided by 4 = __2⅜"__

15. Back crotch extension = back body width (*2) = __10"__ divided by 2 = __5"__

16. Front grainline/creaseline = front crotch line = __11⅞"__ divided by 2 = __5¹⁵⁄₁₆"__
plus ¼" (6mm) = __6³⁄₁₆"__

17. Back grainline/creaseline = back crotch line = _____ divided by 2 = _____
plus ¼"(6mm) = _____

Step 8

You will also need to determine the front and back creaseline and grainline. To do this for the front, add the total of point #14, which is the front body width and the crotch extension. Place that total in the space provided on point #16—in our case 11⅞" (30.2cm). Then divide that number by 2, our measurement is 5¹⁵⁄₁₆" (15.1cm). Then add ¼" (6mm) to get a final total of 6³⁄₁₆" (15.7cm).

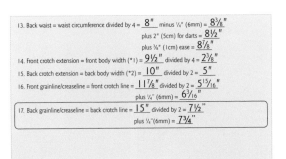

13. Back waist = waist circumference divided by 4 = __8"__ minus ¼" (6mm) = __8⅜"__
plus 2" (5cm) for darts = __8½__
plus ⅜" (1cm) ease = __8⅞"__

14. Front crotch extension = front body width (*1) = __9½"__ divided by 4 = __2⅜"__

15. Back crotch extension = back body width (*2) = __10"__ divided by 2 = __5"__

16. Front grainline/creaseline = front crotch line = __11⅞"__ divided by 2 = __5¹⁵⁄₁₆"__
plus ¼" (6mm) = __6³⁄₁₆"__

17. Back grainline/creaseline = back crotch line = __15"__ divided by 2 = __7½"__
plus ¼"(6mm) = __7¾"__

Step 9

To determine the back grainline/creaseline, add the total of point #15, which is the back body width and the crotch extension. Place that total in the space provided on point #17, in our case 15" (38cm), divide it by 2 for a total of 7½" (19cm), then add ¼" (6mm) for a total of 7¾" (19.6cm).

Module 4:

Drafting the Pant Guidelines

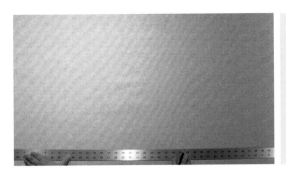

Step 1A

Place your pattern paper on the table, with the long edge facing you and running left to right.

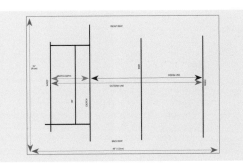

Refer to Plot Sheet #1 (see p.308) for the orientation of the paper and draft.

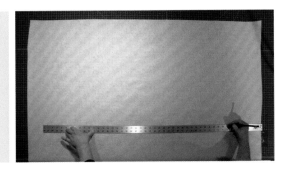

Use your 48" (122cm) metal ruler and draw a line beginning at 4" (10cm) in from the left side of the paper, across the center of the paper. End the line at your #1 outseam measurement and place a cross-mark. This is the ankle. Here our outseam measures 40" (102cm).

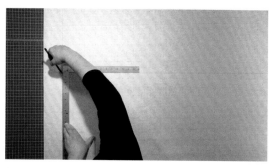

Step 2

Use your L square to square a line off the right side of the outseam line, at the waistline, for approximately 15″ (38cm).

This is the front waistline.

Step 3

Reposition the paper, flip the L square over, and square a line off the outseam line at the waistline for approximately 15″ (38cm). This is the back waistline.

Step 4

Reposition the paper and square a line off the outseam at the front ankle mark for 15″ (38cm), applying the same technique used for the waist.

Step 5

Reposition the paper for the back ankle line. Flip the L square and square a 15″ (38cm) line on the lower right side of the outseam line, to create the back ankle line.

Step 6A

Align your L square with the outseam line and the front waistline. Measure down along the outseam by your final crotch measurement, including the ¾″ (2cm) ease, and place a mark. Our crotch measurement is 11″ (28cm).

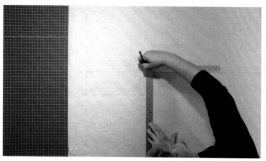

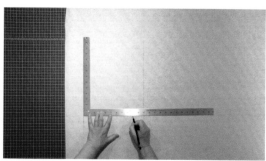

Step 6B

Reposition the L square at the crotch mark/outseam intersection, and square a line for 15″ (38.1cm) to form the back crotch line.

Step 6C

Flip the L square over and square a 15″ (38.1cm) line off the outseam at the crotch mark to form the front crotch line.

Step 7A

Next, you will square a line for the hip, by measuring down from the waist on the outseam line by a hip depth measurement of 9″ (23cm) and place a mark.

Step 7B
Square a 15" (38cm) line from the outseam line, at the hip mark, to form the front hipline.

Step 7C
Reposition the paper and then square a 15" (38cm) line off the outseam, to form the back hipline.

Module 5:

Drafting the Upper Section

CALCULATIONS FOR DRAFT

10. Front body width = hip circumference divided by 4 = $\underline{9\frac{1}{4}}''$ minus ¼" (6mm)

= $\underline{9''}$ plus ½" (1.3cm) ease = $\underline{9\frac{1}{2}''}$ (*1)

11. Back body width = hip circumference divided by 4 = _____ plus ¼" (6mm)

= _____ plus ½" (1.3cm) ease = _____ (*2)

12. Front waist = waist circumference divided by 4 = _____ plus ¼" (6mm) = _____

plus 1" (2.5cm) for darts = _____

plus ⅜" (1cm) ease = _____

13. Back waist = waist circumference divided by 4 = _____ minus ¼" (6mm) = _____

plus 2" (5cm) for darts = _____

plus ⅜" (1cm) ease = _____

14. Front crotch extension = front body width (*1) = _____ divided by 4 = _____

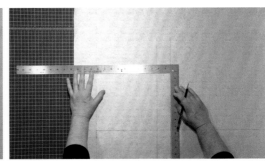

Step 1
Calculate your front body width (#10), using the Calculations for Draft section of the Pant Measurement Form. Take your hip circumference—here 37" (94cm)—and divide it by 4 to get 9¼" (23.5cm). Subtract ¼" (6mm) to get 9" (22.9cm), then add ½" (1.3cm) of ease for a final total of 9½" (24.2cm).

Step 2A
Position the L square at the front outseam/crotchline intersection. Measure over by your front body width measurement and place a mark. In this case, at 9½" (24.2cm).

Step 2B
Reposition your L square at the crotchline/front width mark intersection, then draw a line from the waist to the crotchline.

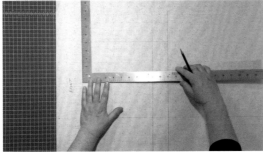

CALCULATIONS FOR DRAFT

10. Front body width = hip circumference divided by 4 = $\underline{9\frac{1}{4}}''$ minus ¼" (6mm)

= $\underline{9''}$ plus ½" (1.3cm) ease = $\underline{9\frac{1}{2}''}$ (*1)

11. Back body width = hip circumference divided by 4 = $\underline{9\frac{1}{4}}''$ plus ¼" (6mm)

= $\underline{9\frac{1}{2}''}$ plus ½" (1.3cm) ease = $\underline{10''}$ (*2)

12. Front waist = waist circumference divided by 4 = _____ plus ¼" (6mm) = _____

plus 1" (2.5cm) for darts = _____

plus ⅜" (1cm) ease = _____

13. Back waist = waist circumference divided by 4 = _____ minus ¼" (6mm) = _____

plus 2" (5cm) for darts = _____

plus ⅜" (1cm) ease = _____

14. Front crotch extension = front body width (*1) = _____ divided by 4 = _____

This is your center front line.

Step 3A
To calculate the back body width measurement (#11), refer to the Calculations for Draft section of the chart. Take your total hip measurement—in our case 37" (94cm)—and divide by 4 to get 9¼" (23.5cm). Add ¼" (6mm) to that number to get 9½" (24.1cm), then add ½" (1.3cm) of ease to get the final width of the back waist. In our case, this final total is 10" (25.4cm).

Step 3B
Position your L square at the back outseam/crotchline intersection. Measure over by your back width measurement and place a mark. In this case, at 10" (25.4cm).

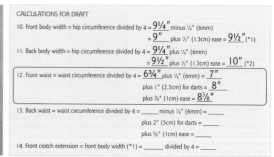

CALCULATIONS FOR DRAFT

10. Front body width = hip circumference divided by 4 = $9\frac{1}{4}$" minus ¼" (6mm)

= 9" plus ½" (1.3cm) ease = $9\frac{1}{2}$" (*1)

11. Back body width = hip circumference divided by 4 = $9\frac{1}{4}$" plus ¼" (6mm)

= $9\frac{1}{2}$" plus ½" (1.3cm) ease = 10" (*2)

12. Front waist = waist circumference divided by 4 = $6\frac{3}{4}$" plus ¼" (6mm) = 7"

plus 1" (2.5cm) for darts = 8"

plus ⅜" (1cm) ease = $8\frac{3}{8}$"

13. Back waist = waist circumference divided by 4 = _____ minus ¼" (6mm) = _____

plus 2" (5cm) for darts = _____

plus ⅜" (1cm) ease = _____

14. Front crotch extension = front body width (*1) = _____ divided by 4 = _____

Step 3C

Now flip the L square so that it aligns with the back outseam/back width mark intersection, then draw a line from the waist to the crotchline.

This is your center back line.

Step 4A

Now calculate your front waist (#12), using the Calculations for Draft section of the Pant Measurement Form. Divide your waist circumference—27" (68.6cm)—by 4 to get 6¾" (17.2cm). Add ¼" (6mm) for a total of 7" (17.8cm). Add 1" (2.5cm) for dart pickup (8"/20.3cm), and ⅜" (1cm) ease to get 8⅜" (21.3cm).

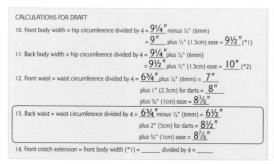

CALCULATIONS FOR DRAFT

10. Front body width = hip circumference divided by 4 = $9\frac{1}{4}$" minus ¼" (6mm)

= 9" plus ½" (1.3cm) ease = $9\frac{1}{2}$" (*1)

11. Back body width = hip circumference divided by 4 = $9\frac{1}{4}$" plus ¼" (6mm)

= $9\frac{1}{2}$" plus ½" (1.3cm) ease = 10" (*2)

12. Front waist = waist circumference divided by 4 = $6\frac{3}{4}$" plus ¼" (6mm) = 7"

plus 1" (2.5cm) for darts = 8"

plus ⅜" (1cm) ease = $8\frac{3}{8}$"

13. Back waist = waist circumference divided by 4 = $6\frac{3}{4}$" minus ¼" (6mm) = $6\frac{1}{2}$"

plus 2" (5cm) for darts = $8\frac{1}{2}$"

plus ⅜" (1cm) ease = $8\frac{7}{8}$"

14. Front crotch extension = front body width (*1) = _____ divided by 4 = _____

Step 4B

For the back waist measurement (#13), take your waist circumference—in our case 27" (68.6cm)—and divide it by 4 to get 6¾" (17.1cm). Because the back waist is smaller than the front, subtract ¼" (6mm) to get 6½" (16.5cm). Add 2" (5cm) for dart pickup, to get 8½" (21.5cm). Then add ⅜" (1cm) ease and record the final measurement of 8⅞" (22.5cm).

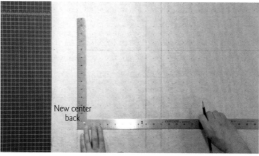

Step 4C

With your L square positioned at the waistline/back width intersection, measure in ¾" (2cm) on the waistline and place a mark. This will be your new center back line.

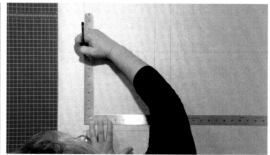

Step 4D

Shift the L square over to the ¾" (2cm) mark on the waistline. Measure over from that mark by your final back waist measurement (#13) and place another mark. Ours measures 8⅞" (22.5cm).

Step 5

So that you will not get confused while you draft the front and back pant legs, it is good practice to annotate the pattern with "Back" above the back waistline, and "Front" above the front waistline.

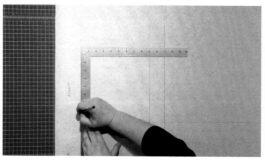

Step 6A

With the L square positioned at the waistline/front width intersection, measure over by your final front waist measurement (#12) and place a mark. Ours measures 8⅜" (21.3cm).

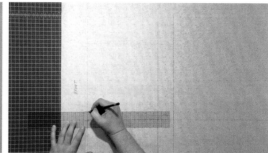

Darken the mark with your pencil and ruler.

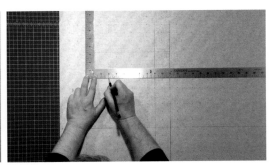

Step 6B

To locate the center of the dart closest to center front, position your L square at the waist and measure over from center front by your front princess line measurement (#7)—here 3⅜" (8.5cm)—and place a mark. Square a guideline down from the mark for approximately 3" (7.5cm).

The placement of the first waist dart is dependent on the shape of the abdomen. A fuller abdomen may benefit from a placement more toward the side seam and require only one dart.

Step 6C

Measure 3" (7.5cm) down from the waist for the dart length and make a mark.

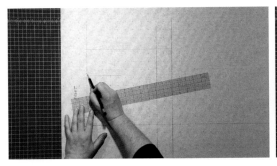

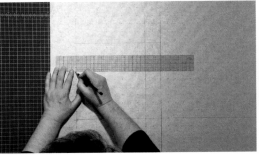

Step 6D

At the waistline, use your clear plastic ruler to measure out ¼" (6mm), first on one side of the front waist dart ...

... and then on the other side of the dart.

Step 6E

Then draw a ¼" (6mm) perpendicular line at the dart end point.

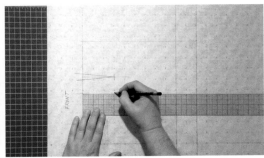

Step 6F

Finish the front waist dart by connecting the ¼" (6mm) mark on both sides of the dart to the dart's vanishing point. Note how we extend the lines past the waistline when drafting the dart.

Step 6G

The second dart's centerline is measured at the waist, approximately 1½" (3.8cm) away from the center of the first dart. Place a mark.

Step 6H

Square a guideline down from the second dart's center mark at the waist, for about 4" (10cm). For the length of the second dart measure down 3" (7.5cm) from the waist and place a mark.

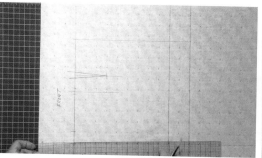

Step 6I
At the waistline measure out ¼" (6mm) on each side of the center dart line.

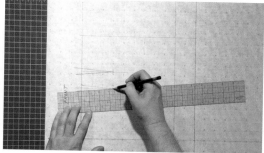

Step 6J
Connect the ¼" (6mm) marks on the waist to the dart's vanishing point.

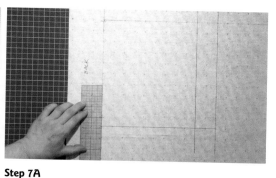

Step 7A
Next, you will plan the back darts. Start by measuring over from the new center back mark by your back princess line measurement (#8) and place a mark. This is the centerline of the first dart. Here our measurement is 3" (7.5cm).

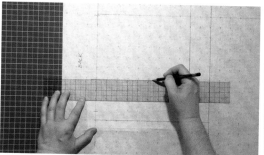

Step 7B
Square a line down from the back waist on the centerline of the first dart for approximately 5" (12.5cm).

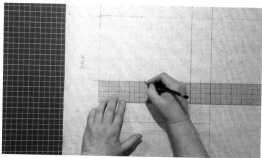

Step 7C
Measure down 4½" (11.5cm) on the centerline of the dart from the waist. Then mark the vanishing point of the dart.

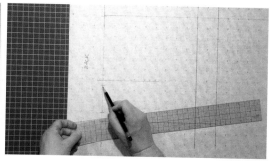

Step 7D
To draft the dart pickup, measure out ½" (1.3cm) at the waistline on each side of the dart centerline. Place a mark, first on one side of the centerline, then on the other side.

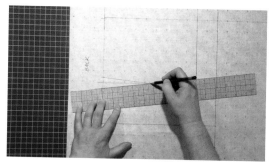

Step 7E
Next, connect the ½" (1.3cm) waist marks to the dart vanishing point, first on one side of the dart and then on the other.

Step 7F
The centerline placement of the second back dart for this size 6 (UK 10) is 1¾" (4.5cm) away from the centerline of the first back dart. The dart placement will vary according to the figure type, increasing in width by ⅛" (3mm) for each larger size.

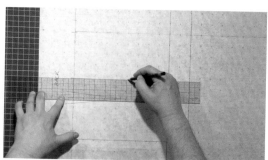

Step 7G
Place a mark at the waist centerline of the second dart and then square a line off the waistline for approximately 4" (10cm).

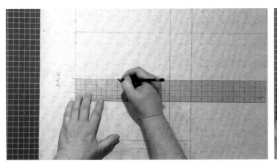

Step 7H
Measure the second dart's length at 4″ (10cm) and place a mark.

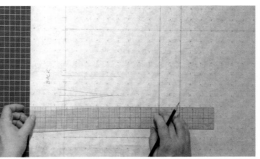

Step 7I
Draft the second dart pickup, by measuring out ½″ (1.3cm) at the waistline on each side of the dart centerline. Place a mark, first on one side of the centerline, and then on the other side of the centerline.

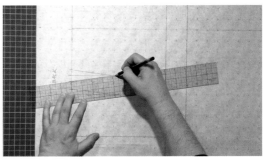

Step 7J
Next, connect the ½″ (1.3cm) waist marks to the second dart's vanishing point, first on one side of the dart and then on the other. Once the draft is tested in muslin (calico), the length and location of the darts may change.

Module 6:
Drafting the Crotch

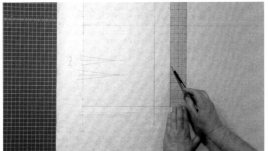

Step 1A
Now draft the back crotch extension. Begin by finding the outseam line to the center front measurement and dividing that number in half.

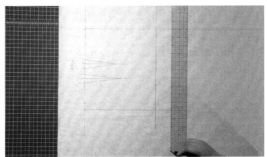

13. Back waist = waist circumference divided by 4 = $\underline{8''}$ minus ¼″ (6mm) = $\underline{8\frac{3}{8}''}$
plus 2″ (5cm) for darts = $\underline{8\frac{1}{2}''}$
plus ⅜″ (1cm) ease = $\underline{8\frac{7}{8}''}$
14. Front crotch extension = front body width (*1) = $\underline{9\frac{1}{2}''}$ divided by 4 = $\underline{2\frac{3}{8}''}$
15. Back crotch extension = back body width (*2) = $\underline{10''}$ divided by 2 = $\underline{5''}$
16. Front grainline/creaseline = front crotch line = _____ divided by 2 = _____
plus ¼″ (6mm) = _____
17. Back grainline/creaseline = back crotch line = _____ divided by 2 = _____
plus ¼″(6mm) = _____

Record these measurements as #15 on the Pant Measurement Form. Our back hip width at the crotch measures 10″ (25.4cm), divided in half is 5″ (12.7cm).

Step 1B
Slide the ruler along the back crotch line, and draft the back crotch by extending the divided back hip measurement beyond the center back line. Then place a mark. Here we are marking the back crotch extension at 5″ (12.7cm).

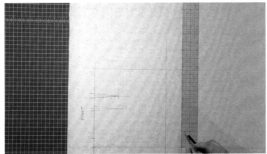

Step 2A
Now reposition the paper in preparation for marking the front crotch extension.

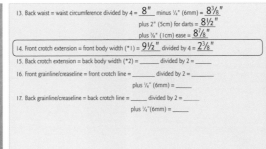

13. Back waist = waist circumference divided by 4 = $\underline{8''}$ minus ¼″ (6mm) = $\underline{8\frac{3}{8}''}$
plus 2″ (5cm) for darts = $\underline{8\frac{1}{2}''}$
plus ⅜″ (1cm) ease = $\underline{8\frac{7}{8}''}$
14. Front crotch extension = front body width (*1) = $\underline{9\frac{1}{2}''}$ divided by 4 = $\underline{2\frac{3}{8}''}$
15. Back crotch extension = back body width (*2) = _____ divided by 2 = _____
16. Front grainline/creaseline = front crotch line = _____ divided by 2 = _____
plus ¼″ (6mm) = _____
17. Back grainline/creaseline = back crotch line = _____ divided by 2 = _____
plus ¼″(6mm) = _____

To calculate this, divide the front body width measurement by 4, and record these measurements on the Pant Measurement Form as #14. Our front hip width at the crotch measures 9½″ (24cm), divided by 4 equals 2⅜″ (6cm).

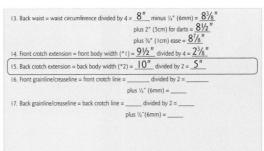

Step 2B
Slide the ruler along the front crotch line, and draft the front crotch by extending the divided front hip measurement beyond the center front line. Then place a mark. Here we are marking the front crotch extension at 2⅜″ (6cm).

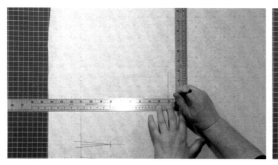

Step 3A
To establish the front crotch curve, align your L square with the center front line and crotch line, and mark a point on the inside corner of the L square.

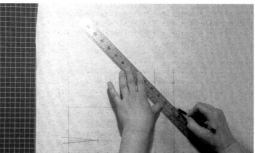

Step 3B
Draw a 2" (5cm) diagonal guideline from the center front/crotch line intersection through to the new mark.

Step 3C
Position your L square, and place a mark at 1½" (3.8cm) away from the corner of this diagonal line.

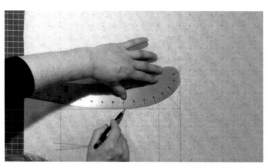

Step 3D
Position your hip curve so that it intersects the front crotch extension mark, the diagonal line, and rests on the center front.

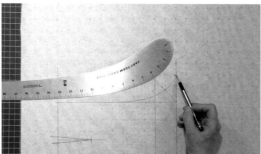

Step 3E
Check to be sure that you have connected all three points on the front crotch.

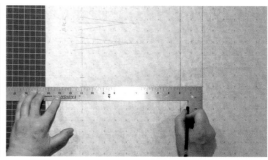

Step 4A
To establish the back crotch curve, align your L square with the center back line and crotch line, then mark a point on the inside corner of the L square.

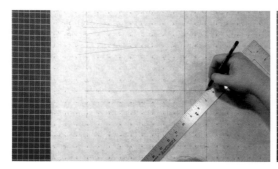

Step 4B
Draw a 2½" (6.3cm) diagonal guideline from the center back/crotch line intersection through to the new mark.

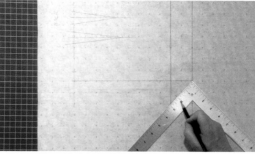

Step 4C
Then place a mark 2" (5cm) away from the corner of this diagonal line.

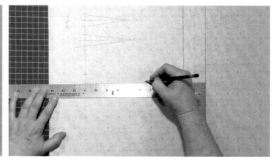

Step 4D
With your L square aligned with the back crotch and center back lines, place a mark midway between the waist and the crotch, on the center back line. Here our midway point is 5½" (14cm).

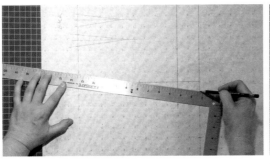

Step 4E
Next, draw a straight line for the center back seam, connecting the new back waist mark, through the midway point, ending at the crotch line.

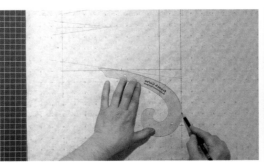

Step 4F
Now you will draft the back crotch by connecting the midway point, the diagonal mark, and the back crotch line.

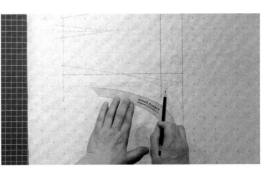

Step 4G
Find the best position on your French curve before drawing the curved line to form the back crotch. Note how the French curve rests on the crotch line and does not actually intersect with the crotch extension mark, yet forms a nice smooth, curved line.

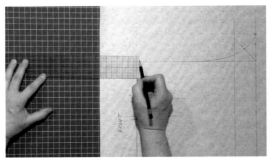

Step 5A
You will now move to the center front in order to lower the front waist. Place a mark ¼" (6mm) below the waistline on the center front line.

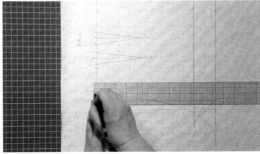

Step 5B
For the center back, you will raise the center back waist. Place a mark ¼" (6mm) above the center back waist.

Module 7:

Drafting the Lower Section

Step 1A
To establish the grainline for the back of the pant, find the midway point on the crotch line from the side seam to the back crotch point. Divide this measurement by 2, using your ruler, and place a mark.

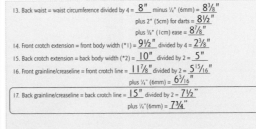

13. Back waist = waist circumference divided by 4 = __8"__ minus ¼" (6mm) = __8⅜"__
plus 2" (5cm) for darts = __8½"__
plus ⅜" (1cm) ease = __8⅞"__
14. Front crotch extension = front body width (*1) = __9½"__ divided by 4 = __2⅜"__
15. Back crotch extension = back body width (*2) = __10"__ divided by 2 = __5"__
16. Front grainline/creaseline = front crotch line = __11⅞"__ divided by 2 = __5¹⁵⁄₁₆"__
plus ¼" (6mm) = __6³⁄₁₆"__
17. Back grainline/creaseline = back crotch line = __15"__ divided by 2 = __7½"__
plus ¼" (6mm) = __7¾"__

Step 1B
Referring to #17 on the form, record your back crotch line measurement—in this case, 15" (38cm). Next, record the divided measurement; here 7½" (19cm). Add ¼" (6mm) to that measurement and record this total. This is the top of the back creaseline. Our final measurement for the back grainline/creaseline is 7¾" (19.6cm).

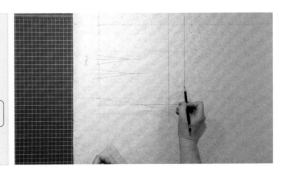

Step 1C
Place a mark on the back crotch line at the final measurement of #17. Again, our measurement is 7¾" (19.6cm).

Step 2A
Reposition the paper so the back ankle is in view. Place a mark on the back ankle line, 7¾" (19.6cm) over from the side seam.

Annotate the ankle line by writing "Ankle" below the line.

Step 2B
Next, connect the back top creaseline mark to the back ankle mark. Align your 48" (122cm) metal ruler with the top creaseline mark and ankle mark, then draw a line that extends beyond the waist and the ankle. This is the grainline and creaseline for the back pant.

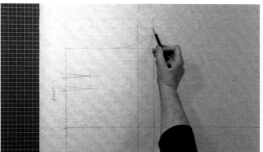

Step 3A
Next, you will find the front grainline/creaseline for the front pant leg, by first finding the midway point on the front crotch line from the side seam to the front crotch point.

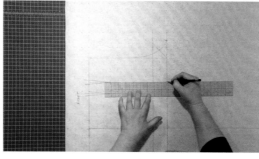

Step 3B
Refer to the Pant Measurement Form and record your #16 front width measurement; ours measures 11⅞" (30cm). Divide that measurement by 2 and record that measurement. Ours measures 5¹⁵⁄₁₆" (15cm). Then add ¼" (6mm) to get the final measurement of 6³⁄₁₆" (15.6cm).

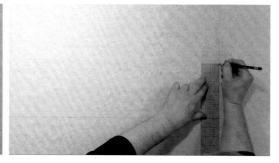

Step 3C
Reposition the paper to get the front ankle in view. Measuring over from the outseam line, place a mark on the ankle line at 6³⁄₁₆" (15.6cm).

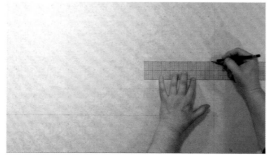

Now darken this mark using your pencil and ruler. This will be the bottom creaseline.

Step 3D
The next step is to connect the front crotch mark with the front ankle mark, to form the front creaseline and grainline. Position your 48" (122cm) metal ruler, connecting the two points. Draw a line that will align with the center of the front dart and extend beyond the ankle of the pant.

Step 4A
Reposition the paper in preparation for marking the front and bottom width of the pant. For our draft the total hem circumference will be 16" (41cm)—7½" (19cm) wide for the front leg, and 8½" (22cm) wide for the back leg.

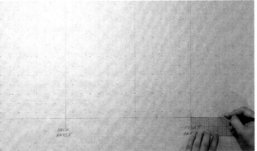

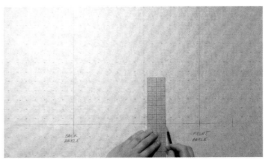

Step 4B

From your front ankle creaseline, measure over on the ankle line, half the width of the front hem width measurement, and place a mark. In our case, half of 7½" (19cm) is 3¾" (9.5cm).

Step 4C

Now repeat this step by placing a mark using the same measurement—3¾" (9.5cm)—on the other side of the front creaseline at the ankle line.

Step 4D

Use your ruler to darken the front ankle marks, so that they are at right angles to the ankle line. These will be the ankle inseam and outseam lines for the front pant leg.

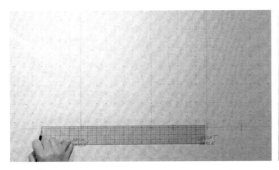

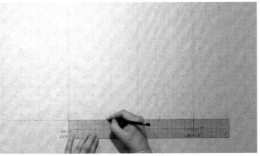

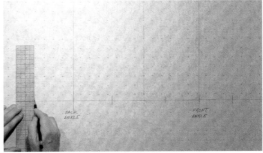

Step 4E

Now you will draft the back ankle's inseam and outseam by measuring over from the back creaseline by the back hem width. Here our total back hem width is 8½" (21.6cm); half of that is 4¼" (10.8cm).

Step 4F

Measure over and place a mark on one side of the back creaseline—ours measures 4¼" (10.8cm)—then slide the ruler over and place a mark at the same measurement on the other side of the creaseline.

Step 4G

Darken the front ankle marks with your ruler, so that they are at right angles to the ankle line. These will be the ankle inseam and outseam lines for the back pant leg.

Total hem circumference
Leg width

16" (41cm) = Back 4¼" (10.8cm)	Front 3¾" (9.5cm)
17" (43cm) = Back 4½" (11.4cm)	Front 4" (10cm)
18" (46cm) = Back 4¾" (12cm)	Front 4¼" (10.8cm)
19" (48cm) = Back 5" (12.5cm)	Front 4½" (11.4cm)
20" (51cm) = Back 5¼" (13.3cm)	Front 4¾" (12cm)

Step 4H

To customize the width of the pant leg, measurements for a wider leg are included on the Pant Measurement Form.

Step 5A

Reposition the paper in preparation for completing the pant side seams. Start by connecting the front outseam of the pant from the hip to the ankle. Use your 48" (122cm) metal ruler to connect the two points, continuing the line past the ankle line.

Step 5B

Now connect the back outseam from the hip to the ankle. Position your metal ruler at the hip and connect a line to the front ankle mark that extends beyond the ankle line.

Pants

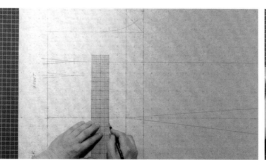

Step 6A

To establish the side seam curve above the hipline, place a mark 2" (5cm) above the hipline on the outseam line. Darken that mark using your ruler.

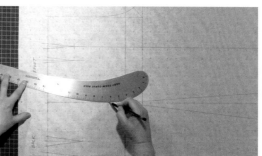

Step 6B

Now connect the new front waist mark with the 2" (5cm) hip mark to create the front side seam. Position your hip curve so that the straighter end of the curve intersects the waist mark, and the fuller end of the curve rests on the outseam at the 2" (5cm) mark.

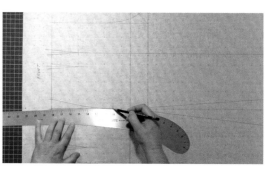

Step 6C

Now connect the new back waist mark to the 2" (5cm) hip mark to complete the back side seam. The back curve will be flatter than the front curve, due to the wider waist darts on the back waist.*

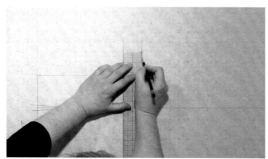

Step 7A

To establish the front inseam line, place a mark ½" (1.3cm) in from the front crotch point.

Step 7B

The first step will be to connect the ½" (1.3cm) mark on the front crotch to the front inseam ankle mark, using your 48" (122cm) metal ruler.

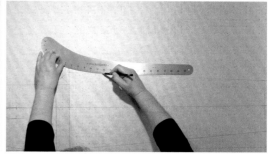

Step 7C

The second step is to place the curved end of your hip curve at the front crotch point and then blend the line to the inseam line, approximately 5" (12.5cm) below the crotch point.

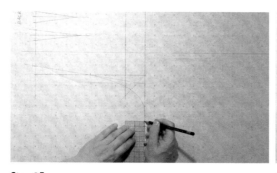

Step 8A

You will repeat the process for drafting the back inseam line by first coming in ½" (1.3cm) on the back crotch point, and placing a mark on the crotch line.

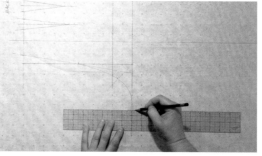

Step 8B

With your ruler at a right angle to the crotch line, darken the ½" (1.3cm) crotch mark.

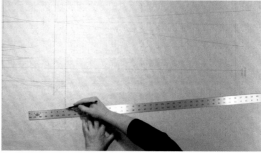

Step 8C

Now you will connect the back crotch mark to the back inseam ankle mark. Use your 48" (122cm) metal ruler to connect the two marks to complete the first step of drafting the back inseam.

Step 8D
To complete the back inseam, use the curved end of your hip curve to blend a line from the back crotch point to approximately 6" (15cm) down the inseam line.

Module 8:

Drafting the Side Seam & Waistline

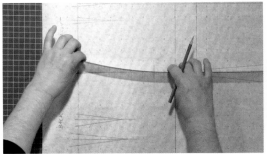

Step 1A
You now need to find the measurement from the front waist intersection to the 2" (5cm) mark on the side seam. Use your plastic ruler to find that measurement, then record it.

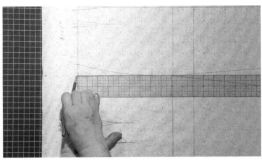

Step 1B
Now find the measurement from the back waist to the 2" (5cm) side seam measurement, and compare to the front side seam measurement. Here the back side seam needs to be raised to match the front. Mark the adjustment with a red pencil.

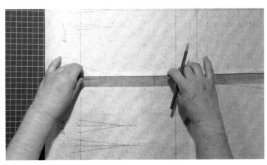

Check again to be sure that they both match.

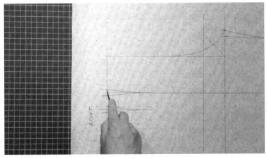

Step 2A
Next, you will close the darts to true the waistline.

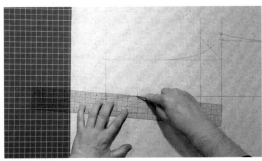

Step 2B
A trick when folding darts for trueing is to first score the dart stitching line using an awl and a ruler. Score the dart line closest to center front. Be careful not to press too hard on the awl or the paper will tear.

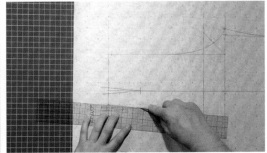

Step 2C
Next, score the stitching line of the second front dart leg, closest to center front.

Pants

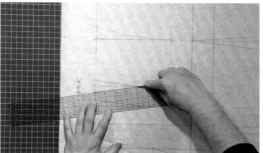

Step 2D

Reposition the paper then score the back waist darts. Again, score the dart leg closest to the center back.

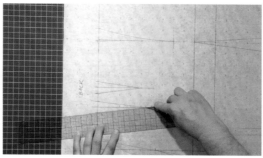

Step 2E

And finally, score the second dart's leg closest to center back.

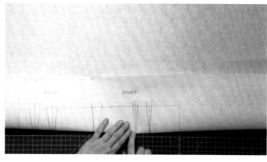

Step 3A

Softly fold the draft in half with the waist facing up. Crease the paper at the vanishing points of the front waist darts to make it easier to close the darts.

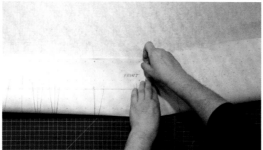

Step 3B

Close the first front waist dart by fingerpressing the scored dart leg. Then fold the paper at the vanishing point to close the dart. Secure the dart with a piece of tape above the waistline.

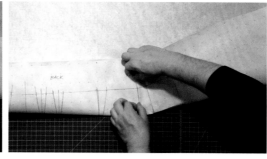

Step 3C

Fingerpress the second dart as you did the first, along the scored dart leg, then tape it closed above the waist.

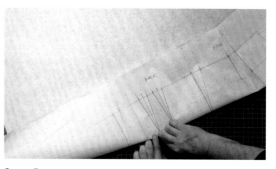

Step 4A

Now reposition the paper to close the back darts. Crease the paper at the vanishing points of the back waist darts to make it easier to close the darts.

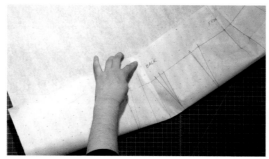

Step 4B

Fingerpress and close the dart and dart leg closest to center back. Tape the dart above the waistline.

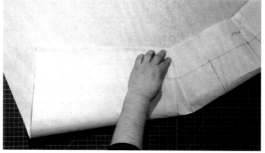

Step 4C

Then crease the vanishing point of the second dart and repeat the process of fingerpressing and closing the dart leg closest to center back. Tape the dart closed above the waistline.

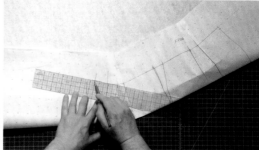

Step 5A

Next, you will true the back waistline. Start by squaring a ½" (1.3cm) line off the intersection of the new raised center back waist and crotch line with your clear plastic ruler and red pencil.

Step 5B
Now move to the front waist and repeat these steps, squaring a ½" (1.3cm) line off the new lowered center front waist/crotch intersection with your red pencil and ruler.

Step 6A
In preparation for trueing the waist, reposition the waist portion of the draft and gently flatten the paper with your hands.

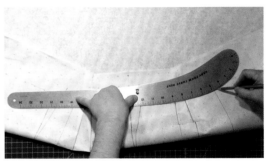

Step 6B
You will true the center front waist to the side seam next. Position your hip curve and blend a line, using your pencil, from the lowered center front waist mark to the front side seam. Note how the waistline changes above the darts as a result. Also, be sure that the center front/waist intersection remains a right angle.

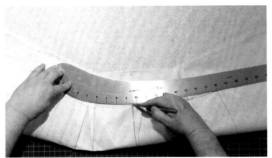

Step 6C
Now you will true the back waist. Position the hip curve and blend a line with red pencil connecting the raised center back waist mark to the back side seam. Once again, note how the waistline changes above the darts. Ensure that the center back/waist intersection remains a right angle.

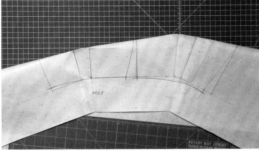

Step 6D
Reposition the draft and re-blend the waistline, if you think you can improve on the curve. Here we are re-blending the back waistline to get a better waistline shape.

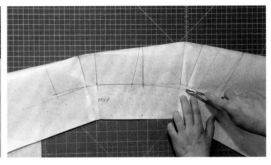

Step 6E
Sandwich a smaller cutting mat in between the waistline seam and the wrong side of the folded pant draft.

Step 6F
Next, you will use your tracing wheel to true from the center front waist to the front side seam on the red pencil line. Then you will true from the back side seam to center back, again tracing on the red line.

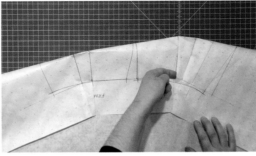

Step 7
Remove the small cutting mat from the table and carefully remove all of the holding tape from the darts.

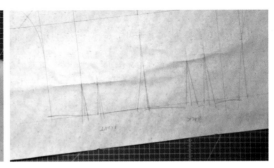

Step 8A
Open the draft up and then flatten the pattern on the table with your hands.

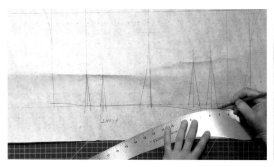

Step 8B

With your hip curve, extend the back waist dart leg lines with your red pencil, following the waistline tracing wheel marks for both of the back darts.

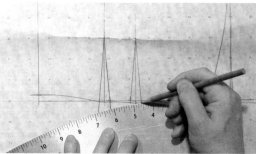

Step 8C

Repeat the process of trueing the dart leg lines at the waistline for both front darts, using the red pencil and following the tracing wheel markings.

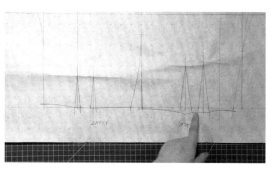

Step 8D

Next, you will extend all of the dart legs with the red pencil and ruler, starting with the back waist darts. Note how the lines extend beyond the new waistline of each dart.

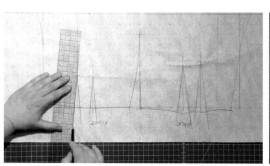

Step 8E

Move to the front pant waist and repeat the process of extending the dart leg lines with your red pencil.

Step 9A

To establish the knee depth, align your L square with the side seam and front waistline. Referring to #6 on the Pant Measurement Form, measure and mark your waist-to-knee measurement on the outseam line.

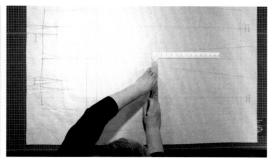

Step 9B

Now reposition the L square, and square a line off the outseam/knee mark intersection onto the back pant leg to form the back knee guideline.

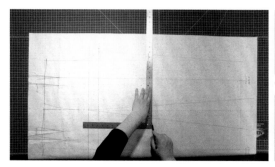

Step 9C

Reposition the paper, then flip the L square over, aligning it with the outseam and the knee mark, to draft the front knee guideline for the front pant leg.

Step 10A

Annotate the front pant knee by writing "Knee Line" above the knee guideline.

Step 10B

Reposition the draft, and annotate the back pant knee with "Back Knee" above the guideline.

Step 10C
Now write "Crotch Line" above the back crotch line, and "Hip" above the back hipline.

Step 10D
Shift the draft over and annotate the front hipline and the front crotch line.

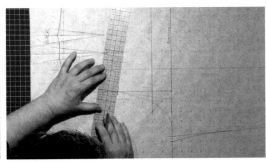

Step 11A
The last step is to add notches to the draft with your ruler and red pencil. Add the first notch on the back crotch at the reference point. Notches should always be at a right angle to the seam line and extend no more than $\frac{1}{4}$" (6mm) into the seam allowance.

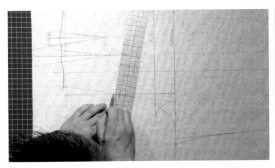

Measure up $\frac{1}{2}$" (1.3cm) and place another mark for the second back crotch notch.

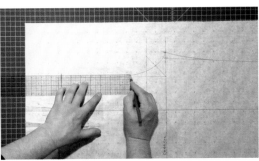

Step 11B
Next, mark the front crotch notch. The front crotch gets a single notch, positioned 7" (18cm) below the waistline and, again, at a right angle to the seam line.

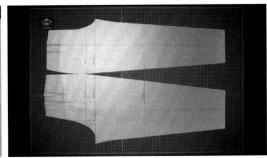

Step 11c
Once the pant draft is completed, cut a fit-muslin adding the $\frac{1}{2}$" (1.3cm) seam allowances and $1\frac{1}{2}$" (3.3cm) hem allowances and make any corrections to the draft before transferring the pant sloper to oaktag.

Self-evaluation

☐ Have I extracted the necessary measurements correctly and recorded them on the Pant Measurement Form?

☐ Did I accurately calculate my front and back waist darts?

☐ Have I drafted my front and back crotch extensions correctly?

☐ Did I remember to adjust my waist at the back side seam to match the front?

☐ Are my front and back pant leg width measurements accurate for my desired hem circumference?

☐ Did I close my waist darts and true the front and back waistline in one operation?

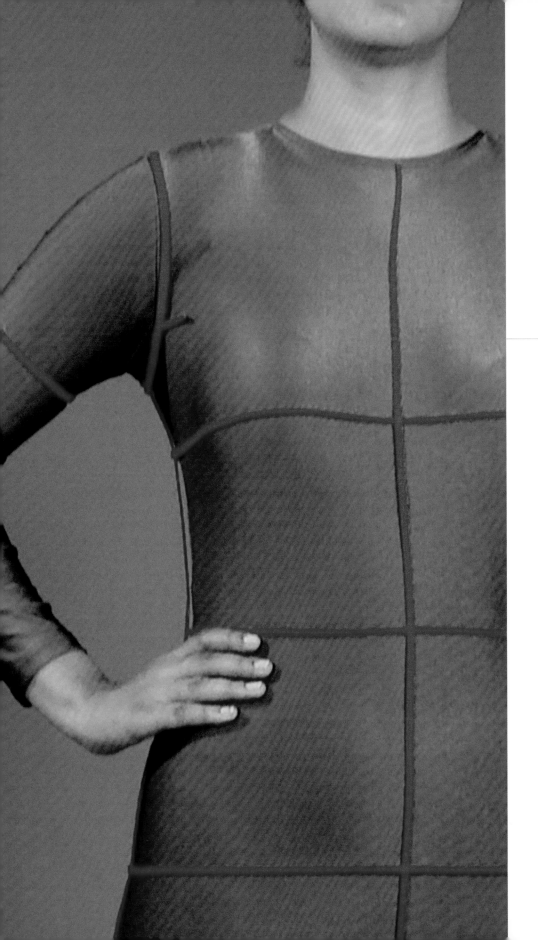

Appendix

A supplement to Lesson 3.1:
Drafting a Shoulder Dart Bodice from Measurements

- **Women's Body Measuring Points Chart**

- **Women's Global Size Range Bodice Chart Chart**

Women's Body Measuring Points Chart

#	Point	Figure	Description	Total
	UPPER BODY – FRONT			
1	Crown	1	top of head	
2	Head/Head Circumference	1	measured around the head at the widest part	
3	Collarbone/Center Front-Neck base	6	prominent front neck bones connecting the clavicle (collarbone) to the sternum (#15). The center of the collarbones is known as the center front-neck base	
4	Head Height- Center Front Neck to Crown	1	vertical measurement from center front neck (#3) to the crown (#1) with the head upright	
5	Head Height from High Point Shoulder to Crown	2	head height from high point shoulder (HPS #8) to crown (#1) with head upright	
6	Mid-Neck Circumference	1	circumference measured midway between head and neck base (#3)	
7	Side Seam	3	vertical measurement from armhole (#43), along the side of the body, to waist and continuing to the ankle (#92)	
8	High Point Shoulder (HPS)	1	intersection where shoulder (#14) meets neckline	
9	High Point Shoulder to Collarbone	1	vertical measurement from high point shoulder (#8) to collarbone (#3) level	
10	Front Neck Width Level	1	horizontal measurement from high point shoulder – collarbone (#9) level to center front (#25)	
11	Neck-Base Circumference/ Neckline	1	neck circumference measured from center front-neck base (#3) to back-neck base (#55)	
12	Shoulder Joint	6	bone known as the acromion formed by the union of the humerus (upper arm), the scapula (shoulder blade #68), and the clavicle (collarbone #3) allowing the arm to rotate around its axis at the shoulder	
13	Shoulder Circumference	1	horizontal distance measured at the level of the arm crease points front (#20) and back (#57), measured with arms down	
14	Shoulder/Shoulder Length	1	distance measured along shoulder from high point shoulder (#8) to armhole (#43)	
15	Sternum	6	flat bone in the middle of the chest, also known as the breastbone	
16	Front Neck Width	3	measured from high point shoulder (#8), around the front neckline curve, to center front neck base (#3)	
17	Shoulder Drop	1	vertical measurement taken from high point shoulder (#8) to the shoulder joint (#12)	
18	Shoulder Slope	3	measurement in degrees, taken with a goniometer, positioned on the shoulder drop line [horizontal line from high point shoulder (#8) to shoulder joint (#12)] and moved until the baseline is parallel to the floor	
19	Front Shoulder Slope	3	diagonal distance measured from intersection of shoulder (#14) and armhole (#43), to center front waist (#25)	
20	Front Arm Crease Point	3	location on the front where the arm separates from the body, positioned where armhole begins to curve	
21	Front Shoulder Width	3	horizontal distance across the front from shoulder joint to shoulder joint (#12)	

#	Point	Figure	Description	Total
22	Front Chest Width	3	horizontal distance across the chest – from front arm crease point to front arm crease point (#20)	
23	Waist/Waist Circumference	1	circumference distance around the body indicating the narrowest portion of the figure	
24	Front Waist Width	3	measurement along front waist (#23) from side seam (#7) to center front (#25)	
25	Center Front/Center Front Waist Length	1	vertical line denoting the center of the body – from center front-neck base (#3) to waist (#23)	
26	Apex	6	location of front bust point representing the most projected part of the bust	
27	Bust Radius	2	contour vertical measurement from under the breast to the apex (#26)	
28	Apex to Apex	3	bust point to bust point at the widest part of the bust	
29	High Point Shoulder to Apex/Bust Depth	3	vertical measurement from high point shoulder (#8) to apex (#26)	
30	Bustline	1	widest part of the bust at apex (#26), level with the floor	
31	Bust Circumference	1	horizontal circumference measurement around the body at bustline (#30)	
32	Front Width Depth	3	vertical distance from center front-neck base (#3) to front chest width (#22)	
33	Front Width Shoulder Depth	3	vertical distance from high point shoulder (#8) to front chest width (#22) level	
34	Full Front Length	1	distance measured from high point shoulder (#8), over apex (#26), down to waist (#23), contoured to the body	
35	Upper Chest Circumference	1	horizontal measurement around the body, taken slightly below the armhole (#43) and above the bustline (#30)	
36	Under Bust Circumference	1	horizontal measurement around the body under the bust (#30)	
37	Bust Arc	6	horizontal distance along the bustline, from side seam (#7), across the apex (#26) to center front (#25)	
38	Bust Span	6	horizontal distance from right apex (#26) to center front (#25)	
39	Princess Line – Front Upper Body	6	line positioned midway at shoulder (#14), through apex (#26), down to waist (#23)	
40	Princess Line to Center Front Waist	6	distance measured from front princess line (#39) to center front (#25) along the waist (#23)	
41	Princess Line to Side Seam at Waist	6	distance measured from front princess line (#39), to the side seam (#7) at the waist (#23)	
42	Underarm	2	hollow area under the arm	
43	Armhole/Armscye	2	circumference measured from shoulder joint to shoulder joint (#12) through the front (#20) and back (#57) arm crease points, approximately 1" (2.5cm)–2" (5.1cm) below the underarm (#42) depending on the size	
44	Side Waist Length	2	measurement taken at the intersection of the side seam (#7) and armhole (#43), to the waist (#23). This is also known as the tight bodyline	

#	Point	Figure	Description	Total
45	Armhole Depth from Shoulder	2	vertical distance measured from the intersection of the shoulder (#14) and armhole (#43), down to the intersection of the side seam (#7) and underarm (#42)	
46	Bicep/ Bicep Circumference	6	circumference at the fullest part of the upper arm, located between the underarm (#42) and the elbow (#47)	
47	Elbow/Elbow Circumference	6	maximum distance around the elbow (#47) with arm bent at 90° angle	
48	Shoulder to Elbow Length	6	distance from shoulder joint (#12) to the back elbow (#47)	
49	Elbow to Wrist	6	distance from elbow (#47) to wrist (#51)	
50	Underarm Length/Sleeve Inseam	6	measurement taken from the armhole (#43) to the bottom of the wrist bone (#52) with arm bent at 90° angle	
51	Arm Length – Shoulder to Wrist	6	measured from the intersection of the shoulder (#14) and armhole (#43) to the bottom of the wrist bone (#52) with arm bent at 90° angle	
52	Wrist Bone/Wrist Circumference	6	distance measured around the wrist bone (prominent bone between forearm and hand)	
53	Hand Circumference	6	measured at the widest part of the hand with fingers together, including the thumb	
54	Hand Length	6	measured at the wrist bone (#52) to the longest finger	
	UPPER BODY BACK			
55	Back-neck Base/Nape	4	prominent bone at the back of neck when head is bent forward	
56	Head Height- Center Back-Neck to Crown	4	vertical distance measured from the center back-neck base (#55) to the crown (#1), with the head upright	
57	Back Arm Crease Point	4	location on back where the arm separates from the body, positioned where armhole begins to curve	
58	Back Neck Width	4	measured from high point shoulder (#8), along the back-neckline curve, to center back-neck base or nape (#55)	
59	Back Width	4	horizontal distance across back from back-arm crease point to back-arm crease point (#57)	
60	Back Full Width	4	horizontal distance across back at widest part, from center back (#64) to side seam (#7)	
61	Back Shoulder Slope	4	diagonal distance measured at the intersection of the shoulder (#14) and armhole (#43) to the intersection of the center back (#64) and the back waist (#23)	
62	Back Width Depth/ Shoulder Blade Level	4	vertical distance from center-back neck (#55) to shoulder blade level (#63)	
63	Shoulder Blade Level Width	4	horizontal distance along shoulder blade level (#62), from center back (#64) to armhole (#43)	
64	Center Back/Center Back Waist Length	5	vertical line denoting the center back of the body – from back-neck base (#55), to back waist (#23)	
65	Across Back Shoulder Width	5	horizontal distance across back, from shoulder joint to shoulder joint (#12)	

#	Point	Figure	Description	Total
66	Back Waist Width	4	measurement from side seam (#7) to center back (#64), along the back waist (#23)	
67	Princess line – Back Upper Body	5	line positioned midway at back shoulder line (#14) down along mid-back to back waist (#23)	
68	Shoulder Blade	4	two bones located at upper back, connecting the upper arm bone with the clavicle (collarbone #3). Also known as the scapula or wing bone	
69	Back Full Length	5	vertical measurement from high point shoulder (#8), over shoulder blade (#68), down to back waist (#23)	
70	Arm Length – Center Back to Wrist	6	distance from back-neck base (#55) to the wrist (#52) with arm bent at 90° angle and measured from the back-neck base (#55), along the shoulder (#14) and shoulder joint (#12), down the outside of the arm, and over the elbow (#47) to the wrist bone (#52)	
71	Armhole Depth from Back-Neck	5	vertical armhole depth measured from center back-neck base (#55) to level of back-arm crease point (#57)	
72	Torso/Total Torso Length	2	central part of the body from which the neck and limbs extend, known as the trunk. Also, vertical measurement from center front neck-base (#3), through the crotch (#76), up to the center back-neck base (#55)	
	LOWER BODY			
73	Hip/Hip Circumference	1	horizontal distance measured at 7" (17.8cm) down from waist (#23), or the widest part of the hip, parallel to the floor	
74	High Hip Circumference	1	horizontal measurement taken around the hip from 4" (10.2cm) below the waist (#23), parallel to the floor	
75	Low Hip Circumference	1	horizontal distance around the hip measured at 9" (22.9cm) below the waist (#23), parallel to the floor	
76	Crotch/Crotch Level	2	level where the legs join the torso (#72), parallel to the floor	
77	Crotch Length (total)	2	combined measurement taken from the front waist (#23), through the crotch (#76) to the back waist (#23)	
78	Crotch Rise/Depth	2	vertical distance from the waist (#23) to the crotch (#76), measured using an L square, or measured from a seated position. Also known as true rise	
79	Crotch Extension	2	area on a pant where the crotch measurement extends out from center front (#25) and/or center back (#64), to the leg inseam (#102). Also known as the saddle	
80	Front Body Width	1	distance along hipline (#73) from center front (#25) to side seam (#7)	
81	Back Body Width	4	distance along hipline (#73), or widest part of the hip, from center back (#64) to the side seam (#7)	
82	Hip Bone	1	prominent bone that projects out on the front hip	
83	Front Princess Line	3	vertical line positioned midway between center front (#25) and side seam (#7), and continuing down the center of the front leg	
84	Back Princess Line	5	vertical line positioned midway between center back (#64) and side seam (#7), and continuing down the center of the back leg	
85	Back-Neck Base to Knee	5	vertical distance measured from the back-neck base (#55) to the knee (#91) level	
86	Back-neck Base – Floor	5	vertical distance measured from the back-neck base (#55), to floor level	

#	Point	Figure	Description	Total
87	Thigh/Thigh Circumference	2	measurement taken at widest part of thigh (area between hip and knee)	
88	Mid-Thigh Circumference	2	measurement of upper leg, midway between crotch (#76) and knee (#91)	
89	Calf/Calf Circumference	2	measurement around calf (muscle on lower back leg) at widest part	
90	Waist to Knee–Back	5	vertical distance measured from waist level (#23) to knee (#91) level	
91	Knee/Knee Circumference	2	measurement around knee joint – between upper and lower leg – at widest part	
92	Ankle Bone	2	joint between the lower leg and foot	
93	Knee to Ankle	2	vertical distance from knee (#91) level to bottom of outside ankle bone (#89) level	
94	Ankle Height	2	vertical distance from outer ankle bone (#92) to floor level	
95	Ankle Circumference	3	measurement around the ankle (#92)	
96	High Point Shoulder to Crotch Level	4	back vertical distance from high point shoulder (#8) to crotch level (#76). Also known as Torso Length	
97	High Point Shoulder to Floor	5	vertical distance measured on the back from the high point shoulder (#8) to floor level	
98	Waist to Ankle	3	vertical distance measured along the side of the body, from the waist (#23) to the bottom of the ankle level (#92)	
99	Waist to Floor	3	vertical measurement taken along the side of the body, from waist (#23) to floor level	
100	High Hip to Floor	5	vertical distance from high hip at 4" (10.2cm) down from waist (#23) to floor level	
101	Hip to Floor	5	vertical distance from hip at 7" (17.8cm) down from waist (#23) to the bottom of the ankle bone (#92) level	
102	Inseam	3	vertical distance from inside leg at crotch level (#76) to the bottom of the ankle bone (#92) level	
103	Outseam	3	vertical distance measured along the side seam (#7), from waist (#23) to the bottom of the ankle bone (#92) level	
104	Foot Length	2	measured from the back of the heel to the tip of the longest toe	
105	Foot Width	3	measured with foot flat on the floor, across foot at widest part	
106	Heel/Foot Circumference	5	distance taken around the upper foot and heel at widest part	
107	Total Body Height	2	vertical measurement taken from crown (#1) down to the floor level	

Appendix

Color codes correspond to those on Women's Body Measuring Points Diagram

▢ Vertical measurement

▢ Circumference measurement

▢ Body contour measurement

▢ Point

▢ Horizontal measurement

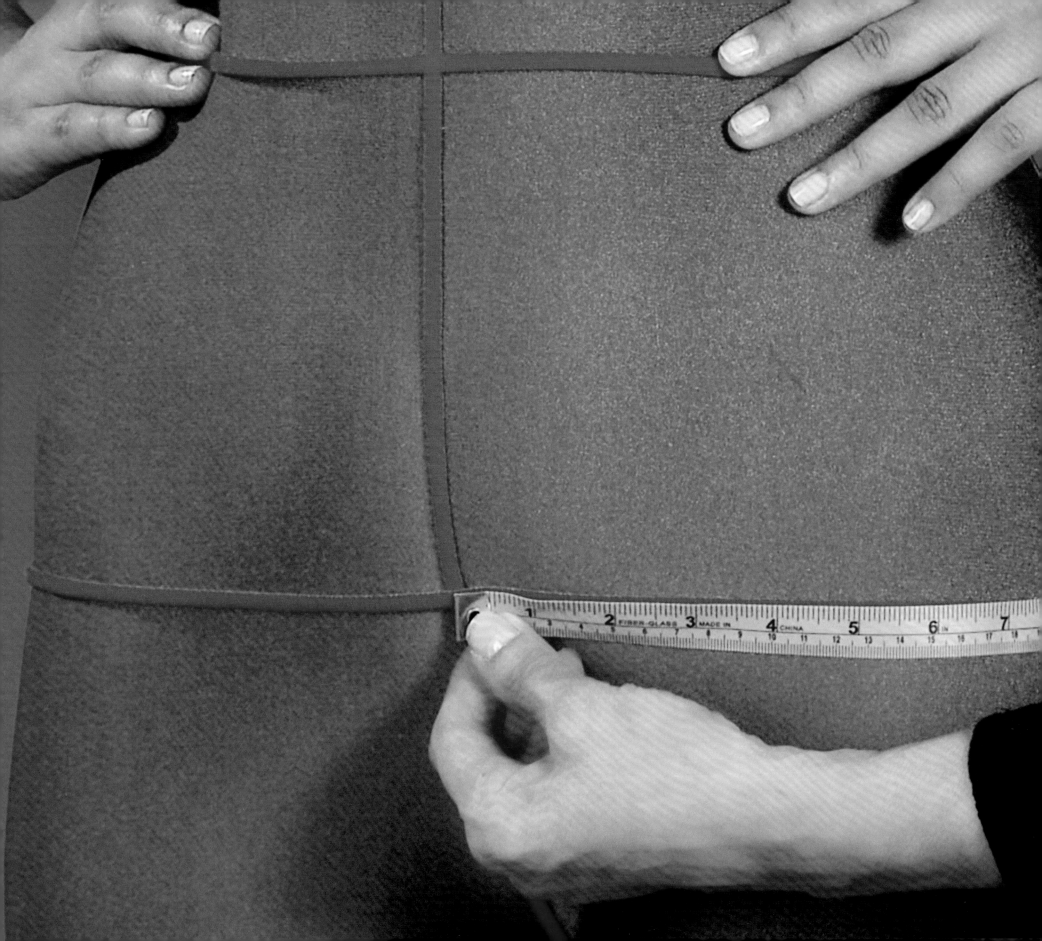

Women's Global Size Range Bodice Chart

Size Category	Size (inches)	cm	Size (inches)	cm	Size (inches)	cm	Size (inches)	cm	Size (inches)	cm	Size (inches)	cm	Size (inches)	cm	Size (inches)	cm	Size (inches)	cm
US	2		4		6		8		10		12		14		16		18	
UK/AU	6		8		10		12		14		16		18		20		22	
DE/NL/DK/SE	32		34		36		38		40		42		44		46		48	
FR/ES/IT	34		36		38		40		42		44		46		48		50	
Grade Rule	1"	2.54	1"	2.54	1"	2.54	1"	2.54	1 1/2"	2.54	1 1/2"	3.81	1 1/2"	3.81	1 1/2"	3.81	2"	5.08
#30 Bust Circumference	33 3/8	84.8	34 3/8	87.3	35 3/8	89.9	36 3/8	92.4	37 7/8	96.2	39 3/8	100	40 7/8	103.8	42 3/8	107.6	44 3/8	112.7
#23 Waist Circumference	25	63.5	26 1/8	66.4	27 1/4	69.2	28 1/2	72.4	29 3/4	75.6	31 1/4	79.4	32 3/4	83.2	34 1/4	87	36 1/4	92.1
FRONT																		
#9 HPS to Collarbone	−1/16; 2 3/8	6.1	−1/16; 2 7/16	6.2	2 1/2	6.4	+1/16; 2 9/16	6.6	+1/16; 2 5/8	6.7	+1/16; 2 11/16	6.9	+1/16; 2 3/4	7	+1/16; 2 13/16	7.2	+1/8; 2 15/16	7.5
#10 Front Neck Width Level	−1/16; 2 1/4	5.8	−1/16; 2 5/16	5.9	2 3/8	6	+1/16; 2 7/16	6.2	+1/16; 2 1/2	6.4	+1/16; 2 9/16	6.6	+1/16; 2 5/8	6.7	+1/16; 2 11/16	6.9	+1/8; 2 13/16	7.2
#14 Shoulder Length	−1/16; 4 7/8	12.4	−1/16; 4 15/16	12.5	5	12.7	+1/16; 5 1/16	12.9	+1/8; 5 3/16	13.1	+1/8; 5 5/16	13.5	+1/8; 5 7/16	13.8	+1/8; 5 9/16	14.1	+1/8; 5 11/16	14.4
#22 Front Chest Width	−1/8; 6 1/2	16.5	−1/8; 6 5/8	16.8	6 3/4	17.2	+3/16; 6 15/16	17.6	+3/16; 7 1/8	18.1	+3/16; 7 5/16	18.6	+3/16; 7 1/2	19.1	+3/16; 7 11/16	19.5	+1/4; 8 3/16	20.8
#24 Front Waist Width	−1/4; 6 5/8	16.8	−1/4; 6 7/8	17.5	7 1/8	18.1	+1/4; 7 3/8	18.7	+3/8; 7 3/4	19.7	+3/8; 8 1/8	20.7	+3/8; 8 1/2	21.6	+3/8; 8 7/8	22.5	+1/2; 9 3/8	23.8
#25 Center Front Waist Length	−1/4; 13 7/8	35.2	−1/4; 14 1/8	35.9	14 3/8	36.5	+1/4; 14 5/8	37.1	+1/4; 14 7/8	37.8	+1/4; 15 1/8	38.4	+1/4; 15 3/8	39.1	+1/4; 15 5/8	39.7	+1/4; 15 7/8	40.3
#29 HPS to Apex	−1/8; 10 1/4	26	−1/8; 10 3/8	26.4	10 1/2	26	+1/8; 10 5/8	27	+1/8; 10 3/4	27.4	+1/8; 10 7/8	27.7	+1/8; 11	28	+1/8; 11 1/8	28.3	+1/4; 11 3/8	28.9
#32 Front Width Depth	−1/16; 4	10.2	−1/16; 4 1/16	10.3	4 1/8	10.5	+1/16; 4 3/16	10.6	+1/16; 4 1/2	11.4	+1/16; 4 9/16	11.6	+1/16; 4 5/8	11.8	+1/16; 4 11/16	11.9	+1/16; 4 3/4	12.1
#34 Full Front Length	−1/4; 16 7/8	42.9	−1/4; 17 1/8	43.5	17 3/8	44.1	+1/4; 17 5/8	44.8	+5/16; 17 15/16	45.6	+5/16; 18 1/4	46.4	+5/16; 18 9/16	47.2	+5/16; 18 7/8	48	+5/16; 19 3/16	48.7

Size Category	Size		Size		Size		Size		Size		Size		Size		Size		Size	
US	2		4		6		8		10		12		14		16		18	
UK/AU	6		8		10		12		14		16		18		20		22	
DE/NL/DK/SE	32		34		36		38		40		42		44		46		48	
FR/ES/IT	34		36		38		40		42		44		46		48		50	
	inches	cm	inches	cm	inches	cm	inches	cm	inches	cm	inches	cm	inches	cm	inches	cm	inches	cm
FRONT																		
#37 Bust Arc	$-1/4$		$-1/4$				$+1/4$		$+3/8$		$+3/8$		$+3/8$		$+3/8$		$+1/2$	
	8 7/8	22.5	9 1/8	23.2	9 3/8	23.8	9 5/8	24.4	10	25.4	10 3/8	26.4	10 3/4	27.4	11 1/8	28.3	11 5/8	29.5
#38 Bust Span	$-1/16$		$-1/16$				$+1/16$		$+1/16$		$+1/16$		$+1/16$		$+1/16$		$+1/8$	
	3 5/8	9.2	3 11/16	9.4	3 3/4	9.6	3 13/16	9.7	3 7/8	9.8	3 15/16	10	4	10.2	4 1/16	10.3	4 3/16	10.6
#44 Side Waist Length	$-1/8$		$-1/8$				$+1/8$		$+1/8$		$+1/8$		$+1/8$		$+1/8$		$+1/8$	
	8 1/4	21	8 3/8	21.2	8 1/2	21.6	8 5/8	22	8 3/4	22.2	8 7/8	22.5	9	22.9	9 1/8	23.2	9 1/4	23.5
#45 Armhole Depth from Shoulder	$-1/8$		$-1/8$				$+1/8$		$+1/8$		$+1/8$		$+1/8$		$+1/8$		$+1/8$	
	5 1/4	13.3	5 3/8	13.7	5 1/2	14	5 5/8	14.3	5 3/4	14.7	5 7/8	15	6	15.2	6 1/8	15.6	6 1/4	15.9
BACK																		
#60 Back Full Width	$-1/4$		$-1/4$				$+1/4$		$+7/16$		$+7/16$		$+7/16$		$+7/16$		$+1/2$	
	7 7/8	20	8 1/8	20.6	8 3/8	21.3	8 5/8	21.9	9 1/16	23	9 1/2	24.1	9 15/16	25.2	10 3/8	26.4	10 7/8	27.6
#62 Back Width Depth	$-1/8$		$-1/8$				$+1/8$		$+1/8$		$+1/8$		$+1/8$		$+1/8$		$+1/8$	
	3 7/8	9.8	4	10.2	4 1/8	10.5	4 1/4	10.8	4 3/8	11.1	4 1/2	11.4	4 5/8	11.7	4 3/4	12	4 7/8	12.4
#63 Shoulder Blade Level Width	$-1/8$		$-1/8$				$+1/8$		$+3/16$		$+3/16$		$+3/16$		$+3/16$		$+1/4$	
	6 3/4	17.2	6 7/8	17.5	7	17.8	7 1/8	18.1	7 5/16	18.6	7 1/2	19	7 11/16	19.5	7 7/8	20	8 1/8	20.6
#64 Center Back Waist Length	$-1/4$		$-1/4$				$+1/4$		$+1/4$		$+1/4$		$+1/4$		$+1/4$		$+1/4$	
	15 7/8	40.3	16 1/8	41	16 3/8	41.6	16 5/8	42.2	16 7/8	42.9	17 1/8	43.5	17 3/8	44.1	17 5/8	44.8	17 7/8	45.4
#66 Back Waist Width	$-1/4$		$-1/4$				$+1/4$		$+3/8$		$+3/8$		$+3/8$		$+3/8$		$+1/2$	
	6	15.2	6 1/4	15.9	6 1/2	16.5	6 3/4	17.2	7 1/8	18.1	7 1/2	19	7 7/8	20	8 1/4	21	8 3/4	22.2
#69 Back Full Length	$-3/8$		$-3/8$				$+3/8$		$+3/8$		$+3/8$		$+3/8$		$+3/8$		$+3/8$	
	16 1/2	42	16 7/8	42.9	17 1/4	43.9	17 5/8	44.8	18	45.7	18 3/8	46.7	18 3/4	47.6	19 1/8	48.6	19 1/2	49.5

*horizontal measurements are one-quarter body circumference

* measurements may be rounded to the nearest 1/16 of an inch

Glossary

2HB pencil A hard black graphite pencil used in draping and pattern making.

Across Back Shoulder Back width on a body/dress form, measured from right back shoulder point to left back shoulder point.

Across Front Shoulder From right front shoulder point to left front shoulder point on a body/dress form.

Ankle Joint connecting the foot and the leg.

Annotate Notes made on pattern pieces that identify each part of a garment pattern, such as the name of the part, any grainlines, the size of the garment, how many pieces need to be cut, whether the piece requires interfacing, or any other relevant information.

Apex Location of front bust point representing the most projected part of the bust.

Arm Length Measured from either center back to the wrist, or from the shoulder to the wrist.

Armhole Section of a garment through which the arm passes, and where a sleeve can be inserted.

Armhole Dart Bust dart that emanates from the armhole and vanishes to within ½" (1.3cm) of the apex.

Armhole Depth Measurement taken from the shoulder/armhole intersection down to the armhole/side seam intersection.

Armhole Ridge Area on the dress form where the shoulder seam and the natural armhole intersect.

Armplate Metal plate on a dress form covering the arm socket.

Armscye Diameter measurement of an armhole.

Asymmetric The principle of informal balance, rather than formal balance, with each side of the garment offering a different silhouette.

Awl Pointed tip tool used to punch holes into fabric, paper, oaktag, and other materials.

Back Balance Guideline A guideline used in draping that is at a right angle to both the center back and the shoulder blade level, to help balance the back drape of a bodice, torso, or dress sloper.

Back Length Measurement from center back/neckline intersection to the waist or to the hem, on a body/dress form.

Back Neck Dart Back dart positioned at the back neckline, mid-way between center back and the shoulder seam and angled towards the top of the back waistline or dart/princess seam.

Back Shoulder Dart Back dart positioned mid-way on the back shoulder seam and angled toward the top of the back waistline dart or back princess seam.

Back Width Fullest part of the back on a body/dress form, from side seam (breakpoint) to side seam (breakpoint).

Balance A garment is considered balanced when the front and back hangs perfectly at the side seam. When working with horizontal stripes and plaids, balancing a garment's side seam is critical.

Band Collar Narrow stand collar, usually between ¾" to 1 ½" (1.9–3.8cm) wide, with or without a closure.

Bell Sleeve Sleeve that is set into normal armhole, is narrow at the top and flares wider at the hem.

Bias Grain Diagonal direction of a fabric, that yields the most stretch. "True bias" is bias that is a 45° angled bias, as compared to "garment bias," which is bias other 45°.

Bicep Fullest part of the upper arm circumference, located between the elbow and the shoulder/armhole intersection.

Bicep Line Line that denotes the bicep and is perpendicular to the sleeve center.

Bicep Circumference Circumference of the bicep area of the upper arm.

Bifurcated Form Dress form that is inclusive of legs. Available neck-to-thigh, neck-to-ankle, or waist-to-ankle.

Bishop Sleeve Sleeve that is full at the bottom and usually gathered into a cuff or band.

BL Acronym for bust level.

Blend Process of joining and perfecting drafting lines to form a smooth line or curve.

Blue Pencil Blue-colored lead pencil used in draping and pattern making for making corrections and adjustments.

Bodice Sloper A fitted upper body silhouette with: a front and back waist dart; with either a side bust or a shoulder bust dart; and a back neck or back shoulder dart. It is used as a foundation sloper (block) from which stylizations are created.

Boxy Torso Sloper Silhouette that sits away from the body, is not fitted, and ends at the hipline.

Bust Dart Dart that ends at approximately ½" (1.3cm) or more away from the apex. It can emanate from either the neck, shoulder, armhole, side seam, or from center front. But dart length varies, depending on the fullness of the bust. The fuller the bust the shorter and smaller the dart.

Bust Ease The amount of ease that is needed between the left and right apex points. When draping, the area between the right and left apex points is never pinned to the dress form.

Bust Guideline A vertical guideline used in draping that begins at the apex, is a right angle to both the center front and the bust level, and whose function is to help balance the front drape of a bodice, torso, or dress sloper and becomes the center of the waist bust dart.

Bustline A horizontal line at the apex, or fullest part of the bust, that is parallel to the floor.

Button Decorative ornament used as a trimming or as a functional fastener. Buttons are made out of a variety of materials and are available with holes or a shank back. They are stitched to a garment and then slipped through a buttonhole or loop.

Buttonhole Hole in which a button passes through to close a garment.

Button Extension Amount of space that is needed when planning a button closure.

Cage Metal wire portion of a dress form below the torso.

Calf Fullest part of the leg between the knee and the ankle.

Cap Height Vertical measurement from the shoulder/armhole intersection to the side seam/armhole intersection.

Cap Notches Marks indicating the upper portion of a sleeve. One notch denotes the front sleeve cap, 2 notches spaced ¼" (6mm) apart denotes the back sleeve cap.

Cap Sleeve Short sleeve ending at or above the bicep with little to no cap ease.

Capline Horizontal line at the top of the cap, parallel to the bicepline.

CB Acronym for center back of the body/dress form.

Center Back Vertical line denoting the center back of the body or of a garment.

Center Front Vertical line denoting the center front of the body or of a garment, from collarbone to waist.

Centerline A line that denotes the center of a pattern or drape. For example, the center of a sleeve or center front or center back of a garment. On a sketch it indicates the plum line.

CF Acronym for center front of the body/dress form.

Chemise/Shift Straight-cut dress silhouette with few darts and no waistline.

Circle Skirt Skirt whose hem circumference forms either a quarter circle, half circle, three quarter, or full circle.

Circumference Distance measurement around a particular area, such as the circumference of a waistline, bicep, wrist, or hip.

CL Acronym for crotch level.

Clear Plastic Ruler A transparent tool for measuring and marking, printed with measurements and a grid of lines.

Clip The action of snipping notches or releasing seam allowances, especially on curves and at waistlines.

Closures Any type of garment closure such as buttons, frogs, snaps, clips, toggles, buckles, D-rings, loops and buttons, Velcro, lacings, or zippers.

Collar Fall Area from the collar roll to the collar's edge.

Compass A technical drawing device that can be used for drawing circles or arcs.

Concave Curve Curve that goes in, not out.

Contour Dart Dart with shape: curved, convex, concave, or fisheye.

Convertible Collar A rolled collar that can be worn two ways: either meeting at center front or, when the top button is unbuttoned, can create a notch collar effect.

Convex Curve Curve that goes out and not in.

Crease Technique used to form a fold or line such as: down the middle on the front of trousers; in pattern making to help fold paper; or in draping to form a mark on the fabric.

Creaseline Line formed when folding a pattern over to form a crease.

Cross Grain Fabric grain that goes from selvage to selvage, also known as the weft. Ways to identify muslin cross grain are: 1) perpendicular to length or warp grain; 2) has some stretch to it but not as much as bias grain; 3) fuzzier yarn with more slubs than length grain; and 4) when folded, will not lay flat as will length grain, but instead will be a bit bouncy.

Cross-marks Marks in the shape of a plus sign, which indicate an intersection in draping, such as at the side seam/underarm, the shoulder/armhole, or any place where 2 lines

intersect.

Crotch Part of the human body where the legs join the torso.

Crotch Depth The vertical distance from the waist to the crotch on a pant, plus desired ease.

Crotch Extension Area on a pant where the crotch measurement extends out from center front and center back.

Crotch Length Combined measurement on the front and back crotch seamlines, taken from front waist to back waist.

Crotch Level Area on a pattern measured from waist to where the crotch starts.

Crotch Line Horizontal line at the position of the crotch.

Cuff Band that ends the bottom of a sleeve, or a detail on the bottom of pants or shorts that turns up over itself.

Cup & Fold Method In pattern making and draping, the technique of cupping the paper or fabric to make it easier to true a dart.

Cut-Away Armhole A stylized sleeveless armhole that is recessed in from the natural armhole.

Cutting Line In pattern making and draping, the cutting line refers to the outside line of the seam allowance on a pattern and the stitching line on a sloper.

Cutting Mat A flexible self-healing surface, with a thin layer of colored vinyl on top, that is used in draping, pattern making, and sewing to protect a table top.

Dart Term for a V-shaped stitched tuck that is used to create shape in a garment. Examples are darts that control fullness in the bust area such as those at the shoulder, side seam, and at the waist. Darts can be concave, convex, fisheye, straight, or curved.

Dart Direction The direction in which the dart intake is positioned. On front and back vertical darts, the dart intake should point in

the direction of the center. For horizontal darts, the dart intake points in a downward direction.

Dart Intake Amount of dart material inside a dart's stitching lines.

Dart Legs The stitching line of a dart, from start to vanishing point.

Dart Length The length of a dart, from start to vanishing point.

Dart Manipulation Concept of how to move darts to different areas on the body.

Dart Pickup The amount of dart material or dart intake formed in the draping and pattern making process.

Dart Shape Shape of a dart, concave, convex, fisheye, straight, or curved.

Dart Size Width and length of the dart pick-up.

Diameter The width of a circle, such as the diameter of a button.

Draft A schematic plan made of a garment using the pattern making process before seam allowances are added. The act of making (drafting) a pattern.

Drafting The process of drawing the lines and curves from measurements to create a pattern or sloper.

Drawing Compass A technical drawing device that can be used for drawing circles or arcs.

Dress Form A replica of the human body made out of either paper mache, fiberglass, or foam and then covered in padding and linen cloth. For use in draping and fitting garments. Pins must be able to be sunk directly into the form. Dress forms are also available as bifurcated forms, that is with legs.

Dress Maker Pins Pins made of nickel-plated steel used in sewing, draping, and pattern making. The ideal size for working with light to medium weight fabrics is a size #20, for medium weight fabrics a #17, and for heavyweight fabrics a size 24.

Ease Allowing for extra measure to a pattern or drape for wearing comfort. Areas where ease is added are: at the bust, waist, hip, underarm/side seam intersection, sleeve, crotch, or anywhere else on the pattern so that the garment fits comfortably.

Ease Notch Marks on patterns that indicate where ease is encapsulated.

Ease Pinch Adding an extra measure to the drape, usually between 1/8" to 1/4" (3mm–6mm), so that the garment fits comfortably.

Elbow The joint that connects the forearm with the upper arm.

Elbow Circumference Total measurement taken around the elbow of the arm.

Elbow Dart One or 2 darts at the elbow to create a fitted sleeve.

Elbow Line Line that is perpendicular to the sleeve center at the level of the elbow.

Extension Area on a garment where the button and buttonhole closure is positioned, or where a zipper fly or pleat is planned.

Extract Measurements Taking accurate measurements on a body/dress form, in preparation for draping or pattern drafting.

Facing Section on a garment used to clean finish that area, for example on a neckline, armhole, curved hem, sleeve, waistline, or pocket top.

Fingerpress Using your fingers to press an area flat on fabric or paper, such as a dart or seam allowance.

Fisheye Dart Curved, almond, or eye-shaped dart that adds shape to a garment.

Fitted When a garment sits close to the body.

Fitted Sleeve Sleeve that has a dart or darts at the elbow and is also used as a sloper.

Fitted Torso Sloper Silhouette that is fitted to the body and ends at the hipline.

Fitting Process of checking to see how a muslin or garment fits, so that adjustments can be made to the pattern.

Flare Extending out from a straight or natural line, such as on a sleeve or the side seam of a skirt, pant, or dress.

Flare Point The point where a flare originates or is dropped from.

Flared Skirt Skirt that extends out from the waist at the side seam and/or from other points along the waistline.

Flat Collar Collar with little to no stand around the neck.

Flat Pattern Two-dimensional pattern making technique used to create designs on paper.

Flex Curve A flexible measuring device used to measure armholes or other curved areas of a dress form, pattern, or garment.

Fold When a fabric or paper is folded over itself to form an edge.

Fold Line Pattern position indicating where to turn up or under, such as on the hem of a garment.

Form-Fitting Fitting the body with little to no wearing ease.

French Curve Tool used to create curved lines in draping and pattern making.

French Dart Bust dart that emanates from the side seam and is positioned close to the waistline, resulting in a semi-fitted shape.

Front Balance Guideline Guideline used in draping that is at a right angle to both the center front and the bust level, to help balance the front drape of a bodice, torso, or dress sloper.

Front Dart Guideline Guideline used in draping that is positioned at the apex and at a right angle to both the center front and the bust level, to help balance the front drape of a bodice, torso or dress and where the center of the front waist dart is located.

Front Extension Excess material, usually 1" (2.5cm), that is added to center front and back muslin panels. It is then folded back in

preparation for pinning the center front/back to the dress form.

Front Length Measurement from center front/ neckline intersection to the waist or to the hem, on a body/dress form.

Full Circle Skirt A skirt that is fitted at the waist and flares out at the hem, forming a hem sweep of a full circle.

Fusible Interfacing Support material with a press-on adhesive backing, which when ironed, with pressure, onto the wrong side of a fabric, adds structure to that area. Fusible interfacings are available in various weights and colors and offered as woven, non-woven, and knitted.

Full Circle Radius Calculations Chart Chart with waist circumference and radius measurements for drafting a full circle skirt.

Garment Bias Any bias grain that is not a 45° angled bias. A 45° angled bias is known as "true bias."

Gather Compressing fabric into a smaller amount, such as when gathering/shirring fabric into a waistline to create a gathered skirt.

Grain Term used to describe the yarn direction of a fabric: crossgrain (weft), length grain (warp), or diagonal (bias).

Grainline Direction of yarns in a fabric weave: crossgrain (weft), length grain (warp), diagonal (bias).

Guide Lines Marks made on muslin or paper and used to balance or control the grain lines during the draping process and pattern making process.

Half Body Form Dress form that goes from the neck to the end of the torso.

Half Circle Skirt A skirt that is fitted at the waist and flares out at the hem, forming a hem sweep that is one-half of a full circle.

Half Circle Skirt Radius Calculations Chart Chart with waist circumference and radius measurements for drafting a half circle skirt.

Handkerchief Hem Full circle skirt with a pointed, uneven hem.

Hem Finished bottom edge of a garment such as a sleeve, blouse, skirt, dress, or pant bottom. Or, the act of finishing the bottom edge of a sleeve, blouse, skirt, dress, or pant bottom.

Hem Allowance The amount of fabric allocated to hemming an area of a garment.

Hemline Line that denotes the bottom of the hem before it is turned up and finished.

HH Acronym for high hip.

High Hip Horizontal styleline positioned 4" (10cm) down from the front waist and parallel to the floor.

High Point Shoulder The shoulder/neck intersection point on a dress form or a garment.

Hip Area of the figure measured at 7" (18cm) down from the natural waistline.

Hip Curve Tool with a curve that is used in draping and pattern making to true the hip and assorted other areas of a pattern.

Hip Level Horizontal styleline that is measured at 7" (18cm) down from the natural waistline and is level to the floor.

Hipline Located 7" (18cm) down from the front waist, and parallel to the floor.

HL Acronym for hip level or hipline.

Imperial Measurement System A measurement system used in the United States, Myanmar, and Liberia with units of measure calculated in inches, feet and pounds. The metric system is used in all other countries.

Inseam Seam area on a garment such as the inside of a pant leg or the inside length of a sleeve. Men's pants sizes are measured from this length.

Iron A device used to flatten an area or areas of a fabric or garment, often using pressure and steam.

Ironing Board Padded and covered table device that is used to press fabrics and garments.

Jewel Neckline A rounded neckline that sits close to the neck and accentuates the wearer's jewelry.

Kimono Wrap robe silhouette of Japanese origin where either the body and sleeves are cut as one, or where sleeves are straight and set in at right angles to the body.

Kimono Sleeve Sloper Sloper where body and sleeves are cut as one, and used as the foundation block for design variations calling for deep armhole silhouettes such as dolman and batwing sleeves.

L Square L-shaped metal tool used in draping and pattern making with inches/centimeters markings, used to square-off drafting lines.

Length Grain In a plain weave textile the lengthwise, also known as the warp, is the strongest grain. Ways to identify muslin length grain are: 1) parallel to the selvage; 2) has little to no stretch; 3) length grain yarns are stronger and smoother, unlike crossgrain yarns which are slubby; and 4) when folded it lays flat unlike the crossgrain, which will be a bit bouncy.

Lowered/Extended Side Seam The amount of ease given to a bodice, torso or dress drape or pattern, based upon whether the garment is sleeveless or has a sleeve.

Mandarin Collar Standing-band collar that extends up on the neck, not quite meeting at center front.

Manipulate Darts The process of moving a dart from one position on a garment drape to another. For example, moving a bust dart from the shoulder to the side seam.

Marker Schematic plan of graded pattern parts by size of a particular garment style. Markers can be made manually or by computer.

Marking The act of placing pencil, chalk, or pen marker notations while draping to indicate areas that will later be trued on the table.

Master Pattern Name given to the original graded patterns for a particular style from which copies or tracings are made.

Match To line up, as in matching notches or a plaid or stripe, at the side seam on a given style.

Mechanical Pencil Lead pencil with a plastic or metal case and a thin replaceable lead that extends by twisting the outer casing, as the point is worn away.

Metal Ruler Straight edge metal ruler used in draping, pattern making, and sewing. Available 36" (91cm), 48" (122cm) and 60" (154cm).

Metric System A decimal measuring system based on the meter, liter, and gram.

Middy/Sailor collar Flat collar that is wide in the back then tapers into a "V" in the front.

Muslin/Calico Plain weave, unbleached, and unsized fabric used in draping and available in a variety of weights, from fine to heavy. Muslin qualties for draping include: #1, coarse weave; #2, fine weave; and #3, tailoring canvas, which is heavier weight.

Muslin Block A piece of muslin that has been measured, cut to size and blocked, in preparation for draping.

NB Acronym for neckband.

Neck Dart Darts that emanate from the neckline. Front neck darts positioned at the neckline must vanish at least ½" (1.3cm) away at the apex. Back neck darts are positioned approximately 1½" (3.8cm) away from center back. They are approximately 3" (7.6cm) in length and vanish in the direction of the back princess seam.

Neckband On a garment, a neckband finishes the neckline. On a dress form the neckband is located above the neckline.

Neckline Contour of the neck from front to back.

Nehru Collar Type of stand collar popularized by Jawaharlal Nehru, the Prime Minister of India from 1947 to 1964.

NL Acronym for neckline.

Notcher Metal tool used to make notches on patterns.

Notches Marks made on patterns to indicate where seams align, where hems are turned and other key matching points that are necessary when constructing a garment.

Needlepoint Tracing Wheel Tool with pointed edges, used in conjunction with tracing paper, to transfer lines and markings when draping and pattern making.

Off-grain Garment that is not draped or cut on the proper fabric grain. Draping or cutting a garment off-grain results in a poor fit and a garment that is unbalanced.

Outseam The pant side seam from waist to ankle, or any out-facing seam, such as the center seam on a 2-piece raglan sleeve.

Oaktag A heavy weight paper used in pattern making for creating slopers (blocks). Available as manila-colored right side/green underside, or both sides manila or white. Also known as card.

Pant Form Bifurcated dress form, waist to ankle.

Pant Sloper Foundation pant sloper that can be used to create many different types of pants.

Pants A garment that is worn on the lower half of the body, with separate tubular sections for the legs.

Parallel Dart Darts that are positioned side by side.

Pattern A schematic plan of a garment design, which is either draped and then transferred into a paper pattern or drafted directly on pattern paper. A pattern will always include necessary seam allowances.

Pattern Layout Arranging pattern pieces of a garment on fabric or paper to get the best possible yield.

Pattern Making Method of creating a two-dimensional diagram or template of a garment

on a flat surface. Also known as pattern cutting and flat patterning.

Pattern Paper Solid white, or dotted/numbered paper used to draft patterns, available in several widths: 36" (91cm); 45" (114cm); 48" (122cm); 60" (154cm); and 66" (168cm).

Pencil Sharpener Device used to sharpen lead pencils during the draping and pattern making process.

Perfecting In patternmaking, a term that refers to defining your lines.

Perpendicular Relationship between two lines that meet at a right angle (90°).

Petal/Tulip Sleeve Sleeve that wraps across the front creating a petal effect.

Peter Pan Collar Flat rolled collar with rounded front edges.

Pin Nickel-plated steel device used in draping, pattern making, and sewing to hold fabric or paper while cutting and in draping to secure fabric to the dress form. Available in assorted sizes, thicknesses, and lengths, and chosen based on the fabric weave and project.

Pin Cushion A small cushion that needles and pins are stick into until needed. Armband pincushions and magnetic pin holders are also available for use in draping and fitting garments, in sewing and pattern making.

Pivot The act of holding the pattern in one place with a pencil or pin and then rotating it on that point, for example when shifting a dart from shoulder to the side seam.

Pivot Method In pattern making, the process of rotating the pattern. For example when shifting a dart from neck to shoulder.

Pivot Point The position where a pivot takes place, such as at the apex when manipulating bust darts.

PL Acronym for princess line.

Placket An opening on a garment, such as on the bottom of a sleeve or the front of a

shirt, usually finished with a separate fabric band or facing.

Plate Screw Screw in the middle of the metal plate of a dress form's armhole.

Ply The act of laying one layer on top of another.

Point The end of something, such as the end point or vanishing point of a dart.

Press Ironing a garment or fabric to flatten an area. It is always best to iron in the direction of the grain.

Presser Foot Sewing machine attachment that is affixed to the presser foot lifter. Its function is to hold the material in place during the sewing process.

Pressing Cloth Cloth used when pressing a fabric or garment to avoid damaging the fabric or creating shine marks.

Princess Bodice Bodice with vertical stylelines that on the front start at mid-shoulder, go through the apex, and continue straight down to about the mid-waist. On the back, the princess line starts at mid shoulder, curves along the middle of the back and ends at about the mid-waist.

Princess Lines Vertical stylelines that on the front start at mid-shoulder, go through the apex, and continue straight down to about mid-waist. On the back, the princess line starts at mid shoulder, curves along the middle of the back and ends at about mid-waist. Other princess line variations can be created, however, all front princess lines must either transect the apex, or be placed within 1" (2.5cm) of the apex, to ensure a proper fit.

Princess Seam Seams of a princess line design.

Puff Sleeve Short sleeve that is gathered at the top and at the bottom and set into a band, cuff, or elastic casing.

Pushpin A short sturdy pin with a long, cylindrical head made of plastic or metal.

Quarter Circle Skirt A skirt that is fitted at the waist and flares out at the hem, forming a hem sweep of a quarter circle.

Quarter Circle Radius Calculations Chart Chart with waist circumference and radius measurements for drafting a quarter circle skirt.

Radius The line measured from the center of a circle.

Raglan Armhole Stylized armhole that starts either at the neckline, the shoulder, or at center front and ends below a traditional set-in sleeve armhole.

Raglan Sleeve Sleeve silhouette with a lowered armhole seam that extends from the front neck to the back neck. It can be drafted as a one or two-piece sleeve.

Re-true The act of re-marking or adjusting lines on a drape or pattern.

Red Pencil Red-colored lead pencil used in draping and pattern making for making corrections and adjustments.

Right Angle An angle of 90°, as in a corner of a square or at the intersection of two perpendicular straight lines.

Roll Line The line at which a collar turns over as in a roll collar.

Rolled Collar Collar that sits/stands high on the back neck and whose neck shape is a straighter line than that of a flat collar.

Ruching A French term meaning to gather, ruffle, or pleat fabric into tight folds.

Running Stitch Small even stitches, made either by hand or machine, that run in and out of fabric without overlapping. They are used to hold down a hem, a pocket, gathers, folds, pleats, or any area of a garment where a temporary stitch is needed.

Removable Tape Clear cellophane tape with a small amount of adhesive backing so that it can be easily removed during the pattern making process.

Sailor Collar Flat square-back collar tapering to a "V" in the front.

SBL Acronym for shoulder blade level.

Scissors Handled instrument with two opposing sharp blades for cutting paper and fabric. To maintain the sharpness of the blades, it is advisable to dedicate each pair of scissors to a specific function; one for only cutting paper and one for cutting fabric only.

Scotch Tape A brand name clear cellophane tape with an adhesive backing used in pattern making.

Seam Allowance Amount of extra material that extends beyond the stitching line. Seam allowances range from ⅛" (3mm) to 1" (2.5cm) and vary depending on the type of seam.

Seamline The stitching line of a garment.

Selvage Finished edges on fabric in the length/warp grain.

Set-in Sleeve Sleeve that sits within a natural armhole as compared to a sleeve that sits in a drop shoulder or stylized armhole.

Setting a Straight Sleeve Process of shirring a sleeve cap and carefully mounting it into an armhole.

Shears Instrument with two opposing sharp blades for cutting fabric. Fabric shears are generally longer, heavier, have a stronger fulcrum, and one handle bigger than the other, for better balance when cutting through layers of fabric. It is advisable never to use your fabric shears for cutting paper as this will dull the blades.

Sheath Dress Semi-fitted dress that gets its shape by adding a waist dart or a French dart.

Shift Dress Dress that hangs straight from the underarm to the hem.

Shirring Running one or more stitches parallel to the other for the purpose of forming gathers.

Shirring Foot Sewing machine attachment that is affixed to the presser foot lifter and used to gather or shirr fabric.

Shirring Stitch A hand or machine stitch used to gather or shirr areas of a garment. Stitch length for machine or hand gathering

is approximately 7 to 9 stitches per inch with longer stitches for heavier weight fabrics. A sewing machine gathering foot attachment is also available.

Shirring Thread Heavier thread used for gathering or shirring fabric areas of a garment.

Shoulder Blade Level A horizontal position located on the back of a dress form/body that is one-fourth the distance down from center back neckline to center back waistline. It is used to balance the fabric grain while draping.

Shoulder Dart Darts that are positioned in the middle of the shoulder. On the front, a shoulder dart vanishes at least ½" (1.3cm) away from the apex. On the back a shoulder dart is approximately 3" (7.6cm) in length and aligns or is parallel with the princess seam.

Shoulder Seam Distance between shoulder/neck intersection to shoulder/armhole intersection.

Shoulderline Position on a body/dress form indicating the shoulder, from shoulder/neck intersection to shoulder/armhole intersection.

SHS Acronym for shoulder seam.

Side Dart Bust dart emanating from the side seam to within ½" (1.3cm) away from the apex.

Side Seam Side of the body/dress form, which is a straight line down from the middle of the underarm.

Silhouette The line or shape of a particular design.

Skirt Garment starting from the waist to above or below the knee or ankle. Can also be the lower portion of a dress.

Skirt Length Length of skirt from waist to hem.

Slash The act of cutting into material to release it, as in releasing the neckline while draping and sewing, or slashing into the waist when dropping a flare for a flare skirt.

Slash & Spread Method Process used in patternmaking when adding fullness to a

garment design, such as slashing a sleeve sloper to create a puff sleeve.

Sleeve Band Piece that is attached to the bottom to finish off a sleeve.

Sleeve Board A small, narrow ironing board used to press sleeves and other areas of a garment.

Sleeve Cap Top portion of a sleeve.

Sleeve Centerline On a straight sleeve, the line that is in the center of the sleeve cap and wrist, perpendicular to the bicep and elbow line. On a fitted sleeve, the centerline starts at the center of the sleeve cap but shifts at the wrist, once the elbow dart is closed.

Sleeve Sloper A basic sleeve block that is made from body measurements and is the basis for all other sleeve stylizations.

Slit Opening on a garment that adds movement such as on the side seam of a skirt, shorts, or jacket.

Sloper Basic foundation block without seam allowances from which various design stylizations are created. Slopers can be developed through the flat pattern process, using body measurements, or by draping them on a dress form.

Squared Off Pattern making term that refers to creating a right angle at an intersection such as when trueing centerfront neckline and centerfront waistline.

SS Acronym for side seam.

Stand The base of a dress form with wheels and a stand petal so that the form can easily be moved and raised and lowered.

Stand Collar Collar with a neckband and collar attached.

Staystitch Machine or hand stitch used to control an area and keep it from stretching.

Stitching Line The part that will be sewn on a garment such as a seamline or any area that will need a stitch.

Straight Grain In the natural direction of the

weave, such as in line with the cross grain yarns or in line with the length grain yarns.

Straight Skirt Sloper Skirt that hangs straight from the hip and acts as a basic block, without seam allowances, from which other skirt styles can be created.

Straight Sleeve A basic sleeve that falls from the underarm to the wrist with a slight amount of ease. It can be used as a basic block for other sleeve stylizations.

Straight Sleeve Sloper Sleeve that is straight from the underarm to the wrist and acts as a basic block, without a seam.

Style Lines Lines on a pattern or a drape that indicate the desired look and design of a garment.

Style Tape By-the-yard tape used in draping when creating design lines on a dress form. It is offered in various widths and available as a woven tape or as a plastic tape with an adhesive backing.

Stylepoint Mark placed on the dress form indicating a desired design point.

Styling Curve Tool used to true armholes and other curves areas on a pattern.

Sweep The amount of circumference area at the bottom of a skirt, top, pants, or other area of a garment.

Sweetheart Front neckline that is in the shape of a heart.

Symmetric A mirror image from one side of a garment to the other.

Tailored Sleeve Set-in sleeve with darts at the elbow.

Tailored Sleeve Set-in sleeve with a dart or darts at the elbow.

Tape Measure Measuring device marked with units of measure, in inches or centimeters, used in draping, pattern making, and sewing.

Thigh Fullest part of the leg between the crotch and the knee.

Thread Thin, twisted yarns available in different fibers, weights, and colors, that are wound on a spool and used for sewing. Choosing the correct type of thread for a particular project is important.

Three Quarter Circle Skirt A skirt that is fitted at the waist, flares out at the hem, forming a hem sweep that is three-quarters of a circle.

Three Quarter Circle Skirt Radius Calculations Chart Chart with waist circumference and radius measurements for drafting a three quarter circle skirt.

Tight Bodyline A draping term used to identify a side seam prior to lowering the armhole and adding wearing ease at the side seam/armhole intersection.

Toile A full muslin drape of a garment design that is ready for fitting.

Torso The area on a dress form, from the neckline to the end of the dress form, before the start of the cage.

Tracing Marks Markings made on a pattern draft with a tracing wheel.

Tracing Paper Transfer paper used in pattern making, draping, and sewing to copy stitching lines when used with a tracing wheel.

Tracing Wheel Tool with smooth, serrated or pointed edges, used in conjunction with tracing paper to transfer stitching lines and markings when draping, pattern making, and sewing.

Trim To cut away an area of a pattern or garment. A decorative detail, such as ribbon, braid, or piping.

True Bias Diagonal direction of a fabric, that yields the most stretch. "True bias" is bias that is a 45° angled bias, as compared to "garment bias," which is bias other 45°.

Trueing/Truing In pattern making and draping, a term that refers to connecting lines to create a finished pattern.

Under Collar Bottom or under collar

patterned smaller than the top collar, depending on the thickness of the fabric.

Underarm Length Length of the sleeve from underarm to sleeve hem.

Upper Armhole Top section of an armhole.

Upper Collar Top portion of a collar.

Upper Front Chest Width Horizontal chest position on a body/dress form located 1" (2.5cm) above mid-armhole, from left armhole to right armhole.

V-Neck Neckline that forms a "V" on the front. However, a garment can also have a "V" back design detail.

Vanishing Point The position where a dart ends.

Vent/Slit Opening on a jacket, skirt, dress, blouse or pants to give movement.

Waist Dart Dart that emanates from the waist and vanishes in the direction of the bust on a bodice and dress, and in the direction of the hip on a pant, skirt or dress.

Waist Tape Tape used to denote the waistline on a dress form.

Waistband A band that is attached to the waistline of a skirt or pant (trouser) that provides a clean finish at the waist.

Waistline Horizontal line around a body/dress form indicating the narrowest portion of the figure.

Walk the Tape Measure Using the edge of a tape measure to measure a curve.

Warp Refers to the lengthwise grain of a woven fabric.

Wearing Ease Planning an extra amount in a drape or pattern draft for the wearer's comfort.

Weave Refers to the three most common types of fabric weave: plain weave; twill weave; satin weave.

Weft Refers to the crosswise grain of a woven fabric.

Weights Tool that is used to hold down

fabric or paper during draping, pattern making, or sewing.

WL Acronym for waist level or waistline on a body/dress form.

Woven Fabric that is made through the interlacing of yarns, either at a right angle to each other to create a plain weave, or in a combination diagonal weave to create a twill and satin weave.

Wrist The joint that connects the forearm with the hand.

Wrist Circumference Distance measurement around the wrist.

Yardstick A straight edge ruler measuring 36" (91cm) in length, used in draping, pattern making and sewing.

Zipper Closure device with metal, plastic, or nylon-coiled teeth and a metal pull. Available in various lengths and colors as well as in different styles such as all-purpose, invisible, and separating.

Zipper Notch Single or double notch, either at the side seam, center front or back of a skirt, dress, or pant, to indicate the opening/length position of the zipper.

Index

Picture Credits

Laurence King Publishing Ltd, the authors, and the picture researcher wish to thank the institutions and individuals who have kindly provided photographic material for use in this book. Every effort has been made to trace the present copyright holders; if there are any unintentional omissions or errors, we will be pleased to insert the appropriate acknowledgment in any subsequent edition.

All images except those listed below are courtesy the University of Fashion.

Page 12 bl & cl Godey's Lady's Book and Magazine, July, 1863, Volume LXVII, (Volume 67); **12 c** Courtesy TreasureEpicurean, San Ramon, CA; **12 cr & r** Private Collection; **15 l** De Agostini Picture Library/Getty Images; **15 r** Sasha/Getty Images; **16 l** George Hurrell/Condé Nast via Getty Images; **16 r & 17 l** Chicago History Museum/Getty Images; **17 r** Victor Virgile/Gamma-Rapho via Getty Images; **18 l** Olivier Morin/AFP/Getty Images; **18 r & 19 l** Guy Marineau/Conde Nast via Getty Images; **19 r** Pietro D'aprano /Getty Images; **20 l** Mike Marsland/WireImage /Getty Images; **20 r** Pierre Vauthey/Sygma/Sygma via Getty Images; **21** Courtesy Julian Roberts; **25** Slaven Vlasic/ Getty Images **29** Slaven Vlasic/Getty Images for NYFW: The Shows; **31** Frazer Harrison/Getty Images; **37** Dominique Charriau/WireImage/Getty Images; **41** Jemal Countess/Getty Images; **53** S. Alemdar/Getty Images; **63** Pier Marco Tacca/Getty Images; **69** Sebastian Reuter/Getty Images for IMG; **85** Victor Virgile/Gamma-Rapho via Getty Images; **97** Peter Michael Dills/Getty Images for Michael Kors; **100** Thomas Concordia/WireImage/Getty Images; **107** Kristy Sparow/Getty Images; **110** Arun Nevader/Getty Images for Art Hearts Fashion; **119** Ernesto Ruscio/Getty Images; **122** Ian Gavan/Getty Images for IMG; **133** Victor Virgile/Gamma-Rapho via Getty Images; **150** Estrop/Getty Images; **153** Richard Bord/Getty Images; **159** VCG via Getty Images; **163** Eduardo Parra/Getty Images; **167** Victor Boyko/Getty Images; **169** Lintao Zhang/Getty Images; **183** Peter White/Getty Images; **185** George Pimentel/Getty Images for IMG; **197** Pascal Le Segretain/Getty Images; **213** Edward James/FilmMagic/Getty Images; **239** Yuriko Nakao/Getty Images; **261** Francois G. Durand/WireImage; **267** Frazer Harrison/Getty Images For NYFW: The Shows; **273** Peter White/Getty Images; **280** Thomas Concordia/WireImage/Getty Images; **281 t** Vittorio Zunino Celotto/Getty Images; **281 c** Frazer Harrison/Getty Images for Mercedes-Benz Fashion Week; **281 b** Matt Jelonek/WireImage/Getty Images; **293** Peter Michael Dills/Getty Images for Lena Hoschek; **303** Kristina Nikishina/Getty Images; **305** Antonio de Moraes Barros Filho/WireImage.

Front Cover: Skirt and blouse by Marina Hoermanseder Defilee – Mercedes-Benz Fashion Week Berlin Spring/Summer 2017. Photo Sebastian Reuter/Getty Images for IMG